THE METROPOLIS
IN
MODERN LIFE

COLUMBIA UNIVERSITY
BICENTENNIAL CONFERENCE SERIES

"Man's Right to Knowledge and the Free Use Thereof."

The Principal Contributors

William Anderson
Sir Alexander Morris Carr-Saunders
J. V. Langmead Casserley
Louis Chevalier
Sir George Clark
P. Sargant Florence
Joseph Folliet
Luther H. Gulick

A. V. Hill
Myres S. McDougal
Richard J. Neutra
Stuart Piggott
Richard U. Ratcliff
Harold L. Reeve
Albert J. Reiss, Jr.
Donald Young

THE METROPOLIS
IN
MODERN LIFE

Edited by

ROBERT MOORE FISHER

NEW YORK / RUSSELL & RUSSELL

Printed in the United States

Preface

The growth of cities has been one of the outstanding phenomena of the last two hundred years. During that time, most nations of the world have changed from rural to urban societies. Within these countries, at least one city has developed to the point where it can be called a metropolis. The metropolis, therefore, symbolizes the basic change in modern civilization from rural to urban.

As its name suggests, a metropolis is a mother city. From it emanates the principal features of the cultural, social, political, and economic life of the nation. At the same time, the metropolis displays many of the most advanced and most retarded aspects of national life. It is a breeder of slums and palaces; an incubator of artistic and scientific progress and of disease, crime, and delinquency. In London, Paris, Rome, and New York, the most commendable and most disgraceful facets of British, French, Italian, and American life lie openly exposed.

Since cities are the handiwork of men, fundamental questions have been raised about the process of adjusting man and his institutions to the environment which he himself creates. For as cities multiply and thrive, they draw an increasing proportion of their population from rural areas. These people come to the city with social attitudes and institutions which are sometimes poorly adapted to urban life. To them, the metropolis, above all, offers many ideals which cannot be realized in a simpler environment. Yet it also offers the possibility of being broken on the wheel when an adjustment to metropolitan ways of life cannot be made.

Many problems have arisen in the course of this transitional process. Although numerous specific questions have been previously explored, an integrated analysis of the metropolis has seldom been attempted. Thus the first conference held in 1954 in connection with the Bicentennial Celebration of Columbia University focused attention upon problems of modern city life. The topic of the conference was appropriately called "The Metropolis in Modern Life."

Since the metropolis seems to be a permanent feature of contemporary civilization, the conference considered the problem of how to enhance its advantages and how to minimize its disadvantages. To that end, the conference was designed to promote an understanding of the basic forces which are manifested in the modern metropolis.

vii

Some of the questions discussed during the conference follow: How significant has the role of cities been in the progress of civilization? As cities have grown, what changes have occurred in social institutions like neighborhoods, clans, families, taboos, and moral standards? What personal characteristics have become more pronounced or have been repressed? How have the organs and practices of politics and government been altered? What changes have come in the meaning and content of the law of property? What economic advantages and disadvantages have been encountered? What demands have been made upon science and technology and how have they, in turn, influenced the size of the metropolis? How have professional men like lawyers and physicians been affected, particularly in their relationships to their clients, to each other, and to their professions? In what ways have man's spiritual aspirations and realizations been altered? Why have philosophers always searched for the "ideal city" and what forms have their conceptions taken?

These questions imply that a broader understanding of the metropolis is important, not only to the growing number of scholars who are studying it, but also to members of the legal and medical professions, business men, religious leaders, welfare workers, and public officials who are assuming more and more responsibility for the development and management of cities. This concern is not limited to the boundaries of any city or nation. It pervades every modern society.

For the conference on "The Metropolis in Modern Life," papers were prepared by a distinguished group of scholars from Great Britain, France, and the United States. The papers were circulated to members of the conference prior to its meeting and other participants were asked to prepare commentaries on each paper. The papers and commentaries are presented in this book with the editor's summary of any open discussion as an introduction to the main parts.

For publication, it was necessary for the editor to condense all the material presented in order to keep the main features of the book in proportion. The participants who have contributed papers and commentaries have kindly consented to this procedure, although they have not had an opportunity to read the edited versions.

The book begins first with a consideration of the dynamic role of cities in social development. On this topic, Professor Piggott examines the place of cities in the civilizations of prehistoric times. Professor Chevalier analyzes demographic materials to ascertain whether the growth of cities, particularly in France, has been evidenced by changes in physique, fertility, life expectancy, or moral and social behavior. Professor Reiss explores some of the general characteristics of urban culture and suggests that cities are characterized not so much by unique social institutions as by the frequency with which certain relationships occur.

In subsequent parts, eminent scholars discuss the adaptation of political, economic, and legal institutions to metropolitan life. They trace the impact of science and technology upon the metropolis, and the influence of metropolitan conditions upon the professions, man's spiritual life, and his search for the ideal city.

This book is notable, then, not for any solutions it offers but for its thoughtful discussions of metropolitan problems that should stimulate the thinking of everyone who is concerned about modern city life.

To the scholars who have contributed to the conference and this book, Columbia University, the officers of the Bicentennial, the chairman, and the session leaders all express their sincerest appreciation.

ERNEST M. FISHER, *Chairman*
First Bicentennial Conference

Contents

xi

PART EIGHT The Search for the Ideal City

PART ONE

The Dynamic Role of the City in Social Development

INTRODUCTION

Although most people still live in predominantly rural countries, the trend toward urbanization is rapidly advancing. According to the best estimates, approximately 2 per cent of the world's population in 1850 resided in cities of 100,000 inhabitants or more. By 1950, the proportion had reached 13 per cent. Even this picture will soon change, since the rate of urbanization is steadily mounting.

Over the last one hundred years, the rise of cities has produced a new phenomenon—the urbanized society. In a few nations, it is by far the principal way of life. For instance, about 70 per cent of the population in England and Wales lives in places of 20,000 inhabitants or more. In comparatively new, sparsely-settled Australia, more than one-half of the population lives in cities of 100,000 inhabitants or more.

The emergence of the urbanized society raises the question of what its ultimate consequences will be. It has appeared so recently that its implications are not fully known. Not all of them look favorable, even for underdeveloped countries where urbanization is now proceeding at its fastest rate.

Thus it seems desirable to study the dynamic role of the city in social development through history. To begin with, Professor Piggott considers the process of urbanization during the first rise of urban communities several thousand years ago. He traces the conflicting development of urban agricultural communities and pastoral communities in ancient civilizations. Here the conflict between the city and the camp—between the so-called civilized peoples and the barbarians—is brought into sharp focus.

The same opposition between outlanders and city dwellers was also a feature of the early history of pre-Columbian America, Mexico, and Peru. There, however, the part played by pastoral communities was far less important than in ancient Mediterranean and Middle East civilizations. This fact seems to indicate that the hostility between pastoralism and urbanism, based on agriculture, is not the only factor in the fundamental antagonism between outlander and city dweller. Perhaps the outsider, whatever his occupation may be, has always been envious of the city and its civilization.

Professor Chevalier examines demographic data pertaining mainly to French cities. He finds that metropolises no longer exert the same influences on the social evolution of nations as they have in past centuries. From both a quantitative and qualitative standpoint, urban centers are less pathological than they once were. Professor Reiss analyzes contemporary urban phenomena in attempting to isolate some of the unique features and implications of urbanization. All three chapters implicitly touch upon the possible future role of cities in a world that is becoming increasingly urbanized.

1

The Role of the City in Ancient Civilizations

STUART PIGGOTT

Professor of Archaeology
University of Edinburgh

This survey will be limited in space to Western Asia and Europe—the area within which the earliest manifestations of city life can be traced. In time, it will be concerned mainly with the period between the sixth and first millennia, B.C. During that span, the early evolution of the city took place and its relationships to other communities became established as a recognizable pattern.

WHAT IS CIVILIZATION?

In common with many other abstract concepts, the term civilization today has become confused by emotional overtones to a degree which often renders its use meaningless or dangerously misleading. Each modern community tends to regard civilization as its peculiar property, with barbarism or its equivalent as the portion of other men.

By origin and primary definition, civilization was the exclusive property of city dwellers or citizens. The antithetic division of mankind into civilized and barbarian peoples was a natural concept within the classical tradition of Greek and Roman thought.[1] Such a world picture was the product of citizens in stable communities with a relatively advanced technology, economically based on agriculture. It was conceived reasonably enough with such an economy as a touchstone. In our own times, some historians tend to select as historically significant only those communities which approximate their own ideals.

Today the dominant human societies are heirs of ancient societies based on an agricultural economy where circumstances and tradition favored technological development. Thus the modern concept of civilization is likely to be colored by inherited attitudes of thought which equate an advanced technology with a high degree of civilization. Such ideas date chiefly from the nineteenth century and derive from materialistic and utilitarian doctrines. Accordingly, the growing complexity in man's material culture through prehistory and

5

history has been interpreted as a natural law of development and an inevitable progress from savagery to civilization.

In this chapter, the term civilization will be avoided as much as possible. It carries an implicit judgement of values and is limited, in its usually accepted sense, to one type of human society. But so far as the "city community" is concerned, little confusion can arise. For it appears to be essentially a product of just those stable, technological, active economies ordinarily comprised under the modern Western usage of the word civilization. Nevertheless, such agricultural economies represent only one kind of human response to the problems of subsistence and adaptation to environment.

THE RISE OF URBAN AGRICULTURAL COMMUNITIES

In the following discussion, the city will be studied as a unit within the earliest human societies in the Old World. It will be analyzed in prehistory and in later periods when archaeological evidence still bulks large and may predominate over written evidence. We are concerned, then, mainly with tangible manifestations provided by walls, fortifications, and the architecture, planning, and layout of buildings for public or private use, and with the material culture of the population as an index to its arts and manufactures, organization and trade, and war and peace.

What Is a City?

The limits between village, town, and city in remote antiquity are difficult to define. For communities which have passed beyond the stage of subsistence farming, certain vague standards of size, implications of social cohesion, and evidence can be used. In general, civic status will be given to settlements which were evidently more than a cluster of huts occupied by peasant farmers. They must have some evidence of centralized government and organization, often focused on a court or temple or both. Their population must be largely engaged in occupations other than direct and exclusive agriculture and hence concerned with trade to some extent. Such settlements may frequently be bounded by walls or fortifications, symbolic and preservative of the corporate individuality of the unit.

The Origins of the City

In seeking the origins of the city, we must search for the origins of stable agricultural communities dependent mainly on cereal crops. Archaeological evidence has confirmed numerous inferences drawn from considerations of climate, botany, and zoology in the post-glacial Old World. They indicate that the origins of grain growing and stock breeding are likely to have developed in areas with a favorable climate where the wild ancestors of the domesticated plants and animals known to antiquity were to be found.

Such conditions existed in the region which is now Western Asia from perhaps 10,000 B.C. or so. Here, too, there has been an apparent transition from the Palaeolithic hunter-fisher, food-gathering economy to one involving at least the collection of plant seeds as food by a simple process of cutting or reaping. A vast period of time must have elapsed in the transition from such tentative beginnings to the establishment of village communities of agriculturalists, and again from these settlements to the first townships to which a date can be given by historical means (around 3,000 B.C.). During this transition, the novel techniques of the farmer slowly supplanted those of the hunter.

The recent use of radio-carbon in computing dates, however, indicates that the completion of the transition from agricultural communities to townships probably required no more than two or three thousand years. Sites like Jarmo, in east-central Mesopotamia, appear to date from approximately 5,000 B.C. About that time, Jarmo was a settlement of stone-using people eating a wheat closely akin to the wild form (though showing evidence of cultivation) and as yet without the technique of pottery making or the use of metals.

But within little more than a couple of millennia, townships appeared with the beginnings of literacy and applied science, an evolving technology, and a more than rudimentary code of laws and formal religion. Indeed, if permanent houses within a defensive wall are taken as archaeological evidence of the beginnings of the city idea, this social and architectural unit had been achieved at Jericho in Palestine as early as 5,000 B.C. by a people with a material culture similar to that of Jarmo.[2]

While more evidence is needed, it looks as though Childe's thesis may have to be revised.[3] Childe maintained that two successive economic and technological "revolutions" took place long ago. One marked the change from a hunter-fisher economy to that of the agriculturalist. The other marked the development of the city concept closely linked with the first use of metals.

But as Childe realized, it was difficult to sustain such a sequence of development outside the Old World. In Central and South America, stone-using communities had achieved a notable degree of urban development without any accompanying metallurgy save the use of gold for ornaments. In Old World archaeology, we may be faced instead with a situation in which the beginnings of agriculture were associated with the appearance of a social unit in which the main elements of an urban economy were already present.

The City as an Economic, Social, and Religious Community

By the third millennium B.C., the city was established as an essential feature of all settled agricultural communities in Western Asia. In large measure, it owed its existence to techniques of farming sufficiently advanced to provide a surplus over and above the needs of the farming community itself. Economically, such towns or cities would be dependent on trade within their own boundaries as well as within the surrounding countryside under their jurisdiction. In response to increased technological developments, the cities and towns would also be dependent on trade with more distant regions for necessary raw materials.

Spiritual cohesion for the citizens would be provided by a centralized authority embodied in a temple and its priesthood, or by a court of a ruler whose attributes were at least semi-divine. Only in modern times have societies emerged without embodying any form of religion which gives significance to human activity at every level.

The city, then, early became the seat of moral authority for an area beyond its own walls. This authority was backed by spiritual sanctions and enforced, if necessary, by juridical or military action based on the seat of government. In the city, dogma and liturgy would be defined and promulgated, custom and tradition codified into laws, local usages regularized into a general system, and diversity replaced by uniformity.

Inevitably, the city would become the focus of aspiration for the surrounding population. It offered a market for the produce of the farm as well as the skills of craftsman and artist. Court and temple often acted as patrons to the artist. In these early city communities, the sculptor and painter first became preoccupied with the human form as subject matter. Their tradition became so much of a commonplace in the Western world that it is usually accepted as inevitable. Actually, however, this convention was peculiar to city communities in antiquity. As an indication of how deeply engrained it was in the traditions of the early agriculturalists, Jericho has recently shown again that naturalistic portrait modelling was carried out by the town dwellers even before they made pottery or used metals.[4]

Archaeological evidence and the earliest historical records of the ancient Orient, therefore, indicate that the town or city represented the fullest achievement of the stable agricultural societies in Western Asia from their earliest inception. Such settlements represented the sum of man's capabilities in thought, emotion, and technical ability.

Were Urban Developments Inevitable?

Was the creation of the urban unit inevitable? Did all food-producing communities tend to develop this pattern? If some did not, had they failed to fulfill their destinies in some mystic way? And how were other forms of economy—dissimilar from the stable agricultural communities but coexisting with them—related to the city tradition?

An answer must begin by briefly surveying the degree of town and city development achieved in Western Asia and Europe around 2,000 B.C. To start in the east, a complex city economy had been established in northwestern India some time before about 2,500 B.C. Outside the great desert areas of Persia, ancient cities already lay along the trade routes in Turkestan to the north; thence to the Elburz Mountains at the south end of the Caspian Sea; and southwards through Fars into ancient Elam and the kingdoms of Sumer and Akkad. In Syria, the Levant, Cyprus, Egypt, and Asia Minor, townships had stood beyond human memory. The second walled city on the site of Troy had been built. Around the shores and islands of the Aegean, fair-sized villages existed, sometimes with citadels and walls. Settled peasant communities were establishing themselves up the Danube and in Central Europe. Along the Mediterranean sea routes, similar little colonies were being founded. In southern Spain, there were even small townships beginning to be built which recall the Aegean world. By Oriental standards, these innovations of stable agriculture came late and in simple form to the hunter-fisher population. Yet there seemed every chance that such communities would flourish and develop in Western Asia and Europe as they had farther east.

But a second survey, made five hundred years later around 1,500 B.C., would have indicated that in Europe, the city concept had not expanded. In India it had collapsed altogether. Despite the fact that Italy was still wholly a land of peasant farmers and Mycenaean Greece a rustic version of the Minoan culture, the familiar classical pattern, with the East Mediterranean civilized world surrounded by the world of the barbarians, was beginning to form. Spain had become a backwater. North of the Alps lay the simplest peasant economies, although they were technologically competent in such crafts as bronze-working.

A half millennium later, the city tradition west of the Levant was on the defensive or at a low ebb nearly everywhere. Even the bastion of the Hittite Empire had crumbled.

THE ROLE OF THE PASTORAL COMMUNITIES

This brings us to the question of why the city complex in antiquity did not develop in certain regions where the antecedent economic and social conditions seemed to be as favorable as they were in areas where it nourished. How did the duality of civilization and barbarism, as apparent to classical thinkers, come about?

At least part of the answer is contained in the fact that we have so far been considering only one type of human economy in the ancient world—the economy of the sedentary peasant. It should be remembered, however, that alternative modes of existence and social organization presented themselves to mankind with the slow amelioration of climatic conditions after the final withdrawal of the ice sheets. Not everyone adopted the role of the farmer and townsman.

In surveying the decline and fall of the Roman Empire, Gibbon saw that even at a comparatively late date in history a "line of separation" could be drawn "between the civilized and the savage climates of the globe; between the inhabitants of cities, who cultivated the earth, and the hunters and shepherds, who dwelt in tents."[5] This antithesis was already in men's minds by the beginning of the second millennium B.C. At that time, an inscription of the Third Dynasty of Ur described its dangerous opponents, the Amurru (or Amorites), as "a host whose onslaught was like a hurricane, a people that from of old had never known a city." In other words, communities with a mobile and often nomadic structure associated with pastoralism existed side-by-side with the stable agricultural settlements.

Pastoralism and Settled Agriculture

The evidence of archaeology and history seems to show consistently that pastoral nomadism represented a self-sufficient economy. Nomadism was not only "a mere stage on the way from food-collecting to agriculture" but also "a highly specialized mode of life enabling man to utilize vast tracts" of country in which settled agriculture or stable pastoralism would be very difficult under the conditions of simpler economies.[6]

By its very nature, a pastoral nomadic economy does not leave archaeological traces which are so marked or permanent as the economy of the peasant or citizen. A pastoral society is far more elusive and may leave few memorials other than tombs. Nevertheless, evidence from Western Asia and Europe indicates that one or more forms of mobile pastoral communities, at least seminomadic and with a minimum dependence on grain growing, existed before 2,000 B.C. as counterparts of the stable agricultural economies. Moreover, the pastoral communities were moving over territories immediately beyond the frontiers of the agricultural settlements. Thus the city and the camp were complementary aspects of life.

The first clear archaeological evidence of probable seminomadic pastoralists comes from South Russia, dated somewhere before 2,000 B.C. In support of the view that a mature pastoralism depends upon the mobility conferred by the mastery of the horse as a riding animal, these people evidently used horses extensively. In Hungary, tangible evidence of bridles shows that tamed animals had been acquired and probably ridden by neighboring agriculturalists before about 1,700 B.C. A couple of centuries later, the horse-drawn chariot was becoming a decisive war engine in Asia Minor and Greece, though documentary evidence of horse riding does not appear there until the fourteenth century B.C.[7]

Around 2,000 B.C., a series of communities can be recognized, stretching from the Pontic Steppes to the Elburz Mountains, and including at least north Anatolia. They were mainly characterized by royal tombs, often of warrior chieftains, furnished with a barbaric magnificence which draws some of its inspiration and probably some of its actual materials from the city communities to the south. The tombs and other evidence imply that these communities made up the southern fringe of a nomadic province which, by its proximity to the rich and technologically advanced mercantile communities in Sumerian and other cities, was able to obtain by barter or plunder the costly trappings desired by its ruling families.

We do not know how early this relationship was established. But a kinship of ideas perceptible between such princely graves and the famous Royal Tombs of Ur, dating soon after 3,000 B.C., has been pointed out. It may indicate that there were contacts between the steppe and the town, with a foreign dynasty bringing in barbaric ideas, even at that time. Whatever the case, the warrior cultures of the European and Asiatic grasslands were ancestors of historical nomad groups like the Scyths, the Huns, and the Tartars. Here the hunter-fisher strains of the circumpolar zone mingled with the pastoralism of the steppe and drew upon the resources of the stable agricultural communities, if necessary, by force of arms.

Beyond the zone of contact with the earliest urban communities, warrior cultures can be traced northwards and westwards into Europe from the Pontic region. At first, these cultures were impoverished in technological resources, with the stone battle-axe as the symbol of authority and weapon of prestige appropriate to the chieftain. But they soon acquired a command of metallurgical techniques. A mixing of traditions can be perceived between the warrior societies and the stable, if simple, agricultural communities established in western and northern Europe since the eve of the second millennium B.C. Analogies from historical precedent and modern ethnological parallels suggest that the agricultural communities were rendered a substrate population under a warrior aristocracy embodied in the pastoralists.

The Camp Versus the City

From about 2,000 B.C. through the next half millennium, the centuries mark one of the great turning points in Old World prehistory and history. During this time, a decisive trial of strength took place between the traditions of the camp and the city. As an outcome of the events resulting from this contest, the foundations of classical and modern Europe were laid. Among the significant factors involved was that many groups of pastoral nomads (or communities closely associated with them) spoke dialects within the Indo-European family of languages. By virtue of their comparatively simple construction, flexibility, and capacity for adaptation without loss of identity, these languages became characteristic of the major achievements in expressed thought and imaginative literature in the ancient world from India to Ireland.

History, philology, and archaeology suggest how the problem resulting from the clash of conflicting philosophies of life was at least temporarily resolved. In the East, sometime before 1,500 B.C. or so, the city civilization of the Indus fell defenseless before the onslaughts of the Sanskrit-speaking herdsmen. The conquerors commemorated their victory in triumphant hymns to their gods, transmitted by oral tradition to the modern world as the *Rigveda*. In Persia, too, the peoples who introduced the Indo-European language (later to be enshrined in the *Avesta*) were appearing as raiders and conquerors at much the same time.

But the most ancient centers of stable agriculture and townships from Sumer to Egypt held their own against invaders like the Guti, Amurru, Mitanni, Kassites, and Hyksos, and eventually absorbed them. In the process of absorption, however, the old tradition was modified; survival was obtained at a price. In Asia Minor, absorption seems to have taken place between horse-breeding warriors and the old city populations. As a consequence, the Hittite Empire rose with its mixed languages which included Indo-European dialects. The Minoan kingdom succumbed to raiders from the mainland. And though Mycenaean culture was heavily tinged with Minoan coloring, it was more akin to the culture of the Hittites with which it shared an Indo-European language, in this instance Greek.

Further north and west lay the world of peasant-farmer communities established late and sporadically in the period 2,000 to 1,500 B.C. In south Spain, little townships may have persisted until after the middle of the millennium. Elsewhere they did not develop until after they were re-established from the east at about 800 B.C. onwards.

The Pastoral Nomad Tradition in Its Mature Form

What is the explanation for this tardy and partial development of the city tradition in Western Europe in the clash of contending cultures around 2,000 B.C.? The question cannot be answered without further considering the nature of the pastoral nomad tradition in its mature form during the middle second millennium B.C. How did it differ from the tradition of the city, and how did it affect the successor states which arose after the initial impact?

The pastoral nomad economy has recently been defined as based upon "a complex of animals rather than a single species, balanced in terms of grazing characteristics to utilize all the grass cover of each locality," so that the long grass is eaten by cattle or horses and the shorter growth by sheep and goats.[8] The mobility necessary in such an economy reflects the wanderings of the hunters following the wild herds from grazing ground to grazing ground. It was maintained and developed by using horses as riding animals. (On the other hand, a form of pastoralism may have existed in remote antiquity without the horse as it did during recent times in communities like the Masai of East Africa.)

In such a setting, the social structure is characterized by strong personal relations within a family, clan, or tribe, although the individual is largely self-sufficient. This structure inevitably tends to be organized and held together by a warrior aristocracy. The civil corporations of a settled agricultural economy are unknown.

Nevertheless, patronage of the arts and technology may flourish to some extent. In the simpler system of personal loyalties of the pastoral economy, such patronage becomes an individual attribute of the chieftain and the members of his court rather than of an institution such as a temple. Representational art is severely subordinated to abstract matter. The artist shows little or no interest in the human form as subject matter, but may often demonstrate a passionate absorption in animal motifs. Although monumental architecture would be irrelevant to a nomad, demands of the warriors and their retinue for equipment may stimulate technological advances in crafts, like those of the metal smith and the wheelwright.

In such societies, a normal absence of writing does not preclude the composition and technical elaboration of imaginative literature transmitted by word of mouth and retained by the enhanced capacity for memory characteristic of nonliterate peoples. In fact, this is the milieu of the world's epic and heroic poetry. The *Rigveda* shows that philosophical speculations embodied in verse of great metrical virtuosity could also be achieved under these conditions.

Nomad–City Warfare

In nomad societies, the warlike element may often become dominant. It may take the form of inter-tribal cattle raiding, as related in the early Irish heroic tales. Or where the borders of the nomads are adjacent to the frontiers of settled agriculturalists, warfare may take the form of plundering nearby villages and townships.

The future relationship of pastoralist and city dweller depended upon the success or failure of such raids. The equilibrium maintained between the contrasted economies remained uneasy so long as military initiative and innovations stayed largely in the hands of the nomads. But once adequate weapons were adopted by the cities and could be multiplied through the facilities for mass production inherent in a stable economy, potential victory rested in community hands.

The events of the second millennium B.C. show that the older city states were often able to acquire the power and capacity to withstand the onslaughts of the predatory nomads in this way. Military ascendency, however, was obtained at a price. The city states had to be transformed into semi-military communities which were in a position to defend themselves as well as wage aggressive wars on an increased scale within and beyond their own borders.

Moreover, the antinomy between the nomad and the agricultural traditions could not be resolved through the adoption by one side of the economy of the other. From the first, the contrasted traditions were irreconcilable. The settled life of village or township presented no attractions to the pastoralist warrior. For him the town was there to be looted, perhaps, but otherwise to be shunned and avoided. On the other hand, there is no evidence that city merchants ever left their counting houses to join the horsemen of the steppes.

At the mature stage of evolution in which the two economies confronted each other in Western Asia in the second millennium B.C., any amalgamation was out of the question. A choice had been made on each side. Once made, it became an innate way of life, acceptable to the other side only when imposed by sheer force. It is misleading to think of the ancient city cultures as an ideal for which all men yearned. "We needs must love the highest when we see it" is a sentiment for which human history offers singularly little support. At all events, ideals are many. Each is peculiar to a restricted tradition and presents itself as a goal only to those brought up within the framework of that particular world of ideas.

Before 1,500 B.C., the nomads had achieved priority in the use of the horse for military traction and to a less extent in its employment as cavalry. In Asia Minor, the hegemony of the Hittites must have been largely based on chariotry as well as the use of iron which was exclusive to them at this time. So far as the use of the chariot is concerned, the same may be said for the Mycenaeans. The Egyptians adopted the technique as a result of their wars in the Levant; by the end of the fifteenth century B.C., they were importing chariots from the Mitanni of Asia Minor. Under the dynasty of the Amurru —people who had never known a city—rose the kingdom of Babylon. While Hammurabi is remembered for his noble code of laws, to his contemporary panegyrist he was "the great hero, the destroyer of foes, the stormwind of war, smashing the hostile land." The city states were not only on the defensive, but were becoming increasingly engaged in aggressive wars. And in the hands of the Indo-European Kassites and later under the Assyrians from the end of the second millennium B.C., the chariot was to become the characteristic equipment of the warrior aristocracy now firmly established in command.

But in India, the ancient city tradition did not change in this manner into the character of the warrior state. It succumbed completely to the attacking forces of the Aryans and seems only to have slowly re-established itself after centuries of submergence beneath the ruder traditions of the steppe.

The city, and all that it connoted in the ancient world, survived the crisis of the early second millennium B.C. only when it was able to place itself on a level equal to or higher than that of the nomad hordes in the matter of active warfare. Having established supremacy, the city was inevitably prone to use its military prestige to wage wars of aggression with other city states. These wars were fought on a far larger and more decisive scale than the internal disputes and changes of dynasty which chequer, for instance, the history of Sumer and Akkad in the third millennium B.C. The city survived, indeed, only at the cost of becoming a warrior state which devoted much of its resources to territorial aggrandizement by force but was constantly on the defensive against other ambitious states and against the still-present warlike pastoral nomads.

Trends Outside the Aegean World

In Europe outside the Aegean world, there was a different sequel to the encounter of opposing peasant-farmer and nomad-pastoralist traditions. On both sides, the situation was on a lower technological scale than in the Orient. Even by the beginning of the second millennium B.C., the social unit achieved by the prehistoric population of Europe had not advanced substantially beyond the small village. In many regions, it may have been little more than the croft or farmstead of a single family of farmers. In northern Europe, considerable remnants of the old hunter-fisher economies of Palaeolithic lineage continued to exist.

Any spread of pastoralists from the eastern steppes into this loosely-knit pattern of scattered communities could have been gradual and without any overt contest for land in a sparsely populated Europe. Indeed, indigenous areas of pastoralism may have been established as early as the first introduction of domesticated animals from Western Asia.

The meeting of the two traditions resulted, in fact, in fusion and amalgamation. Up to the Roman conquest, prehistoric Europe remained a land of simple economies in which both settled agriculture and pastoralism played a part. But pastoralism permeated the fabric of society so deeply that evolution of township and city could not take place.

With the decisive mixture of traditions in Europe at the beginning of the second millennium B.C., it might be assumed that the city tradition would develop along lines familiar in other regions where settled agriculture flourished. However, human communities do not necessarily develop in comparable sequences according to natural laws. Moreover, natural deterrents to this development existed in the form of dense forest cover in the deciduous woodlands over much of the area beyond the zone of the Mediterranean flora. Toward the north, there were increasingly adverse climatic conditions.

But difficulties like these were no more insuperable to early agriculturists than were other environmental problems which had been overcome in Western Asia. Evidence appears to show that the barbarians of the classical world were not merely passive products of geography. Rather they were the result of an accidental mixture of contrasted traditions at a stage of development where neither had the technological advantage of the other. Neither tradition had evolved its own set of ideas to a degree which gave it the force of long-inherited conviction.

Here tentative pastoralists encountered tentative agriculturalists. In so doing, they produced a mutual modus vivendi which inhibited development along either path. The instability and inchoate structure of such an economy did not favor the constructive evolution of any part of the mixture. If the city idea was to appear in Western Europe, it could do so only by being transplanted directly from its ancient home.

Once such a transplantation occurred, it resulted in the establishment of the Roman Empire. It was achieved after about 800 B.C. through the founding of the first Etruscan settlements in Italy by immigrants of Asiatic origin (perhaps from Lydia as Herodotus believed) and by the planting of the western Greek colonies. These movements had their precursors in the Mycenaean trading posts set up in the fourteenth century B.C. as far west as Sicily and probably beyond. Along these routes also came the "grave Tyrian trader" to found the Phoenician depots as far as the Straits of Gibraltar at the beginning of the first millennium B.C. Thus city civilization in the west was in no sense the product of slow indigenous evolution from simple peasant economies. It was the result of deliberate settlement *in partibus* by colonists coming from highly-developed urban centers in the east who brought the new tradition in a complete and intrusive form.

The Worlds of the Citizen and the Barbarian

With the establishment and growth of the Roman Empire, we have reached
the antithesis of citizen and barbarian. They were separated by a so-called
moral barrier between two worlds of different ideals between which no mutual
comprehension could be reached.[9] Transalpine Europe presented to the
Romans a land of technologically undeveloped agriculturalists. It also offered
a land in which mobile warrior bands existed as an active opponent to colonial
expansion. A succession of events then resulted in the formation of the Celtic
peoples. From the second century onwards, much of the aggressive warfare
of the Roman army was directed against them.

The character of the Celtic world of this time fits naturally enough into the
framework of contrasted economies. In it was a substrate population de-
scended from the ancient mixed population of pastoralist and agricultural
traditions dating from the early second millennium B.C. There was also
probably a new and forceful infusion of a warrior aristocracy. The cattle-rear-
ing, horse-breeding, chariot-driving heroes of the Ulster epics at the dawn of
the Christian era are closely akin to the warriors of the *Rigveda,* and later to
the Scyths.

The Roman conquest of Gaul and Britain repeated once again the contests
between city states and warrior pastoralists which occurred in the ancient East
from the beginning of the second millennium. With the consolidation of the
Roman Empire in Europe, the ancient interplay of contrasted economies was
for a time held in check. The events leading to the Empire's fall and the
coming of the Dark Ages of Europe are not new in themselves. They were the
resumption of an immemorial order of things, the renewing of a contest between the incompatible ways of thought embodied in the city and the camp.
Nor was there anything new in the so-called migration period; peoples had
been on the move from choice rather than from compulsion since remote
antiquity.

By the Middle Ages, the city tradition in Europe had established itself
sufficiently to resist the impact of the remaining nomadic war bands. It with-
stood even the Tartar assault of the mid-thirteenth century when nomadic
attacks were pressed home to the frontiers of Germany, and it "might be appre-
hended that the shepherds of Scythia would extinguish her cities, her arts, and
all the institutions of civil society."[10] Such must have been the feelings of the
citizens of Ur at the news of raids of the Amurru, in Harappa as the Sanskrit
war cries were heard across the city walls, or in Knossos when the Minotaur
was doomed.

CONCLUSION

All that we and the great thinkers of the past call civilization—not in the
sense of technological achievement or political dominance, but man's mastery
of his own powers—finds its most favorable environment in the conditions of

security and leisure made possible by settled agricultural economies and their townships. Civilization does not come by accident and is no easy or casual process. It is a conscious but disinterested pursuit which involves an uninhibited range of inquiry into all knowledge, the achievement of a sense of values at once fastidious and tolerant, and the refining and enhancing of the intellectual, spiritual, and emotional perceptions and experiences of man.

By reason of its inherent difficulty of attainment, civilization can never be the endowment of the majority. For in any epoch, the influence of the few determines the climate of thought. However imperfect in conception or execution, the fragmentary rough drafts of civilization have been sketched out, piecemeal and by rare individuals, within the framework of the city societies of the past.

Nevertheless, the thesis outlined in this chapter has no greater validity than any other interpretation of history. It is a personal estimate of what appear to be significant factors, not perhaps sufficiently stressed before, in the formation of the ancient and not-so-ancient world which we have inherited. Like beauty, patterns in history may well exist only in the eye of the beholder. Still, a subjective interpretation of the past is better than no interpretation. After all, it is the only one possible to the human mind. At least, a subjective interpretation recognizes that it cannot claim finality or be all-explanatory. Its very subjectivity allows for as many alternative and correlative perceptions of the innumerable facets of human history as there are historians.

Footnotes to Chapter 1

1. See A. Alföldi, "The Moral Barrier on Rhine and Danube," in *Roman Frontier Studies* (Durham: University of Durham, 1949), pp. 1–16.

2. For Jarmo, see *Antiquity*, XXIV (1950), 189–195. For Jericho, *ibid.*, XXVI (1952), 116–122.

3. V. G. Childe, *Man Makes Himself* (London: Watts and Company, 1937), and *What Happened in History* (Harmondsworth: Penguin Books, 1942).

4. See *Antiquity*, XXVIII (1953), 105.

5. E. Gibbon, *The Decline and Fall of the Roman Empire*, Ch. 34.

6. E. Minns, "Art of the Northern Nomads," *Proc. Brit. Acad.*, XXVIII (1945), 47–99.

7. See R. W. Hutchinson, "Battle-axes in the Aegean," *Proc. Prehist. Soc.*, XVI (1950), 52–64. There is evidence for the domestication of the horse in Kashan and Turkestan as early as the fourth millennium, B.C.

8. See Beardsley, "Hypotheses on Inner Asian Pastoral Nomadism," *Mem. Soc. Amer. Arch.*, No. 9, 1953, 24–28.

9. See Alföldi, *op. cit.*

10. Gibbon, *Decline and Fall*, Ch. 64.

2

Urban Communities and the Social Evolution of Nations

LOUIS CHEVALIER
Professeur, Sciences Philosophiques et Sociologiques
Collège de France, Paris

Present-day research about the influence of large cities upon the development of nations continues earlier work that goes back nearly as far as urbanization itself. To understand the subject, a consideration of these early efforts is helpful. For many similarities exist between historical and contemporary urban problems and studies.

Most of the problems growing out of the concentration of people in limited geographical areas must have been formulated in almost identical terms for major cities of the past like imperial Rome or mighty Constantinople. The same problems have been encountered in the history of Paris or London in later ages. Thus a sociological study of Paris or any other city in the twentieth century can scarcely be detached from inquiries of earlier periods. Because of its extension in time, historical material often places a problem in perspective which enables us to see the solution more clearly.

Important aspects of urbanization were considered, for example, in studies of mortality which were drawn up in London from the second half of the seventeenth century on. The economic and demographic development of Paris, and comparisons between Paris and London, were subject to many investigations during the eighteenth century. Men like the Abbé de Saint-Pierre, the Marquis de Mirabeau, and most of the *philosophes* concerned themselves with some of the essential phases of the general problem of urbanization. Others, like Deparcieux, Moheau, the Abbé d'Expilly, and Buffon, laid the foundations for later demographic and social studies. Much of the material in these investigations is still valid at the present time, and solutions to some of our contemporary problems may be found in them.

Despite the continuity of urban phenomena and the importance of historical

18

data in studying them, new facts have nonetheless emerged in recent years. For the sociologist, the most significant facts pertain to changing trends in mortality and fertility. These tendencies are greatly different from those previously ascribed to urbanization in general. They have resulted in considerable demographic, social, and moral changes in the urban environment.

Although this chapter is concerned with the role that large cities play in the social evolution of nations, the discussion will be limited largely to French cities and particularly to Paris. Relevant data from other countries will be included wherever possible. But there are several reasons for limiting the coverage attempted here.

First of all, little work has been done on an international level. Only in the United States has a preliminary synthesis of research in urban sociology been made. Thus valid comparisons among nations are difficult to draw.

Secondly, important differences appear among cities in various countries which make comparisons all the more complicated. Between cities in Europe and the United States, for instance, there is a marked variation in geographical extent. Large European cities have a tight texture; despite the torn fringes of their suburbs, they have relatively well-defined limits. Large urban centers in the United States, on the other hand, sprawl and break up into veritable urbanized zones. The different compositions and trends within the two types of cities cannot fail to bring about social differences which affect the more mobile middle classes as well as the working classes.

Finally, important differences occur among countries according to the proportion of the national population living in cities, the number of large cities in a given nation and the competition existing among them, and the degree of economic, administrative, and spiritual attraction that each exerts. In this respect, large cities in the United States have a significance that is entirely different from the importance of large European capitals like Paris or London.

In the following analysis, a demographic approach will be used, with special reference to the work of the Institut National d'Etudes Démographiques in Paris. Social phenomena will be considered insofar as demographic methods allow their determination and measurement, within the framework of the social history and structure of Paris and the Parisian region.[1] The role of large cities in the social evolution of nations will be studied from the point of view of the size of the population, the quality of the population, and the relations that exist among the inhabitants.

LARGE CITIES AND THE NUMERICAL SIZE OF THE POPULATION

The growth of cities generally brings about a heightening of living standards and progress in moral and material civilization. But considering that urbanization also causes an apparent decline in fertility of the urban population, it seems to endanger the very standards of living and civilization it sustains. Thus, the influence of the development of cities on the numerical size of populations will first be investigated.

Historical Aspects

Demographic evolution or change is such a slow process that certain older phenomena play a larger part in the actual make-up of a population than do other more recent phenomena whose effects may not be evident until much later. In the aggregate, therefore, large centers at the present time are generally still very close to what they were in days not long gone by. Few changes would have to be made to bring the descriptions of the late nineteenth century up to date. They, in turn, curiously resemble the accounts left by most of the philosophers and economists of the eighteenth century.

But no matter what the period, cities are believed to have lower fertility and higher mortality rates than the rest of the nation. In addition, they supposedly gain in population only through immigration from the countryside. As a result, the rural birth rate declines, since the persons who migrate from rural to urban areas are mainly of child-bearing age. The development of large cities thus seems to be detrimental to the growth of a nation's population.

MORTALITY. Until the end of the nineteenth century, cities are described as being far more evil because of their high mortality rates than because of their low fertility rates. In ancient times, famines and epidemics were more deadly in the cities than in the country. They caused such havoc that only powerful immigrations were able to assure the survival of ravaged cities. From 1575 to 1577, the plague in Venice killed fifty thousand people, about a quarter or a third of the population. In 1581, an epidemic in Marseilles spared the lives of only five thousand people.

In England from the end of the seventeenth century on, and in France from the middle of the eighteenth century, statistical analyses show a continued wasting away of the urban population resulting from a high general mortality, particularly from infant mortality. The analyses of Deparcieux and Buffon and later statistical series indicate how the general urban mortality rate remained higher than the national rate despite some improvement at the end of the nineteenth century.

From 1885 on, the crude death rate in Paris was lower than that of the rest of France. Yet actual mortality, which does not appear if one merely sets the number of deaths alongside the number of inhabitants, is quite a different question. The unequal division of the urban population according to age, and the high proportion of younger persons in urban areas, gives a false impression of a lower actual mortality rate in the more urbanized departments, such as the Seine, the Mediterranean coast, and the northern and northeastern regions of France.[2]

Actually, the highest comparative mortality rates within departments between 1935 and 1937 appeared in the Rhône and the Lyons region, the Alps, the Meurthe-et-Moselle, the Parisian region, the Bouches-du-Rhône, the Gironde, the Haute-Garonne, and the Bas-Rhin. In other words, the highest comparative rates occurred in all the departments containing large cities. On the other hand, the lowest comparative mortality rates were found in agricultural regions.

By age groups, mortality rates in Paris during the same period were lower than those in France for the 0 to 1 year group, higher from 1 to 5, and approximately the same from 5 up to the 15-year-old level. For females, the mortality rate was not so high in Paris from the age of 20 on. But for males, it was lower from 15 to 35 years of age, approximately equal from 40 to 50, and much higher beyond 50.

FERTILITY. Migratory movements in large cities have long prevented any accurate measurement of the fertility of an urban population and the establishment of sure comparisons. Research in the nineteenth century seemed to indicate that the fertility of certain large cities, especially Paris, was lower than that of the whole of France. Yet the findings of the census in 1856 suggest that low fertility rates are not necessarily typical of urban areas alone. At that time, the lowest fertility rates were localized in certain rural regions, such as Normandy, while high rates were observed among some of the departments which were most urbanized, like the Mediterranean coast and the department of the Nord.

One of the most remarkable economists of those days, Louis Passy, observed that the restriction of births was perhaps more prevalent among peasants than workers. According to him, it is not apparent why urban workers would avoid having children if the industrial economy maintained its prosperity. But in the country, ancient factors come into play even more readily as prosperity increases. Montalembert and Le Play suggested that the most important rural factors are the law of succession and the enforced sharing of inheritances.

Subsequent research confirms these observations concerning the true fertility of large cities. First of all, it seems that low fertility in France is not a specifically urban phenomenon. Moreover, urban populations are not by definition sterile, nor are rural populations inherently fertile. In fact, a *decline* in French fertility appeared immediately after the end of the eighteenth century in a nation which was still greatly rural.

The proportion of the population which is urban is only one factor accounting for variations in the birth rate. The geographical locality also plays an important role. The northeastern and western regions have a high birth rate in both urban and rural areas. Similarly, the southwest has a middling or low birth rate and the Mediterranean south has a very low birth rate. The geographical location is significant because it includes different social structures resulting generally from ancient evolutions like regulations on property, inheritance customs, and religious attitudes.

Yet from a certain size upward, large urban centers escape this local determinism. The low fertility of cities results from urban structures that blot out the diversity of regional tendencies. In the northern urban centers, the high rate of fertility reflects in part the relatively high fertility of the whole of the northern population and comes under the influence of the regional environment. But the low fertility of the Parisian region can be explained by the urban environment itself and reproduces a phenomenon which was accentuated in most large European capitals between the World Wars I and II.

During this period, the generally-falling fertility rates in the European capitals sank most rapidly. Whereas the crude reproduction rate for Austria was 0.92 in 1933, it was 0.38 for Vienna. For France, it stood at 1.09 in 1930 and in Paris at 0.57. The differences between the rates shown by the capitals reflected variations in the make-up of the population and probably also differences in national structures. But most important of all was the coincidence between large capitals and low fertility.

Contemporary Aspects

MORTALITY. Probably the most significant recent phenomenon in the demographic evolution of large French cities is the decline in infant mortality. Just before and after World War I, infant mortality was approximately the same in the Seine region and in all of France. Since that time, it has declined more sharply in the Seine region. In 1952, the standard rate of infant mortality in France was over 40 per thousand live births, whereas in the Seine it stood at 25 per thousand.

This decline is far more striking if one differentiates between endogenous and exogenous infant mortality. Endogenous mortality is due to prenatal causes or to causes resulting from the birth itself. Exogenous mortality is due to causes that follow birth, and depends on the environment in which the child lives.

Data indicate that endogenous mortality in France in 1952 was about the same as thirty years previously. But while exogenous mortality in France dropped from 52 per thousand to 42 per thousand between 1948 and 1952, it declined by approximately one-half in Paris from 50 per thousand to 25 per thousand. Since 1952, the decline has intensified. By 1954, exogenous mortality amounted to 15 per thousand for the Seine and to 30 per thousand for the whole of France.

By size of commune in 1950, aggregate infant mortality rates for legitimate children rose from 46.1 per thousand live births in rural communes to 48.1 in small towns of 5,000 to 10,000 inhabitants. Then they dropped to 37.4 in medium-sized cities from 50,000 to 100,000 inhabitants. After a slight increase to 38.4 in centers of over 100,000 inhabitants, the aggregate rates reached their lowest point of 30.9 in the Seine department. This figure was well below the aggregate rate of 43.5 for all communes. (See Table 1.)

A similar tendency was evident for mortality rates computed on the basis of the number of children already born of the same mother. In each case, the highly-urbanized Department of the Seine showed the lowest rates. Generally, the most important factor accounting for lower infant mortality rates in the larger cities seems to be the better quality of the medico-social equipment

Table 1

INFANT MORTALITY OF LEGITIMATE CHILDREN IN FRANCE IN 1950*
(RATES PER THOUSAND BORN ALIVE)

Type of commune**	Number of children already born of the same mother				
	0	1 or 2	3 or 4	5 and over	Aggregate
Rural communes	39.0	43.0	55.2	69.8	46.1
Urban communes:					
Up to 5,000 inhabitants	38.0	43.9	58.6	75.5	46.4
5,000 to 10,000 inhabitants	40.3	46.4	59.3	73.7	48.1
10,000 to 50,000 inhabitants	37.3	41.7	56.8	67.6	43.8
50,000 to 100,000 inhabitants	30.7	35.4	53.4	56.2	37.4
Over 100,000 inhabitants	34.2	37.6	47.4	57.6	38.4
Department of the Seine	28.5	30.4	37.2	54.5	30.9
All communes	—	—	—	—	43.5

* From a recent study by J. Bourgeois-Pachat.

** A commune is a territorial administrative subdivision headed by a mayor who is assisted by a municipal tribunal. In France there are approximately 38,000 communes.

available there. The minimum rates in the Department of the Seine indicate how much the rates in other places might be reduced in the future.

Recent research seems to indicate a lessening of this differential mortality rate between cities and the countryside. In the country, there is no difference between the the death rates of managers and agricultural laborers, since the influence of natural environment is so much stronger than that of standards of living. In French cities, on the contrary, death rates vary considerably according to professions. With an over-all average adult death rate of 100, the mortality rate for *agricultural* managers and laborers is 65. Within the *urban* working class, the rate is around 125 with a range between 100 and 360.

In Amsterdam, at least, a leveling of the mortality rate according to social classes appears for the first time.

These results confirm other recent observations concerning general mortality during wars and crises. In countries with sufficient medico-social care, the death rate has remained remarkably low despite circumstances that would have elevated it in other times or places. In short, the so-called level of existence has ceased to be an important mortality factor in certain advanced countries. Medical attention and the general way of life play a more important role than the economic status of the individual. If social conditions still have a bearing on the death rate, they do so through living habits and educational levels rather than through income considerations. Research in progress by the authors on mortality rates by professions already confirms this important point by showing the dominating influence of the medico-social machinery and, in particular, of social security. If social equality before death is not yet completely achieved, it is nevertheless taking on new aspects.[3]

FERTILITY. Today, as in the past, fertility is generally lower in cities than in the country. Fertility rates even appear to decrease with increases in city size.

Since 1946, the Institut National de la Statistique has published registered birth figures together with data about "domiciled births" according to the mother's place of residence. These were totaled up by department, by commune, and by category of commune.

Thanks to this innovation, the importance of fertility according to categories of communes can be measured for the first time. Taking into account the breakdown according to age (which is generally more favorable in cities), P. Gasc found the following reproduction rates in 1946 for "domiciled births:" for large towns, 1.23; for medium-size towns, 1.43; for small towns, 1.56; and for rural communities, 1.66. Thus, total fertility (legitimate and illegitimate) is one-third higher in the country than in the large towns. If the factor of marriage were eliminated, the difference would be reduced from one-third to one-fifth, which is still significant.

Interpretation

Are large urban centers irremediably sterile and does the growth of large cities endanger the very existence of the nation? The question might be answered only if the problem of differential fertility were first resolved so that rates could be put on a comparable basis.

In this respect, important work has been carried on in the United States,[4] although the conclusions cannot necessarily be applied to other countries. French research at best emphasizes the difficulty of the inquiry. Is there, for example, a relation between the low fertility within the Parisian center and bad housing conditions? An inquiry undertaken by A. Girard and H. Bastide through polls reveals that certain households delay the birth of children because of housing difficulties. It is not certain, however, that these young couples would act differently under different housing conditions or that they would have more children.

Lacking additional French research, we can draw upon the remarkable work of the Milbank Memorial Fund in studying the fertility of households in Indianapolis, Indiana.[5] The survey found that despite the relatively poor fertility of couples adopting planned conceptions, this fertility tended to be in direct rather than in inverse relation to the economic and social status. It is certainly not easy to apply these results to populations in other urban centers in the United States. Yet the American inquiries as well as work in other countries suggest the importance of the conscious adaptation of fertility to circumstances.

Experience in Paris apparently confirms this tendency. It contradicts earlier data suggesting that a rise in urban population ought to be followed in all nations by a diminishing fertility, a rising mortality, and a general aging of the population. Nations with constantly growing urban centers would be at a disadvantage in comparison with less urbanized countries. But such is no longer the case. Recent changes in mortality and fertility rates now indicate that urbanization is not necessarily synonymous with depopulation.

LARGE CITIES AND THE QUALITY OF THE POPULATION

Here we shall be concerned with the physical, intellectual, and moral characteristics of countries with large urban populations. These characteristics will be interpreted in terms of the quality of the inhabitants in large cities and also the quality of the population within the entire nation.

The Quality of the Inhabitants in Large Cities

HISTORICAL PHENOMENA. Some demographic facts remain virtually unchanged with time. Others can be explained only by reference to previous changes from the eighteenth or nineteenth century. The permanence of such social phenomena shows that despite economic, social, or political transformations, the influence of urban living conditions perpetuate themselves no less than do rural ways of life.

Physical characteristics: In the eighteenth century, the interpretations of Deparcieux, Messance, and Buffon are useful in analyzing numerous descriptions of the Parisian population and its health, mores, and physical and moral appearance during the fifty years that preceded the Revolution. Thanks to this sort of demographic investigation, it is possible to discern in Mercier's *Tableaux de Paris* or in Restif de la Bretonne's *Nuits de Paris* what is fiction and what is observed fact.

Over the first half of the nineteenth century, demographic research achieved its greatest extension. At that time, the rapid growth of the main urban centers, especially Paris, brought about social, political, and moral disturbances that could not be ignored. Efforts were then made to renew Condorcet's earlier attempts to apply the science of measurement to all human studies, even to social, political, and moral sciences. The efforts and ambitions of the statisticians engaged in this work are best embodied in the writings of Quételet.

Early attempts to measure physical differences between urban and rural populations included a comparison of heights in different provinces. In the first half of the nineteenth century, the Seine was ranked among departments exhibiting the lowest heights, although it is located in the north which generally had the tallest population. This situation can be explained by the fact that at that time many immigrants into Paris came from the south, where the average height was lower than in the north. Other data supported the tendency for large cities like Paris to be physically pathological.

Moral characteristics: As far as the moral characteristics of urban and rural populations are concerned, mortality and crime statistics may be used as indicators. Both are expressions of the same unhealthy condition, and both show the same geographical, professional, economic, and social localizations. Their chronological phases correspond to the seasons as well as the years.

The demographic analysis of mortality in Paris during the first half of the nineteenth century throws light upon certain great literary works that embody the pathological nature of the Parisian environment. Interpreted in the light of

contemporary statistics, works like *Les Misérables* or *Les Mystères de Paris*
are veritable documents of the unhealthy physical and moral state of the
Parisian population at that time. The importance of such descriptions of the
dregs of the underworld, the confusion between the proletariat and the dangerous classes, and the prevalence of poverty and crime, has been shown
elsewhere.[6] This is not fiction, belonging to what might be termed "crime
literature," but the masterful evocation of an over-all situation.

Phases of development: The pathological nature of the urban environment
has not been equally apparent in every age. Trends in mortality, illegitimate
births, and criminality would seem to indicate that their peaks correspond to
periods of rapid urban population growth by immigration, even in prosperous
times. Their low points ordinarily occur when urban growth rates fall and even
in the face of poor economic conditions.

During the greater part of the eighteenth century, the Parisian population
increased slowly. Immigration was partly nomadic and the Parisian population
incorporated only a small part of its numbers. But the years that preceded the
Revolution paralleled a sudden rise in immigration. During the Revolution,
immigration was rapid and probably had an effect on the Revolution in Paris
and its violence.

In the first years of the Restoration, the rate of population increase remained fairly low. Morbidity and mortality rates were approximately stationary and the moral, social, and political climates were favorable. Thus there is a
marked contrast between the descriptions of Victor Hugo and Eugène Sue in
the Revolutionary age and the Restoration accounts of Balzac, in which
workers hardly appear and where criminality remains exceptional, in spite
of Vautrin.

In 1821, the *faubourg* of Saint-Antoine, an eastern section of Paris, was described in these terms: "Everything there betokens the blissful calm of indus-
trious people of small means with regular habits, love of work and peace,
simple and clean clothes, harmony in households. Vice and debauch are
equally foreign here; there are no places open to prostitution or dissolute
idleness. I saw only two public houses beyond the barrier, and few exist inside.
Those outside are filled only on holidays and I noticed only family groups in
them, relieving through the unconstraint of open and gentle mirth the weari-
ness of their regular walk through the bois de Vincennes."[7]

The violence that followed this calm coincided with the July Monarchy. In
the Second Empire and the first years of the Third Republic, it was succeeded
by a long period throughout which demographic changes were less violent,
more regular, and better adapted to economic conditions and the urban framework.

Over the last two decades of the nineteenth century, there was an upsurge of
illegitimate births, infant mortality, criminality, and an accumulation of social
conflicts and of all manner of violence which partly reflect an unfavorable
economic situation, but mainly an increase in immigration beyond the eco-

nomic and material capacities of the city. Throughout those years, the importance of sexual irregularity, venereal disease, and syphilophobia in literary descriptions of Paris are aspects of the phenomenon.[8]

CONTEMPORARY PHENOMENA. Although the above-mentioned tendencies remained in force for the Parisian metropolitan area until after the first World War, recent demographic research has uncovered new phenomena as well as considerable alterations in the older ones.

Physical characteristics: Research has been conducted by the Institut d'Hygiène on the height and weight of 20-year-old males and of children throughout France during the nineteen forties.[9] The findings reveal that marked changes occurred between the two World Wars and afterward. They contradict all pessimistic forecasts that were made during the second world conflict. Here, in brief, are the main conclusions.

The study of stature and weight of 20-year-old men, based upon military statistics, shows first that regional differences which were so marked during the nineteenth century had considerably lessened. With the exceptions of Brittany and Corsica (where the average height is definitely lower than elsewhere) and Alsace-Lorraine and the Basque region (where it is superior), the averages were pretty even. From department to department, height did not differ by more than one centimeter (0.39 inch) and remained pretty close to 167 centimeters (5 feet $5\frac{7}{10}$ inches). The average weight of 60 kilos (132 pounds) did not vary more than one kilo (about 2⅕ pounds).

Secondly, the average height of recruits seems to have increased by 5 to 6 centimeters (1.97 to 2.36 inches) during the preceding 40 years, more through the elimination of small-height groups than by the increase of tall groups.

Finally, urbanization tends to raise the average height. In the nineteen forties, the stature of the 20-year-old man in Paris was between 168.8 and 172.8 centimeters. It was nearly always greater than the height of draftees from the department that boasted the highest average, the Haut-Rhin (169). The lowest average was in a Breton department, the Ille-et-Vilaine (164.6). The weight of draftees of the Seine department did not show such a marked superiority but still belonged amongst the highest of France (60.7 kilos as against 62.10 in the Haut-Rhin).

This urban height advantage results from particular circumstances shown by certain correlations. Height tends to increase, for example, as the level of education rises. It tends to decrease with the number of brothers and sisters in a family. The urban height advantage also reflects a general improvement in the standard of living throughout the nation between World Wars I and II. Proportionately, the improvement is far less remarkable in the Parisian center than in certain rural regions. These new tendencies, therefore, do not indicate any considerable change in the former picture of the influence of a large urban agglomeration on the physical quality of the population.

More remarkable is the change of height and weight for children which was revealed by the research of the Institut d'Hygiène in 1950. Within the same age bracket, the height and weight of 300,000 children in public and private schools was generally greater in the city than in the country, although certain differences appeared among cities. The averages for Strasbourg, for instance, were distinctly higher than those of Paris; on the other hand, in Lyons and Marseilles, they were generally lower.

The averages for cities in 1950 were greater than in the recent past. In the fifteenth arrondissement of Paris, for example, the average heights for boys below 11 years of age were 2 to 3 centimeters above the 1934 average. For children above 11 years of age, height was also slightly superior to previous averages, but only by one centimeter. Weight variations were less distinct. These facts, correlated with the lowering of infant mortality in Paris, confirm the urban advantage and the increasing influence of the availability of medico-social equipment which partly counteracts unfavorable factors.

How long may this initial advantage last? Up to what point will favored generations continue to be privileged? It does not appear that urban death rates can be expected to continue falling for long. For the urban center keeps on imposing the same unfavorable conditions upon the biological quality of its inhabitants.

Among the biological aspects, one of the most important appears to be the greater opportunity offered by urban centers for contagion. The probability of infection is greater in a large city than in the country. Tuberculosis, for example, accounts for a far higher percentage of positive tuberculin skin-tests among city school children than among those of the country.

Among the socio-economic factors, work conditions and the type of urban life appear to play a more important role than housing conditions. The Parisian center has no monopoly of slums. Overcrowding is typical of all cities that became industrialized from the second half of the nineteenth century on.

Moreover, large centers impose special working and living conditions whose physiological consequences are obvious. Statistics on occupational mortality are indeed hard to interpret; their results do not tally exactly for all countries.[10] However, they show that in France, mortality for the same occupation is generally higher in Paris than in the rest of the nation.

To these constraints must be added other phenomena characteristic of large cities—lack of isolation, noise, insufficiency of sleep, psychosomatic ills, and so on.

Intellectual characteristics: Writers describing the civilization of capitals have always asserted that large urban centers offer a particularly favorable environment for the intellectual development of their inhabitants. This contrast between moral and intellectual effects is constantly stressed by the eighteenth century *philosophes.* It finds expression in many articles of the great *Encyclopédie.*

According to the Abbé de Saint-Pierre, for instance, the intellectual superiority of urban populations results from an initial selection that draws the most gifted individuals away from the country and small towns to the city. He underlines the causes and effects of a complex phenomenon which researchers are now trying to resolve and of which only a few aspects will be summarized here.[11]

Essentially, the causes of the apparent intellectual superiority of urbanities are attributable to the pathological aspects of the urban way of life with its accelerated rhythm of activities. This appears in every trait, including leisure where movies and radio occupy the forefront in all urban concentrations.[12] Cities are much more pressured by timetables than are rural areas.

Such differences between urban and rural environments have psychological consequences which sociological descriptions of large cities are attempting to uncover in various countries. These inquiries agree that large differences exist between intellectual behavior under urban and rural conditions. It seems difficult, however, to attribute the differences to a uniform intellectual superiority of large-city populations, or to conclude that urban residents are more intelligent than people in other regions, particularly in rural areas. All that can be said is that the intelligence of city populations is of a different quality than that of rural inhabitants, and is on the whole better adapted to the exigencies of urban life.

What of the demographic area? The remarkable decline in infant mortality in the Parisian center cannot be explained solely by the higher cultural level of the population. It is the result of a particularly concentrated medico-social apparatus, which does not necessarily have the same effect on all urban environments.

Nor can a conclusion be drawn in favor of the asserted superiority of large urban populations in the occupational realm. This is so because certain economic occupations find more favorable conditions in large cities than in small towns or rural areas. Cities offer better organized occupational training, and more opportunities for varied experience which workers acquire themselves through repeatedly changing their jobs. At the same time, the decline of trade guilds and apprenticeships has given city workers a great advantage over laborers from the country.

It is not surprising, therefore, that the output per man-hour is lower in the country than in metropolitan centers. Research carried out in France on the decentralization of industries and industrial centers, particularly within the aviation industry, has stressed this inferiority but shows that it was not irremediable. The use of industrial methods adapted to the area in question produces approximately equivalent results after a while.

Similar conclusions may be drawn from research bearing on the intellectual level of children. In 1950, 95,237 children from public and private elementary schools, aged from 6 to 12 years, were given a collective test to measure their intellectual aptitude.[13] This inquiry indicated that, for all ages and in every case, the performance of children from the country was below that of city children. The difference was especially apparent for test questions concerned with an understanding of the logical relations between abstract signs.

Yet these results do not necessarily demonstrate that children from the country are less intelligent than those from cities. City children are exposed to stimuli that qualify them better for a test of this nature which, by its very make-up, is more suitable for city than for country children.[14]

A study made by Louis Henry of the intellectual level of school children in various districts of Paris and the suburbs has brought to light important differences. With some exceptions that seem to reflect the inferior socio-economic level of the population of certain districts, schools with a low average mark are found in the suburbs and schools with a very high average mark are in Paris. This means that belonging to a large metropolitan center does not necessarily endow all of the inhabitants with equal intellectual aptitude.

The large city, in other words, does not diffuse its opportunities and resources to every resident. In nineteenth century Paris, for example, just beyond the city lay an area where an economically and socially underprivileged population camped within the ruins of old villages. At that time, Parisian naturalization had only uneven effects, and even now regional groups remain tenaciously at the gates of Paris. Veritable Breton colonies still exist in certain communes of the Parisian outskirts that are particularly ill-favored economically and socially. Of course, material changes and improvements in school equipment and transportation have tended to increase contacts and lessen the differences between the city and the suburbs.

Moral characteristics: The influence of contemporary urban life on the moral quality of the inhabitants can be studied by considering the normal behavior of the population as well as the criminal behavior.

As previously indicated, criminality may appear in different countries at certain times as one of the consequences of rapid urbanization. Although this deviant behavior is not necessarily representative of the moral status of the entire population, certain data do show a higher crime rate in the Parisian center than in France as a whole. In 1952, the juvenile delinquency rate stood at 85 per 100,000 inhabitants in Paris. For all of France, it was 43 per 100,000.

But these data do not indicate that urban criminality is generally higher than rural criminality in France. They merely suggest that the demographic behavior of urban populations is different from that of other populations. In other words, different demographic structures—represented by different distributions of the population by age and sex—account for different demographic behavior.

In large cities, the distribution of the population by age and sex is generally abnormal. There is a preponderance of young adults and a numerical superiority of women over men. The ratio of females to males tends to increase with the degree of urbanization, and is especially high among age groups from 15 to 30 years old.

In the Parisian center, a chart showing the distribution of women would emphasize their numerical superiority in the wealthiest west districts. The workingman's suburbs, on the other hand, would show a predominantly male population. Thus, "one might compare this chart with others established according to certain socio-economic criteria, such as the average returns per taxpayer in 1949, the percentage of non-communist votes during the general elections held on November 10, 1946, the proportion of dwellings having a bathroom, the height of recruits in 1948."[15]

The inequality in the sex distribution, however, has not always been the same. In fact, the predominance of women in Paris did not appear until the last years of the Second Empire. In eighteenth century Paris, alongside an old indigenous, normally-formed population, immigration of a nearly exclusively male population was concentrated in the poorer districts. The Revolution and the Empire brought great upheavals in the sex distribution of the capital's population.

Following the immigration of the first decades of the nineteenth century, men easily got the better of women during the July Monarchy. Certain sections in the center of Paris were then inhabited solely by workers living in furnished rooms. It is impossible to understand the violence that rocked Paris during those years without bearing in mind the abnormal composition of the city by districts. Generally, it can be said that large cities are hard put to maintain a numerical balance of sexes which immigration tends to destroy. In Paris, the result at first was a male surplus; from the end of the nineteenth century on, a female surplus.

The study of the demographic consequences of this unequal distribution according to age and sex also has a significant bearing with respect to urban mortality rates, marriage statistics, birth rates, and frequency of sexual relations.

Within large cities, the frequency of sexual relations is difficult to determine since it does not depend on marriage. In estimating the number of households composed of unmarried couples living together in Paris in 1880, Bertillon relied upon data concerning illegitimate births. From them, he concluded that there was probably one unmarried household for every ten regular ones. Since about 825,000 married couples lived in Paris in 1876, Bertillon figured on a very conservative basis that there must have been at least 82,500 unmarried households.

The higher percentage of bachelors by age groups and the rise in the age at which men marry are also statistical indications of the city's abnormal population distribution by sex. The "choice of the partner" is made under particular circumstances which Ilse Schwidetzky has studied especially well within the framework of German cities.[16] But Jean Sutter has noted that inbreeding is fairly high in a number of French departments containing a large urban center,[17] and analogous observations were made in Amsterdam. In France, marriage itself appears more fragile[18] in large cities and the correlation between juvenile delinquency and family break-ups is clear. A statistical survey of 300 cases in Paris showed that 67 per cent of the children who committed theft belonged to a broken-up home. Moreover, it has been noted that marriage tends to be less fertile. In 1949, in the Department of the Seine 65 per cent of the separations occurred in childless households.

Important studies[19] show identical tendencies in most countries and an apparent link between urban concentration and the weakening of family ties. Everywhere essential factors include the work of the wife that wrests the prestige as chief breadwinner from the husband, and the vulnerability of the family head in urban surroundings.[20] Nevertheless, considerable differences do appear between various ways of life and between social classes within the same city.[21]

Large Cities and the Quality of the Inhabitants of a Nation

The study of physical and moral characteristics of large urban concentrations does not suffice to resolve the general problem of the influence of metropolitan centers. The greater part of a country's population is ordinarily concentrated within several large cities. These cities usually have identical economic and social characteristics and a same type of civilization. Thus they impose upon their inhabitants ways of life that are scarcely different.

The rest of the national population may be in the minority, as a sort of residual matter existing only in relation to the large cities and doomed to wane progressively. Its subsistence depends solely on anachronistic circumstances that will eventually disappear, or on the value which large cities still find in the present state of things.

But it sometimes happens that this secondary population group is quantitatively more important than that of the great cities. Though linked to the large city through economic, cultural, and occasionally administrative and political bonds, it nevertheless has an independent existence. Against the absorption and competition of the large centers, it sets up a resistance that varies among nations.

A long historical description would be required to describe the influence of the development of large cities on the physical and moral quality of the inhabitants of a nation. Historical documentation is so abundant, convincing, and well-known that there is no need for repetition here. Pirenne writes: "The day when towns are born, the irremediable decadence of the feudal and mystical Middle Ages begins. New tendencies that are more human, more worldly, more modern are felt in western Europe. The Crusades are followed by peaceful commerce between Christians and Mohammedans in Mediterranean harbors; the *chansons de geste* are replaced by the fabliaux; Latin by vulgar tongues. And it is rightly claimed that in the new spirit of the middle classes is to be found one of the most active causes of the success of the Renaissance."[22]

Thanks to the development of urban economies, the standards of living of entire national populations have risen. Along with the standards of life, modes of life have also progressed through declines in mortality and morbidity. As for culture, it might be an exaggeration to view urban development as *the* essential cause for the decline of illiteracy. But it would be no less a mistake to disregard the part played by cities in the evolution and the diffusion of ideas.

Until recently, the urban and the rural spheres were not sharply separated. It would be easy to show that the past economic and social evolution of France has resulted at least as much from the efforts of the middle classes in places outside of Paris as from the initiative of the Parisian middle class, which is constantly rejuvenated by a provincial influx.

Even in the life of political ideas, the province plays as important a part as the city. The history of republican feeling in Paris from 1848 to the end of the Second Empire shows that the capital generally borrowed political themes from the provinces more frequently than she exported them to the provinces. As for the capital's cultural contribution in fine arts and letters, the civil status of 2,000 well-known Parisians during the July Monarchy indicates that 1,560 had been born in the provinces. By the end of the nineteenth century, this ratio had grown even further. In all fields, historical investigation shows a reciprocal influence of capital upon province and province upon capital.

The influence of large cities on the quality of the inhabitants of a nation is particularly difficult to determine when urbanization has reached a stage at which good and evil effects merge and so minimize the possibility of distinguishing each clearly. Such is the case in France where the influence of the Parisian center and other large cities is related to the problem of the nation's present and future economic modernization. Studies have been made in France concerning some of the economic aspects of the problem.[23] Others are of broader interest. Each will be merely summarized here.

If the growth of large cities has fostered economic development and a general rise in the standard of living, migrations from the country and from small towns towards the main urban centers have depopulated certain regions. Some of these regions are among the most fertile in land and resources in France. This represents a loss of wealth for the particular regions as well as for the nation itself. It eventually results in either a lowering of the standard of living or a slowing up of the rise in that standard.[24]

As far as France is concerned, it is a mistake to confuse industrial development with the growth of large cities. Research indicates that the industrial effort must now be directed toward the small and medium-sized towns. Since the end of the nineteenth century, these places have suffered the most from industrial growth in the main cities, especially in Paris. Any further development of the Parisian region is not desirable. Not only would it aggravate present problems of the city, but it would also proceed at the expense of the economy of other regions of France. In other words, the cost of Parisian industrialization would ultimately swallow up the profits.

With reference to the effect of the development of large centers on the intellectual level of the inhabitants, many demographs have investigated the possible consequences of the differential fertility. From this point of view, the development of large centers may bring about a lowering of the intellectual level of the national population through the selection of the most gifted individuals which marks the emigration towards cities and by the weak fertility which the urban center brings about. At the present stage of research, it seems difficult to maintain such a conclusion.

In the United States, work of *The Milbank Memorial Fund Quarterly* has studied this problem at length. As has been shown, a causal relationship cannot necessarily be established between large cities or certain intellectual and social characteristics and weak fertility. Moreover, the problem is a long-range one, since the growth of large urban centers within a nation cannot fail to change the psychological characteristics of an increasingly important part of the population.

Social Relations in an Urbanized Nation

Social relations between individuals in large cities or in smaller communities can be viewed in two ways. They may be analyzed through the facts or through the consciousness which the inhabitants have of the facts and the attitudes which they have adopted toward them. This involves the question of what differences in inequality or mobility may exist, how aware the people are of them, and how both factors affect social behavior.

Social Differences

INEQUALITY. Until after the first half of the nineteenth century, social inequality was so important within the old European capitals that it was reflected by a veritable biological inequality. During the *Ancien Régime* before the Revolution, for example, Paris grew slowly by the natural development of indigenous aristocratic, middle-class, or craftsmen families. Only a small proportion of population growth resulted from immigration. The greater part of the immigrants remained nomadic or lived in the poor sections on the fringes of the capital.

The differences between the indigenous and immigrant population were so marked that each was considered to belong to a separate race. There were the Parisians and also the other "people," referred to in literary works of the time by names that suggest a racially different population. In describing the suburban *quartier* of Saint-Marcel in the southeast section of Paris, Mercier wrote in 1781: "In this neighborhood, the people are more dishonest, more inflammable, more quarrelsome, and more disposed to riot than in the other districts. The police are afraid to provoke the populace, which is treated with respect because it is capable of going to the greatest excesses. . . . These people have nothing in common with the Parisians—the refined residents along the banks of the Seine." Similar discriminations can be found in the descriptions of the Abbé d'Expilly. They are supported by statistics of marriages, births, and especially mortality.

In the nineteenth century, racial and demographic differences in Paris were further emphasized by a large and accelerated immigration into the capital.

The contrast is summarized by the title of Victor Hugo's *Les Misérables*. It makes up the heart of Eugène Sue's *Les Mystères de Paris,* the first page of which reads: "We shall attempt to place before the eyes of the reader certain episodes in the lives of other barbarians who dwell as much beyond the pale of civilization as the wild tribes so well depicted by Cooper. Only the barbarians of whom we speak are in our midst."

The bases of these social differences were biological, as revealed by a real inequality in birth and mortality data. But they also existed in popular belief. The two peoples faced each other and lived side-by-side on racial terms, both influenced in their behavior by physical attractions and dislikes.

Modern data are marked by a considerable lessening of the biological inequality that was one of the primary aspects of social inequality during the nineteenth century. Undoubtedly, certain biological differences still remain. In France, the work of the Institut d'Hygiène indicates that in 1948 the average height and weight of 20-year-old men corresponded approximately to the social morphology of Paris. The west sections, inhabited by a middle-class population, showed a higher average than did the workers' sections in the east. Similar differences appeared among the children.

With some exceptions, biological inequalities are no longer so strongly marked. They no longer represent the most apparent expression of social inequality. In large cities, social differences are now of another sort. Even if present-day inequality appears important, a brief glance at the historical past suggests that these inequalities are far milder than they were less than a century ago, because they are no longer expressed in birth and death statistics.

Does the lessening of biological inequality give new meaning to other forms of social inequality—primarily to forms concerning living standards? From this point of view, is the social contrast more marked today in the large centers than in towns of lesser importance or in the country? The solution of such a problem encounters well-known difficulties. For, within the same country, the economic and professional structures of urban centers by regions and also the local customs and ways of life are so diversified that the living standards are often not absolutely comparable.

One study has brought out contrasts of this nature which occur between the United States and France.[25] A comparison of social inequality within large cities in the United States and in Europe would reveal less the differences that exist between these cities than it would the differences between the entire economies and societies.

For France, no findings yet justify the statement that social inequality is more or less strong in the Parisian center than in other towns or the country. Moreover, any such data could not be truly comparable since the ways of life and the needs are so varied. Only one conclusion seems possible: even if the contrasts between the standards of life within large cities may be stronger than elsewhere and affect a larger number of people, it is certain that such centers also develop intermediary situations that are numerous and varied and that soften the contrast between the most privileged groups and the least favored. This social diversity is particularly apparent in the capitals. Not only is the variety of conditions greater but the passage from one condition to another is facilitated. Social mobility within large centers helps reduce social inequality.

MOBILITY. Social mobility has always been stronger in the cities than in the country. In past times, the contrast was striking between the slow evolution of rural society described by Marc Bloch and the mobility of the Parisian society which can be measured in part through bankruptcy statistics and registry office files.[26] The contrast appears in the changing social status of individuals as compared with the status of their fathers, and also in a large percentage of social promotions received within a single individual career.

From the middle of the nineteenth century on, marriage statistics in Paris show a high percentage of heterogeneous marriages. Although present-day research does not permit a precise description of social mobility in Paris, a contrast of the relative importance of cities in the United States and France is pertinent. "Over two-thirds of the Americans find for themselves a different professional class from that of their fathers and so do nearly half of the French. Effective mobility in France is about three-fifths of what it might be if its society were completely open. In the United States, the corresponding proportion amounts to four-fifths."[27]

Urban structures themselves facilitate social mobility. From the demographic standpoint, cities are apparently incapable of insuring the rebirth and the increase of their population solely by balancing birth and death rates. Migrations from the country and towns of lesser importance toward the large cities and internal social migrations resulting from the relative fertility of the various classes in relation to each other all favor social mobility.

Social Behavior

The violence of social antagonism within metropolitan centers contrasts strangely with the facts that social inequality is no more marked in large cities than elsewhere, and that social mobility is greater in cities.

Yet social struggle is more constant, intense, bloody, and nationally important in cities than in the country. The political evolution of the Parisian center from the beginning of the Third Republic until the present time is a sufficient illustration of this tendency.[28]

Until around 1900, election results show that Paris was more to the left than the rest of France. But the suburbs—which were still only slightly industrialized—were much less advanced than Paris. From 1900 on, Paris moved right and the suburbs, as they grew industrialized, moved towards the extreme left wing of socialism.

Between the first and second World Wars, the moderate parties were generally stronger in Paris than in the rest of France, but they were far weaker in the suburbs. The left-wing parties like the radicals and socialists were constantly weaker in Paris than in the provinces. The Communist extreme left wing was invariably stronger in Paris and even more so in the suburbs than in the rest of France. In short, the extremist parties were stronger in the Parisian center than were the middle-of-the-road parties, but the extremists belonged to the right wing in Paris and to the left wing in the suburbs.

The political evolution from 1946 to 1954 showed the same tendencies. The traditional strength of right-wing predominance in Paris was maintained. In 1951, right-wing parties received 41.1 per cent of the registered vote in Paris against 34.6 per cent for all of France, but only 29.8 per cent in the suburbs. The weakness of the middle-of-the-road parties continued. The Communist party reached its high point in the Parisian region in 1936 and then declined. But it remained a little stronger in Paris (20.9 per cent) than in the whole of France and considerably stronger in the suburbs (31.4 per cent).

Finally, it should be noted that the percentage of potential voters staying away from the polls has always been weaker in the Seine area than in the whole of France. Before 1939, it was stronger in the suburbs than in Paris; since 1946, it has been stronger in Paris than in the suburbs. The Parisian center is thus marked by more extremist political tendencies than are those characteristic of the rest of France.

Most of the European capitals would show similar observations and con- clusions. From these facts, the conclusion might be drawn that the growth of large cities could bring about a worsening of social strife and of political in- stability in a nation. The violence of such strife results mainly from the number of individuals which this strife divides. There are few reasons why workers or those of the middle classes should be more hostile to each other in a large urban center than in a small town or in a rural community. On the contrary, there are many reasons why these attitudes ought to be more mod- erate. But the sole fact of their numbers, grouped in one particular spot, exaggerates their differences, multiplies their dissension, and accumulates the feelings of uneasiness or of fear which they might feel toward each other.

These feelings become all the stronger when great changes of population take place in large cities, such as the history of Paris shows from the eighteenth century up to the present times. The opposition between two segments of the population—the old-stock Parisians and the newcomers, which Frégier, con- fusing rabble and proletariat, calls in a famous work "the dangerous classes"[29] —accounts for the feverish aspect of the July Monarchy.

During the last years of the nineteenth century, a new upsurge of immigra- tion coincided with an economic crisis and had similar consequences. The history of the Popular Front had demographic as well as economic aspects. To a large extent, the quantity of the inhabitants and the rhythm of demo- graphic progression caused the large city to experience exacerbated social antagonism which was not always entirely revealed by its economic and social structures.

To this must be added a change in attitude brought to light by the work of collective psychology. In cities, various forms of propaganda have every chance of gathering larger groups than elsewhere. This purely material factor is particularly apparent in European nations. It explains in part the contrast between the political and social extremism of capitals and the more moderate attitude of the rest of the country. It is less important in nations that have a higher percentage of urban populations.

CONCLUSION

Urban centers no longer exert the same traditional influences on the social evolution of nations as they have in the past. Several recent phenomena stress this fact. These findings concern only limited demographic aspects of the problem, but they provide a comparative and incontrovertible interpretation.

For one thing, large urban centers can no longer be considered as the place where generations wane and die. From the quantitative standpoint, present mortality and fertility tendencies show that cities do not irreparably endanger the rebirth of mankind and that urban civilizations are not necessarily deadly.

From the qualitative point of view, the traditional picture of the pathological effects of urban life cannot be preserved any longer. The bad social state of the capital city is not necessarily expressed in monuments of misery and death like hospitals, prisons, pawnshops, or cemeteries. Admittedly, the sanitary and moral state of large cities may not be better than that of smaller areas. Certain physical and moral ills that would not develop anywhere else thrive in the urban center and are in a way revealed by it. But essentially the physical and moral pathology of large cities is different from—not greater than—the pathology of other towns or of the country. And certain changes in large cities portend at least the emergence of conditions favorable to superior physical and moral qualities.

Similarly, from the social standpoint the intensity of political strife within European capitals results much more from external than internal circumstances. There is no reason why economically favorable conditions, high standards of living, and intense social mobility should not bring about at least a considerable lessening of social conflicts.

Many of these indications have appeared only recently. Certain current trends may not yet be sufficiently well established to be significant. In the future, they may change once again. Moreover, the conclusions relating to the Parisian center do not necessarily apply equally to all urban societies. The greatest demographic differences, of course, appear between the United States and Europe. Solutions valid for one nation may be highly inapplicable to another.

FOOTNOTES TO CHAPTER 2

1. Louis Chevalier, Leçon Inaugurale du Cours d'Histoire et Structure Sociales de Paris et de la Région Parisienne.

2. [A department is one of 94 principal administrative divisions of French territory headed by a préfet who is assisted by a general tribunal. Each department is divided into arrondissements or sub-préfectures, and further subdivided into cantons and communes.]

3. A. Sauvy, "La Mortalité à Amsterdam Selon Les Quartiers," *Population,* VII, No. 3 (1952). This journal is published in Paris by the Presses Universitaires de France and issued by the Institut National d'Etudes Démographiques.

4. See F. Lorimer and F. Osborn, *Dynamics of Population* (New York: Macmillan, 1934).

5. See P. K. Whelpton and C. V. Kiser, *Social and Psychological Factors Affecting Fertility* (New York: Milbank Memorial Fund, 1946), 3 Vols. Reprinted from articles which previously appeared in *The Milbank Memorial Fund Quarterly,* Vols. XXI to XXIII.

6. Louis Chevalier, "Description Littéraire et Description Historique de Paris, pendant la Première Moitié du XIX° Siècle," un communication au Congrès des Etudes Françaises de septembre, 1953.

7. Pierre Joseph Spiridion Dufey (dit Dufey de l'Yonne), *Mémorial d'un Parisien* (Paris: Dalibon, 1821).

8. The best example is Charles-Louis Philippe, *Bubu de Montparnasse* (Paris: Librarie Universelle, 1905).

9. J. Tremolieres and J. J. Boulenger, "Contribution à l'Etude du Phénomène de Croissance et de Stature en France de 1940 à 1948," *Recueil de Travaux de l'Institut National d'Hygiène,* I (1950).

10. Such differences are pointed out in the volume of the B.I.T., *Méthodes de la Statistique de la Morbidité et de la Mortalité Professionnelle* (Geneva, 1930).

11. Among the investigations, the most important are those of the Bureau of Applied Social Research at Columbia University, New York, directed by Paul F. Lazarsfeld, Kingsley Davis, and Robert K. Merton, and those directed by Georges Friedmann in France.

12. See P. F. Lazarsfeld, "Audience Research in the Movie Field," *The Annals of the American Academy of Political and Social Science,* CCLIV (November, 1947), 160–168.

13. See Heuyer, Pieron, Pieron, and Sauvy, *Le Niveau Intellectuel des Enfants d'Age Scolaire* (Paris: Presses Universitaires de France, 1950), Cahier n° 13, a study of the Institut National d'Etudes Démographiques.

14. See Jean Sutter in *ibid.,* pp. 56–57.

15. Jean Daric, "Le Repartition des Sexes dans les Populations Urbaines," *Population,* VII, No. 4 (1952), 604.

16. Ilse Schwidetzky, *Grundzüge der Völkerbiologie* (Stuttgart, 1950), pp. 184–206.

17. Jean Sutter and Leon Tabah, "Les Notions d'Isolat et de Population Minimum," *Population,* VI, No. 3 (1951), 489.

18. See Sully Ledermann, "Les Divorces et la Separation de Corps en France," *Population,* III, No. 2 (1948), p. 328.

19. In particular, see the publications of René Koenig and "The American Family," in *The American Journal of Sociology,* LIII, No. 6 (May, 1948).

20. R. C. Angell, "The Moral Integration of American Cities," *The American Journal of Sociology,* LVII, Part 2, No. 1 (July 1951).

21. P. Fougeyrolles, "Prédominance du Mari ou de la Femme dans le Ménage," *Population,* VI, No. 1 (1951). This article summarizes the findings of a study made in the working-class suburb of Paris by Malakoff and shows large differences among social environments.

22. H. Pirenne, *Les Villes et les Institutions Urbaines* (Paris: Librairie Félix Alcan, 1939), I, p. 1.

23. G. Dessus (ed.), *Rapports et Travaux du Comité d'Etudes sur la Décongestion des Centres Industriels* (Paris: Ministère de l'Economie Nationale, 1947).

24. For further discussion, see Alfred Sauvy, *Dépeuplement Rural et Peuplement Rationel* (Paris: Presses Universitaires de France), Cahier n° 8, a study of the Institut National d'Etudes Démographiques.

25. N. Rogoff, "Social Stratification in France and in the United States," *The American Journal of Sociology,* LVIII, No. 4 (January, 1953), 347–357.

26. Louis Chevalier, *La Formation de la Population Parisienne au XIXᵉ Siècle* (Paris: Presses Universitaires de France), Cahier n° 10, a study of the Institut National d'Etudes Démographiques.

27. Rogoff, "Social Stratification in France and the United States," *op. cit.*

28. See François Goguel-Nyegaard, *Géographie des Elections Françaises de 1870 à 1951* (Paris: Colin, 1951), and *Initiation aux Recherches de Géographie Electorale* (Paris: Centre de Documentation Universitaire, 1947). Also André Siegfried, *Tableau Politique de la France de l'Ouest sous la Troisième République* (Paris: Colin, 1913).

29. H. A. Frégier, *Les Classes Dangereuses de la Population dans les Grandes Villes* (Paris, 1840).

3

An Analysis of Urban Phenomena

ALBERT J. REISS, Jr.

Professor of Sociology and Anthropology
Vanderbilt University

According to sociologists, the city is a form of community organization with a characteristic way of life. It is "a relatively large, densely concentrated aggregation of heterogeneous individuals living under conditions of anonymity, impersonal relations, and indirect control."[1]

This definition fails, however, to differentiate clearly among human communities. Sociologists maintain that because cities are unique demographically, they possess a unique set of social characteristics. But these characteristics can also be found in other types of communities and in varied socio-cultural situations. Moreover, they are perhaps generic only to particular value contexts. If so, exactly what is generic to city life as compared with other forms of community existence?

Formative Factors in Urban Communities

Sociologists often distinguish rural from urban communities in terms of basic variables in community formation. The four variables most frequently considered are invention and creativity in science, technology, and art forms; agricultural as distinct from non-agricultural pursuits; the complexity of the division of labor; and the size and density of settlement.

Accordingly, the city is assumed to be a large and densely concentrated settlement with a complex division of labor based on non-agricultural pursuits. It is supposedly the source of invention and creativity whose forms are diffused to a rural hinterland. But evidence shows that these variables are not independent. In fact, it is questionable whether they actually serve to differentiate urban from other forms of human communities. Apparently they do not, except in the sense that invention and creativity, non-agricultural pursuits, and a complex division of labor are more frequently localized in large and dense settlements.

Even if the four variables are considered to be preconditions for an urban way of life, they are not by definition urban factors. For they also occur under

41

other structures of living. If, for example, the inventions of the wheel, the domestication of animals, or the use of another man's labor are preconditions to urbanization, then they must have arisen under non-urbanized conditions. Thus urbanization itself cannot be a sufficient source of invention or creativity.

Invention and Creativity in Urban Areas

The idea that only cities serve as centers of invention and diffusion seems to be a provincial one.[2] Human creativeness as well as its preconditions are not limited to city dwellers. Crop control, soil terracing, plant hybrids, and the monastery and the university are not necessarily urban inventions. Nor has it been demonstrated that inhabitants reared in cities are more creative than those reared elsewhere.

Louis Sullivan once noted that the creative forms of the American farm-house served as models for "modern urban architecture." Religious sects and fundamentalist schisms often originate in rural areas and then diffuse to the city. The Church of God and the Church of God of Prophecy, for example, spread from the rural areas of Tennessee and North Carolina to New York City and Chicago.

An investigation is needed, therefore, of the conditions of social organization which give rise to specific creative forms. We need to learn whether these conditions may be found in communities of different sizes. Are certain forms of invention unique to cities? Although universities and monasteries are found in both large and small communities, do their organizational forms and institutional processes vary with community size?

Agricultural and Non-agricultural Pursuits

Contrary to popular opinion, a distinction between agricultural and non-agricultural pursuits does not differentiate clearly between rural and urban communities. Historically, rural communities always contained people, like teachers, preachers, or the medieval classes above serf and villein, who seldom engaged in agriculture. Even today, farmers sell their produce to an urban market and trade there as well.

In fact, the production and processing of food for consumption may occur under different types of conditions. The plantation or "single cash crop" economy, for instance, imports food from many sources, and may raise it for local consumption only as a secondary consideration. The generalization that the "average" rural person ordinarily produces his own food supply, whereas the "average" urban inhabitant does not, holds true only for a non-specialized rural economy. It is seldom the case for extractive industrial communities or plantation-type economies which grow cotton, tobacco, rubber, or coffee. On the other hand, most of the large urban settlements in antiquity did not rely on a rural countryside for agricultural products, because many urbanites raised their own food within the confines of the city.[3]

Furthermore, specialization in non-agricultural enterprises occurs in different kinds of communities. For example, the mountain dwellers in the south-eastern states are often thought to be an isolated, rural, agricultural folk. But many of them are not engaged in agriculture at all. They may work in extractive industries, such as coal mining, or may practice bootlegging or similar activities.[4] The hillbillies commonly live in rather large and densely concentrated settlements. Yet the social interaction in these communities could not be characterized as anonymous or impersonal.[5]

The dispersion of manufacturing in the United States and the location of industrial establishments in underdeveloped areas no longer support the assumption that manufacturing is primarily an urban activity. However, some kinds and processes of manufacturing may be more adaptive to large than small communities. The point is that agriculture, as a sustenance activity, is not a valid basis for distinguishing between rural and urban structures. As a matter of fact, forms of sustenance relations are organized in communities of various sizes and density of settlement. Under these circumstances, we need to examine the manner in which particular forms of sustenance relations are so organized.

Complex Division of Labor

Urban theorists usually maintain that a complex division of labor is an important prerequisite of a city as well as a generic urban characteristic. However, a high degree of occupational specialization may exist in non-urban communities. It has been found among coal miners in small, mountain, folk settlements. In the long run, it is a doubtful measure of urbanization, since technological advances tend to decrease occupational specialization.[6]

As a community expands, the complexity of the division of labor accordingly increases. The larger the population, the greater the number of occupational roles needed to facilitate interaction and maintain a particular level of living. Careful investigation of this form of occupational specialization is required before it can be considered as a requisite for cities under *all* cultural conditions.

Size and Density of Settlement

The size and density[7] of a population in space varies considerably. Some sociologists suggest, therefore, that urban communities should be defined in terms of variations in the ratio of absolute population to absolute space. But such a criterion fails to account for the fact that no differentiation can be observed among communities of different sizes and densities in the United States. Empirically, at least, "urban" can be independent of size and density. If this is true, then large size and high density of settlement are not always conditions for an urban way of life in any given community.

UNIQUE URBAN CHARACTERISTICS

The size and density of a settlement are supposed to affect the way of life carried on within it. Thus cities are frequently said to be characterized by an increase in social heterogeneity, impersonality and anonymity of interpersonal relations, toleration of social differences, social and geographic mobility, participation in voluntary associations, and the indirect control of human behavior. These are thought to be unique urban characteristics.

Social Heterogeneity in Urban Areas

The assumption that social heterogeneity is greatest in urban areas is based on the statement that "the greater the number of individuals participating in a process of interaction, the greater is the *potential* differentiation between them."[8] But this postulate refers only to potentiality, not reality. Actually, cities may standardize interaction in such a way that very little of the potential is realized.

The question also arises whether empirical studies always show a marked social heterogeneity in urban centers. A study of stratification in Aarhus, Denmark, indicated that the inhabitants were culturally quite homogeneous.[9] By contrast, studies in the United States suggest that the frontier often was a settlement of very heterogeneous population groups.[10] Today, many of our rural counties show a rather marked cultural heterogeneity just as our cities do. Heterogeneity, therefore, may be a function of the processes of settlement, growth, and mobility in a society as well as a function of the "interaction potential."

Impersonality and Anonymity

Because no one can know everybody else in a large city, social relations are said to be impersonal. Yet impersonality is not necessarily a valid criterion for distinguishing between urban and rural communities. If it were, the lower limit of size for an urban settlement might be as few as 100 to 200 inhabitants.

As a matter of fact, not all urbanites lead anonymous and impersonal lives. Most of them form some intimate interpersonal relationships with other urban dwellers. In studying time budgets, the writer found that urban dwellers spend as much time in intimate interpersonal contacts as rural dwellers do. Indeed, the present day urbanite spends more time in intimate association than either rural or urban inhabitants did fifty years ago. Today many urbanites engage in primary social contacts and also in a number of segmental social contacts. But the proportion of time spent in segmental contacts is generally small.

Although densely-settled areas may provide conditions favorable to anonymity, other environments do also. The frontier, the sparsely-settled regions of our western states, and the community based on extractive industries often offer a high degree of anonymity. Nevertheless, the city may be unique because it provides special institutions which facilitate both an individual and a collective existence for anonymous individuals. A study of the dweller in furnished rooms supports this viewpoint.[11] Perhaps one reason why a city has specialized living arrangements for the anonymous is that anonymity is so difficult to maintain there. While an individual may be anonymous to many residents, he may be well known to the underworld and the police. Only by investigating the various circumstances in which anonymity may arise can we determine whether large settlements produce more anonymous relationships than small ones.

Toleration of Social Differences

The higher the density of settlement, the greater the necessity for interacting with the unlike. Thus urbanites are supposedly more tolerant of social differences than non-urbanites. Yet we know that residential segregation is likely to be *greater* in large communities than in small ones. On the other hand, class and other value orientations can be maintained more easily in smaller communities, although actual interaction among class representatives is greater. So far, we are not certain what kinds of situations in themselves produce toleration.

It has been found, for example, that white urbanites accept Negroes as factory employees because such behavior facilitates worker goals. But the same white people are very intolerant of Negroes living close to them in a residential area.[12] If residence is a unique urban condition, then urban residence may be negatively related to tolerance, in the absence of other factors.

A toleration of "deviant behavior" is said to be marked in cities. Still, members of armies, prisoners and prison authorities, and residents of rural communities and frontier settlements also tolerate a considerable amount of deviation from conventional norms. Given a variation in cultural norms among societies, it is doubtful whether toleration is solely an urban phenomenon. Studies of voting frauds in rural areas, the high incidence of homicide in rural Sicily and in our southern rural or mountain communities, the existence of prostitution communities,[13] the high rates of premarital pregnancy among rural peasants in Scandinavia and the Low Countries, the cattle rustlers and other organized criminal groups of our western frontier, and most so-called indexes of vice—all occur with greater frequency in some rural areas than in some urban contexts.[14]

An examination of the social situations in which vice or deviance arises probably will show that the conditions are not peculiarly urban, though many forms of deviance usually will be found in urban communities. Value orientations, rather than the size of the community, probably account for observed differences in the toleration of deviant behavior among communities.

Social and Geographic Mobility

The city allegedly promotes social and geographical mobility to a greater extent than rural communities do. This belief rests on certain historical-cultural conditions. It is based on a relatively open system of social stratification and a high rate of urban growth in a society with an expanding economy. However, some urban social systems have a more closed system of social stratification and correspondingly lower rates of mobility. Thus urbanism and mobility are not necessarily co-related.

While many urban inhabitants change their status through mobility, so do agricultural and mining workers. The rural frontier of the United States was characterized by high geographic and social mobility. Small frontier settlements often became points through which large numbers of persons passed in their migration westward. Among such settlements were the Cumberland Gap in Tennessee, Kentucky, and Virginia, the Moccasin Gap in Virginia, and the Flower Gap in North Carolina.

The frontier land settlement movements and the various gold, silver, and oil rushes all contributed to mobility in the United States. The planter aristocracy of the Old South originally appears to have been a fluid mobility matrix which became stationary later.[15] Even with the so-called passing of the frontier, social mobility still is enhanced through success in farming occupations.

Urban or rural conditions, therefore, do not enhance mobility by themselves. For mobility is a function of opportunities—a geographic frontier which can be settled by agricultural inhabitants, a lumbering or mining frontier, an open economic structure in manufacturing, or a military bureaucracy. And all these structures *may* actually restrict rather than promote mobility, regardless of the type of community.

Considering the facts regarding farm tenancy, nomadic peoples, and drifters in frontier settlements, it is doubtful whether residential mobility is far greater in urban than in rural communities. A current investigation of the writer shows that residential mobility in Chicago and Augusta, Georgia, was no greater than in many rural counties in the United States during the period 1930 to 1935. In fact, the variation in residential movement for *urban* residents compared with that for *farm* residents was greater than the variation in mobility between *urban* and *rural* residents.

It appears that *high* residential mobility is a function of conditions which can arise in agricultural areas, communities with extractive industries, metropolitan centers, and other places. On the other hand, *low* rates of residential mobility have been reported for many European cities. Thus we need to explore further the nature of the conditions which lead to such high or low rates.

Participation in Voluntary Associations

Voluntary associations are said to be generic to urban communities. Yet it is known that voluntary associations exist in rural areas as well. Consider, for example, the Ku Klux Klan. Political associations abound in rural districts. The many rural homemaking and agricultural associations sponsored by the United States Department of Agriculture are not so much the result of urban influences as they are the consequence of a particular level of political-cultural development in this country. Voluntary organizations based on church or kinship affiliations seem to have been more common in both urban and rural areas during the pre-industrial revolution than today. Then, too, the spread of rural cooperatives and the various agrarian social movements of the West were apparently responses to producer-consumer relations rather than rural or urban phenomena as such.

Among urban residents, evidence indicates that participation in voluntary associations varies according to social class. High participation in voluntary associations is not characteristic of an urban working class. In New Haven, Connecticut, for instance, ". . . the majority of the urban working-class do not participate in formally organized voluntary working associations. . . . The central fact which emerges in this connection is the important role which family and kinship continue to play in providing for the companionship and recreational needs of persons interviewed. Approximately two-fifths of the husbands and wives in the sample had no intimate friends outside the family and kin groups."[16]

From the time of de Tocqueville to the present, visitors to our country have remarked about the American penchant for voluntary associations. An understanding is needed of the conditions under which voluntary associations arise before we can characterize any kind of community as the locus of such activity.

Indirect Control of Human Behavior

Is indirect control of human behavior unique to urban communities? It is claimed that competition and formal mechanisms of control in cities replace the bonds of kinship and neighborliness in rural areas. But this generalization is very difficult to test against empirical reality. Gossip and other informal controls, for example, may not control behavior in most residential areas within large cities. Yet gossip does influence behavior in the urban factory or office, in slum peer groups, and in other urban situations. In contrast, the interaction of rural neighbors may be subject to direct social control in the neighborhood, whereas their relationships with a "manorial lord" or the state are effected in large measure through indirect modes of control.

No matter what the size of a community may be, when a person acts in small situational contexts his behavior is apparently subject in a large degree to direct primary group controls. For instance, investigations made by the writer of worker productivity in large urban factories indicate that a man's output is highly subject to direct group controls. Similarly, studies of small neighborhoods show that the behavior of residents is highly subject to direct controls. But when a person acts in large contexts—as a resident of a large apartment house or as an inhabitant of a populous rural county—his behavior is probably more subject to personal and indirect forms of social control.

URBAN INFLUENCES

In assessing the relative influence of a city upon its hinterland, no differentiation has yet been made between the effects of urban influences and the effects of a particular level of cultural development. Even among cities, a great deal of variation exists in the actual amount of influence exerted. Prior to 1900, the great cities of China, India, and the U.S.S.R. appear to have exercised less influence upon their hinterlands than did the historic cities of London, Rome, or New York. Unless this variation in relative dominance is accounted for, it will be difficult to assess the net influence of any given city on its hinterland.

Although the level of cultural development may be advanced more by urban than by rural communities, it is not an independent product of urbanization. Considering the influence of religious groups and rural folk in establishing elementary and higher education, it cannot be said that urban centers alone led the mass education movement in the United States. In fact, the gift of federal or public lands to rural townships or counties was motivated primarily by rural legislators. The majority of our Christian or church-related colleges were founded by religious folk in primarily rural areas, and were often located in rural districts or small towns. Rather than being subject exclusively to urban influences, education in the United States is more an institutionalized goal of both rural and urban America.

The degree of integration among communities is also important. Recent studies indicate that considerable variation prevails among different cultural and social levels.

> It can now be stated that only about half of the almost nine hundred large cities in the world are located in countries whose level of socio-economic development is high enough to approximate that taken for granted by most writers on urbanism. This is demonstrated by the distribution of large cities according to the degree of literacy, of urbanization, of industrialization, and the per capita income of the countries where they are found.[17]

It is often alleged that rural or small communities are passive or neutral agents in exerting communal influence. But such a viewpoint is hardly suited to an ecological theory of community structure or an interactive theory of social organization. We need to consider the influence, if any, of the hinterland on the city as well as the effect of the city on the country. From a theoretical standpoint, we need a theory which accounts for relations among communal units in terms of factors of reciprocal influence. Empirically, we may have to abandon our concern with variations in the degrees of dominance among communities until we know more about migration flows, educational systems, technological developments, and other phenomena upon which dominance is based.

A Starting Point for Urban Studies

The previous discussion suggests that so-called "urban" traits are not entirely unique to urban communities. Nor do they necessarily occur under all urban residential and sustenance situations. If so, under what situations do they arise?

The Situational Context

An examination of social traits, such as anonymity, mobility, impersonal relations, or indirect control, under various conditions will probably fail to disclose any direct relationship between the occurrence of the traits and the size, density, and heterogeneity of a community. However, by studying the traits under various situations, we may be able to discover something that is generic to them in every case. Then we can learn whether large and dense settlements always provide sufficient conditions for their occurrence.

With regard to anonymity, for instance, it is possible that the larger the community, the greater the *number* of anonymous individuals in it. But is it true that the larger the community, the greater the *likelihood* of anonymity? We may find that only the urban environment develops a characteristic set of institutions for the anonymous person, ranging from "taxi" dance halls for the living to hired pallbearers for the deceased. Although anonymity may not be limited to large urban areas, cities alone may provide a unique set of institutions for the anonymous.[18]

Communities as Social Systems

In analyzing urban phenomena, community systems should be studied as a special type of social systems. A community system may be defined as a number of interacting people whose relations with one another are regulated by common symbols or values resulting from the fact that they share the same geographical area for residential and sustenance activities.[19] The properties of community systems may be identified, then, by indicating the variables in question and the geographical area under study.[20]

Perhaps the major advantage of the community-system approach is that the occurrence of any phenomenon within a community does not identify it per se as a community trait. Just because a school, church, or office is located in a community does not necessarily imply that it is a typical community institution. Nor does the characteristic recurrence of a high or low birth rate inevitably indicate an urban influence. Only when an institution contributes to the integration of residential and sustenance relations of the inhabitants should it be classed as a community institution under this method of approach.

CONCLUSION

Many phenomena are said to be characteristic solely of urban communities. But evidence indicates that the same traits may generally occur in other community systems as well. Further research is needed to discover whether urban communities can be distinguished from other types of communities in terms of anything more than a certain frequency of interaction patterns.

FOOTNOTES TO CHAPTER 3

1. L. Wirth, "Life in the City," in L. Carnovsky and L. Martin, *The Library in the Community* (Chicago: University of Chicago Press, 1944).

2. This is part of the "urban pastoral" ideology. See D. Riesman, "The Study of Kansas City: An Informal Overture," *The University of Kansas City Review,* XX (Autumn, 1953), 15–22.

3. See M. Weber, "Die Stadt," in *Grundriss der Sozialoekonomik* (Tubingen, 1947), pp. 518–519.

4. From July 1, 1950 to June 30, 1951, Alabama, Florida, Georgia, Kentucky, Mississippi, North and South Carolina, Tennessee, and Virginia accounted for 83.4 per cent of the 10,384 persons arrested for the illegal manufacture of alcohol; 91.5 per cent of the 10,777 stills in illegal operation; and 93.5 per cent of the 5,545,411 gallons of mash in unlawful manufacture. *Annual Report of the Commission of Internal Revenue, 1951* (Washington, D.C.: U.S. Treasury Department, 1952). Revenue agents report that most of the illegal manufacture of alcohol in these states occurs in isolated mountain or lowland areas.

5. Located in Tennessee and Kentucky, the isolated Pruden Valley has approximately 6,000 inhabitants who live in contiguous company housing settlements. These people are so far removed from agriculture that few of them have gardens. Another example of a non-agricultural folk community is the "French shore" of the southeastern Acadian French in Nova Scotia. Some pre-literate fishing and hunting communities are also quite large and densely settled.

6. Technology is correlated with occupational specialization in such a way that nothing but a marginal differentiation often remains among occupations. In these cases, the specific machine or process then becomes the basis for occupational differentiation. Yet the high degree of transferability of skill among so-called diverse occupations belies significant qualitative differentiation. Although less reliance is placed on skill, it is interesting to speculate whether or not increased technology in farming makes it easier to become a farmer.

7. Density, or relative concentration, is always relative to some measure. When open country is sparsely settled, as in Utah, Nevada, and Idaho, no "community" arises among the inhabitants.

8. See L. Wirth, "Urbanism as a Way of Life," *The American Journal of Sociology,* XL (July, 1938), 11.

9. See T. Geiger, *Soziale Umschichtungen in einer Danischen Mittelstadt,* Universitessforlaget I, Aarhus, Enjar Munksgaard-Koebenhaven, 1951. Geiger's work suggests the error in generalizing about urban phenomena from investigations solely of cities which are gaining in population and within which there is considerable social mobility.

10. See T. P. Abernathy, *From Frontier to Plantation in Tennessee* (Chapel Hill: University of North Carolina Press, 1932). Abernathy maintains that there were always many "drifters" at the frontier. He presents a great deal of historical evidence to document the heterogeneous character of the frontier settlement. See also W. J. Cash, *The Mind of the South* (New York: Knopf, 1941).

11. H. W. Zorbaugh, "The Dweller in Furnished Rooms: An Urban Type," *Proceedings* of the American Sociological Society, XX (1925).

12. J. D. Lohman and D. C. Reitzes, "Note on Race Relations in Mass Society," *The American Journal of Sociology,* LVIII (November, 1953), 240–247.

13. In 1940, the writer estimated that Hurley, Wisconsin (population 3,375) had approximately 400 prostitutes. Their clientele were iron miners of the northern Michigan peninsula rather than residents of Ironwood, Michigan (population 13,369), the only census urban center within 75 miles of Hurley.

14. Kinsey's data on sexual deviance among males are instructive in this context. See A. C. Kinsey, W. B. Pomeroy, and C. E. Martin, *Sexual Behavior in the Human Male* (Philadelphia: W. B. Saunders, 1948), p. 457 ff. The study of single-sex communities indicates how communal structure leads to various forms and organization of sexual deviance. See. E. G. Ericksen, "Barrack Town: Social Irrationality in the One-Sex Company Town," an unpublished Ph.D. dissertation, University of Chicago, 1947.

15. For the volume and character of mobility in the planter aristocracy of the South, see Cash, *op. cit.*, Ch. 1.

16. F. Dotson, "Patterns of Voluntary Association among Urban Working Class Families," *American Sociological Review*, XVI (October, 1951), 693. See also R. Freedman and M. Axelrod, "Who Belongs to What in a Great Metropolis?" *Adult Leadership*, November, 1952.

17. N. Rogoff, "The Universe of Cities: Some Preliminary Considerations," Columbia University Bureau of Applied Social Research: Project AFIRM, January, 1953, i. See also K. Davis and H. Hertz, *The Patterns of World Urbanization* (a forthcoming publication by Macmillan, 1954).

18. Other large system contexts, like armies, similarly develop unique institutions providing for anonymous living. However, they are not entirely generic to size. See E. A. Shils and M. Janowitz, "Cohesion and Disintegration in the Wehrmacht in World War II," *The Public Opinion Quarterly*, XII (Summer, 1948), 280–315.

19. For similar approaches, see A. Hawley, *Human Ecology* (New York: Ronald, 1950) and T. Parsons, *The Social System* (Glencoe: The Free Press, 1951).

20. See E. T. Hiller, "The Community as a Social Group," *American Sociological Review*, VI (April, 1951), 189–202.

PART TWO

Contributions of the Metropolitan Community to the Political Institutions of a Free Society

INTRODUCTION

Many contributions of the metropolitan community to the political institutions of a free society have come through the work of non-salaried citizens' commissions. Throughout the United States, our boards of education are unpaid, and most communities have unsalaried boards of health. Other kinds of citizen action in government continue to maintain democratic participation at the local level.

Despite the nature of their volunteer work, however, these public-spirited men and women are constantly attacked in the newspapers. Thus it has become increasingly difficult to get responsible people to serve on metropolitan commissions which are charged with planning for the future of our cities. Moreover, the scale of problems in question is often so huge that volunteer work requires more and more time. Under these unfavorable circumstances, how can administrative decisions continue to be made democratically by citizens' commissions?

This is a universal problem of self-government. To solve it, the public must be educated to understand what it means to get busy people of ability to devote part of their time to civic service. Perhaps some sort of public appreciation should also be expressed. In Britain, the Honors List recognizes a man nationally for what he has done for the country by the time he reaches the age of fifty-two.

This educational venture must stress the point that all citizens have a responsibility for bringing on the next generation. There ought to be a systematic method of putting young men and women on citizen boards to provide for future leadership. Without adequate leadership, the future of our metropolitan areas will be questionable indeed. In addition, there should be a well trained and paid administrative staff to take the burden of work off citizens' groups while leaving them an opportunity to shoulder the responsibility for the welfare of their community.

Problems of metropolitan planning are emphasized by the fact that many legislatures are dominated by rural points of view. Although the importance of suburban county planning has recently increased through welfare, highway, and educational programs, the area of its concern with the metropolitan community as a whole has never been properly delineated.

Moreover, state legislatures frequently are hostile toward the big cities. The legislatures cook only by pressure, and the pressures exerted upon them by the big city, the suburbs, and intermediate administrative bodies are so conflicting that no clear program for community metropolitan development may emerge.

Yet most of our leaders in social evolutionary thought have come from urban areas. Most organized groups for political action are based in the metropolis. Here, perhaps, lies the possibility for an improved relationship between various jurisdictional authorities. It should help to develop political institutions better suited to modern urban life.

4

Political Influences of the Metropolis

WILLIAM ANDERSON
Professor of Political Science
University of Minnesota

Christian literature contains many references to the city as embodying some of the highest ideals of the good life for men. We read of the city foursquare, the Heavenly City, and the City of God. Contributions to the Old Testament reveal an even earlier interest in the construction and adornment of cities. So do the monuments and records of various ancient civilizations. Greek writers of the golden age extolled the city-state as the highest form of political community, and as the sign and guaranty of the best in civilization. The Romans took an inordinate pride in their Eternal City.

To many of the barbarian tribes which overran the Roman Empire, however, the city was a hateful thing. Many cities were reduced or destroyed during successive barbarian invasions. Even today, the fears and dislikes of certain rural leaders provide a seeming justification for keeping political power in rural hands by the under-representation of urban people in legislative bodies. This process goes on despite the tendency for rural folkways to become increasingly urbanized with the growth of modern metropolitan areas.

CHARACTERISTICS OF A MODERN METROPOLITAN AREA

A Non-political Entity

A modern metropolitan community is a great agglomeration of people living, working, and playing in a congested area in and around a great city like New York, London, Paris, Chicago, Philadelphia, Los Angeles, or Boston. Within its roughly-defined area, each agglomeration may have a certain unity of social and economic structure. But from the political and legal point of view, it is a congeries of many overlapping, conflicting, often selfish and disputatious units of government, including counties, cities, villages, boroughs, towns, and special districts.

The entire metropolitan community, therefore, is politically amorphous,

57

without structure or unity. It is not a corporate person. In the eye of public law, it does not exist; even in the field of politics, it speaks with many contradictory voices. It is a place of divided loyalties and conflicting allegiances. In short, it is a community that is not fully a community.

What is more, the typical metropolitan community is a part of some larger and constitutionally higher political entity like a state or a nation. Consequently, there is seldom any strong desire at state or national political levels to unite the entire metropolis into one strong unit of local government. This would only antagonize the citizens who are loyal to the lesser political units that would be absorbed into the new metropolitan political entity. And it would produce a political unit sufficiently strong to capture increasingly the loyalties of its people, and possibly even to challenge the authority of the state or nation that created it. To keep the powers of local self-government well dispersed may be justified from a number of viewpoints. But one result is clearly to prevent a metropolitan community from speaking with a single voice on any public question.

A Far-reaching Political Influence

One characteristic of the great metropolitan community gives it an influence that few national and state governments have been able to curb. This attribute results from the fact that the metropolitan community is a main center of human activities for areas wider than its own, and a center that tends to increase in influence as population increases and civilization tends to advance.

Many American states in their early days tried to assure decentralization and to prevent metropolitan domination by putting the state capital in one small community, the state university in another, and other state institutions elsewhere. To some extent, this policy of decentralization has been successful, but not wholly so. Even if the state capital is elsewhere, the largest city in the state tends to be the center for important state political meetings and decisions. Indeed, there have been instances in which a metropolis *outside* a state's boundaries has been the principal meeting place and place of decision for the actual rulers of the state. Similarly, if a state spends its money on a state university in a small community, the town will tend to become bigger and more influential, and the larger cities in the state will also tend to develop their own large universities. In short, a metropolitan place is naturally the center of high politics and higher education.

A Center of Essential Activities

The metropolitan community is a center of banking and finance and commerce and industry. Along with these things, it is the center of book and magazine publishing; great newspapers and news gathering services; essential communications media such as telegraph, telephone, cable and radio; theaters, moving pictures and television; railroads, steamships, truck and bus lines, and airlines; in fact, of all the great media of communication and transportation.

In strictly metaphorical language, metropolises are the nerve and communication centers for the larger body politic.

These important facilities of modern communication and transportation find it to their advantage to center in the great cities. As they do so, they give extra drawing power to the metropolis for uncounted other purposes. Great religious organizations, insurance companies, advertising agencies, fraternal organizations, foundations, hospitals and medical centers, and untold other organizations make their headquarters in the great cities. Leaders in finance, business, the professions, education, literature, music, art, the theater, and most other lines of endeavor that carry prestige and power, tend to congregate in the great cities. The influences exerted from such centers upon the nation's life are not derived from the whole metropolitan community itself. They are produced rather by the numerous outstanding individuals and organized groups that make up the community.

SOME METROPOLITAN POLITICAL CONTRIBUTIONS

In the following discussion, a number of terms will be used that should first be defined. The word *politics* refers to all the various activities of men that relate to the formation and performance of public policies in political communities. *Political communities* themselves exist at international, national, state, provincial, and local levels. These political communities are not in any sense complete unless they have *organized governments* with the power to perform their functions over fairly definite areas and populations.

Political institutions, on the other hand, are more or less regularized and enduring patterns of political activity or behavior within political communities. They arise when political activities are carried out according to established and fairly regular methods and patterns. In free societies, political institutions include not only the ordinary governmental agencies and procedures, but also the organization and activities of political parties, the conduct of campaigns and the holding of free elections, the protection of life, liberties, jobs, and property, among other things.

The *institution of private property* exists in various forms in all free societies. Without this institution, a free society itself might not endure. The influence of the institution of private property pervades all parts of the social order. It has economic, social, and moral as well as political aspects.

Finally, *freedom of religion,* or the separation of church and state, is another significant political institution in modern free societies.

Metropolitan Versus Non-metropolitan Contributions

The great cities of the past were important centers of empires and civilizations. In their physical structures and social orders, they represented something of men's ideas as to the good life. But the cities themselves were essentially the creations of men and not the creators. As they were made by men, so some of them were destroyed by men.

Ancient city planners drew up plans for the physical features of the cities and lawgivers drew up their laws. No doubt these planners and lawgivers were influenced in their thinking by the cities in which they lived. No doubt, also, that the cities they planned and the laws they drew up had some influence in turn on city populations. But this is a far cry from the idea that the cities as such molded themselves and the civilizations of which they were a part.

As in the case of ancient cities, we must also be careful not to attribute to modern metropolitan communities any contemporary political institutions unless the evidence is entirely convincing. The fact that certain things happen within great cities should not be confused with the theory that the cities make them happen.

Political Institutions in the United States

Before appraising metropolitan influences on our political institutions, some of the more obvious ones that exist in the United States should be mentioned. Among others, they include:

1. The idea and practice of having *written constitutions* that are supposed to emanate from the people and to be supreme over the ordinary branches and officers of government.

2. *Bills of Rights* to protect the rights and liberties of individuals against encroachments by governmental authorities. These liberties include the freedoms of speech, press, religion, and assembly, the right to form and to join political parties and other voluntary groups, and due process of law in the courts for protecting all rights.

3. A *federal system* set up under a supreme Constitution to divide the powers and functions of government between a central or national government and a layer of state or provincial governments. Each state government and the national government has the autonomous right to initiate and carry through its own measures in accordance with its own views as to its constitutional powers.

4. The so-called *separation of powers* in both national and state governments between legislative, executive, and judicial branches. This is a means of preventing excessive concentration of governmental powers in any one group of men, and also a means of protecting individual rights and liberties more fully against government.

5. Various *checks and balances* set up in both national and state constitutions to preserve the separation of powers and to make for at least a minimum of cooperation between the several branches.

6. *Presidential government,* an aspect of the separation of powers in both the nation and the states, whereby the chief executive, president or governor, elected for a fixed term of years, is held responsible to the voters of state or nation and is not directly responsible to the legislative branch.

7. The system of *party government in legislative bodies* exercised mainly through a series of *powerful committees,* which frequently defeats executive leadership.

8. The system of *judicial review* over both legislative and executive acts, whereby the courts can exercise some restraining influence to prevent violations of the constitutional rules. This restraint is exerted by keeping national and state governments from encroaching upon each other, by hold-

ing legislative, executive, and judicial branches within their proper channels, and by helping to keep all parts of the government from violating the individual liberties ensured by the bills of rights.

9. Within the states and under state laws, a widespread system of *local self-government* exercised in great numbers of local governmental units of many types, representing an astounding and apparently unsystematic decentralization of local governing powers.

10. A great variety of *innovations* in state and local government, including municipal and county home rule, and the council-manager plan of city and county government.

Among this array of federal and state political institutions, none seems to be the direct result of metropolitan influences. In fact, when the United States Constitution and the original state constitutions were framed, there were no great cities in America to exert any influence. The same situation prevailed for the new states that were carved out of the frontier and brought into the Union in the course of the next 120 years. From Vermont and Kentucky in 1791 and 1792 to Arizona and New Mexico in 1912, all were essentially frontier states when they entered the Union. Even the basic system of local units of government was established before the era of great cities.

This does not imply that the leaders in the urban communities of the time had nothing to do with the framing of national and state constitutions. For we know that the merchant and professional classes residing in the seaboard towns from Boston to Charleston had a leading role in the struggle for the Constitution of the United States. Even at the first census in 1790, however, the largest seaboard town was New York City with only 33,000 inhabitants. Philadelphia had about 28,000 citizens, with 14,000 more in the suburbs. Although such places would not be called metropolitan communities at the present time, in their day they were centers of communication and ideas and political movements.

The Influence of Metropolitan Problems

Alongside the major governmental institutions in the United States, there are numerous political practices and organizations of a private or only semiofficial character. They include political parties, pressure groups and lobbyists, leagues of municipalities, associations of public officials, voters' leagues, governmental research associations and bureaus, taxpayers' associations, and local, state and national organizations of citizens organized to influence public policy on almost every conceivable subject. Industry, finance and commerce, workers and farmers, the professions, religious and fraternal groups and law-enforcement leagues, and groups interested in both international and domestic public policies, are all represented. The membership, forms, objectives, and methods of these organizations are almost infinitely varied. The ease with which such groups can be formed to influence public policy is a strong testimonial to the freedom of political participation that prevails in the United States.

What has been the influence of metropolitan communities on this broad range of political groups and institutions? Clearly, most local organizations are formed in state and regional urban centers. In national metropolitan communities, nationwide and international organizations establish their headquarters and hold their meetings. The great metropolis provides the financial means and the physical facilities for such purposes as well as the people with specialized knowledge and interests to take the leadership in organization.

In the United States, New York City appears to be the principal center for launching movements and organizations for national welfare and policy purposes. But many organizations that have large memberships, such as labor, commerce, church, and professional groups, locate in other metropolitan centers like Washington, D.C., and Chicago. Because of its special significance as the nation's capital, Washington has become the center for a great number of the biggest national organizations, including the principal agricultural ones.

All these national, regional, state, and local organizations are parts of the political institutions of the people in the United States. They exert influences upon each other and upon the government at all levels. They are private organizations in that their membership and financing are voluntary. But this fact does not exclude them from having public objectives, or from engaging in activities to influence governments to adopt policies favorable to them.

Although it is not possible to distinguish absolutely between rural, small town, and metropolitan political viewpoints, it could probably be shown that leaders in the great metropolitan centers have been more aware of some problems than have the leaders in smaller communities. The pressures that metropolitan leaders and their organizations have put upon the government have been primarily to produce *action* on the part of public authorities and not so much to *change* the forms of government or political institutions. These actions have related to various metropolitan problems concerning immigration, social welfare, public services, liberty, and civilizing institutions.

IMMIGRATION. As the main immigrant centers, the large cities were called upon by their more perceptive leaders to provide decent housing and health protection for the immigrants, and to bring the immigrants into their social, religious, and political systems in an orderly way. At the present time, this sensitiveness to immigrant needs is revealed in activities to improve inter-racial relations and fair employment practices, as well as in public housing programs and other ameliorative measures.

SOCIAL WELFARE. In large cities, movements to promote social welfare through public action had their most important developments. The drives against child labor, against the hazards of industry and slums, against crime and disease, arose most clearly in the large cities. It was there that social centers and settlement houses were established, and there the concepts and practice of social work reached higher intellectual and professional levels.

City planning and zoning also originated where the need was greatest, in the large cities, notably in New York, Chicago, and Los Angeles. From thence came the concepts later accepted by state and national governments of regional, state, and national planning for public works and human well-being. Out of these and other movements of urban origin arose also the concept that private property has public responsibilities and can be justified only as it performs its public functions. Over the years, older notions of "absolute property" have been modified into more social and functional concepts of the role of private property. Thus the basic political institution of private property has undergone considerable change from influences that appeared most clearly in the great urban places.

PUBLIC SERVICES. The expansion of public services was primarily a large-city phenomenon in the nineteenth century and even the early part of the twentieth century in the United States. As life in the growing cities became more and more congested, many necessary services could not be supplied by individuals and families for themselves. Technologies were then developed to make communal services effective and relatively economical. Communal water supplies, waste disposal systems, fire protection, full-time police and law-enforcement systems, pavements, and sidewalks, and a wide range of related public works, parks and recreational facilities, public health services and hospitals, comprehensive systems of public and private education, and many other services were developed by major cities before the national and state governments became aware of similar needs.

In time, the rise of the urban public services helped to overcome earlier rural objections to organized public action. The people on farms and in small towns found reasons to establish public services of their own, such as rural mail delivery, better roads, rural electrification, and a number of others. Then the scope of the national and state services also began to expand. The urban influence spread outward into rural places, and the rural population became more urbanized.

LIBERTY. Liberty has also received special support in large urban places. The substantive liberties set forth in constitutional bills of rights—freedom of speech, press, religion, and assembly—have a special significance in large urban places. There the friends of civil liberties organize and carry on their work most effectively.

All this does not mean, of course, that freedom is always best protected in big cities. For many elements in metropolitan populations are ready to suppress every form of deviation from their own self-legislated norms, whether in books, periodicals, or newspapers, or on the stage or other public rostrum.

Although the victory sometimes goes to the forces of repression, metropolitan communities in free societies usually have within themselves the people and the power to fight back successfully. Great newspapers and publishing houses, non-conformist economic, social and religious groups, and educational and scientific groups, find their most congenial habitat and their opportunity for greatest usefulness and influence in the large cities. They give strength and support to every sincere effort to protect American civil liberties.

CIVILIZING INSTITUTIONS. It seems obvious that the most potent civilizing institutions of our time are developed primarily in metropolitan communities. Moreover, in these great centers men carry on civilizing activities that influence government and public policies throughout the nation and the world. Things of the heart and things of the mind develop in conjunction with each other. The spirit and the intellect are both uplifted as a result.

The position of the great newspapers and the other media of mass communication like radio and television has already been mentioned. But in addition, there are other distinctively metropolitan institutions like the theater, the motion picture industry, art museums, opera, great orchestras, music halls, and schools of music. There are museums of natural history, great collections of scientific objects, exhibits of all kinds, research institutes, and great philanthropic, educational and scientific foundations and institutes.

Furthermore, there are the private and public universities that adorn the great metropolitan centers and shed their light throughout the nation and the world. Are not their programs of advanced instruction, research, publication, and public services, indispensable to the advancement of all nations and all peoples? Primarily from them, men see and contribute to the advance of science and of international understanding and cooperation. Their contribution to the government and politics of the nation raises and sustains both the moral and intellectual level of all political action.

Consider, for example, the role of Columbia University in the City of New York. From its founding as King's College in 1754, it paid attention in its curriculum to the education of men in moral science, history, economics, and government. In 1880, Columbia established the first American graduate school for the study of public law, government, and the related social sciences. As a part of the program of this school, it has continuously published the scholarly *Political Science Quarterly,* and it began to publish doctoral theses in the field in its very valuable series on *History, Economics and Public Law.*

Shortly thereafter, it also started to send out into the colleges and universities of the land young men with the Ph.D. degree to teach government, politics, history, economics and related subjects. In these ways, Columbia University was a great innovator. It was an outstanding contributor to the political education of a nation, and indeed to the education of men in other lands as well. The fact that several other metropolitan universities began at about the same time to advance political education to the level of graduate instruction in no way detracts from the honor due to Columbia University for having established the first graduate school in the United States in this distinctive field.

A development such as this could have taken place only in the great urban centers. It illustrates the point that great cities, great universities, and great ideas for raising the moral and intellectual level of mankind go hand in hand. When the leaders in Columbia University undertook in 1880 to begin political education at its highest level, they started a movement that has spread throughout the nation and that has immeasurably raised the level and the quality of public discussions on policy questions for all levels of government—local, state, national, and international.

CONCLUSION

The concept of political institutions used here is highly comprehensive. Whatever moves men significantly and measurably to higher, nobler, and more humane views and actions cannot be excluded from a consideration of metropolitan influences on politics and government. In the future, men will always have to struggle to establish and maintain these high ideals of humanity, integrity, and intelligence in government and politics. To that end, everyone can make a distinctive contribution, whether in rural communities, small towns, or metropolitan areas.

But the seamy side of city life must not be denied or glossed over. Great cities have long been centers of political corruption and concentrations of sin in other forms. Yet this side of the picture should not be exaggerated beyond its intrinsic importance.

For the forces of education and enlightenment, liberty and humanity, human dignity and integrity, find most of their greatest and most effective exponents and leadership in the great cities of our land. There men and women are most alert to invasions of human liberties, and are most sensitive to acts of injustice and the needs of others. In the great cities, the forces of education, reason, and justice mobilize most quickly and spring into action to protect the free institutions that are the crowning achievement and the true glory of this beloved nation of ours.

5

Metropolitan Political Developments

LUTHER H. GULICK
President, Institute of Public Administration
New York

Historically, it could be shown that the more important institutions of our free society originated in the thinking of men who lived in the larger population centers of their day. It could also be demonstrated that the historic struggles for freedom, including the violent revolutions of the eighteenth and nineteenth centuries, were centered in the great cities, and that the resulting political institutions were given an extensive trial, if not initiation, in urban areas.

But the importance of these past connections between metropolitan life and the development of political institutions is not certain. After all, our free institutions were mainly developed in the Western world while the bulk of the population lived outside of metropolitan areas. The biggest city was everywhere regarded as a danger and a source of unrest. Even in examining what we mean by political institutions, it is difficult to identify any considerable number of key developments which have come from the metropolitan community as such.

OUR POLITICAL INSTITUTIONS

During the last generation, there has been a notable return to a broader understanding of the content of our political institutions. Much of the damage caused by the separation of economics, statistics, sociology, and group psychology from political science is now being repaired. Political science is being greatly strengthened and enriched by the recent contributions of sociologists, historians, journalists, economists, ecologists, and psychologists. Viewed from this vantage point, our free political institutions include an extremely complex array of social arrangements and doctrine. Among them, an observer from Mars would probably list:

Constitutionalism; that is, the defined system of restricted ultimate power, and its corollary, a
Responsible bureaucracy; involving on one side an

66

Executive power displaceable without bloodshed; and on the other a

Legislative and judicial apparatus empowered to change the basic laws and enforced customs; this entire government resting on

Elections and representative institutions, which are given democratic reality through

Constitutional protections and social traditions which maintain

Freedom of thought and speech; freedom of organization; extensive areas which are independent of the state, including religion, education and research; universal free education and literacy; a free press and other channels of mass communication; and a social and property system which does not bind the individual by law or custom to any place or class.

With these basic institutions of a free society are associated many techniques and procedures. Some are highly important, though they are facilitative and might be performed equally well by other techniques. Such procedures include specific systems of election, party machinery, budgeting and civil service administration; the division of governmental work into executive, legislative and judicial functions; the structure of federalism; local home rule and the techniques of delegation; the machinery of prosecution, courts and juries, both for indictment and trial; the development of techniques for distributing the costs of government in relation to ability to pay as well as benefit received; and the specific structure of voluntary educational and civic organizations and associations (mostly tax exempt as a matter of state policy) which complete the web of government.

This list does not exhaust the catalogue of governmental machinery and bodies of accepted doctrine which give us our free society. Nevertheless, it indicates the kind of governmental structure prevailing in the United States in the middle of the twentieth century. Moreover, each of these institutions has been influenced by the existence of the metropolitan centers of power. But none of them is a unique contribution of metropolitan culture.

Perhaps federalism, with its highly important philosophy and practice of geographic association and delegation, was a contribution derived in part from the city confederations of Italy, Germany, Switzerland, and the southern coast of England, which formed toward the end of feudal times. Although federal arrangements influenced the thinking of the framers of our constitutional system, only the Swiss federation negotiated the transition from feudalism to the current national state. The constitutional structure of the great federal states of the modern world was not conditioned by metropolitan communities, most of which arose subsequently in point of time.

Metropolitan areas have made important contributions, however, toward the subordinate governmental technologies and programs of modern free society. These have arisen from three totally different circumstances. The first contributions derive from the struggle for power; the second from the effort to ameliorate difficulties incident to congestion; and the third from the attempt to meet the managerial requirements of big units of government.

THE STRUGGLE FOR POWER

With the rise of industrialism and finance capitalism, the shift from rural to urban preponderance, and the transition from landed to other types of wealth, much of the machinery of modern government has been established or maintained to deal with forces centered in growing metropolitan communities.

Men in positions of power generally tend to seek a larger share of the productive or distributive processes than other people feel is justified. Historically, the division of shares was determined by long-established communal custom mitigated by conquest. But this system broke down completely in the West with the discovery of the New World in the fifteenth century, the development of the machine in the nineteenth century, and the more recent rise of technology based on science.

When these explosive forces rose to endanger the customary structure of shares, status, and control, individuals who were threatened turned to the overriding authority of the state to protect their position and prevent a change in their rights, privileges, and immunities. Similarly, people who wished to alter the established social, political, or economic order sought to effect the change in part through the powers of the government. Where the resulting conflict occurred between nations, the solution was often found in war. Where it arose between elements in a single country, the solution was sought through modifying governmental policies and through political action, including the capture of governmental offices. In extreme cases, this produced internal revolution.

The great cities were deeply involved in both of these revolutionary situations. When the American colonies were unwilling to put up with the restrictions of the British Board of Trade, an armed conflict resulted between metropolitan England and the colonies, not unlike the more contemporary conflict between metropolitan France and her colonies. And when the powers of economic and social control passed to the American states, the struggle to dominate governmental policies eventually broke out into the war between the states, a rear-guard action of the southern aristocracy against the temporary coalition of the metropolitan east and the small-farm west.

Since at least the days of the walled medieval city, the metropolis has always been the center of trade and commerce. Subsequently, it also became the center of industry and finance. Not infrequently these metropolitan forces have established control over the government and dominated its economic, social, and political measures.

Furthermore, culture, education, art and philosophy have always flourished in close association with metropolitan centers. This is so because they depend on the possibility of specialization and leisure and also because of the stimulation which comes from the contacts which arise inevitably in the crossroads of the world.

In comparison with most rural areas, it can well be argued that the urban centers—because of their livelier structure of communication, freer flow of thought, richer pattern of individual association, and greater readiness to depart from past traditions—have given an important twist to the social evolution-ary process evident in our governmental and political history. Certainly this metropolitan impact is no less real than is the so-called influence of the frontier in our institutional development.

In any case, the metropolis has been deeply involved in the struggle for political, economic and social power throughout history. This struggle to maintain or change the status quo through capturing the government has conditioned our constitutional system and our party structure. It has produced important governmental measures such as monetary, banking, land, and tax laws; tariffs and commerce controls; labor laws; housing and health ordinances; corporate and security controls; grants-in-aid, and social security and agri-cultural provisions. Generally, metropolitan communities have contributed to such governmental arrangements by creating the problems and stresses in question rather than by inventing new political programs and institutions which are metropolitan in essence.

MAKING THE METROPOLIS LIVABLE

As men crowd together in great cities, they make possible an increasing specialization and interdependence. Cities loosen the old ties of family and community in an ever-new structure of mobility and anonymity. They expand the range of individual free activity. Men in cities also become subject to great catastrophes and hazards against which the individual is less and less able to protect himself. Finally, congestion necessitates cooperative services which are unnecessary and completely impossible in a rural area. The greater the city, the more these tendencies are in evidence. Here lies the field in which the metropolitan community has made its distinctive impact on demo-cratic institutions.

Zoning and Planning

The first metropolitan contributions pertained to the use of land. They were designed to keep the streets open against the encroachments of abutting land owners. In the United States, such controls date back to the earliest days. But they were not developed comprehensively until zoning came into vogue follow-ing the first broad zoning ordinance of New York City in 1916.

Though there can be planning without zoning, and zoning without planning, and great construction programs without either, the three generally go hand in hand. Fortunately, city planning, with its dream of efficient and beautiful cities and a rationally-designed physical and social environment, is more and more capturing the imaginations of individuals who control the destinies of the great cities. Here again, metropolitan areas and lesser urban concentrations have created the problem. The dreamers, the planners, the builders come forth from the total culture, and many programs reach far beyond the metropolitan areas. Some go to the extent of urging the end of the great cities.

Fire Protection

Another sort of metropolitan contribution to government is fire protection and its extraordinary body of law and administrative control. These controls are designed to save an individual from his neighbor's conflagrations, and to protect tenants against the carelessness of the landlord. For this purpose, we have fire fighting organizations with summary powers over persons and property, subject to exercise by a single commander. We also have elaborate fire codes, specifying in great detail how structures may be erected and equipped, and enforced by a skilled corps of inspectors. Here is a clear illustration of the limitations of freedom which are imposed on the individual by the community as an essential element of our free institutions.

Public Health

Even more spectacular are the powers and institutions developed in the large cities to deal with communicable diseases. Only since the early nineteen hundreds have public health measures been developed to free the populations of the great Western cities from epidemics spread by contact or by contaminated water or food. The powers entrusted to the commissioner or the board of health are extremely broad. The summary powers of municipal health authorities over persons and property rest with public health doctors and technical inspectors.

Traffic

Traffic control on the streets is a problem which emerged at first only in the great cities. While horse racing on the highways was prohibited long before the time of automobiles, only in the last generation have specialized institutions and engineering techniques been developed to formulate and enforce the rules and regulations which endeavor to rationalize the use of the streets.

Noise and Pollution

The most recent extension of the limitation of individual freedom in the great cities arises in the effort to limit noise and prevent the pollution of air and waters.

Freedom and Anarchy

The doctrine in all these cases is the same. It is intensely practical. The problems arise in acute form because of congestion. The individual cannot protect himself against the dangers or discomforts arising from the free acts of others. Therefore, the community establishes rules of action to maximize welfare by rationing freedom. It increasingly places enforcement of controls in the hands of a responsible and technically trained bureaucracy.

This is not a new problem of freedom. It has been the center of political and philosophical speculation since Plato. Indeed, the major domestic problem of Greek city life, with which Plato and Aristotle struggled, was "how to give freedom to the citizen without producing anarchy."[1] The major laboratory for this long testing of human experience and the continual revision and application of the philosophy of freedom has been in the greatest metropolitan areas. There the problems are sharpest and the intellectual climate most suitable for experimentation and reflection.

The Settlement House and Organized Public Recreation

Among the products of the great cities, there are two highly significant institutional developments which deserve special mention. These are the settlement house and the public recreation program.

The social settlement movement began in London when Toynbee Hall was established in 1884. Two years later, the University Settlement was founded in New York. In 1889, Hull House appeared in Chicago, and in 1891 what is now known as South End House in Boston. As the charter of Hull House indicates, the settlement houses established a localized community headquarters designed "to provide a center for a higher civic and social life, to institute and maintain educational and philanthropic enterprises, and to investigate and improve conditions. . . ."

This was not an idle boast. We need only remember that many of the leaders of American social and civic reform, including Florence Kelly, Lillian D. Wald, Mary K. Simkhovitch, Graham Taylor, Julia Lathrop, Grace Abbott, Jane E. Robbins, William J. Tucker, Edward T. Devine, Robert A. Woods and Paul Kellog, came directly from the settlement houses of our great cities. The shape and content of American programs in public health, child welfare, labor legislation, tenement legislation, adult education, prison reform, urban crime analysis, housing, recreation, and our social security provisions derive much of their inspiration and form from the individuals who lived in settlement houses. These houses were located in substandard, crowded, and sweated sections of the great cities where the industrial revolution and population migration combined to make it all but impossible for the individual to cope with the downward drag of the isolating and anonymous forces of the metropolis.

Although the settlement house and the family welfare society were not governmental institutions, they are among the fundamental seminal institutions of our free society. Here were produced in the metropolitan centers the ideas and the drive which found political expression in the economic, social, and political developments of the first half of the twentieth century. If neighborhood community life is ever re-created in the great cities, it will rise in part on the foundation laid by the settlement movement.

The recreation movement sprang from the same desperate needs of urban populations. A sand garden for slum children in Boston opened in 1885; an outdoor gymnasium for men and boys followed in 1889. In 1898, New York City opened various school buildings for evening recreation centers. Chicago in 1903 voted $5,000,000—then a stupendous sum—for parks, following the lead of New York City which had purchased Central Park for recreation purposes in 1853.

Seward Park in New York was a 3-acre slum clearance project carried through under the leadership of Jacob A. Riis. Other great names are associated with the effort to bring sunshine and wholesome activities into the drabness of the congested city. They include Joseph Lee, Jane Addams, Henry S. Curtis, Felix M. Warburg, Robert W. DeForest, Mary McDowell and Mary Simkhovitch, Luther Halsey Gulick, and Theodore Roosevelt. Here again, there has arisen in the darkest alleys of the metropolitan areas a program of deep significance for the future of our urban institutions. This program is now being profoundly affected by the advent of the automobile and the change in the length of the working day and week.

MEETING MANAGERIAL REQUIREMENTS

The third area of metropolitan influence on our governmental institutions is reflected in political and administrative developments. While these matters are not strictly constitutional in character, they are so important that certain constitutional arrangements might well miscarry without them.

Political Developments

THE POLITICAL MACHINE. Metropolitan centers in the United States have produced a series of political situations which depart drastically from the democratic idea. Tempered by ballot box revolutions and uprisings of good government at intervals of twenty to thirty years, the normal pattern of party politics in our great cities shows a vote-producing organization dominated by a boss. This machine is in politics for profit. It derives its revenues from kickbacks or contributions from contractors, protected gamblers, race tracks, and other businesses which derive an advantage from the selective non-enforcement of laws, ordinances, and regulations; assessments on public employees; returns from the favored assignment of bankruptcies and estates and the facilitation of legal business; and gifts or blackmail from special interests.

Such is the typical big city and urban county machine. (Fortunately, there have been some heartening exceptions, and there have also been bosses who were genuinely devoted to the community and were more concerned with power than with plunder.) Usually, one or more powerful state or national politicians stand in the background. They may not participate in the local patronage, but are in league with the local machine because it delivers to them the city vote in state and national elections. The net result is not a pretty picture. It is a miscarriage of our democratic theory.

The attack on this political problem of the older metropolitan areas in the United States has produced few constructive contributions to the political institutions of a free society. The reason is not far to seek. The fathers of our constitutional system paid no attention to the problem of government in great cities because there were no big cities until well along in the nineteenth century. Even the constitution of New York State was not concerned with cities until 1822.

Moreover, most people who have studied the political evils of the big cities from Thomas Jefferson down through de Tocqueville, Dorman B. Eaton, Frank J. Goodnow, Albert Shaw, Woodrow Wilson, James Bryce, Charles Austin Beard and Howard Lee McBain placed the blame largely on recent immigrants. They thought that political parties should be abolished in local municipal elections, and that this could be done principally through the short ballot, municipal home rule, abolition of spoils, separate elections, direct primaries and the initiative, referendum, and recall.

Only the scholars of this generation have begun to see that party organization is an inescapable and desirable instrumentality of democratic life in large population groupings, where self-government requires representative institutions in political party leadership as well as in government. It is unquestionably desirable to keep national problems out of local elections, to disassociate local election dates and parties from national elections and parties, and to stimulate independent civic groups. But those persons who have sought to abolish local political parties have only opened up a vacuum into which the political machine has been sucked.

In addition, the Australian ballot, direct primaries, regulated party elections, proportional representation, and the voting machine have all contributed toward curing the bad situation in the metropolitan communities. But only the voting machine is clearly the product of the great cities.

EMERGENCE OF THE MAYOR. Another important political development of the last century in the big cities is the rise of the office of the mayor. Starting in the pattern of the English mayor, our first mayors were generally short-term presiding officers of the city council with no powers over administration and no important political following. About 1825, the mayors were made elective. This brought them to the top politically, especially when council committee management broke down and technology reared its head in the public service.

In metropolitan areas, the mayor has now become what the governor is at the state level and the president is at the national level. While further analysis is needed, it would seem that a single focus of responsible political leadership in the mayor, the governor, or the president makes it possible for masses of voters to reach genuinely democratic decisions without unduly fractionalizing the political unit or creating an irresponsible dictator. Our experience in testing this hypothesis in the great cities is not without significance.

THE GOVERNMENTAL RESEARCH MOVEMENT. Beginning in New York City in 1906, the so-called municipal research movement has developed in the United States and Canada. The municipal research idea rests on two discoveries. First, modern city government is so complex and so reliant on highly-developed technologies and professionalized skills that the ordinary citizen, even the experienced man of affairs, cannot keep track of his own local government. He cannot act intelligently about elections and matters of policy unless he has staff help from men who can give continuous, professional attention to the work and performance of the government. Secondly, it has been found that a bureaucracy tends to succumb to inertia. Thus continuous, functionalized professional work is required to revise established methods and procedures of government in line with changing arts of operation available in the private sector of the economy and in other governmental units.

Starting with these two ideas, Robert Fulton Cutting, Henry Bruere, Frederick A. Cleveland, William H. Allen, Edwin R. A. Seligman, George McAneny, and Frank Tucker launched in New York the first well-staffed citizen agency. It was designed to bring business reforms to government and to enable the citizen to have an informed impact on the governmental management of his local municipality.

From this small beginning in 1906, the municipal research idea has spread over this country. It has expanded sometimes through the organization of separate bureaus of governmental research, sometimes through special departments of the local or statewide chambers of commerce or other civic agencies, and sometimes through a special bureau of a university. The idea has also been extended to the state and national sphere.

Great changes have come in the activities of the bureaus of governmental research over the past forty years. Many of their technical and procedural functions have been taken over by the organization and methods agencies of government, or by consultant or professional groups. As a result, the bureaus of research are dealing less and less with mechanics and are increasingly serving the citizen through analyzing the broader problems of management, co-ordination, intergovernmental relations, and policy.

From the standpoint of our political institutions, the research bureaus are staff agencies, independent of government, which are designed to help community leaders, the press, and the citizen to deal effectively with the broad management problems of the community. As such, they deserve special mention in discussing our free institutions and the possibility of effective citizen action in an age of increasing technology.

STATE ASSUMPTION OF LOCAL METROPOLITAN FUNCTIONS. Most large metropolitan areas have lost a considerable part of what is normally regarded as a local responsibility to the superior layers of government. Historically, we find that at one time or another in many urban areas of the United States, a public service which was in collapse has been entrusted to a state-created commission, like the Chicago Sanitary District, the Boston Metropolitan District Commission, or one of thirty similar agencies now extant.

As their titles indicate, the state agencies usually extend beyond the boundaries of the central city. They were created partly because the local municipal boundaries were too constricted and too deeply imbedded in law, sentiment, and politics to handle the problem involved. But some state commissions were designed as much for political purposes as for the improvement of administration. There have been many controversies over the invasion of local power through the creation of superseding state commissions. The struggles have occasionally been furious and bloody.

Many years ago in New York City, the state took the police function away from New York City and set up a Metropolitan Police Force to include the cities of New York and Brooklyn, which were then separate, and Westchester and Richmond Counties. When this new police force tried to assume command under an appointee of the state governor, the mayor of New York, Fernando Wood, ordered his city police to repulse the effort. More than one bloody ruckus ensued. On the very steps of City Hall, *The New York Times* of June 17, 1857, reported that 850 policemen and hundreds of onlookers joined in a fight. "Blows fell upon naked heads thick and fast and men rolled helplessly down the City Hall steps." Finally, General Sandford and the Seventh Regiment marched down Broadway and occupied City Hall green. This ended one day's fighting between the "Municipals" and the "Metropolitans." The controversy went on for over a year, however, until a decision of the Court of Appeals finally settled the matter and the municipal police force was dissolved.

In many states, the effort to solve the problem of state-local conflict became a mere struggle of political machines for control of patronage. In others, it fostered the move for "local home rule." As a result of this drive, state constitutions were changed and it became politically unfashionable for the states to dabble too openly in local affairs. This movement reached its height in about 1920.[2]

But soon thereafter, the big cities became increasingly unable to function with boundaries too narrow for their problems, with revenues tied primarily to real estate, and with non-businesslike administrations. Their incapacity brought on a new wave of state and federal supervision and control, hastened by the final collapse of city finances in 1930. This time, the objectives of state interference were not the control of patronage so much as the control over programs, activities, standards, and finance. The latter controls are not exercised directly by state and national political officers, but indirectly through the state and national bureaucracy. The new turn of events has profoundly altered the nature of the problem of local home rule.

REGIONAL PLANNING. In certain metropolitan areas, as we have observed, super-municipal agencies have been created by state law in response to specific problems concerning transportation, water supply, sewerage, parks and recreation, or public health and policing. But it has remained for the planners and the governmental researchers to think about the whole problem in the large.

The first tentative moves have been purely voluntary. They include efforts such as the Regional Plan Association, Inc., of New York, the monumental studies conducted in Chicago and Los Angeles, and the work of the Greater

Boston Area Council, the Pittsburgh and Allegheny County groups, and the Committee on Metropolitan Problems of Cincinnati and Hamilton County. In addition, there are fourteen official regional planning agencies, topped by the National Capitol Regional Planning Council set up by the Congress, and a dozen more unofficial groups.

Without official status, the oldest of these ventures—particularly the Regional Plan Association, Inc., of New York—have exerted a very real influence on the development of co-ordinated highway and other plans among governmental jurisdictions which are independent of each other. This is as much as can be said of the few official agencies which have generally hesitated to apply such positive powers as they theoretically possess.

Through state and federal action and local voluntary initiative, therefore, we have created in metropolitan centers new structures of local government and citizen action which ignore the antiquated boundaries of the core cities. These political developments should be watched, for they may prove to be transitional steps toward overriding governmental institutions of the future metropolitan community. For in coming years, our great sprawling metropolitan areas will certainly lose their rights of local self-government (as they have in other nations) unless dramatically new local instrumentalities are developed to meet the requirements of people who live in parts of the metropolis which are so far undefined and unincorporated. Here again, the metropolitan communities have created a problem, but little has been accomplished by way of inventive political solutions.

Administrative Developments

NEW TYPES OF PLANS. Since 1910, the shift of administrative functions from the legislature to the executive has produced the "strong mayor plan" of city governmental organization which is still the dominant constitution in the big cities of the United States. The "commission plan," widely adopted between 1901 and 1920, has now virtually disappeared. Starting in 1913, the soundly-conceived "council-manager plan" has been adopted in over one thousand cities and a few counties. Except in the largest cities, it is now widely recognized as the most effective structural plan for giving administrative efficiency in a framework of effective democracy, particularly where there is a past tradition of machine politics.[3]

For the largest cities, a combination of the manager plan and the strong mayor plan is undergoing practical tests in New York, Philadelphia, and New Orleans, and to some degree under earlier plans in San Francisco and Los Angeles County. According to the combination plan, the elected mayor, without curtailing his political responsibility, appoints a professional, non-political city administrator to discharge, under his direction, the managerial functions of the mayor's office. The city manager is supposed to bring to his top management job non-partisan supervision as well as professional leadership in the administrative management of governmental business.

PROCEDURAL CHANGES. In the governments of our metropolitan centers, there have also been some important procedural changes. Among these are:

> *Personnel administration,* which began somewhat negatively as civil service reform in New York City in 1883. Now it has become a constructive program of recruitment, training, position specification, salary standards, and career service.
>
> *Public budgeting,* which began in New York City in 1907 and has subsequently been adopted on the New York pattern in the national government, in most states, and in virtually all cities and other large units. It is now being developed in New York City and elsewhere as program or performance budgeting.
>
> *The evolution of planning agencies* as part of top policy direction, with responsibility for development of the capital budget, the enforcement of zoning, and the formulation of master plans.

MUNICIPAL UTILITIES AND AUTHORITIES. In the great urban centers, there has been a remarkable expansion of entrepreneurial services together with an experimentation in their form of organization and management. At present all of the big cities are deeply involved in public ownership. Water supply, public markets, public baths, the generation and distribution of power, urban transportation and park facilities, auditoriums, and public housing are undertaken as governmental ventures in the most capitalistic metropolitan communities without any thought of socialism. In many cases, the utilities were originally privately developed and operated, as some still are even in the largest cities.

This drive for public ownership and operation of public utilities resulted from the breakdown of private operation and the unsatisfactory standards which were maintained under conditions imposed by the communities which generally held the rates down in the face of inflation and refused to accept interruptions of service which arose in labor disputes. In the face of these conditions, private investors pulled out and the properties were socialized. Except for a very few isolated instances, the extensive socialist ventures were undertaken without a single voice being raised pro or con on the basis of any underlying political or economic philosophy. The decision to build, own, or operate was entirely a practical one, recognizing solely the need for service and investment.

It is particularly interesting to note how little influence this urban socialism has exerted on the thinking of socialist and communist leaders. Marx, who lived in London while doing his major writing, based no part of his economic interpretation of history, his theory of the class struggle, or his doctrine of surplus value on metropolitan developments. In the *Communist Manifesto,* Marx and Engels mention urbanism but once, and then to say that bourgeois society "has created enormous cities . . . and has thus rescued a considerable part of the population from the idiocy of rural life." Only the Fabians— particularly George Bernard Shaw and the Webbs—looked to municipal socialization as one of the steps toward a socialist society. Thus municipal public ownership seems to have exercised a surprisingly slight influence on the philosophies or programs of socialism or communism. In the United States, public ownership has certainly exercised an even lesser force on political doctrines.

During the most recent phase of urban development in the United States, we have used again the old device of the ad hoc governmental corporation. The best-known example is the Port of New York Authority, established by interstate compact in 1921 and approved by the Congress of the United States under the treaty clause of the federal constitution.

At the present time, there are several score of these so-called authorities throughout the country, each with its own function and structure. Most authorities are at least partly self-supporting. They are tax exempt and draw their current revenues from rates and tolls rather than from taxation. The governing boards are administratively independent and politically irresponsible. They adopt their own budgets and fix their own collections. In some cases, their independence has been arranged precisely to free the enterprise from the normal political and fiscal controls. Some conspicuously successful enterprises have operated under this program, although they have been criticized for tending to decide for themselves what is good for the public without much thought of other needs and activities.

The development of politically floating ad hoc governmental agencies is nothing new. It is characteristic of any period of burgeoning local governmental services in the face of somewhat static and inelastic governmental institutions. Many similarly independent activities arose in the period after the Civil War, though their services were more of a governmental than a commercial nature. The classical exposition of this development is to be found in Sidney and Beatrice Webb's four volumes on *Statutory Authorities for Special Purposes.*

In both British and United States history, the ad hoc agencies were ultimately abolished in the main and consolidated into the structure of local government. This was done to make possible an effective democratic community control over their policies and to interrelate their otherwise disparate and often competing programs and finances.

THE FUTURE

In reviewing the political institutions of our free society, it seems evident that the great metropolitan centers have problems rather than solutions, difficulties rather than answers, and mostly defeats rather than happy inventions.

The major institutions of our free society were not evolved by or for metropolitan communities. However, the struggle for power within the modern state has found important economic, social, and political protagonists arising with the metropolitan areas and culture. Thus, much of the constitutionalism of free government, and many of the basic economic and social controls, have evolved to hold in balance the forces developed within the metropolis.

The metropolitan way of life, thought, and association has also imparted a twist to our evolution. The intolerable difficulties of city life, resulting from congestion, have lead directly to extensive and successful experiments. These experiments were designed to balance individual freedom with community welfare, based on a reliance upon a responsible technical bureaucracy; to socialize many services; and to develop community agencies created to afford the otherwise helpless individual an opportunity to achieve the fuller realization of his humanity even in the overbearing metropolis.

Finally, in the great metropolitan centers creative efforts have been directed to meet the managerial requirements of big units of self-government. On the political front, these efforts include the effective development of responsible political leadership, the demonstration that technical staff agencies can serve the citizen as well as the bureaucracy, and the experiments with super-municipal agencies and area-wide community planning which may well lead toward the metropolitan governments of the future. On the administrative front, there have been advances in the organization of top municipal management, with the council-manager and mayor-administrator structures, as well as advances in personnel, budgeting, and planning administration.

We must admit, however, that the basic political institutions of our society were not designed for great and changing metropolitan areas. Nor do they meet certain of the most important metropolitan needs. In fact, many of our institutions stand squarely athwart the dynamic flow of social, economic, and political life in the great cities.

The time has come when the people of the great metropolitan areas, working through their state governments, should undertake a fundamental and imaginative examination of the governmental requirements of their spreading population and activities, and should develop new instrumentalities of governance suited to their political and administrative needs.

Thus far, the metropolitan communities have made few unique contributions to our free political institutions. Now is the opportunity to create new contributions, fundamental in scope, which are sorely needed. In this quest, no group has more to offer than the university which feels a sense of responsibility toward the metropolitan community of which it is a part.

FOOTNOTES TO CHAPTER 5

1. R. H. S. Crossman, *Plato Today* (New York: Oxford University Press, 1939), p. 7.

2. A new movement to establish constitutional home rule for cities developed in 1950.

3. Omitting Washington, D.C., the patterns of big-city government organization in 1954 were as follows: for 23 communities with 250,000 to 500,000 inhabitants, 8 had mayor-and-council plans, 6 had commissions, and 9 had manager-and-council plans. For 12 communities with 500,000 to 1,000,000 inhabitants, 11 had mayor-and-council and 1 had manager-and-council plans. For 5 cities over 1,000,000 population, all had mayor-and-council plans.

PART THREE
Economic Advantages
and Disadvantages
of Metropolitan Concentration

INTRODUCTION

Efficiency in producing and distributing goods and services is the main economic advantage of a metropolitan concentration. In one spot the metropolis offers the greatest number of opportunities for work and leisure. Within its confines it provides the means for making and marketing the widest possible range of goods, services, and ideas.

During recent years the efficiency of our largest urban concentrations has been frequently questioned. Traffic congestion has increasingly hampered the ability of the metropolis to assemble and distribute goods and persons quickly and cheaply. Cities like New York, London, and Paris, in fact, are said to be slowly choking themselves to death. Could it be that under modern technological conditions, metropolises are now too big to be efficient? If so, why have them?

These problems are highlighted by the threat of nuclear warfare. If necessary for safety, dispersal of our biggest cities might bring a permanent loss in economic efficiency and a lower standard of living, provided the metropolis really offers net economic advantages. On the other hand, if metropolitan areas are actually disadvantageous, dispersal might favor economic efficiency as well as survival probability.

Problems of the economic advantages and disadvantages of metropolitan concentrations are also emphasized by the rapid expansion of suburban areas around central cities. According to one view, the "suburban trend" is an inevitable and desirable tendency toward decentralization. New outlying residential subdivisions, regional shopping centers, and peripheral industrial and office facilities allegedly offer the best solution to overcoming the disadvantages of metropolitan congestion. Indeed, they may represent one phase of a gradual physical transformation in the normal pattern of the city itself. If this position is accepted, decentralization from central cities should be facilitated as much as possible through appropriate city planning and other public policies.

Another view interprets the suburban trend as a process of natural growth which accompanies any rise in urban population. It is said to be a logical adaptation to outlying residential development rather than a flight of metropolitan activities from the center. In fact, this trend may enhance the economic efficiency of the center as more specialized activities displace less intensive ones which migrate toward the outskirts. Any congestion should be counteracted by measures designed to minimize travel time within the metropolitan area. Decentralization is undesirable because it weakens the vitality of the most useful centralized activities and also increases travel time to and from central locations.

These viewpoints may be resolved by inquiring in greater detail about the economic nature of metropolitan concentrations. What is the potential role, if any, of the metropolis in economic progress and the advancement of living standards? Professor Florence deals with this question and weighs more fully the economic advantages and disadvantages of urban agglomerations in general. Professor Ratcliff is concerned with the efficiency of specific land-use patterns which bear directly upon the economic well-being of any particular metropolitan area. Commentaries by Professor Mayer and Larry Smith seem to support the position of Professors Florence and Ratcliff that, although much needs to be done to improve our urban areas, the age of the great cities is still with us.

6

Economic Efficiency in the Metropolis

P. SARGANT FLORENCE
Chairman of Research Board
Faculty of Commerce and Social Science
University of Birmingham, England

Before discussing the functions and consequences of the metropolis, the question first arises whether the subject actually exists. Is there really such a thing as a metropolis?

If the metropolis is defined as the chief city of a country, the answer is clearly yes. Thirteen out of nineteen of the world's largest countries have one city that is at least twice as populous as the next largest city.[1] Table 2 lists twenty-two countries with major cities. In China, Turkey, and the United

Table 2

THE METROPOLIS IN COUNTRIES WITH A POPULATION OF FIFTEEN MILLION
OR MORE INHABITANTS

Country	Largest city at least twice as populous as second largest city	Country	Largest City	Cities more than one half as populous as largest city
Argentina	Buenos Aires*	Brazil	Rio de Janeiro	Sao Paulo
China	Shanghai**	Yugoslavia	Belgrade	Zagreb
Egypt	Cairo	India	Bombay**	Calcutta
France	Paris*	Italy	Rome	Milan, Naples
Germany	Berlin	Pakistan	Karachi	Lahore
Great Britain	London*	Poland	Warsaw	Lodz
Korea	Seoul	Spain	Madrid	Barcelona
Japan	Tokyo	U.S.S.R.	Moscow	Leningrad
Mexico	Mexico City*			
Philippines	Manila*			
Rumania	Bucharest*			
Turkey	Istanbul**			
Thailand	Bangkok*			
U.S.A.	New York**			

* Over five times as populous as the next largest city.
** Largest city not the capital city.

States, the metropolis—defined as much the largest city—is not the capital. Further confusion can be avoided by eschewing altogether the words capital city.

In this discussion, the term metropolis will refer to the biggest city of a country. But metropolitan, city, or area will refer to the next few largest concentrations of population. These definitions are in accord with the facts of Table 2 which indicate that most countries have one outstanding city as well as several large secondary cities.

Just as there is usually a steep drop from the population of the largest to that of the next largest city, so there are a series of steep drops down the ranks. Indeed, the late Professor Zipf maintained that a harmonic degression is involved —the symptom of some law of least effort.[2] Lawfully or lawlessly, there is undoubtedly a fairly steep cliff effect. Consequently, a few very large cities loom above merely large cities and include a substantial proportion of a country's total population. As a clear boundary line, a population of one million might qualify *absolutely* for metropolitan city status, and two million for metropolitan area status. Or the four largest cities or areas of a country might qualify *relatively*. These rubrics qualify the eight American and four British cities and areas given in Table 3.

THE ECONOMIC STANDPOINT

One test of the economic advantage or disadvantage of a metropolitan concentration is whether or not the concentration is comparatively efficient as indicated by a high measurable return (or output) in relation to measurable costs (or input). Measurement is mainly in terms of money or physical quantities exchanged. Professor Pigou in his *Wealth and Welfare* (1912) also added stability and equal distribution of returns as other tests of economic advantage. These considerations will be discussed later along with the advantages of variety and the distinction between current efficiency and efficiency for future progress.

In an economy where men and capital and management are free to move from one place to another, the more efficient or fittest structure may be presumed to survive and grow larger. Hence a prevailing large size and growth may be taken as a first approximation to a test of economic efficiency. Although some cities like St. Petersburg (Russia), Madrid, and Washington, D.C., were artificially planned as capitals, their subsequent growth or lack of growth is what counts in this essentially ecological criterion.

In Western as well as Eastern civilization, big cities contain a large proportion of the total population. They often appear to have grown out of proportion to the growth in the population generally. The trend toward urbanization is a common lament and, by and large, is strongest toward the largest cities.

In the United States, for example, the four largest cities contained 8.2 per cent of the population in 1890 and 11.0 per cent in 1940. The eight largest

Table 3

American and British Metropolitan Cities and Areas[a] with Their Populations
(In Thousands)

	United States, Census of 1950 Total Population 150,697,000			Great Britain, Census of 1951[b] Total Population 48,840,100			
City	Population of City	Population of Standard Metropolitan Area		City	Population of City	Area or Conurbation	Population of Conurbation
New York	7,892	12,912		London	3,346 (London County)	Greater London	8,344
Chicago	3,621	5,495		Birmingham	1,112	West Midland Conurbation	2,237
Philadelphia	2,072	3,671		Glasgow	1,089	Central Clydeside	1,758
Los Angeles	1,970	4,368		Manchester	703	S. E. Lancashire	2,421
Detroit	1,850	3,016					
Boston	801	2,370					
San Francisco	775	2,241					
Pittsburgh	677	2,213					
Total	17,405[c]	36,296		Total	5,549[c]		14,760
Percentage of Aggregate Population in United States	11.5	24.1		Percentage of Aggregate Population in Britain	11.4		30.2

[a] City of a million or area of two million inhabitants.

[b] One per cent sample tables.

[c] Cities of over a million inhabitants only.

cities contained 10.6 per cent of the population in 1890 and 14.0 per cent in 1940. In 1941, the four most populous standard metropolitan areas held 16.8 per cent of the population and 17.5 per cent in 1951. The eight most populous areas in 1941 contained 22.9 per cent of the population; in 1951, they held 24.0 per cent.

Comparisons of this sort are weighted against the large cities and metropolitan areas. For changes, if any, in boundaries usually fail to keep pace with the overspill and the joining-up or conurbation of several neighboring cities. Technically, the city of New York grew from 2.5 million inhabitants in 1891 to 7.9 million in 1950. But *in fact,* the city joined with Jersey City, Newark, and other existing cities and grew into the New York–Northeastern New Jersey standard metropolitan area of 12.9 million souls.

The understatement by straight comparison of available statistics is still clearer in European countries. Here, in the last few years, the metropolitan areas often appear to be growing less rapidly than the country as a whole. In most large cities, this is probably due to the spilling of the population over the administrative boundaries.[3]

Even if we accept officially-recognized city or area limits, Table 4 still indicates that, excluding the United States, eight countries have a single metropolis or metropolitan area engrossing more than 10 per cent of the national population. In Canada and Belgium, four metropolitan cities or areas alone hold at least 25 per cent of the population. In Australia, nearly one-half of the population is in four metropolitan areas.

Within almost all large countries, therefore, the metropolis and metropolitan cities are growing in importance. On the assumption of the survival of the fittest, their prevalence constitutes a prima facie case for the *economic* advantage of a metropolis and metropolitan cities. Can this ecological hypothesis be supported by citing specific economic advantages which outweigh specific economic disadvantages?

In Table 5, a list on each side of the argument is presented as a basis for discussion. To the various criteria of efficiency in increasing current production and in bettering the pattern of income are also added the criteria of efficiency in increasing future income and offering a variety of jobs and services.[4]

The list in Table 5 assumes an economic structure of a country in which most production is for the market rather than for the producers' own consumption, and where industrial development has gone some way, but not necessarily very far. Table 2 previously indicated that, on the whole, large countries which are least industrially developed, such as India, China, and Pakistan, have the lowest percentage of population in a metropolis or metropolitan cities.

THE NONECONOMIC BORDERLINE

Since life is a whole, economic considerations cannot be divorced from noneconomic criteria. Nor is the borderline between the two always clear. In discussing the large city, this border is particularly important because of the

Table 4

PROPORTION OF POPULATION OF CERTAIN COUNTRIES IN METROPOLITAN CONCENTRATIONS
ACCORDING TO VARIOUS DEFINITIONS

Country	Date of Census	Percentage of Population in		Population in			
		Largest City or Area	Next Three Largest Cities or Areas	Cities of One Million or Over		Areas or Cities of One Million Population or Other Areas of Over Two Million	
				Number	Percentage	Number	Percentage
Australia	1950^d	19.0	26.0^a	—	17.4	2	34.7
The Argentine	1950^c	17.4	6.6	1	11.4	4^b	30.2
Great Britain	1951	16.5	6.0	3^b	15.2	—	
Belgium	1950^c	15.2	21.0	1	10.2	1	12.0
Canada	1950^d	12.0	13.0	1	11.9	—	
Mexico	1950	11.9	3.6	1		1	11.9
France	1949^c	11.9	3.3	1	10.3	—	
Egypt	1949^c	10.3	5.3	1		—	
United States	1950	8.5	8.9	5^b	11.5	8^b	24.1

[a] One area, two cities.
[b] See Table 3.
[c] United Nations estimate.
[d] Government estimate.

Table 5

ECONOMIC ADVANTAGES AND DISADVANTAGES OF METROPOLITAN CONCENTRATION

Efficiency in Increasing Current Production

Economic Criterion	Advantages	Disadvantages
Distribution by manufacturer to maximum consumer market	Short transport and communication	Congestion*
Procurement by manufacturers from sources of maximum primary production	Transport and communication centers	Long transport and communication
Localization of a large manufacturing industry	Short transport and communication between related factories. Also external economies	Risk of mass unemployment from lack of diversification**
Securing and combining factors of production	Pool of labor and management; finance	Scarcity of land; congestion at center; long journey to work*

Efficiency in Increasing Future Income

Economic Criterion	Advantages	Disadvantages
Economic progress	The intercommunication of designs and inventions	

Efficiency in Pattern of Income

Economic Criterion	Advantages	Disadvantages
Stabilization of income	Stability by large city localizing many industries	
Increasing income	Higher wages	Higher cost of living, especially rent
Equalizing income	Wider free services (parks, sewers, refuse collecting, paving, and so on)	Higher local taxes merely to provide services compensating for losses by urbanization

Efficiency in Offering a Variety of Jobs and Services

Economic Criterion	Advantages	Disadvantages
Variety	Wide selection of industries, occupations, and grades	
Localization	Localization of rarer goods and services, specialization in the arts and sciences, financial and commercial services, communications, and entertainment	No offer of rural amenities
Hierarchy	The larger the metropolitan concentration, the greater the range of goods and services	

* May be counteracted to some extent by the existence of specialized centers within the metropolis.

** May be offset in some degree by localizing many industries.

current belief that the metropolis wins on economic advantages but loses on noneconomic advantages. Purposely, therefore, our economic criteria have been chosen to take into account the polemics of the border. These criteria include tests, like equality and stability, that many philosophers would consider to be relevant to welfare rather than to efficiency economics.

The criterion of variety in goods and services is especially significant when applied to the cultural offerings of cities. Though many persons class cultural offerings as noneconomic, they can be subjected to statistical measures and often demonstrate economic advantages to the large city. One example is the offerings of public libraries. K. S. Lomax[5] has contended that for cities with a population of more than 100,000, no further advantages accrue by reason of larger size because the ratio of available books per head does not tend to increase. But this per-head ratio is a fallacious index of the point at issue. A dweller in a large city of a million souls has access to, say, 500,000 books; a dweller in a smaller city of a hundred thousand souls has access to 50,000 books. In each case, the ratio of books to persons is one-half. But for a given cost, big city people get a far greater variety in the range of books accessible to them. That is the point, and it is not entirely noneconomic.

There is still another example of the variety criterion that most people would class as sociological. Yet it is measurable and can be stated in economic terms. What size of city is required for a person of certain intellectual interests to have access, at a reasonable cost in time or money, to the satisfaction of a sufficient number of congenial friends? In England educated people are "choosey" and higher education is intensive rather than extensive. My own experience is that, apart from the special habitat of intellectuals like Oxford or Cambridge, a city of a million is required to give me, say, the twenty or thirty congenial friends I require!

The wide interpretation of economic criteria, however, does not always favor the metropolis. To cite well-known disadvantages, the congestion and noise of streets and transport and the pollution of air, earth and water can each be expressed as economic costs in performing a given task—costs of delay and fatigue, or costs of washing and illness.

THE ECONOMIC TESTS

With respect to the advantages and disadvantages of metropolitan concentration given in Table 5, four main economic tests may be applied. They refer to efficiency or not in increasing current production, in pattern of income, in increasing future income, and in offering a variety of jobs and services.

Efficiency or Not in Increasing Current Production

COST OF DISTRIBUTION BETWEEN MANUFACTURERS AND CONSUMERS. Other things being equal, the population layout most economical of transport and communication would be for everyone to live concentrated in the same area. The main "other thing" which makes this principle unrealistic is the fact that agriculture, including forestry, and some mining must be carried out extensively over a wide and scattered area.

Mineral wealth is often concentrated by nature, and metropolitan cities could be sited over the main mineral deposits. In fact, all the officially-recognized major and minor British metropolitan conurbations, except London, are either on or very near coalfields. But agriculturalists who raise vegetable crops and animal livestock must physically live dispersed.

Nevertheless, the principle of concentration is important. Transport is of little value in itself. Yet it occupies at least five per cent of the total working force of an industrially developed country and a still higher proportion of capital. In any one country, considerable economies would be effected in manpower, in transport equipment, and in other costs if everyone lived nearer to where the goods he consumed were produced.

Some political scientists and geographers have preached the advantage of the physically large country. But to an economist, a small densely-populated manufacturing country, like England, holds the advantages of minimizing the distance goods must travel to their consumer. To that extent, final costs are diminished.

Even within the small space of England, a certain central area has been suggested as the most economic location for most industries. The area has the shape of a pentagon and extends northwest from London and includes the Lancashire and Yorkshire conurbations. A pentagon is also the shape of certain ancient coffins and the area is scurrilously referred to as "the coffin."

The point remains, however, that a confined industry is often advantageously placed in economizing transport and communication. This economy of concentrated population is evident in public utilities and communications. Large cities can generate and transmit electric power and gas cheaper to their inhabitants and can bring more people into telephonic communication at low local rates than can smaller cities. Postal services and door-to-door delivery are also economized. All England can be served by daily London newspapers hot from the press with a far larger circulation and consequent saving in cost than any daily in the United States.

COST OF PROCUREMENT BY MANUFACTURERS FROM PRIMARY PRODUCERS. To an economist, lengthy distances from the primary extraction of food and materials are the main disadvantage of the large city. If all primary production were fairly evenly dispersed, the pattern of population settlement would be in villages and equally-spaced small market towns. An actual example of this symmetry is the English county of Hereford, devoted largely to mixed farming, fruit growing, and its famous breed of cattle.[6]

But in so far as primary production is unevenly distributed, long transport from one place to another is often required and the big city may emerge as a transport center. In fact, many a great metropolis of today, like New York and London, found its origin as a seaport or, like Chicago, as a lake port and railroad center. Of the forty cities of the world with a population of over one million, at least two-thirds are on naturally-navigable waters. In short, although the cost of procurement of materials is mainly a centrifugal force, it may give the metropolitan city an economic advantage in certain circumstances.

LOCALIZATION OF A LARGE MANUFACTURING INDUSTRY. Through *external* economies, industrial localization allows a cluster of small plants in the same industry to obtain (on the principle of multiples) the economies of bulk transport, massed resources, and balanced production which large plants enjoy *internally*. For example, goods can be carried cheaply from one factory to another on publicly-owned roads. In the jewelry-making quarter of Birmingham, one short street "contained forty businesses, twenty-five in the jewelry trade and ten working for it as bullion dealers, stone-merchants and scrap and sweeping merchants. Work was 'put out' if orders were too many, thus adjusting output to capacity. Porters and errand boys and girls 'toting' goods from plant to plant linked processes, like the internal transport system of a large factory, and formed a substantial part of each firm's staff."[7] Much the same interdependence of small plants seems to hold in the clothing section of New York.

This economy of localization arises independently of market or material orientation. Few of the most highly localized United States or British manufacturing industries are particularly near their material or markets.[8] Yet a branch of manufacture may locate in one place, even though neither its markets nor its materials are concentrated there.

Where a large industry is so localized, its localization in one center implies a large city or area. Examples are the Manchester–South Lancashire metropolitan sized conurbation, which is the locus of the English cotton textile industry; and the Pittsburgh and Detroit metropolitan areas, loci of the American iron and steel and automobile industries.

The larger and more complete the concentration of any industry, the greater are certain economies. A buyer can visit and shop around in only one or a few centers and still find all he is looking for. Moreover, if trucking occurs between two large concentrations, the trucker can be assured of a full load in both directions. By cheap local telephone rates, if not by personal contact, everyone engaged in the industry can communicate easily. It should be noted that at least three relatively modern innovations—transmission of electrical power, the telephone, and motor transport—charge for their use on the basis of cost of production in each case. They appear to favor large concentrations as against the older postal service and railroads which charge either a flat rate, or whatever the traffic can bear, regardless of the cost of production in any particular case.

There is a counterbalancing disadvantage, however, to the specialization of an area in one industry. If that industry slumps, all the economic activities in that area—retailing, services, building, public utilities—will slump with it and a pocket of mass unemployment results.

Now it happens that localized industries are also the industries subject to severe unemployment. This may be a mere coincidence. But coincidence or not, the correlation is remarkable, at least in Great Britain. Here detailed unemployment rates were collected throughout the depression years 1929–36, with its *Schwerpunkt* of August 1932. As a rough index of an industry's liability to heavy unemployment, we may take a rate of 30 per cent or more in August 1932; as an index of relative immunity, a rate of 15 per cent or less. To demarcate industries with a low degree of localization—that is, dispersed industries—a coefficient of localization of 0.40 may be taken.[9] Both a coefficient of localization and an unemployment rate are calculable[10] for 32 British industries. By this demarcation, 17 of these industries were dispersed and 15 were localized. Among the *dispersed* industries, 13 had a low, only 4 a high, unemployment record. Among the *localized* industries, 2 had a low and as many as 13 a high unemployment record.

Some of the largest of the 13 unstable industries were pottery, cotton, linen, and jute—located respectively at Stoke-on-Trent, South Lancashire, Ulster, and Dundee. These four communities suffered intense mass unemployment. Other large unemployment-liable industries were steel smelting, tin plating, shipbuilding and coal mining, located in the depressed areas of South Wales and the Northeast.

SECURING AND COMBINING FACTORS OF PRODUCTION. Economic organization and enterprise is largely a matter of bringing together the four productive factors of land, labor, management, and capital, in the most efficient proportions. Three of these classical four factors become easier to secure as concentration intensifies. The greater the population within the daily commuting radius, the greater is the available pool of skilled or unskilled *labor* and of *managers* from which to draw. For modern economic undertakings, *capital* is also required in large supply. To judge from evidence offered later, only the largest cities seem to provide a sufficiently pooled supply of capital available for financing industry.

The factor of *land,* however, presents economic disadvantages in the large metropolitan concentration. A large concentration means a large number of men on a limited area of land. As men compete for this limited land, its price or rent goes up. Normally, though with plenty of exceptions, land prices are highest in the center of the concentration and along transport routes radiating out, star-like, from that center.

These high prices or rents give priority to uses of land that profit most from a central site or access to central site. They drive out uses which find this centrality relatively less profitable. Economists speak of the hierarchy of possible uses of a piece of land[11] descending from the most to the least profitable.

Without any deliberate city planning, the restrictions of the land factor by the price mechanism ecologically will produce some kind of logical pattern. Land-use maps for large cities in all countries bring out clearly the central sites of professional specialists, of financial and commercial houses and of public administration, entertainment facilities, and specialty stores. They also indicate the radiating star pattern of more general stores and the grouping of factories and homes, usually separately, in the sections between the radii. Factories processing heavy goods tend to group around rivers, canals, railways, and other means of transporting their materials and products.

Logical as this pattern may be, it has two main economic disadvantages that increase as the size of the city increases. The first disadvantage is that the various uses profiting especially from centrality may become so numerous that the center approaches complete congestion. At the same time, prices and rents of central sites may become prohibitive. Most metropolitan cities have tended to counteract this disadvantage either through simple decentralization or through the device of a series of coordinated centers each specializing in different uses.

London, for example, contains some of the most famous specialized centers or quarters. It has the City for finance; West End, Oxford, and Bond Street (three miles from the City) for specialty shops; Whitehall for public administration; Harley Street for doctors; the Inns of Court around Chancery Lane for lawyers; Soho for restaurants; Piccadilly Circus and Leicester Square for entertainment of various sorts; and Pall Mall for clubs. New York has Wall Street for finance, Fifth Avenue for specialty shops, and Broadway for entertainment. Paris has its Quartier Latin as a university and art student haunt, and its Rue de la Paix and Montmartre for visitors' shopping and night life.

The second main disadvantage of the land-use pattern of the big city is the distance of family homes from the place where the family breadwinner works. The fully apprenticed medieval worker used to be known as a journeyman. The modern city worker might be called so, too, for much of his time is spent in daily journeying. True, the journey to work is relieved by transport systems ranging from surface streetcars and buses to elevated buses, subways, and tubes. But, though the time thus cut down may compensate for the longer distances, as the city grows the cost to the journeyman grows in proportion.

In the period 1929 to 1944, when fares were lower than they are now, several British city surveys included the cost of these journeys. Table 6 attempts to put the costs on a comparable basis. At Worcester, England, a town of 60,000 inhabitants, it was found[12] that three-quarters of the employed population walked or cycled to work at no direct cost. In Birmingham, a city of a million, half of the employed population paid fares to get to work, and 3.7 per cent paid over 5s. a week. In London, a city approaching ten million, more than half of the employed population paid fares; 6.4 per cent paid over 5s. 6d. a week.

The principal wage-earner who journeys to work may not incur the only travel cost of the large-city family living in the suburbs. There is usually at least one other wage-earner, and he or she may have to journey to work just as far as the principal earner. In the London survey, the "sons, brothers, daughters, sisters and wives"[13] of the principal wage-earner apparently worked

Table 6

THE COST OF THE JOURNEY TO WORK IN THREE BRITISH CITIES

Cost per Week	Percentage of Principal Wage-earners in Cities of Varying Populations		
	Worcester* 60,000 (approx.)	*Birmingham** 1,000,000 (approx.)	*London*** 10,000,000 (approx.)
None	75.5	50.8	46.4
0 – 2s. 6d.	16.7	26.9	24.8
2s. 6d. – 5s.	5.8	18.6	22.4 (to 5s. 6d.)
Over 5s.	2.0	3.7	6.4 (over 5s. 6d.)
Total	100.0	100.0	100.0

* J. Glaisyer and others, *County Town* (London: John Murray, 1946), pp. 106–107. The data for Birmingham are expressed here as a percentage of those wage-earners (89 per cent of the total) who had a fixed place of work.

** K. K. Liepmann, *The Journey to Work* (London: Kegan Paul, Trench, Tribner and Co., 1944), p. 187.

locally (without cost of travel) only slightly more frequently than the principal wage-earner himself. In one of the four boroughs surveyed (Tottenham), they actually worked locally *less* frequently and paid fares over 5s. 6d. *more* frequently.

Long daily journeyings occur not only to work but to school or university. Weekly or bi-weekly journeys are taken to central stores. Now and then journeys are taken to hospitals and other central facilities necessary to living and earning. The London Transport Board calculated in 1939 that "the burden of cost which falls upon the average family in London for transport is about £ 15 per annum, a sum which is estimated to be equivalent to 8 per cent of the average income of working class families."[14]

In addition to the monetary cost of travel, there is a human or real cost.

One must add on the human cost, the psychological wear and tear, the psychological boredom and harassment and depression brought about by this daily shuttling between dormitory and workplace. Consider the number of man-hours reckoned in multiples of a million stupidly expended in the daily transportation of the human body: minutes and hours which, at the peak of traffic, cannot even be utilized in achieving the trivial anesthesia of the daily newspaper. Add to this the depression of the uncomfortable journey, the exposure to infectious diseases in the overcrowded car, the disturbance to the gastro-intestinal functions caused by the strain and anxiety of having to reach the office or factory on time.

Emerson said that life was a matter of having good days; but it is a matter of having good minutes, too. Who shall say what compensations are not necessary to the metropolitan worker to make up for the strain and the depression of the twenty, forty, sixty minutes he spends each night and morning passing through these metropolitan man-sewers.[15]

The metropolitan city worker is indeed on three horns of a trilemma. He either lives more or less centrally and economizes on the land required for other purposes by squeezing his family into an apartment house. *Or* he lives in suburbia with some land for himself and his family to enjoy, but has a long and costly journey to his work and misses many a metropolitan advantage. *Or* he must do without a family. Only occasionally will his family and his work be at the same point on the periphery.

Efficiency or Not in Pattern of Income

THE STABILIZATION OF INCOMES. An advantage of the large city (and often a cause of its growth) has already been mentioned in the possibility of a localization of a large industry with the attendant external economies. A localization of a single industry, however, will not produce a metropolitan-sized city or area unless the industry is very large indeed. More frequently, a metropolitan city or area contains a localization of several industries offering employment to a variety of persons. As measured by my location quotient, seventeen industries were found to be localized[16] in the British Midland conurbation centered on Birmingham. Industrially, this localization of several industries is perhaps the outstanding advantage of a metropolis. It means that a city can have the economies of a localization without its major disadvantage of instability and risk of mass unemployment in the whole community.

The highly documented *locus classicus* of mass unemployment is the British depressed area of 1929 to 1935. In South Wales or the Northeast Coast, whole districts had two out of three producers unemployed over several years with consequent bankruptcy of retail and other service firms. In these areas, as already said, only two or three industries were localized, notably coal mining and iron and steel mills, and either shipbuilding or tin plating. There was little work fit for women. Unoccupation was piled on unemployment.

The danger in the specialization of a city or area upon a few industries can be overcome, without losing the advantages of localization, only by the paradox of specializing upon many industries. To be exact, the danger can be surmounted if the city becomes the *locus* of the localization of many industries. Unless the industries are very small, this multiple localization implies a very large city, if not a metropolitan one.

The seventeen industries localized in the Birmingham conurbation, for instance, employed about 350,000 workers. This figure would imply a population, including nonindustrial workers, of at least 1,200,000. These industries varied in the percentage of women to total employees from 3.0 per cent to 66.8 per cent. In their peak unemployment rate in August 1932, they differed in the percentage of women to total employees from 49.3 per cent for iron and steel to 16.3 per cent for electrical engineering and 13.7 per cent for the chocolate and candy industry.

To gain the full advantage of multiple localization, different industries should be linked and economically helpful to one another. But they should not fluctuate in unison. In the Birmingham conurbation where metal industries form the basis of the economy, four types of such linkage occurred among industries performing successive processes; industries serving a number of other localized industries, such as die sinkers, stampers, and platers; various industries producing parts for other localized assembly industries; and various industries using the products of scrap of other local industries.[17] These four types of linkage have been named vertical, diagonal, convergent, and divergent. The net result is a colocalization of concatenation that carries forward and amplifies the external economies of localization. If *different markets are supplied and different types of labor employed,* the whole industrial and commercial structure will presumably not collapse together. Moreover, there will be more growing points from which increasing employment in new industries can compensate for falling employment in old industries.

This presumption was tested in the depression of 1929 to 1935. Table 7

Table 7

COMPARATIVE MEASURES OF STABILITY OF EMPLOYMENT IN VARIOUS BRITISH AREAS*

Area	Average by Year of Monthly Percentage Rates of Unemployment								Average for 1931–38
	1931	*1932*	*1933*	*1934*	*1935*	*1936*	*1937*	*1938*	
Great Britain	22.0	22.2	20.3	17.3	16.2	13.9	10.7	12.7	16.9
Wales	33.5	37.5	35.4	33.5	33.1	31.4	22.4	24.8	31.5
Birmingham Conurbation**	28.4	27.1	23.6	16.1	11.5	10.1	8.1	11.2	16.7
City of Birmingham	17.7	15.3	12.1	8.1	6.6	5.2	4.3	7.7	9.6

* West Midland Group, *Conurbation* (London: The Architectural Press, 1948), p. 125.
** Median rates of fifteen employment exchange areas.

compares the unemployment rates during the years of the depression for Great Britain as a whole, for Wales (representing a region without any metropolitan conurbation but dominated by one depressed area), for the city of Birmingham, and for the other fifteen employment exchange areas of the Birmingham conurbation. The city of Birmingham had almost the same population as the total of these other areas in the conurbation. Both areas had mixed industries, although industries were more mixed in Birmingham than in the rest of the conurbation. It appears that Birmingham itself maintained employment well above the national average. The other areas of the conurbation started with a higher-than-national unemployment rate but eventually pulled the rate down below the national average. In Wales, the unemployment rate remained high and ended at double the national average.

To the best of my knowledge, no such detailed analysis has been made of the industrial structure of areas other than the Birmingham metropolitan conurbation. During the depression of 1929–37, London, whose localized industries were probably even more mixed than Birmingham,[18] showed an unemployment rate approaching only one-half of the national rate.

In the depression period before 1937, data from the Barlow Commission emphasize the holding power of the London area, which at that time was offering employment to persons unemployed elsewhere. Under the British Unemployment Insurance system, the place where a worker's unemployment book was first issued is noted in the book. Taking all books issued in the London area in the years up to 1937, only 2.1 per cent of men and 2.0 per cent of women workers were found in 1937 to be residing in other regions.

London, in fact, had the highest stability of all areas. The next most stable area was the Midland region containing the metropolitan conurbation of Birmingham, with 4.3 per cent of the men and 2.4 per cent of the women having migrated elsewhere. At the other end of the scale, among men workers who had originally been issued with books in Wales, 15.9 per cent had migrated to other regions; among women workers, 13.8 per cent. In the Northern region, equally without a metropolitan conurbation, 13 per cent of the men and 10 per cent of the women who had been issued with books in that area were found to be working elsewhere in 1937.[19]

The proviso that the colocalized industries must supply different markets applies to both London and Birmingham and ensures that the fluctuations in employment are dovetailed seasonally.[20] In Birmingham, for instance, when the motor car industry slumped during the summer, the jewelry and the chocolate and candy industries boomed. The proviso that different types of labor must be employed also pertains to London and Birmingham and the South Lancashire metropolitan conurbation. As revealed in the census of 1931, the diversification of jobs here ensured that at least 40 per cent of all adult women living in the counties concerned were gainfully occupied. Simultaneously, however, less than 20 per cent of adult women were occupied in the counties of Glamorgan and Monmouthshire, located in the South Wales nonmetropolitan depressed area.

INCREASING INCOME PER HEAD. Large cities localizing many industries may provide more stable income over time than smaller cities localizing a single industry. But do they stabilize at a higher income per head? In Britain, there is little information on local and regional income levels. For the United States, a few data are presented in Table 8.

On the face of it, all the eight large standard metropolitan areas in the United States have a much higher median income per family than the national average. The highest average annual income ($4,063) is found in Chicago. The lowest of the eight ($3,344) occurs in Pittsburgh, but even this low income is 9 per cent higher than the United States average of $3,073. The higher income per family might be due to some economic structure peculiar to large metropolitan areas, with the result that the higher paid categories of occupations were relatively more frequent in those areas. Or it might be due to the possibility that standard metropolitan areas are found in certain sections of the United States where levels of income tend to be high.

To control the factor of economic structure, column 6 of Table 8 lists the

Table 8

INCOME LEVELS AND EQUALITY IN THE LARGEST STANDARD
METROPOLITAN AREAS IN THE UNITED STATES AND
IN THEIR GEOGRAPHICAL DIVISIONS, 1947–1950*

Standard Metropolitan Area and Geographical Division	Median Annual Family Income 1949	Percentage with Income			Average Salary or Wage of Manu- facturing Employ- ees 1947	Aver- age Gross Rent 1950	Net Aver- age Salary and Wage 1947	Percentage of All Factories Employing Less Than Twenty Workers 1950
		Less Than $2000	$2000 to $5000	$5000 or more				
Chicago	$4,063	13.3	48.0	34.7	$3,157	$586	$2,571	64.0
Detroit	3,976	12.5	54.6	32.9	3,322	593	2,729	70.0
East North Central	*3,428*	*21.0*	*54.9*	*24.1*	*3,010*	*545*	*2,465*	—
San Francisco	3,935	15.5	52.6	31.9	3,220	495	2,725	71.8
Los Angeles	3,650	19.9	52.7	27.4	3,118	536	2,582	73.0
Pacific	*3.545*	*21.2*	*53.4*	*25.4*	*3,088*	*511*	*2,577*	—
New York	3,695	17.4	47.8	30.4	3,074	591	2,483	69.3
Philadelphia	3,466	19.4	54.9	25.7	2,876	535	2,341	61.0
Pittsburgh	3,344	18.7	59.0	22.3	3,030	481	2,549	60.0
Middle Atlantic	*3,402*	*20.2*	*54.9*	*24.9*	*2,886*	*556*	*2,330*	—
Boston	3,516	17.1	56.8	26.1	2,775	619	2,156	67.5
New England	*3,246*	*21.7*	*57.4*	*20.9*	*2,670*	*541*	*2,129*	—
United States	3,073	29.2	50.7	20.1	2,777	510	2,267	68.2
All metropoli- tan areas	—	—	—	—	2,937	—	—	63.8
Eight largest metropolitan areas	—	—	—	—	3,088	—	—	66.4
Smaller metro- politan areas	—	—	—	—	2,808	—	—	55.4
Rest of United States	—	—	—	—	2,344	—	—	72.7

* U. S. Bureau of the Census, *County and City Data Book, 1952,* Table II.

average 1947 wage or salary of manufacturing employees only. Here again the average income per head of all the big metropolitan areas (except Boston) appears higher than the national average ($2,777), or the average ($2,808) for the smaller metropolitan areas. Without exception, it is much higher than for the rest of the country ($2,344).

To control the factor of sectional levels of income, data are given for the geographical divisions of the United States where the eight largest standard metropolitan areas occur. None of the eight areas has a median family income in 1949 below the corresponding income of its division except Pittsburgh, where it is 2 per cent below. The proportions above the family income in their geographical division shown by the other seven metropolitan areas range from 2 per cent for Philadelphia to 18 per cent for Chicago.

In seven out of the eight largest metropolitan areas, the average salary or wage of manufacturing employees also is higher than that of the relevant geographical division. The exception is Philadelphia, which falls 0.3 per cent below the Middle Atlantic average. The other seven metropolitan areas range from Los Angeles (1 per cent above its divisional average) to Detroit (10 per cent above). Among the causes of this higher income and earning power of the largest metropolitan areas are the economic advantages of metropolitan concentration in production, already listed. A larger balance of return over costs in production would have as a consequence more income to distribute.

Compared with less concentrated areas, the high money income and high salary and wage of the large metropolitan areas tend, in turn, to attract population into the metropolitan areas and help to account for their growth. Indeed, it is maintained that these metropolitan areas must grow mainly by immigration, since they have a relatively low reproduction rate—a fact, if true,[21] often hurled at them in scorn. This may or may not be a matter of scorn. But the question here is whether the attraction of high money income is a *real* advantage when money terms are translated into commodities.

The chief commodity likely to have a very different money price in towns of different size is housing. Column 7 of Table 8 gives the average gross rent[22] paid in 1950 in the eight largest standard metropolitan areas, in their geographical divisions, and in the United States as a whole. The data show that average rent is certainly higher in the metropolitan areas. But if we subtract average rent from average income, families in the large metropolitan areas still seem to have an advantage in *net* income over other families in the United States or in their own geographical divisions. For the United States, the net salary or wage was $2,267 ($2,777 average income minus $510 average rent). Seven of the eight largest standard metropolitan areas averaged more than this figure; Boston, the single exception, fell 5 per cent below the national average. Net average salaries or wages in the other seven large metropolitan areas ranged from Philadelphia, 3 per cent, to San Francisco and Detroit, 20 per cent, above the national average.

If we compare each of the eight largest standard metropolitan areas with its own geographical division, there is again only one exception to the rule that the metropolitan average salary or wages, net of rent, is higher. Los Angeles and Philadelphia rise less than 0.5 per cent above their divisional average. But the other largest metropolitan areas range above this average from 1 per cent for Boston to 10 per cent for Detroit and Pittsburgh.

On the whole, then, even if the usually higher rents of the largest metropolitan areas are subtracted, these areas show a higher income to their inhabitants. In addition, advocates of metropolitan concentration may maintain that real income should include the free services offered to citizens, such as museums, libraries, parks, sanitation, paved and lighted streets, and policing, which are carried further in larger than in smaller cities and towns.

This argument of greater free services in large cities seems to have a doubtful validity. To start with, it is not true by any means that after a certain size of city is passed, more money is always spent in these ways per head of population, or that spending more means providing more or better services.[23] In any event, this type of spending is often an attempt to compensate artificially for a natural disadvantage of the large city. The provision of parks compensates for the lack of access to country and for the impossibility of city apartment dwellers owning gardens. Judging from crime statistics, the more costly policing of large cities tries to compensate for the higher tendency of larger cities to crime. Pavements and lighting of streets compensate for the slush and danger of their intensive use. More ample sanitary and refuse collecting systems compensate for the greater liability to disease of a large congested city and the impossibility of the private disposal of refuse. Zoos and at least natural history museums might reasonably be considered an artificial compensation for the loss of the chance of nature study in the raw. On the other hand, art museums and higher education in city colleges do provide something free that is new and not usually found in smaller uncongested cities with accessible countryside and room for gardens.

This question cannot be judged adequately without a deeper analysis of the statistics of city expenditures and a deeper insight into what the common man really likes. Books are written and social research carried on by *uncommon* men. Today such writers, unlike Samuel Johnson and his uncommon contemporaries,[24] are mostly country or small-town lovers. But it is more than probable that most common men or women in the United States, England, or Europe value big city life above access to gardens and country which the smaller cities afford. Certainly the typical Cockney felt unhappy when evacuated during World War II to smaller towns; but then again, the big city may be blamed for so conditioning him!

On the one side of the question, there is Lewis Mumford and his predecessors like Ruskin and Cobbett, who wrote of London as "the Great Wen," and Shelley with his "Hell is a City much like London—a populous and smoky City."[25] On the other side, supporting Dr. Johnson, many people seem to prefer window shopping to the equally free nature study. This propensity to take delight in the street sights and life of the great city seems the typical behavior and ideology[26] of the Western masses. The propensity cannot be ignored by the economist since it forms part of the basis for consumer demands and standards of living, and for the townward migration of labor and management. Much of the Londonward location of industry has been explained by the yearning of the location-decision-maker's wife for closer access to Oxford and Bond Streets.

EQUALIZING INCOME. Apart from providing more free services, it is difficult to generalize whether or not metropolitan concentrations in all countries have the advantage of greater equality among incomes. So much depends on the sociological setup. Before its social revolution of 1914 to 1945, which abolished millionaires and deprived all the moderately rich of domestic servants, England showed the widest inequality among incomes in rural areas and small towns rather than in large cities. Next to agriculture, domestic service had the highest occupational location quotients in rural areas and small towns, and agricultural laborers had the lowest wages of any large industry for men. At the opposite end of the scale, rich families made their homes in the rural counties, at least for the fall and winter months, to take the pleasures of shooting, foxhunting, and hunt balls. They were known, in fact, as *The County* families. This rural setup of farmers and peasant proprietors, with some small traders in small market towns but few hired hands or sporting rich, is probably as egalitarian a society as it is possible to have.

In the United States, a measure of economic equality in various localities is provided by the distribution of families into three groups, as in columns 3 to 5 of Table 8. Equality can be measured as a *low* percentage of families with a median income of less than $2,000 per year or a *high* percentage between $2,000 and $5,000.

On the first test of a low percentage below $2,000, all the eight largest standard metropolitan areas had percentages in poverty lower than the national percentage and their own divisional percentage. The difference is particularly noticeable in the East North Central division. There 21.0 per cent of families had incomes below $2,000, but Chicago had only 13.3 per cent and Detroit only 12.5 per cent in this condition of relative poverty.

On the second test of a large middle or lower-middle class, seven out of the eight largest standard metropolitan areas fall at or below their divisional percentages (Pittsburgh is the exception), but six out of the eight rise above the national percentage. This situation can be explained by the fact that a high proportion of families in the lower income brackets live in the nonindustrial divisions of the United States, especially in the South, where no large metropolitan concentrations occur.

The inhabitants of the largest standard metropolitan areas in the United States, therefore, tend to have higher real and nominal incomes than the inhabitants of their respective geographical divisions or even of the whole country. Fewer of them suffer poverty, although compared with the situation in their own geographical divisions there is perhaps less of a middle class.

From these monetary tests measured by income distribution, the criterion of equality may be broadened into the degree of equality in status. In economic structure, status is traditionally a question of being an employer or employee. The prevailing degree of equality is thus measurable in terms of the proportion of proprietors and owners of firms to total employees. It depends largely on the prevalence of small firms.

A big city is sometimes supposed to imply big firms and giant concerns, with no entrepreneurs in the sense of owner-managers, operated by a bureaucracy of top, middle, and supervisory salaried managers. A useful test of this supposition is to find the proportion of factories in the area which contain less than twenty employees, since the vast majority of these factories are owned singly by a small firm. The percentages are given in the last column of Table 8. In contrast to the belief that the largest metropolitan areas have relatively few small factories, the opposite situation appears to hold. Small firms, as we should expect,[27] prevail most in the rural and other nonmetropolitan areas of the United States. But they prevail considerably more in the largest truly-metropolitan areas than in the smaller metropolitan areas.

In the most populous standard metropolitan areas, the percentage of all establishments that employ less than 20 workers is 66.4; in the less populous areas, it is only 55.4. The large metropolitan areas, however, show considerable individuality. Los Angeles, San Francisco, Detroit, and New York are above the national average of small plant prevalence (68.2 per cent); four large areas are below the national average. The trend for the larger cities to have a smaller average size of plant—measured in terms of the average number of wage earners per establishment—becomes clear in Table 9.

Table 9

RELATION OF FACTORY SIZE TO SIZE OF CITY IN
THE UNITED STATES, 1940

Classes of Size of City (Population in Thousands)	Number of Cities	Number of Wage Earners per Establishment (Unweighted moving averages of three size-class averages)
500 and over	14	30.2*
200 to 499	29	42.0
100 to 199	49	51.0
90 to 99	7	59.1
80 to 89	13	60.6
70 to 79	18	60.6
60 to 69	33	64.6
50 to 59	28	65.0
40 to 49	50	65.9

* Simple average.

The explanation for this unexpected negative correlation between factory size and city size is connected with the economics of localization already noted. If a local cluster of small plants can obtain *externally* the economies which large plants enjoy *internally,* localization of an industry in a city will enable small plants to survive by undertaking linked specialized processes, services, or products on a fairly large scale. The small plants can always get the services, materials, and labor they require on the spot. Among specific industries, manufactures with a very high coefficient of localization tend to be enterprises with a medium or small plant size.[28] This correlation is particularly true of Britain; it is traceable in the United States, too.

Efficiency or Not in Increasing Future Income: Progress

Economic progress may be defined as an increase over time in the efficiency or economy with which material or human resources are turned into goods and services. Among the historical examples of economic progress within nineteenth-century Britain and mid-nineteenth to mid-twentieth-century North America, the outstanding factor is the application to industry of scientific observation and experiment. In the early stages of the Industrial Revolution, scientific thought was not typically applied in the larger metropolitan cities. One connects the English developments with Arkwright and Crompton in Lancashire, and with Watt in Scotland, Birmingham, and the mining areas, but not with innovation in London.

Today the application of scientific thought is no longer the work of an individual genius at the industrial front. It proceeds mainly by the systematic research of teams in large laboratories built in certain places specifically for the purpose. The exchange and communication of ideas is now all-important. Research is likely to be localized in the larger centers of the industry, if not in certain centers specializing generally on research. Large metropolitan cities may thus be expected to play a large role in making progress possible.

This hypothesis can be tested by the proportion of scientific workers of different grades located in various places. Table 13 (to be discussed later) includes these facts among its calculations of the industries and occupations which are located in New York, London, and Paris to a greater degree than would be mathematically expected.

In 1931[29] Greater London contained 19.5 per cent of the employed population of Great Britain. But it held 52.7 per cent of all workers engaged in making scientific instruments and apparatus other than photographic and electrical—yielding a location quotient of 2.7.

In 1946, the Department of the Seine (the metropolitan area with its center at Paris) contained 12.2 per cent of the employed population of France, but held:

36 per cent of all engineers, yielding a location quotient of 3.0
37 per cent of industrial designers, a quotient of 3.0
34 per cent of technological agents, a quotient of 2.8
37 per cent of lab workers, a quotient of 3.0
32 per cent of lab chemists, a quotient of 2.6

The New York metropolitan area contained 11.2 per cent of the total employees in American manufacturing industries in 1947, but also held:

56.5 per cent of all workers employed in the manufacture of surgical and medical instruments, yielding a quotient of 5.0
40.5 per cent of all workers employed in making scientific instruments, a quotient of 3.6
32 per cent of all workers employed in making electrical measuring instruments, a quotient of 2.8

17.5 per cent of all workers employed in making mechanical measuring instruments, a quotient of 1.6

In Britain, industrial firms with plants scattered throughout the country tend to place their research laboratories in London or some large metropolitan area like Birmingham or Manchester. In its report for 1948–1949,[30] the British Department of Scientific and Industrial Research lists 37 industrial research associations. Of the total of 41 laboratories or experimental stations in these 37 associations, 19 are in the London area, 3 in Manchester, 2 in Birmingham, and 1 in Glasgow. Though the industries concerned are scattered throughout the country, 25 out of 41 of the research centers are in one or another of the four British metropolitan areas.[31]

Efficiency or Not in Offering a Variety of Jobs and Services

VARIETY. The variety of economic activities carried on in any city or area can be measured statistically. A precise measure is the coefficient of specialization which was applied to each of the states in the United States by the United States National Resources Planning Board in its *Industrial Location and National Resources* published in 1943. A coefficient of 1.00 denotes the highest theoretically possible specialization. The coefficient of 0.00 denotes no specialization; that is, perfect reproduction of the national economic structure.

Specialization is the opposite of variety. Thus a comparatively high specialization coefficient shown by such states as North Dakota (0.354), South Carolina (0.370), and Arkansas (0.371) which specialize in agriculture, or by the District of Columbia (0.390) which specializes in government, may be looked upon as a low coefficient of variety. On this interpretation, the states of widest variety were Missouri (0.107) and Indiana (0.108) with no great deviation from the national structure. These two states mixed agriculture and the various industries and services in ratios much like the national proportions.

Unfortunately, this coefficient has not been worked out for metropolitan areas or cities. But a coarse measure of specialization—in manufacturing only—can be obtained by adding up the number of separate individual industries listed for each metropolitan area in the United States Census of Manufactures. No industry is listed unless it employs at least one hundred workers.

In the standard industrial classification used in the Census, 450-odd individual manufacturing industries are denoted by a four-digit code. Out of a possible 450, the eight largest standard metropolitan areas each have one hundred or more workers in from 68 to 260 individual industries. These areas are ranked in Table 10 by numbers of employees in manufacture. The number of their individual industries declines as the total number of workers falls, but not continuously. Detroit and Pittsburgh, and to a lesser degree Chicago, appear to engage in relatively fewer individual manufactures than their total number of manufacturing employees might warrant—a deviation related to the localization of particularly large individual industries in their midst.

This variety of individual industries offering a substantial chance of employ-

Table 10

LOCALIZATION OF MANUFACTURING EMPLOYMENT IN THE LARGEST
STANDARD METROPOLITAN AREAS IN THE UNITED STATES

Largest Standard Metropolitan Areas	Number of Employees in Manufacture	Number of Individual Industries Employing 100 or More Workers
New York	1,604,184	260
Chicago	945,326	167
Detroit	555,788	83
Philadelphia	532,492	175
Los Angeles	358,772	173
Pittsburgh	337,974	68
Boston	271,273	132
San Francisco	163,641	94

Unweighted Average 148

ment (at least one hundred jobs) contrasts with the situation in the smaller standard metropolitan areas. Each of the eight largest areas has more than 160,000 in manufacture; the average of the substantial variety of their manufactures is 148. But at the other end of the scale, areas with 50,000 to 60,000 employed in manufacture have an average of 17 individual industries with substantial employment; for eleven areas with 40,000 to 50,000 so employed, an average of only 12.[32] Apart from the instability that may result if a few industries are either declining or liable to depression, this lack of variety implies the disadvantage of lack of choice to the worker for his particular likes, abilities, or acquired skills.

LOCALIZATION. Variety within a large city may imply a further advantage. It suggests that certain specialized, rarer activities come into existence which might not otherwise appear if the big city did not supply the market or the necessary conditions for effective full use of specialists.

This point can be illustrated from the localization of the printing and publishing group of industries. General commercial printing is an individual industry that appears in the pattern of practically all metropolitan areas, whether large or small. But the rarer activity of publishing periodicals, and the still rarer activity of publishing books or rendering auxiliary printing services, is reserved for the largest metropolitan areas only.

Fifty-four metropolitan areas in the United States have a sufficient number of manufacturing employees (40,000) to be separately analyzed in the Census of Manufactures. Among the fifty-four, the number of areas containing individual (four-digit code) printing and publishing industries with at least one hundred employees each varied in 1947 as shown in Table 11. All other individual industries with at least one hundred workers in the printing and publishing group were concentrated in no more than three of the fifty-four industrial metropolitan areas.

As Table 11 indicates, commercial printing is carried on in nearly all census metropolitan areas, and newspaper publishing in one-half of them. On the other hand, periodical publication and other printing services, and particularly publishing and printing books, generally take place in only a few of the larger communities. Of the twenty metropolitan areas offering substantial employment (100 jobs or more) in periodical publication, only seven or 35 per cent

Table 11

INDUSTRIAL METROPOLITAN AREAS IN THE UNITED STATES
WITH PRINTING AND PUBLISHING INDUSTRIES
EMPLOYING AT LEAST ONE HUNDRED WORKERS
EACH IN THE YEAR 1947

Industry	Industrial Metropolitan Areas Containing the Industry (Out of a Total of 54 Areas)
Commercial Printing	48
Newspaper	27
Lithographing	22
Periodical	20
Photoengraving	17
Typesetting	11
Miscellaneous publishing	10
Bookbinding	9
Engraving and plate printing	4
Publishing and printing books	4

have a manufacturing population of less than 100,000. This is about half the percentage which would be expected on the basis of population size alone. For 63 per cent of the fifty-four areas listed in the Census of Manufactures have a manufacturing population of less than 100,000. The book publication and printing industry is still more selective of the larger metropolitan areas. New York, Chicago, San Francisco, and Milwaukee are the only four areas where it substantially occurs.

For the eight largest standard metropolitan areas, Table 12 sets forth the distribution of printers and publishers, omitting the more ubiquitous commercial printing. These eight areas hold only 24.1 per cent of the national population but contain 32.6 per cent of newspaper workers and 62.9 per cent of other non-commercial printing and publishing employees. They are also pre-eminent in certain varieties of service, such as wholesaling, finance (with insurance and real estate), and personal business and repair services.[33] With 24.1 per cent of the national population, the eight areas have 35.6 per cent of all active proprietors and paid employees in personal, business, and repair services; 38.2 per cent of all wholesale employees; and 41.4 per cent of all employees in finance. The relevant location quotients are 1.5, 1.6, and 1.7.[34]

New York is pre-eminent among the big eight in three of the four columns of Table 12. Nowhere does its location quotient fall below 1.4; in publishing books and periodicals and printing services it is 4.0. Chicago has quotients of between 1.4 and 3.5; Philadelphia, quotients between 1.2 and 2.6; San Fran-

Table 12

EMPLOYMENT IN VARIOUS INDUSTRIES AND LOCATION QUOTIENTS (LQ) FOR THE LARGEST STANDARD METROPOLITAN AREAS IN THE UNITED STATES*

Employment in Industries

Standard Metropolitan Area	Population as Percentage of National	Printing and Publishing				Personal Business and Repair Service		Wholesale Employees		Finance	
		Newspapers		Periodicals, Books, and Services							
		Per Cent of National	LQ	Per Cent of National	LQ	Per Cent of National	LQ	Per Cent of National	LQ	Per Cent of National	LQ
New York	8.6	11.8	1.4	34.4	4.0	15.0	1.7	15.8	1.8	18.9	2.2
Chicago	3.6	5.0	1.4	12.7	3.5	5.6	1.5	6.6	1.8	5.7	1.6
Philadelphia	2.4	2.9	1.2	6.4	2.6	3.0	1.2	3.0	1.3	3.2	1.5
Los Angeles	2.9	3.6	1.2	2.0	0.7	4.0	1.4	3.9	1.3	4.5	1.6
Detroit	2.0	2.1	1.1	1.4	0.7	2.5	1.2	2.1	1.1	2.0	1.0
San Francisco	1.5	2.3	1.5	1.6	1.1	2.1	1.4	2.7	1.8	2.8	1.9
Boston	1.6	3.1	2.0	3.9	2.5	2.0	1.3	2.5	1.6	2.8	1.8
Pittsburgh	1.5	1.8	1.2	0.5	0.3	1.4	1.0	1.6	1.1	1.4	0.9
Largest eight areas	*24.1*	*32.6*	*1.4*	*62.9*	*2.6*	*35.6*	*1.5*	*38.2*	*1.6*	*41.4*	*1.7*
Other census metropolitan areas	32.0	—	—	—	—	37.3	1.2	55.1	1.7	38.1	1.2
All census metropolitan areas	56.1	—	—	—	—	72.9	1.3	93.3	1.7	79.5	1.4
United States	100.0	100.0	—	100.0	—	100.0	—	100.0	—	100.0	—

* Based on data from U. S. Bureau of the Census, *County and City Data Book, 1950* and *1947 Census of Manfacturers*, Vol. 3, Table V. For a definition of the location quotient, see footnote 34, page 123.

cisco, between 1.1 and 1.9; and Boston, between 1.3 and 2.5. Quotients below unity indicate a lower than national proportion of persons engaged in the activity. Such quotients appear in Los Angeles and Detroit in publishing periodicals and printing services, although for the other three activities, their quotients are 1 or above. Pittsburgh fails, however, to show quotients above unity in the majority of columns.

If certain qualitative structural characteristics possessed by the largest cities are required for metropolitanship, Pittsburgh and Detroit may, perhaps, fail to meet the requirements. In Britain, the same qualitative failure would also have to be recorded by the metropolitan area of Birmingham and the Black Country. Its proportions of the labor force in services associated with most metropolitan areas (including some to be indicated later) fall well below the national averages.[35]

This brings forward the question: when is a metropolis not a metropolis? When, to be exact, may a metropolis possess the disadvantages of concentration without its advantages? Perhaps the best approach is to bring out certain common characteristic qualities of three areas of cities which are acknowledged to be metropolitan by the cosmopolitan world. Table 13 gives the location quotients of certain activities that are highly localized in New York, London, and Paris within their own national structure. Government activities are omitted since we specifically disallowed the metropolis as necessarily carrying the connotation of a national or state capital.[36]

The first characteristic quality of large metropolitan areas is the function of acting as headquarters of finance and of certain business services like accounting and technical advice. As the high quotients in Table 12 for Chicago and San Francisco remind us, in a large country this function requires regional as well as national headquarters. A second metropolitan function is communication, represented by the publishing of newspapers and of periodicals and books and by various publishing and printing services. Here again Table 12 shows that regional as well as national headquarters are required. A third metropolitan function is that of leading scientific progress, a function found pre-eminently in New York, London, and Paris, but not very visible in the statistics of any regional metropolis in the United States.[38] These three metropolitan functions suggest that the metropolis is a clearinghouse as well as a reserve or pool of distributable resources and a brain and nerve center for economic action.

In the metropolis, regional and national inventories or pools of stocks are accumulated for distribution by wholesalers. Pools of liquid funds are accumulated by banks and insurance offices. New scientific ideas and inventions are thought out and experimented upon; if hopeful, they are made public or communicated privately; and if the hopes are accepted commercially as good risks, they are financed so that capital equipment may implement the communicated ideas.

In measuring communication by private contact, we can point to the high location quotients (see Table 13) in London for consulting engineers (2.2) and consultants in chemistry (2.2), in Paris for engineers (3.0) and technicians (3.0), and in New York for business services (1.7). The preponderance of stenographers and clerical workers in all three cities also indicates the concentration on non-printed paper work, which is still the main means of communicating ideas privately between persons. The quotients indicating localization of communication in New York (1.5) and of postal, telegraph and wireless communications in London (1.7) are also significant in this connection.

The comparison of the three cosmopolitan centers makes it possible to find new common functions beyond those of commerce and finance, scientific progress, and publication and communication. New York, London, and Paris are all pre-eminent in economic activities catering to a variety of tastes ranging from cultural to luxurious, from literary and artistic to sheer love of finery. Just as science and the application of scientific invention in industry seem to preoccupy the metropolitan city, so does art and applied art, especially in clothing and in fancy luxury goods, whether of textiles, leather, precious metals or artificial flowers.

Table 13 shows that the number of individual industries of this sort with high location quotients in New York and London is fairly overwhelming. But though Paris is the most famous for art and artifice applied to clothing, the statistical evidence is less plentiful. This is partly due to the fact that the census occurred so soon after World War II. It is also due to the fact that the French census did not distinguish between *haute couture* and plain *couture,* which is so widespread over France. At any rate, no other center for applied arts appears in addition to the metropolis of Paris, and this is also true of Great Britain and the United States. For the whole apparel group of industry, New York has a location quotient of 3.2; Chicago has a quotient of only 0.7.

The cosmopolitan metropolis also specializes in entertainment. In New York a high quotient (1.5) is shown for the amusement, recreation, and related group of industries and in London for the theaters, cinemas, music halls, and concerts group (1.7). Higher quotients appear for individual occupations. Actors are over three times as numerous in New York (3.6) as a level dispersion over the country would warrant. In London the actors' quotient is 2.4. The musicians' quotients are 1.8 and 1.7, respectively, in the two cosmopolitan cities. In Paris, too, there is a preponderance of occupation in spectacles (4.5) and musicians (2.6).

More material entertainment preponderates in all these cities in the form of clubs and cafés. The *garçon de café* is, in proportion to the total number of workers, 1.8 times more numerous in Paris than for France as a whole. Entertainments vary from concerts to coffee houses and suit all tastes and all sorts of economic demand. A peculiar function of a metropolis, and one which may be counted as an economic advantage, is the variety it can offer to the consumer as well as the worker.

Other functions of the metropolis would probably appear if the statistics had

Table 13

OCCUPATIONS AND INDUSTRIES WITH HIGH METROPOLITAN LOCALIZATION
MEASURED IN LOCATION QUOTIENTS FOR NEW YORK, LONDON, AND PARIS

Variety of Function	Standard Metropolitan Area of New York	Greater London	Paris (Department of Seine)
Commerce and Finance	Stenographers (City) ... 1.8	Typists ... 2.0	Administrators ... 2.0
	Other clerical workers (City) ... 1.8	Other clerks ... 1.8	Commercial travelers ... 3.0
	Wholesaling ... 1.8	Managers of commercial office departments ... 1.7	Stenographers ... 2.4
	Business services ... 1.7	Company directors ... 2.1	Storekeepers ... 2.7
	Finance ... 2.2	Accountants ... 1.7	Employees in commerce ... 2.1
	Communication ... 1.5	Bankers and officials ... 1.6	Hommes d'affaire export ... 2.3
	Public utilities ... 1.5	Advertising agents ... 2.2	Accountants ... 2.3
	Other professional services (City) ... 1.6	Stockbrokers and jobbers ... 2.3	Technicians: banks, insurance, publicity ... 3.0
		Other financial insurance employees ... 2.6	Bank employees ... 3.5
		Storage ... 1.9	Bank and finances group ... 3.2
		Postal, telegraph, and wireless communications ... 1.7	
		Insurance, banks, and finance ... 1.9	
		Other professional and business services ... 2.6	
		Wholesale nonfood ... 1.6	
Publishing Industries	Lithographing ... 2.0	Lithographing and other engraving ... 2.3*	Printers ... 3.0
	Miscellaneous publishing ... 3.0	Newspaper and periodicals ... 2.0*	Typographers ... 2.1
	Periodicals ... 3.3	Production of printed books ... 2.4*	Binders ... 4.1
	Books ... 4.3	Process engraving ... 2.6*	Journalists ... 4.4
	Bookbinding (group of 4) ... 3.1	Bookbinding ... 2.6*	
	Engraving on metal ... 3.1	Ink ... 3.5*	
	Printing trades service (group of 4) ... 2.7	Printing machinery ... 2.9*	
	Printing ink ... 2.8		
	Printing trades machinery ... 3.7		

Category						
Science and Applied Science	Manufacture of scientific instruments	3.6	Other scientific instruments and apparatus	2.7	Lab workers	3.0
	Electrical measuring instruments	2.8	Wireless apparatus	2.4	Lab chemists	2.6
	Surgical and medical instruments	5.0	Drugs and fine chemicals	2.4	Engineers	3.0
	Mechanical measuring instruments	1.6	Consulting engineers	2.2	Technological agents	2.8
	Electronic tubes	3.1	Consultants in chemistry, etc.	2.2	Radio electricians	2.4
	Other electrical products	2.6	Laboratory attendants	1.6		
	Medicinal chemists	5.3				
Art and Materials	Authors (City)	2.4	Authors	2.1	Literary, artistic and scientific profession	4.2
	Architects (City)	1.5	Painters, sculptors, etc.	2.5	Industrial designers	3.0
	Designers (City)	1.9	Architects	1.4	Architects	2.9
	Artists and teachers (City)	3.1	White lead, paints, and varnish	1.9		
	Artists' material	2.1	Pencils and penholders	3.0		
	Models and patterns	4.2	Musical instrument makers	3.6		
	Paints and varnish	1.9				
	Lead pencils and crayons	5.2				
	Hand stamps and stencils	2.0				
Applied Art (Clothing)	Women and misses outerwear (group of 7)	4.7	Garment makers	1.5	Tailleurs et coupeurs	1.8
	Women and children's undergarments (group of 2)	3.6	Clothing renovation and repair	2.7	Modiste (includes milliner)	2.0
	Children's outerwear (group of 3)	4.4	Handkerchiefs, scarves, ties	3.3	Clothing group (census of 1936)	1.8
	Miscellaneous apparel and accessories (group of 9)	3.3	Dress, blouse, skirt	2.1	Furriers	4.3
	Millinery	5.7	Tailoring	1.5	Pelleterie	3.3
	Knit outerwear mills	3.7	Millinery	2.7		
	Men and boys neckwear	3.9	"Other" clothing	1.8		
	Men and boys suits and coats	2.4	Furriery	3.6		
	Fur goods	7.8				
	Furs dressed and dyed	6.3				

113

(continued on P. 114)

Table 13 (cont'd.)

Variety of Function	Standard Metropolitan Area of New York	Greater London	Paris (Department of Seine)
Applied Art (Goods for Luxury and Refinement)	Greeting cards ... 2.4 Mirrors and picture frames ... 2.2 Lamp shades ... 3.4 Artificial flowers ... 6.7 Miscellaneous fabricated textiles (group of 9) ... 3.2 Handbags and purses ... 5.3 Small leather goods ... 4.1 Miscellaneous leather goods ... 3.3 Jewelry (precious metal) ... 3.5 Costume jewelry ... 3.4	Hem and embroiderers ... 2.1* Artificial flowers ... 2.7* Wood carve, gild, picture frames ... 1.9 Ornamental feather dressing ... 3.0* Saddlery, harness, and other leather ... 1.9 "Other" precious metals ... 2.0*	*Miscellaneous textile workers ... 2.5* *Artificial flower workers ... 5.6* *Maroquinier ... 3.8* *Jewelry workers ... 4.5* *Jewelers (retail) ... 4.3*
Entertainment	*Musicians and teachers (City) ... 1.8* *Actors (City) ... 3.6* *Eating places (sales) ... 1.9* *Amusements, recreation, and related group ... 1.5*	Actors ... 2.4 Musicians ... 1.7 Waiters ... 1.9 Theaters, cinemas, music halls, and concerts ... 1.7 Restaurants, catering, eating, and coffee houses ... 2.1* Clubs ... 1.9* Entertainment and sport group ... 1.6	*Garçons de café ... 1.8* *Sportifs professionels ... 2.2* *Musiciens ... 2.6* *Spectacles (minus musicians) ... 4.5*

* Based on total employed in England and Wales.
See Footnote 37 for further notes on Table 13 (page 123).

been broken down fine enough in the census. Medical specialists, for instance, concentrate in London. But the census does not distinguish specialists from the more numerous general practitioners who are dispersed, so that the specialists' pattern of concentrated location is blurred.

HIERARCHY OF SERVICES. Can some persistent hierarchical pattern be established in the variety of services offered by cities of different sizes up to metropolitan dimensions? In a survey of Worcester, England,[39] population 60,000, a series of superimposed location patterns of economic and social services were identified. Food stores, primary schools, and pubs were completely dispersed. Clothing stores, cafes, libraries, secondary schools, and clinics were semi-dispersed in suburban centers as well as the main center. Specialty stores, hotels, hospitals, a live-actor theater, and a technical college were only in the main center of town. A larger city, say, of 100,000 to 200,000 or a metropolis of over a million would each provide a further superstructure to these series.

From such data, Colin Clark concludes that "a region can give its inhabitants an adequate range of commercial services when the population of its principal city is somewhere in the neighborhood of 100 to 200,000,"[40] and that in the case of the other service industries, a smaller population will generally suffice. It depends, of course, on what services Clark has in mind. But the actual pattern found in the United States and Britain does not appear to support his dictum so far as the services of financing industry, expert specialist advice, or of scientific industrial research and development are concerned.

Quite the contrary. To be adequate, these services apparently require larger cities than do adequate commercial and wholesaling services. Even adequate wholesaling services may require a city somewhat larger even than 200,000.[41] If servicing is widened to the social and cultural service (Clark himself includes universities), the dictum seems even less true. In the United States, an adequate choice of live-actor theaters seems to require a metropolitan area of twelve million. In England, a good university of 1,000 to 3,000 students (Clark's own test) requires a city of at least 300,000 with a regional population of a million rather than Clark's 250,000.

One conception of the pattern of city-size requirements for various functions is pictured in Fig. 1. It represents three categories of size whose frequency is pictured as 64 to 8 to 1—not too far from reality. The tallness of the upright lines roughly represents the range of variety of a city's activities.

Certain activities, particularly mining and localized manufacturing industries, are sporadic and performed in some cities and towns and not in others. Other economic activities are nearly ubiquitous and regularly performed in most cities and towns, although disproportionately to the population at large. Still other activities are performed disproportionately in most cities and towns above certain sizes and tend to be ubiquitous in large concentrations.

As Fig. 1 suggests, baking and bottling of beverages (in England, brewing) are performed in most towns down to the 25,000 level together with other activities such as retailing, construction activities, and eating and drinking locals ("catering and victualling"). These activities are usually performed disproportionately; that is, workers engaged in them form a larger proportion of the total of all workers in towns than in the nation as a whole.

An example of a persistent retailing pattern was found in English market towns in the West Midland Group's survey of Herefordshire. Each of the six market towns showed only a slight deviation from 22 per cent of the total of workers in retailing, though only 11.7 per cent of workers were retailers in England and Wales as a whole.[42]

Metropolitan Area (over 1,000,000 population)

Finance and business services
Book and periodical publishing and printing services
Science
Arts
Applied arts
Entertainment

Large City (200,000 to 1,000,000 population)

Wholesaling
Public services
Newspaper publishing

Middling City (25,000 to 200,000 population)

Public utilities
Commercial printing
Baking and bottling of beverages
Construction activities
Professional services (school teachers,
　general practitioners, and so on)
Eating and drinking locals
Retailing

FIG. 1. THE HIERARCHY OF CITY FUNCTIONS. In the figure, each vertical line represents one city; its height indicates the extent of the city's functions. For every 64 middling cities, there are approximately 8 large cities and 1 metropolitan area. Middling cities generally perform only the functions listed, such as public utilities, commercial printing, and so on. In addition to all middling-city functions, large cities contain activities like wholesaling which no middling city performs. Finally, metropolitan areas carry on all large-city functions and also other activities, such as finance and business services, found exclusively in metropolitan communities.

In the United States, the structure of 484 cities with more than 25,000 inhabitants shows that 71 per cent of them have over 19 per cent of their workers in trade, though 18.8 per cent is the national average in trade. If we cut out towns that have no hinterland and are mere suburbs next to other suburbs, at least 80 per cent of towns over 25,000 would persistently show this above-average retailing activity.[43] The disproportion of traders on the average of all cities of given size, however, is not so remarkable as the *persistence* of the trend toward some disproportion. While only 4 per cent of the 484 cities had a proportion in trade less than 15 per cent, at the other end of the scale only 3 per cent had over 30 per cent in trade.

Another test of the persistence of retailing applies to 147 census metropolitan areas of all sizes. If they are ranked in order of retail sales and of population,[44] only one-eighth deviate in sales rank more than 20 per cent from population rank. And none of the eight largest truly-metropolitan areas deviates in rank to that extent.

Persistent disproportion could probably be similarly shown by all cities over 25,000 in professional services. Although the persistence appears less, it also occurs in commercial printing and public utilities.[45] In professional services, the average proportion in cities of different size appears to have ranged in 1940 only from 8.3 to 10.0 per cent of total employed persons, and the average for each size range was always above the national proportion of 7.3 per cent.[46]

Other economic activities are not so persistent in all cities. Wholesaling,[47] public services, and newspaper publishing are performed in most of the large and very large cities, and substantially only there. Still other activities, like finance and business services and book and periodical publishing and printing services, are very large city functions which are performed, as already shown, in most of the large metropolitan cities and generally only there.

The variety of activities of a metropolis, therefore, includes highly special activities which only it performs on any substantial scale. The word hierarchy can perhaps again be appropriately applied here. Fig. 1 presents cities of three extensions or heights of function. In hierarchical terms, most cities may, like priests, be performing only routine activities. But rising or towering above this rank, like bishops or archbishops, are cities which conduct routine services like retailing but also spread upward into other and more unusual varieties of work.

Only the metropolis can furnish a market which is sufficiently large to support the performance of the most highly-specialized activities. Though rarely demanded, these functions may be of great importance to the organization, progress, and culture of the whole country. In addition, the variety of activity economically possible in a large metropolis at the top of the hierarchy is of advantage to the individual producer and worker who, without leaving his home, has a choice of occupation and trade to fit his talents, and to the consumer who has a choice of goods and services for life and leisure. If the conception of standard of living includes a wide choice in services and the use of leisure, the metropolis with its variety of services and entertainment presents the higher standard of living.

But this standard of living may be bought at too high a cost. In particular, one variety of the use of leisure is absent—namely, easy access to the country-side—an amenity which many people like and which more, perhaps, ought to like. The more general costs and disadvantages of metropolitan concentration were previously set out in Table 5 above. This Table may, indeed, serve as a summary of the arguments presented on either side of the balance sheet.

CONCLUSION

This discussion has attempted to draw up a balance sheet of the economic advantages and disadvantages of metropolitan concentrations as they have actually developed. But before finishing, some observations should be ventured on the resultant. Is there a net profit or loss in these existing concentrations, or indeed in any concentration of metropolitan dimension?

To the more generalized of these two questions, the answer is probably yes. It is an economic advantage to the business, scientific, and cultural life of a country to have at least one large metropolis, and to have more than one in a country covering a wide area. This metropolis must be a large concentration of population if it is to provide at one spot a sufficient concourse of supply and demand in certain activities where the resources and the market are rare.

Scientific progress, for example, requires contact and discussion between unusual men with a variety of experience, like pure scientists, applied scientists, consultants and experts, business promoters and entrepreneurs. Art equally requires a concourse of able students and teachers and of appreciative discerning and wealthy patrons, all of whom, in Great Britain and the United States at least, are comparatively rare in the population. Nothing less than a city of a million people would yield the necessary minimum of, say, twenty able students, three inspiring teachers, and one appreciative millionaire or two half-millionaires. Able practitioners, teachers, and appreciators of the applied arts, such as the *haute couture,* are more numerous, since there is obviously money in it. But to be economic, their activities must still be localized on a fairly large scale.

Samuel Johnson remarked one day in 1769:

> The happiness of London is not to be conceived but by those who have been in it. I will venture to say, there is more learning and science within the circumference of ten miles from where we now sit, than in all the rest of the kingdom.
> *Boswell:* The only disadvantage is, the great distance at which people live from one another.
> *Johnson:* Yes, Sir; but that is occasioned by the largeness of it, which is the cause of all the other advantages.
> *Boswell:* Sometimes I have been in the humour of wishing to retire to a desert.
> *Johnson:* Sir, you have desert enough in Scotland.[48]

In this passage, Johnson three times hits the nail on the head. *First hit:* the metropolis has a high proportion of scientists and learned men. As a friend of Sir Joshua Reynolds and Dr. Burney, Johnson presumably would include artists and musicians, too. *Second hit:* the metropolis must be large in order to supply and sustain economically the high proportion of scientists and learned men which is necessary for the happiness and other advantages arising from numerous contacts and discussions. *Third hit:* this high proportion in the metropolis unfortunately means that other areas are disproportionately deprived and may become intellectual deserts. It is to avoid such deserts that regional concentrations do occur in large countries in such communication functions as the publishing of newspapers, periodicals, and books. Deserts are avoided also by instituting regional universities, university colleges, and radio stations. This institution is a clear pattern (partly deliberately planned) in England, Wales, Scotland, and Ireland. In small or middling-sized countries, if there is no outstanding metropolis, the activities admired by Johnson might not occur *at all* because of insufficient concourse.

To say that *some* metropolitan concentration is necessary for business organization, for the arts and applied arts, and for science and the applied sciences so important for economic progress, is not to say that the *existing* metropolitan concentrations are justified by a balance of economic advantages. Far from it. All existing concentrations probably have several industries and services that could well be decentralized and dispersed. It is naturally difficult for economists in any given metropolitan area to suggest what activities should be discarded, though some have braved it out.

The West Midland Group, for instance, suggested that certain industries in the Birmingham area were not necessarily so linked with the conurbation's main industries that the area would suffer economically from their removal. One of the main industries of the conurbation is the assembly of automobiles, and the rubber tire industry existed beside it within the city. Such close contact was not necessary. It was argued that "the tire is not such a part of the car as requires continual adjustment (of design) to needs, and more than half the tires are for replacement and not for original assembly. In fact the American rubber-tire industry is localized at Akron, Ohio, some considerable distance from the center of the motor car trade in Detroit and surrounding parts of Michigan."[49]

On the whole, the large manufacturing metropolis can probably be most easily reduced without loss of metropolitan function—in Britain, Birmingham and Southern Lancashire; in the United States, Detroit and Pittsburgh. But undoubtedly every metropolis contains some elements that could be dispersed or at least decentralized without economic loss, thus reducing the total congestion and pressure on land values. It is a question of the scientific selection of activities.

Though this selection is often invidious for local bodies, national authorities have put forward pleas[50] for the greater dispersal of specific activities. In

Britain, at least, some of these pleas have been converted into plans, the plans formally carried into law, and the law actually executed.[51] The most notable planned and executed decentralization has been under the Distribution of Industry Act of 1945. This Act was passed by Sir Winston Churchill's wartime coalition government, not by a purely labor government. Thanks to the refusal of licenses to build and to the nonallocation of timber and steel, since 1945 many factories and extensions to factories have been prevented from being built in the metropolitan areas of London and Birmingham. They have been built instead in regions, called Development Areas under the Act, which were greatly "depressed" in the 1930's. Though the number employed in these development areas in 1939 was only about one-sixth of the number in the whole of Great Britain, the areas were granted two-fifths of the value of all new factories completed or occupied between January 1945 and April 1953.

The policy of dispersion from congested metropolitan areas to a whole new region is being supplemented by a policy of decentralization from congested metropolitan centers to the metropolitan outskirts. The New Towns situated at a radius of about thirty miles from London's center are designed not as dormitories but as self-sufficient employment units. Though not always stated explicitly, this policy of decentralizing industry and population rather than dispersing them over a large area has an advantage in preserving a certain continuity for the life of the metropolitan family and for the life of the firm too. It also preserves certain metropolitan amenities. Even though they live thirty miles away, members of a family can still occasionally consult a metropolitan specialist, visit a metropolitan theater, or attend a metropolitan "streetcar" university. And even though thirty miles from the industrial center, the staff of a firm can consult business experts and make easy contact with suppliers, with markets and with servicers, and thus keep many of the advantages of industrial localization.

How far will such dispersion and decentralization occur ecologically without some form of state planning or regulation? Immediately after World War II some factory dispersion occurred in the United States without state planning.[52] Industrialists at that time found a more ample reservoir of labor in the smaller cities. These small reserve pools may have formed, however, as a result of the lack of new house building during the war which restricted the geographical mobility of labor. As renewed building in metropolitan areas gives additional house-room, it is not certain that labor may not move into the large cities and form pools again.

My conclusion, then, is that *some* degree of metropolitan concentration is an economic advantage, but not *all* of the actual amounts and kinds of metropolitan concentration that exist in the world today. The practical task is to distinguish between the two and to cut out the disadvantageous concentrations. And this task involves the further question as to who is to undertake it. Who, if anyone, is to be charged with discovering the balances of disadvantage and executing the necessary reorientation?

The first question is more easily answered than the second. Research in land economics, so ably pioneered at Columbia University, should itself be dispersed over the universities of the world. The findings of research should be put at the disposal of the executives in reorientation, whoever they may be, whether multiplant business executives, regulatory control commissions, or national, state, and city planners. Here at universities we are concerned with gathering and communicating knowledge to whosoever may make use of it. But the gathering must be scientific and broad-bottomed. This chapter has, I hope, at least illustrated how many of the economic and sociological problems of concentration are common to different nations, and has perhaps demonstrated the scientific value of international comparison.

FOOTNOTES TO CHAPTER 6

1. All of the largest countries had a population of over 15 million inhabitants each in 1947. See *World Almanac, 1952*, pp. 289–353.

2. G. K. Zipf, *Human Behavior and the Principle of Least Effort* (Cambridge, Mass.: Addison-Wesley Press, 1949), especially pp. 374 ff.

3. This effect is most evident in the City of London—an area of 677 acres defined by the medieval wall. There the resident population has been falling continuously for a century. In 1921, the resident population was 13,709; in 1951, it was 5,268. The larger Administrative County of London, with 28 boroughs, fell 2 per cent in population during 1921–1931 and 23.8 per cent during 1931–1951. Meanwhile, London's Outer Ring increased in population by 27.1 per cent from 1921–1931 and 30.9 per cent from 1931–1951. As a result, Greater London (including both the Administrative County and the Outer Ring) grew by 9.7 per cent from 1921–1931 and by 1.6 per cent from 1931–1951. Beyond Greater London is the London Traffic Area with fairly continuous housing developments. In this Area, sizable towns with more than 30,000 inhabitants in 1931, like Slough, Hornchurch and Romford, doubled or trebled in population between 1931 and 1951. Watford, a so-called Rural District just beyond the Outer Ring, rose over 150 per cent in population between 1931 and 1951. By 1951, it had achieved a density of more than 1,340 persons to the square mile.

4. In Table 5, the section on efficiency in income patterns refers to differences which have been distinguished by Professor Pigou as tests of economic welfare. They are largely the result of conditions of production. See A. C. Pigou, *The Economics of Welfare* (London: Macmillan, 1920), chapter 4, section 1.

5. *Statistical Journal*, part I, 1943, p. 54.

6. See West Midland Group, *English County, A Planning Survey of Herefordshire* (London: Faber and Faber, 1946).

7. P. S. Florence, *The Logic of British and American Industry* (London: Routledge and Kegan Paul, 1953), p. 87.

8. *Ibid.*, pp. 83–84.

9. For the method of derivation, see *ibid.*, pp. 37–38, and footnote 34, below.

10. Unfortunately, many industries were defined differently by the British Ministry of Labour (which collected unemployment rates) and by the Census of Production and the Census of Population, on whose data the coefficients are based.

11. J. Robinson, *Economics of Imperfect Competition* (London: Macmillan, 1933), p. 106.

12. J. Glaisyer and others, *County Town, A Civic Survey for the Planning of Worcester* (London: John Murray, 1946), pp. 106–107.

13. K. K. Liepmann, *The Journey to Work* (London: Kegan Paul, Trench, Tribner, and Co., 1944), p. 187.

14. Royal Commission on the Distribution of the Industrial Population Report, 1940, par. 358.

15. L. Mumford, *The Culture of Cities* (New York: Harcourt, Brace, 1938), p. 242.

16. West Midland Group, *Conurbation, A Planning Survey of Birmingham and the Black Country* (London: The Architectural Press, 1948), pp. 105–107. For definition of location quotient, see footnote 34.

17. *Ibid.*, p. 123.

18. W. H. Beveridge, *Full Employment in a Free Society* (New York: W. W. Norton, 1945), p. 61.

19. Royal Commission on the Distribution of the Industrial Population Report, 1940, pp. 318–319.

20. West Midland Group, *Conurbation*, figure 22, p. 124.

21. In 1950, all of the eight largest metropolitan areas in the United States showed a substantial natural increase of births over deaths. The increase ranged from 9.5 per thousand population in the New York area to 16.4 per thousand in the Detroit area. For the country as a whole, the rate of natural increase was 14.0 per thousand.

22. Gross rent is contract rent plus the cost of water, electricity, gas, and fuels, if these items were paid by the renter.

23. See H. S. Phillips, "Municipal Efficiency and Town Size," *Journal of the Town Planning Institute,* May–June 1942. Also K. S. Lomax, "Relationship between Expenditure per Head and Size of Population of County Boroughs in England and Wales," *Statistical Journal,* part I, 1943.

24. "I [Boswell] suggested a doubt, that if I were to reside in London, the exquisite zest with which I relished it in occasional visits might go off, and I might grow tired of it. *Johnson*—'Why, Sir, you find no man, at all intellectual, who is willing to leave London. No, Sir, when a man is tired of London, he is tired of life; for there is in London all that life can afford.' " J. Boswell, *The Life of Samuel Johnson* (London, 1791), entry for September 20, 1777.

25. "Peter Bell the Third," part 3.

26. Early Christian theology, for instance, speaks of "the City of the living God, the heavenly Jerusalem." Heb. 12, 22.

27. Florence, *The Logic of British and American Industry,* pp. 63, 70. The main cause for the survival of small plants is not the difficulty of management (which theoretical economists so often assume and illustrate with galaxies of curves) but physical necessity in cases where transport of materials and products is costly and where materials or markets are dispersed, as in non-metropolitan areas.

28. *Ibid.*, pp. 71–72. For definition of the location quotient, see footnote 34, below.

29. P. E. P. Report on Location of Industry, 1938, appendix Table I.

30. 1950 Cmd. 8045, appendix III.

31. See Table 3 above.

32. We must avoid the fallacy of dividing the number of industries by the number of inhabitants or total of workers. Like the library facilities cited

earlier, the essence of variety is the accessibility of an absolute number of different industries (or books) to any one worker (or reader).

33. Some of the services lumped in are probably dispersed fairly evenly throughout the metropolitan areas and thus mask the real disproportion.

34. The location quotient is the result of dividing the proportion of local-to-national workers in any branch of industry by the proportion of local-to-national residential population. (In place of the residential population, sometimes the measures of local-to-national workers in the entire industry, in all industries, or in all types of employment are used.) In the top line of Table 12, for example, the local area has 15.8 per cent of the national total of wholesale employees, but only 8.6 per cent of the national population. Thus the location quotient is 1.8—computed by dividing 15.8 by 8.6. A location quotient of 1.0 indicates that the location of an industry in a given place is no more and no less than would be mathematically expected from the distribution of population. Location quotients over 1.5 for an industry in a populous area indicate a definite tendency toward localization of the industry in that place.

35. "The lack of services and amenities keeps many managers and salaried staff from working in the Conurbation, and explains the drift to London. It is also a serious matter when firms in the Conurbation try to entertain possible foreign customers. Many an order must have been lost because of dreary evenings spent by potential buyers." West Midland Group, *Conurbation*, pp. 110–112.

36. New York, London, and Paris each have specialties which are not specialized in by the other two cities. Paris has metal, chemical, and furniture manufactures. London also has furniture as well as other industries, such as matches and cattle food, which depend on materials imported through its port. New York has toilet preparations and soap.

37. The method of calculating the location quotient is described in footnote 34. The British industrial quotients in Table 13 are based on the total occupied or employed populations; the American manufactures quotients are based on the total number of workers in all manufactures. At the time of writing, neither the United States Census of 1950 nor the British Census of 1951 was yet published completely. The last completely-published population census for Britain was in 1931; for the United States, in 1940. Wherever possible, later data have been used. The date, however, is not of prime importance, since local concentrations like these are persistent and slow to change.

Sources of the London data are the Census of 1931 Industrial Tables for industries. Quotients based on data for Great Britain are cited as published in the P.E.P. report on Location of Industry, except for calculations from the original Census data of certain individual industries which were lumped together in this report. The lumping was necessitated by differences in the full list of industries of the Scottish and English censuses. For occupations (italicized), sources of data are the Census of 1931 Occupational Tables, except for postal, insurance, other services, wholesale nonfood, garment makers, and theaters, which come from the Census of Great Britain, 1951, one per cent tables. Quotients which are based on data for England and Wales have been specially calculated from original census data. For separate regions, including London, neither occupations nor industries had been fully published in detail at the time of writing. Where totals are small, sometimes men, sometimes women are omitted.

Sources of New York data for industries are the United States Census of Manufactures, 1947, Vol. III. For communication and public utilities only, data come from Census of 1940: Industries and exclude street transport. For occupations (italicized), the source is the Census of Population for 1940, except where noted. Other data come from the *County and City Data Book, 1952.*

The source for the Paris data, except where noted, is the French Census for 1946, Tome V. The quotients refer to the Department of the Seine, which is the metropolitan area for Paris. The classification is occupational—by *profession individuelle*—not industrial.

38. Chicago has a location quotient of 1.7 in manufacturing surgical and medical instruments. But it has a quotient of only 1.1 in manufacturing scientific instruments. The Census does not list any manufacture of mechanical measuring instruments in Chicago.

39. Glaisyer, *County Town,* pp. 278 ff.

40. C. Clark, "The Economic Functions of a City in Relation to its Size," *Econometrica,* April, 1945.

41. Clark, *ibid.,* uses numbers of persons employed in the service industries per million dollars of regional income (rather than per total occupied population) as a measure of the adequacy of services. Although this measure may be sufficient for retaining activities, for other activities regional income is not so logical a basis, particularly where a metropolis may serve a whole country. For example, there is no reason to expect finance and business services necessarily to locate where general income is highest. In fact, the locational relation is partly the reverse of the situation in retailing. The higher average incomes of an area are the result rather than the cause of the habitat of financiers or business experts. Because Clark divides financiers and commercial experts by regional income, he rates New York State very low in commercial and financial services—much lower than North or South Dakota, New Mexico, Oklahoma, or the states of the deep South.

42. West Midland Group, *English County,* p. 86.

43. Eliminating all towns in New Jersey, Massachusetts, and Ohio, where suburbs seem to flourish, we get a net total of 358 towns with over 25,000 inhabitants. Of these, 282 or 79 per cent have more than 19 per cent of workers in trade. *County and City Data Book, 1952,* pp. 442–505.

44. U. S. Bureau of the Census, *Statistical Abstract of the United States, 1952,* pp. 904–905.

45. This analysis could be made from data contained in the *County and City Data Book, 1952.* Nonlinear relations are not excluded. Small and very large cities might show characteristic disproportions while middling-sized cities might not.

46. A. H. Hawley, *Human Ecology* (New York: Ronald Press, 1950), p. 381.

47. Wholesaling is less evenly dispersed than retailing over the United States. This fact is brought out by a diagram in National Resources Planning Board, *Industrial Location and National Resources* (Washington, D.C., 1942), p. 81. The map in E. M. Hoover, *The Location of Economic Activity* (New York: McGraw-Hill, 1948), p. 52, indicates that wholesaling is probably more dispersed than finance.

48. Boswell, *Life of Johnson,* entry for September 30, 1769.

49. West Midland Group, *Conurbation,* p. 136.

50. The British Royal Commission on the Distribution of the Industrial Population, of which Sir Montague Barlow was chairman, reported in 1940.

51. The United States has always had decentralized government. Until the foundation of the University of London, higher education was decentralized in Britain.

52. P. W. Dickinson, *Decentralization in Industry,* National Industrial Conference Board Studies in Business Policy, No. 30 (1948).

7

Efficiency and the Location of Urban Activities

RICHARD U. RATCLIFF
Professor of Land Economics
University of Wisconsin

The subject of efficiency and inefficiency in the locational distribution of urban activities deals with the structure and arrangement of land uses. The presumption inherent in the topic is that locational maldistributions exist in the metropolis which impair its efficiency. This presumption is validated by ample evidence all about us.

But problems of locational maldistribution do not occur exclusively in metropolitan areas. They also crop up with varying degrees of intensity in villages, towns, and cities. To ascribe the problems of the city merely to size is to imply that solutions lie in reversing the growth process through deconcentration. Both this assumption and implication are questionable.

In fact, we shall see that growth is but one of many forces contributing toward locational maldistributions. Size as such is likely to be more advantageous than otherwise if proper adaptations are made.

Efficiency in land utilization, as in other forms of human endeavor, is measured in terms of productivity. We measure the efficiency of a factory, for example, in terms of physical output in relation to costs. Thus to improve the efficiency of a factory or of land utilization, we either increase output without increasing costs, or maintain the same level of output at reduced costs.

One of the basic output costs is that of overcoming space. If everybody and everything were at the same place at the same time, there would be no costs of overcoming space, and the efficiency of the locational distribution of urban activities would be at a maximum. But space costs are inherent in our physical world. This disutility of distance is the joint product of the activities involved, the distance, the available means of overcoming the distance, and the importance of the contact to the persons or activity concerned. No matter why people want to be near something or somebody, their preference is expressed in terms of value and becomes an economic force.

125

In the costs or disutility of distance, we have one test for the efficiency of the locational distribution of urban activities. This cost is economic rather than physical; it is space relationship evaluated in view of its importance to those individuals and firms concerned.

In addition to costs of distance, there is a second measure of urban efficiency. It is the equitable distribution of the burden of locational costs in accordance with benefits received and in proportion to the responsibility for their creation. This is a basic economic criterion which is inherent in the operation of the market mechanism.

Thus two criteria of urban productivity exist. They are to minimize the social costs of distance or space and to distribute locational costs equitably in accordance with benefits received. These are economic tests in the sense that they are made on a scale of costs which serve as the basis of market transactions. They are also social tests in the sense that the underlying criterion is the welfare of the community.

The balance of this chapter will discuss some of the manifestations of urban efficiency and inefficiency and evaluate them in light of our stated objectives. First, however, the principles of urban growth and structure in an economic context will be briefly reviewed.

PRINCIPLES OF URBAN GROWTH AND STRUCTURE

In a study made for the Regional Plan of New York, Robert Murray Haig, a long-time member of the faculty of Columbia University, set forth concepts which are the cornerstone of modern urban land economics.[1] Subsequent land-economics studies have contributed little more of theoretical value to Haig's explanation of why we have cities or his rationale of their internal functional arrangement. Economists, however, have filled out the descriptive material and developed practical applications of theory to business and planning problems. In theory, neo-classical market concepts have been reconciled with Haig's fundamental explanation of human behavior. The human ecologists have also enriched our understanding of cities by applying concepts from the natural sciences to human behavior in urban areas. But all in all, we have not marched forward far from the point to which Haig advanced in 1926.

In discussing problems of urban growth and structure, the urban organization of society may be explained by the socio-economic activities which call for the concentration of people, buildings, and machines within a relatively small area. Cities are, therefore, a physical adaptation to man's requirements, primarily but not exclusively for production and consumption. With respect to their location, Haig notes that "the most favored spots are those from which the richest resources can be tapped with the lowest transportation costs."[2] Since the greater share of the total available labor force is not required to perform the work of primary extraction or to operate the transportation system, it is "economically 'foot free' in the sense that it is under no economic compulsion to live 'on the land.'"

But for the most part, the foot free population must carry on the processes of production and consumption at the same place. It follows, then, that the most advantageous places for both production and consumption are in cities which are most favorably located with respect to raw materials. At these convenient assembly points, employment opportunities are available in processing, manufacturing, distribution, and related business functions. Also the richest assortment of consumption goods may be supplied at the lowest cost. Haig says, "instead of explaining why so large a portion of the population is found in urban areas, one must give reasons why that portion is not even greater. The question is changed from 'Why live in the city?' to 'Why not live in the city?' "

Despite certain qualifications, the fundamental principle of Haig's thesis is that from the standpoint of transportation efficiency, urban concentrations are the points of lowest cost in the processes of production and consumption. Note that the core of this explanation is physical. For concentrations of people and things are the result of efforts to minimize the costs of friction—costs of overcoming the friction of space. Space relationships, then, are primary factors in the existence of our urban organization and in the location of our urban centers. Cost, an economic factor, and more specifically, the minimization of cost, is the controlling force.

The locational pattern of urban areas, consequently, is a reflection of basic economic forces. And one part of the economic mechanism of society is represented by the arrangement of people, buildings, and activities in urban concentrations at strategic points on the web of transportation lines. In extending this point of view further to the internal structure of cities, we shall discuss three essential concepts: location, enterprises as packets of functions, and the dimensions of the cost of friction.

The Concepts of Location, Functions, and Friction

Location refers to the unique complex of space relationships within which each site is fixed at a given point in time. These space relationships refer to all other people, things, and activities both near and remote. Significant space relationships are determined by the use to which the site is put. Each relationship varies in importance according to a given use for the site, and the pattern of variation may change with time.

Haig points out that "each business is a *packet of functions,* and within limits, these functions can be separated and located at different places." Certain functions are loosely tied together; others are strongly cohered. Department stores in large cities, for instance, often separate their storage and order-filling functions from the sales floor. Lawyers keep their old files in cheap and remote warehouse space. But a small-scale business may find it impracticable to separate physically the packet of functions which the proprietor must conduct himself or closely supervise and coordinate.

The physical problem of overcoming the *friction* of space is costly in time and energy. As Haig says, "accessibility . . . means ease of contact—contact

with relatively little friction," that is, at low cost. Transportation is a method
of overcoming the friction of space. But since transportation is never in-
stantaneous or effortless, it remains a costly process.

Transportation costs vary with each activity and the term itself must be
interpreted broadly. For a retail enterprise, transportation costs include costs
of assembling merchandise, costs of employees' travel between home and work,
and above all the travel costs of the customers who come to shop. The convenience of the customers is the prime determinant in location and the basis
for the high rent typically paid for central retail sites.

Transportation costs are only one of two dimensions of the costs of friction.
The other component is site rental. According to Haig, "site rentals are
charges which can be made for sites where accessibility may be had with
comparatively low transportation costs." Thus an enterprise will pay in rent
an amount up to the savings which it can make in transportation costs by
reason of the accessibility of a site. Site rentals and transportation costs are
complementary. In total, they represent the cost of what friction remains.

Patterns of Land Use

With the concepts of location, enterprises as packets of functions, and the
dimensions of frictional costs in mind, the internal land-use organization of
the city can be explained. The structure of the city is determined by the dollar
evaluation of the importance of convenience.[3] Each activity seeks to minimize
the disutilities and costs of friction by locating where its transportation costs
are at a minimum. Each one must be willing to pay site rent up to an amount
which, added to transportation costs, is just less than the total of transport
costs plus site rent for alternative locations.

Any given enterprise will be in competition with others which can also use
the same location to advantage. The successful bidder for a site will be the
activity which can most successfully exploit the aggregate of convenience
which the site offers for its special combination of functions. Assuming perfect
competition, each site thus becomes occupied by the activity which can use
it most efficiently.

The attributes of each location, however, are dependent upon the nature
of the occupants of every other location, and bidding for all sites is not simultaneous. Hence there is a continuous shifting of land uses as locational attributes vary with changes in the occupancies of other locations. Despite
numerous market imperfections and distortions, natural economic forces tend
to create an urban pattern which is relatively efficient in its basic space relationships.

Although the people of a community determine how they wish land to be
used, the citizens (with the exceptions of proprietors) have little direct voice
in the location of urban industrial enterprises. The locational decision of the
industry is a dollars-and-cents matter which depends on the total amount of
frictional costs for alternative locations. The retail pattern, on the other hand,

is largely determined by considerations of convenience for the consumer. Thus the location of stores of various types is conditioned by the buying habits of the potential customers and by the resulting volume of their custom. In the location of home sites, consumers have a strong voice.

In the matter of public land use, the citizens act in unison through their elected representatives and the established governmental machinery. In so doing, they determine where parks, schools, streets, and sewage plants shall be found, and they enter the market to bid for these locations at a market-determined price. If the community is willing to pay the necessary price in a condemnation suit, the citizenry cannot, of course, be outbid in the market. But the decision to proceed with public improvements is, in fact, greatly influenced by the prospective cost of acquisition of the site whether by negotiation or by condemnation.

Citizens exercise another form of control over the pattern of land use where zoning ordinances are in effect. In adopting a zoning ordinance, the people decide how in their opinion costs of friction can be minimized through the arrangement of land uses to be decreed. The zoning pattern affects the convenience of almost every citizen in one way or another, and his own approval, indirect and uninformed though it may be, is a part of a democratic determination of the urban pattern.

Although Haig does not discuss land values as such, he might have pointed out that the pattern of site rentals is the equivalent of the pattern of land values. He does show that a general improvement in transportation, or a general reduction in transport costs, will mean a reduction in total frictions and thus a reduction in the aggregate of site costs. Conversely, when bus fares are raised, total land values tend to increase in the area served because the costs saved by convenience will be greater. It has been shown that the spread in the use of the private automobile has, in fact, tended to reduce land values in central areas by making outlying retail centers more generally accessible.[4] It further follows that the best planned city will have the lowest total of land values.

In discussing the economic basis of zoning, Haig notes that "zoning finds its economic justification in that it is a useful device for insuring an approximately just distribution of costs, of forcing each individual to bear his own expenses." Although this statement is not clearly explained, an explanation may be derived from his general thesis.

In an idealized arrangement of land uses with aggregate costs of friction at a minimum, each site occupant would bear a rent burden properly representative of the savings in transportation cost for his enterprise. But if one enterprise is inappropriately located, then additional costs of transportation are created for all other enterprises by reason of the distortion of the most efficient pattern of space relationships. These extra costs are not borne by the offending enterprise but by the other activities. Thus zoning control, which would prevent such a misplacement, serves to insure a fair allocation of site costs.

As an illustration, Haig uses the men's garment industry on Manhattan

Island which was once appropriately located there, but gave way later to more intensive land uses. Its presence created costs of friction arising from spoiling the character of the choice shopping district, blocking the avenues leading to the shopping district with vehicles, and pre-empting the transit facilities. These costs should have properly been borne by the industry rather than by the community at large.

Haig concludes by stating that "the forces of competition do tend to approximate the ideal layout, and the trends actually in operation are the surest indication as to what is economically sound." Zoning serves to enforce and facilitate the natural forces and to prevent individual exploitation at the expense of others.

Robert Murray Haig was one of the first economists to study metropolitan planning—that "broad and virgin field which the economist is called upon to cultivate in connection with modern city and regional planning." Since Haig's time, social scientists have pointed out that the master plan is no better than the social and economic analysis of which it is the final expression. Haig foresaw the "change in the economic character of the plan from that of a 'consumption good' to that of a 'production good.' Where the early plan was once content to be a noble design, the modern plan aspires to qualify also as a productive piece of economic machinery." He believed that the aim of the modern master plan is to maximize the efficiency of the urban area through an arrangement of land uses which will minimize the costs of friction. The underlying economic forces which mold the urban land-use pattern are working, often imperfectly, toward this same end. The imperfections, lags, and obstacles to the free operation of the forces of adaptation are the origins of urban problems which limit the efficiency of the land-use structure as an economic mechanism.

SOME IMPORTANT URBAN PROBLEMS

During recent years, the rapid growth of urban areas has been accompanied by an equally spectacular rise in the intensity of various urban problems. Most of these problems would have existed in some degree even though growth of cities had been much less rapid. The congestion of traffic and the shortage of parking facilities, for example, are the products of prosperity as well as size. In discussing problems of decentralization, metropolitan integration, and central areas as well as traffic and parking, we shall be concerned with the repercussions and impact on urban productivity. Is each problem the unique product of size? Or is it the continuing accompaniment of a dynamic urbanism in a dynamic society?

Decentralization

In most parts of the country, cities of all sizes are growing in population, in number and complexity of activities, and in physical extent. Additions to the housing stock are being made on vacant land at the edge of the settled area. Occasionally new communities are founded at some distance from the main body of the city and new subdivisions for a time may be surrounded by open country. This is a configuration as old as civilization. For there is no place for a built-up city to expand except at the periphery.

During recent years, the automobile has given greater freedom of location to the householder. Patterns of new growth have been more scattered, irregular and dispersed. But, though the auto age is still new, the interstices are filling in with the main body of settlement. Is this decentralization or the suburban trend? Or is it simply the geographical necessity of urban growth modified in form with advancing technology which gives greater freedom in choice of location?

Certain kinds of qualitative residential decentralization do occur. The upper income groups and the persons who are the most promising potential community leaders are moving to the suburbs. In this case, the arrangement of political boundaries removes these people from the tax rolls of the central city and bars them from office holding or from serving on public bodies. A basic problem of decentralization would, therefore, appear to be political decentralization. It separates the new growth from the main body by creating an artificial governmental galaxy which is functionally inappropriate for the economic and social organism of the metropolis.

But are other functions, such as industry and commerce, decentralizing? A summary of studies about the decentralization of industry is provided in a recent publication which distinguishes between *diffusion*—a redistribution of industrial plants from a major central area to a nearby or peripheral area, and *dispersion*—a wider redistribution, such as from a large city to a number of smaller localities throughout a major economic region. The analysis suggests that over the past half century the chief characteristic of the pattern of industrial location is stability. Until World War II, there was a "slow but rather persistent diffusion of industry within the major areas or districts of industrial concentration . . . indications of dispersion were less strong and . . . varied considerably with general business and industrial conditions."[5] From 1939 through 1947, the tendency toward dispersion was stopped but some diffusion continued. This evidence indicates a species of slow decentralization among primary industrial employers which will ultimately effect some reorientation in the pattern of other land uses.

For several reasons, however, it is likely that the effect of industrial relocation on residential decentralization will be slow and moderate. First, there is no compulsion for a worker to live near his job. His car gives him mobility and his job may change more frequently than his home location. Second, for workers who live in the residential areas of the central city, a shift in plant location from the old industrial core to the edge of the settlement may mean but little travel time one way or the other. The lesser congestion may be offset by the greater distance. A private car or car-pool arrangement may be more costly than public transportation but more pleasant and timely. Thus there is no strong reason for such workers to change place of residence. The rapid rise in home ownership suggests another factor which tends to anchor workers to their residence in spite of change of place of employment.

Third, we can expect no rapid mutation in urban structure as a result of industrial diffusion because the shift is small and slow in relationship to the total industrial plant. The residential and commercial facilities growing up around new outlying industrial developments are only to a minor extent ascribable to decentralization. They are mainly in response to new growth of industrial facilities rather than in response to the movement of existing plants to the outskirts.

With regard to retail establishments, except for a few very large cities there is no evidence of literal decentralization. Many new retail facilities, of course, have appeared in outlying areas, but that process has been going on for a long time. As cities grow, the *proportion* of retail trade done in the central area declines. But decentralization occurs only when the central area suffers an *absolute* decline.

Other minor shifts represent true decentralization. Certain office and clerical type activities are moving from central areas to the suburbs. Most publicized is the shift of office activities from New York to Westchester County. This movement has not bulked large in total employment. It has affected types of activities which have a minimum number of local contacts and which do business largely by mail and telephone. For these activities, costs of friction are not increased by the move. Some of the activities were probably originally misplaced in the congested central commercial district and created extra cost of friction for other land uses which will be reduced when the central site is occupied by activities more appropriate to the location.

Most of the manifestations of urban change which are popularly classified as decentralization, therefore, are not literally decentralized. In most cases, they are merely responses to basic growth taking place at the edge of existing development where land is available. Very little true decentralization has occurred, and this amount has been a natural readjustment in the locations of certain activities as an adaptation to changing locational factors. The effect is to reduce the costs of friction for the enterprise. Where soundly executed, it also reduces aggregate costs of friction in the community.

Decentralization is a symptom of degeneration and decay only if it leaves a vacuum behind. Or we might say that where decentralization is the product of centripetal forces, it is healthy. Much of the outward movement of certain urban functions occurs as they are pushed out of the center rather than as they respond to a pull toward outlying locations.

For example, many of our cities grew up around centrally-located industries. In time these industries were replaced by retail activities which, in effect, were able to outbid the industries for the central sites. In a study of the Madison, Wisconsin, central area to be discussed later, it was found that in 1925 there were 13 centrally-located auto repair shops but only 6 in 1950. In the meantime, numerous repair shops appeared in peripheral locations as more intensive commercial uses pushed out the repair man. The history of the Madison central area is one of a constant replacement of less intensive uses by more intensive uses. This form of decentralization is the complement of centralization and concentration.

Decentralization of certain lower-intensity land uses which are forced out of the center by higher-intensity replacements is a normal and continuing process of urban dynamics which enhances efficiency. But artificially induced dispersion, advocated by the decentralists, is another question. It holds the danger of loss in total efficiency and productivity in return for the presumed advantages of the suburban way of life.

Integration

The arrangement of land uses in a metropolitan area is broadly independent of the boundaries of the political subdivisions which typically lie in irregular patterns about the central city. Each political subdivision, presumably acting in its own interests, controls the assignment of activities within its own boundaries. It may do so in such a fashion that it excludes developments which, from the metropolitan standpoint, would be appropriately located in the subdivision. But despite these and other obstacles to the free play of basic market forces, it is generally true that the over-all pattern of land use in the metropolitan area tends toward the most efficient pattern which minimizes the costs of friction. The political boundaries are only accidentally related to the pattern of development.

It is clear enough that planning and planning controls must be on a metropolitan basis to gain the end of minimum locational frictions. And it is equally true that, coordinated with planning control, a metropolitan fiscal control must exist if all areas and all land uses are to bear their fair share of frictional cost. To understand this point we must see the role of the tax system in equalizing locational costs.

Transportation costs are reduced by improved streets and traffic ways. The costs of improving streets are borne on the general tax roll or they are levied by special assessment against the properties which benefit most directly. If we assume that Haig's definition of site rent includes tax levies, then each site occupant pays a share of the street improvement costs from which he benefits in varying degrees. Of course, the occupant probably does not pay his exact share. Yet when a street improvement benefits a property, the land value tends to rise proportionately, assessed value for tax purposes will rise in response, and, in effect, a share of the cost of the improvement proportionate to the benefit will be borne by the property.

Take the example of a central city and a contiguous residential suburb separately incorporated. The city widens and improves a main artery leading from the vicinity of the suburb to the central business district. The cost of this improvement is paid out of the city's general fund. The benefits are to those individuals and firms who will find this route of travel a speedier and more convenient channel. The businesses in the center benefit from reduced costs of transportation for their employees and customers. The employees and customers who will use the improved route, and residents of the residential suburb, will also benefit. Who will bear the cost?

If the cost of the improvement is met by a general increase in the city tax rate, each citizen of the city will share the cost in proportion to the taxable value of his property. Because some properties will benefit directly, their site values will tend to rise. This rise will be reflected in the next assessment. As a result of the improvement, the properties will bear an increased burden equivalent to the increased value times the total tax rate (including the increase called for because of the improvement).

Thus the benefited properties will bear a greater burden than other properties but not necessarily a burden equivalent to the benefit. The residents of the suburb who benefit will bear none of the direct costs. Some of them work in the central area; most of them visit the center frequently for shopping and recreational purposes. Is any share of the cost passed on to them as workers or customers?

The suburbs and their inhabitants benefit by the employment opportunities which are present in the community and by the centralized shopping and service facilities. In this respect, suburbanites are no different from central city folks. The accident of separation by an arbitrary political boundary has nothing to do with the social and economic relationships of mutual benefit which are the life blood of the metropolitan organism.

It is certain, therefore, that the suburbanites bear a lesser burden on account of the new street improvement than citizens of the central city. Because of the improved access to the center, the values of their suburban homes will rise and yet they bear none of the direct tax cost of the improvement. On the other hand, the next owners of these suburban homes will pay a higher price than did the present owners, and this higher price will reflect the reduced transportation cost to the center. Thus the next owners will bear a share of the costs of friction in the increased site rent (Haig's equivalent of land value) related to the saving in transportation costs. But the present home owners will capitalize upon the increased values without bearing a share of the costs which brought about the increase.

If it could be shown that downtown merchants could pass on some of the burden of the cost of the improvement through higher prices for their goods, then the suburbanites would appear to bear at least some of the cost. In no event, however, would they bear as much of the cost as the citizen of the central city who shares the tax load. In a competitive system, it is doubtful whether merchants could secure higher prices as a result of increased accessibility. For items available in the center only, prices are set with no reference to convenience. For items available in outlying areas as well as the center, prices in the center might rise a little. But the increase would be limited by the level of prices in the competing areas plus a differential reflecting advantages in convenience.

Rather than increased prices at the center, the more likely reaction is an increase in the volume of sales due to expanded accessibility. For competitive items available elsewhere in the city, sales will increase because the center has gained in accessibility relative to other shopping areas. For items sold only at the center, sales will tend to increase as a result of increased potential customers brought into the area and exposed to effective merchandising blandishments. If, as a result of increased sales volume, profits are swollen, the forces of competition will tend to bring about a price reduction.

Thus the suburbanites may bear none of the cost of increased accessibility. And they may benefit from reduced transportation costs (greater convenience), from an increased value of their real estate, and from decreased prices of goods which they buy at the center. The citizens of the central city who use the improved street will benefit in the same fashion but will also carry a share of the cost. The merchants will benefit in increased volume of sales and in increased profits but they will bear a substantial share of the cost of the improvement. Employers might be able to hire workers at lower wages because of increased convenience, although in a competitive system, this saving in labor costs will be passed on to customers in lower prices.

The case of the street improvement is one of many examples of public improvements, paid for out of general taxes, which reduce costs of friction. It indicates that those persons who live beyond the jurisdiction of the taxing body and who use its facilities of employment and service are not bearing their fair share of the costs of reducing the frictions of space.

Traffic and Parking

In applying the Haig hypothesis to the problem of traffic congestion, let us assume that each land use in a community conforms to the ideal pattern. Each one is space-related to every other land use in a manner which maximizes locational efficiency. Now suppose that one artery to the center is used heavily to a point where the time-cost of travel from outlying areas is increased. Increased travel costs on this route might result not only from traffic congestion but also from removal of public transport facilities, changes in the street car or bus schedule, or physical deterioration of the street surface. In the first impact, all persons and activities which are space related through the congested artery will suffer increased costs.

The ultimate tendency, however, is to reduce site rent (land values) at both ends as an offset to increased transport costs. The reduction in site rent will ultimately be expressed in reduced costs of the goods and services and will thus tend to offset the added costs and discomforts of the customers. But this happens very slowly and after a long period of adjustment. Some of the services will act to reduce total costs of friction by moving to a point more convenient to their patrons. Once they have moved, they disrupt the balance in the web of space relationships in the central area of which these uses were component parts. This effect leads to further readjustments and in the end, to substantial shifts in the land-use structure. This process of adaptation is costly. Shifts in location involve moving costs, tend to hasten obsolescence of buildings, and may require public improvements or decrease the efficiency of existing public facilities.

As an example, take the case of a centrally-located home office of an insurance company. Because increased downtown congestion has created hardship for the employees, the home office is moved to the suburbs. The removal of a substantial number of the insurance company clerks and executives from the daytime population of the central area may have a considerable effect on the locational pattern and on central land values. The uses affected are the restaurants which served lunches to the departed office workers, and all the shops, stores, and service establishments where the workers bought goods or services at noon or after hours.

In the new location of the insurance company operation, new service uses will appear to serve such a large and concentrated group. The land uses in line of travel between the homes of the employees and the new location will also be affected. But if the new location is not carefully selected, it may create a cross stream of employee traffic which might produce congestion in yet another place. For the employees of the insurance company, the aggregate convenience in home-to-work travel will be greater than immediately before the move. But it will probably be less than before the time that downtown congestion increased to a point where the advantages of centrality were offset.

Thus the repercussions of increasing traffic congestion extend far beyond the direct effect upon the central business area. The self-correcting adaptations are long-delayed and the costs created by the processes of adjustment are not likely to be recovered quickly. The efforts of individual enterprises to reduce frictional costs will create new frictional costs which others must bear. The realignment of the pattern of land values will probably result in smaller total land values as a tax base. Because of the accidents of political boundaries and the lower tax level in suburban areas, the process of adaptation may push a significant share of the tax base beyond the city limits.

The movement of functions from the central area, resulting from increasing frictions through traffic congestion, creates a net loss to the community in productivity, or at least no gain. The move takes place when, by reason of the increased frictional costs, the outlying location is more favorable than the original central site. But if the central site were originally appropriate to the use, the total community costs of friction are likely to be greater in the new location than they were in the original location before the condition of traffic congestion existed.

On the other hand, when more intensive land uses replace less intensive uses in the central area, there is a net gain in productivity. This is the natural process of adaptation which minimizes aggregate frictional costs by placing in central locations activities which can best exploit local sites.

The parking problem is inseparable from the traffic problem; so long as people travel to the center by private automobile, terminal facilities are as important as streets. The degree of difficulty in parking, including the parking fee, is as much a transportation cost as the delays of traffic congestion or the bus fare. Thus, if we are to maximize downtown daytime population density, we must provide parking as well as reduce other transportation costs.

Who is responsible for financing parking facilities? The community, the merchants who benefit through increased sales, or both? If the cost should be borne by the persons who receive the benefits, then who does benefit? This question has a parallel in the problem of assessing the costs of street improvements. In neither case is the benefit solely assignable to the adjacent property owners. Streets and terminal parking lots are two-way and benefit individuals and firms at both ends. They are rightly a general charge on the entire metropolitan community.

Against this point of view is the argument that individuals do not benefit equally from publicly-provided terminal parking facilities. Some people do not own cars; others rarely come to the business districts. The same line of reasoning could be used against our system of supporting public education. But in both cases, the benefit to the community as a whole, through enhancing its aggregate productivity, is undeniable.

There are certain practical arguments in favor of at least a small service charge for publicly-owned parking. In the first place, where the facilities are intended to serve shoppers, the rate structure can be designed to discourage all-day parking by central area employees. Again, because of the accidents of political boundaries, individuals who come from beyond the limits of the central city would make no contribution whatsoever to the cost of the convenience which they enjoy. These rationalizations are far from satisfactory. But they do partly justify municipal parking fees in addition to the practical consideration that even small fees provide net incomes which, in many cities, support the revenue bonds which are necessary to finance the parking lots.

The Central Area

The dramatic growth of peripheral "one stop" regional shopping centers in the post-war era has once more engendered a widespread fear of retail decentralization. Never, in so short a time, has competitive outlying retail growth been so rapid, so well planned, and so effectively executed. The origins of the present danger which is presumed to face the urban center are popularly associated with traffic congestion and the parking problem. Our streets are overcrowded and there is no place to park—ergo, outlying shopping centers.

But the more thoughtful individuals are wondering whether the urban structure is not undergoing some functional change which is altering significant space relationships and giving rise to basic structural shifts in the arrangement of land uses. In terms of efficiency in the locational distribution of uses, the question is whether certain activities are not now more efficiently located outside the central area. In terms of Haig's concepts, the question is whether certain central area uses can reduce costs of friction by locational shifts to outlying areas.

The centers of metropolitan areas have always been the focal point for various and changing types of activities. In the modern metropolis, retail and wholesale trade are conducted in the central area, though not exclusively there. In addition, there are all manner of commercial services, such as banking houses, investment firms, advertising agencies, and accountants; other professional services, such as insurance company home offices; noncommercial functions, such as centers of government, post offices, and courts of law. Within the central area are also found all manner of eating establishments and agencies of personal service, such as barber shops, as well as other establishments like factories, transportation terminals, and dwelling places.

MINIMIZATION OF TRANSPORTATION COSTS IN CENTRAL AREAS. There are two basic reasons why central locations are advantageous to various activities and functions. First of all, they are useful because they minimize transportation costs. For almost all types of activities, the center is the place most convenient to the greatest number of employees. For many types, it is the place most convenient to the greatest number of customers. In fact, central area businesses may be roughly divided into four groups on the basis of the geographical location of their clientele.

No local clients: Some businesses have contacts largely outside the community. For them, community contacts are a small share of the total. An example is a mail order house with a regional or national market including the community where the home office is located. In this case, centrality is of no great importance from the standpoint of customers but may be important from the standpoint of employee convenience.

Community-wide clientele: The prime example is the downtown department store which serves the entire community and the hinterland for miles about. Convenience to both client and employee is an important aspect of a central area situation.

Neighborhood clientele: The central area is most convenient to householders who live on the periphery in the central slums, in the Gold Coast apartment hotels, and in the adjacent modest homes of clerks and workingmen. Their focus is toward the center for many services and commodities which in outlying residential areas are typically provided in neighborhood and regional shopping centers. Grocery stores, drug stores, barbers, and dry cleaners exist on the fringe of the central area primarily to serve the residential districts which border the commercial core.

Central area clientele: This group of businesses might be termed parasitic except for the fact that it is essential to the productivity of the urban organism. In a sense, the businesses feed off the center, but in another sense they serve the center. Examples are the eating establishments which nourish the day-time population of the center. Another example is the business service, such as the accountant or advertising firm, which finds its clients among the businesses located in the central commercial area. Both examples show how a central location is inevitable in light of the nature of the contacts involved.

The importance of a central location in terms of employee or customer relationships will, of course, vary from business to business. The mail order house has no need for a central location to serve its clients and may be able to recruit enough employees from one sector of the community so that an outlying location is feasible. There are current examples of this situation in the movement of insurance company home offices to suburban locations. The accounting firm serving downtown clients could locate away from the center without much increase in the frictions of its primary services since much of the actual auditing work is done in the clients' own offices. But the extra convenience of central location for face-to-face contact between principal and client is worth the relatively small premium in rent. Where the clientele is community-wide, as in the case of a medical specialist or a department store, the maximizing of customer convenience is of primary importance.

The importance of employee convenience is conditioned by a variety of factors including the tightness of the local labor market, the competitive level of wages, and the proportion of total operating costs which is accounted for by personal services. The pattern of these factors varies from business to business and even from time to time.

COHESION OF FUNCTIONS. The second basic reason why certain activities seek central locations may be given in terms of Haig's concept of the cohesion of functions. Haig first developed the notion to explain the force which tends to prevent the physical separation of the functions of a given enterprise. He indicated that fundamental locational analysis may be described in terms of functions. Each enterprise, in fact, may be viewed as a packet of functions with its proper location determined by the proportioning of the components of the packet.

This concept may be extended to all of the enterprises which make up the central commercial zone. It has long been observed that certain retail store types tend to cluster and attempts have been made to measure these associative tendencies.[6]

Women's shopping goods stores represent the most significant and highly crystallized grouping. In every central business district, closely associated with department and variety stores, are found dress shops, shoe stores, hat shops, hosiery stores, and other women's specialty outlets. There are also other less prominent groupings of store types. Outlets serving men are usually grouped in a men's wear cluster. Restaurants, theaters, and florist shops show a tendency toward clustering. The financial district is a place of banks, investment houses, business services, lawyers, accountants, and insurance companies. There is often a wholesale district with its warehouses and loft buildings and perhaps a manufacturing and processing area. Thus the central area (however delimited) is a galaxy of constellations formed of clusters of activities which appear to have a locational affinity one for the other, and are related in some degree to other clusters in the area.

These constellations are related land-use types which generally are confined in extent to a ground area which can be comfortably covered on foot. Their nature and structure are determined by the locational preferences of the individuals and firms whom they serve. Haig points out that "in a very real sense the people of a community decide for themselves, by their expenditures, how they desire the land to be used."

Among land-use types, there is a hierarchy of "convenience-desirability." Consumers vote by the amount and frequency of their purchases to establish the retail structure in a pattern which maximizes their convenience.[7] This is the basis of the cohesion of the women's shopping district. The buying habits of women call for competitive fashion goods outlets to be in close proximity to facilitate comparison and to provide a wide assortment within small compass. In the same shopping district are other types of non-shopping goods outlets, such as variety stores and candy shops, which serve the women shoppers by providing items which are secondary but nonetheless important objectives of the downtown shopping trip. In each case, the cohesive forces are the maximization of convenience or the minimization of the costs of friction.

The functional constellations of central area activities are bound externally by the same type of cohesive force. The financial district is related to the shopping area in ties of convenience for shoppers who may wish to make deposits or withdrawals as one planned activity in the course of a downtown expedition; for merchants, the convenience in procuring banking service is important. The wholesale and retail districts are tied together where the downtown stores comprise a substantial share of the wholesaler's market. Close to the retail core, the downtown Medical Arts building houses specialists who serve the entire community and offers convenience to shoppers on multiple-purpose visits to the center. Convenient medical service is also available to downtown employees, proprietors, and professionals. In this fashion, then, the clusters are interrelated and form a nucleated pattern in the central zone of our cities.

CONVENIENCES OF CENTRAL AREAS. The central area provides, therefore, a common locational advantage at the focus of transportation, and a mutual advantage in proximity among the central land uses. In other terms, the central area offers a unique convenience of accessibility and availability. *Accessibility* is the ease of movement from some point of origin—the shopper's home—to the destination area, which in this case is the central retail district. *Availability* is the number and kind of services and activities within the destination area. The accessibility of the central area is geographical as well as man-made in the converging transportation facilities. Its availability is a product of the unmatched variety of services and activities, the wide range of choice within each service, and the relatedness, direct and indirect, of most of the central activities.

These dimensions of availability give the central area a tremendous potential advantage in convenience over any other spot in the community. Compare, for instance, two areas, A and B. Suppose that A is the locus of 10 different types of services compared with 5 for B. Then in Area A there are 45 possible combinations of two services while in B there are 10. The greater the number of possible combinations of errands which can be run within a destination area, the greater the aggregate potential saving in transportation costs. Considering also the efficiencies of proximity of related businesses and business services, this web of interdependent functions and space relationships provides the most convenient spacing for a large share of the activities of a high proportion of the people of the community. In addition, it is the most convenient place to get to for the greatest number of people and the most convenient spot to distribute from in serving the whole area.

This analysis of the functional basis for the central area suggests that the center might suffer a decline through reduced accessibility, availability, interdependence, or employment.

Reduced accessibility: Reduced accessibility implies traffic congestion and lack of parking. The usual view is that it is now more troublesome to go downtown than it used to be. But in the aggregate, the central area is potentially more accessible than ever and more people are entering it than ever before. The pain may be greater but the people still come. For certain purposes, the downtown district is *comparatively* less accessible because services of various kinds now appear in outlying areas. But this process is in part a natural accompaniment of community growth.

Reduced availability: So far, the central areas have been moving in the direction of greater rather than lesser availability. The variety of activities has been increasing, and the range of choices offered to the shopper in brand, style, quality, and price has not diminished. Increasing specialization in business functions tends to create more interdependence and thus tends to produce more symbiotic relationships where space-convenience is important. Here the danger to the center lies in losing more functions than are gained, or in losing activities of special significance.

The removal of a single activity may create repercussions on many other activities with which it has had direct contact. In turn, the cessation of direct contacts will have secondary effects on enterprises and activities which have had relationships with the activities directly affected. Thus the removal, without replacement, of a single activity will disturb the web of relationships in a series of impacts of diminishing strength, like the ripples from a stone cast into a mill pond.

The removal of the home office of an insurance company from a central location, for instance, will diminish the convenience of employees in their daily travel to and from work, and of customers who come to the home office on business. It will reduce the ease of contact between investment offices and financial houses; the sales department and advertising agencies; the medical department and medical specialists and laboratories; and between the personnel department and employment agencies. The employees of the company will no longer enjoy the convenience of noon or after-work shopping or errand-running in the compact central area where stores and services are within walking distance.

If the center loses too many functions, a serious decline may result as the web of advantageous space relationships weakens.

Reduced interdependence: To the extent that inter-firm contact is important and frequent, the convenience of the compact downtown arrangement is a perpetuating factor. Changes in merchandising techniques may decrease the number of outlets in relation to the variety of the goods and reduce the cohesion of the shopping district. As the department store extends its lines or expands its offerings in a given line, it becomes less dependent upon the need for close proximity to other outlets which make comparison shopping possible. To the extent that pre-selection through advertising and brand acceptance becomes more widespread, the clustering of competing outlets becomes less demanded. To the extent that business enterprises expand and provide specialized business services within their own organizations through a legal staff, an advertising department or a research staff, the close proximity of business specialists is less important.

Reduced employment: In most cities, the central district is the greatest single point of employment concentration. Historically, cities have grown up around the center of employment and the homes of the workers have been oriented to this focal point. The tendency for workers to seek dwellings near their employment has made the center, in proportion to its importance as a place of employment, a dominant force in determining population distribution.[8] Even off-center places of employment are oriented to the main center in many respects. Thus the central area is the primary nucleus of the whole urban structure. Because of this structural orientation toward employment, the central area is a logical spot for a concentration of services for two reasons. First of all, it is most convenient to the greatest number of places of residence. Secondly, the services are convenient to the employees when at their places of work.

Any reversal of the historical growth process may have a diluting effect upon the center and its dominance. If primary employers move to peripheral locations or if new local off-center concentrations of employment develop, the ultimate effect will be to modify the orientation of the population distribution, and to slowly alter the structure of service activities. The daytime population of the center will be decreased and thus the potential of convenient customers for downtown establishments will decline.

Up to the present time, the major desertions from the central area have probably been manufacturing activities. This is not a recent trend, and, in fact, has nearly run its course in most cities. Of the primary activities around which many cities were built, the manufacturing residue at the center is largely the loft-type industry and the transport terminals. Meanwhile, many other types of primary central employment have developed. The tendency of some activities—such as home offices of corporations with widespread activities and relatively few local contacts—to move to suburban locations could seriously affect some cities if it reaches large proportions.

CENTRAL AREAS AND THEIR FUTURE. Few recorded facts support the view that the decline of central areas is under way. In a few scattered instances, the opening of branch stores has allegedly caused the downtown mother department stores to suffer some loss in volume of sales. But there are also claims of increased business in the central store. In Los Angeles, downtown retail sales volume has apparently dropped 14 per cent since 1948 while store sales in Greater Los Angeles have gone up 18 per cent.[9] On the basis of such limited information, it can hardly be said that the death knell of the central area has been sounded. The phenomena are subject to various possible interpretations and much more study is required.

The recent surge in new outlying shopping developments has led to two alternative explanations. One is that the peripheral retail expansion is taking place at the expense of the central area. As a result, it is claimed that the central retail district ultimately will decline in volume of business and in land values.

The other hypothesis, however, states that the peripheral growth of retail facilities is proportionate to the population increase and spatial expansion of our urban areas. Under this assumption, central areas will continue to grow in productivity and business volume and property values will continue to rise as the total population increases, though perhaps at a slower rate than population. This hypothesis accounts for the recent spurt in outlying retail development as merely a secular and temporary acceleration of a normal growth process. Accordingly, there is no implication that the central area will normally retain a constant or increasing proportion of the total retail business of the community. On the contrary, historical evidence indicates that as cities grow, the central area accounts for a decreasing proportion of commercial activity. Moreover, this phenomenon has long characterized urban growth patterns.[10]

No adequate data are available to test these alternative hypotheses properly. However, by studying the central area functions over a period of time, some light may be thrown on the matter. The main question is whether the retailing function is changing quantitatively or qualitatively to such an extent that serious effects on basic land values may result.

In analyzing the question, a study was made of the changing central area functions in Madison, Wisconsin, a city of about 100,000 population. The analysis started with a classification of land-use types represented in the central area.[11] At approximately five-year intervals beginning in 1921, the extant types of land use were recorded with the number of each type. In this way, it was possible to see which types appeared or disappeared and which multiplied or declined in number.

The study revealed that the Madison metropolitan area almost tripled in population in the last thirty years. But measured by the number of nonresidential ground-floor uses or enterprises, the central area grew little in extent. In 1921, there were 400 separate central land uses; in 1931, 437; in 1941, 450; and in 1950, 448. In the twenty-year period from 1930 to 1950, the increase in uses was small. The physical expansion of the area was correspondingly small and consisted largely of filling-in among the existing nonresidential uses by replacement of residual housing. There was a small increase in the over-all average frontage per unit; certain retail classes of use showed substantial increases in size of outlet.

Contrary to what might be expected, the variety of central area activities in the Madison area did not tend to increase markedly. In 1921 there were 120 different nonresidential ground floor use-types; by 1931, the number had increased to 129 and to 133 by 1950. This information does not include the office type of activity which no doubt showed a greater increase in variety over the period studied.

The Madison central area represents a typical case in which the extent has remained relatively constant while the community has grown substantially. In fact, an indefinite expansion of any central retail area is hindered by certain physical limitations. One well-known limitation is the distance consumers are willing to walk within a destination area to which they come on a shopping expedition. This walking distance limits the geographical spread of the retail district and thus restricts the aggregate volume of business which can be done within its borders. In large cities, the limit applies to the retail core of the central area. But it does not directly include the specialized districts, such as the financial and wholesale segments. In small cities, it is not important.

In a growing community, the central area is not expected to be the exclusive and sole locus of retail distribution for any class of merchandise. As the city expands in population and extent, the number of retail enterprises which can be supported increases more or less proportionately. Enterprises like grocery stores which have relatively small patronage groups will scatter through the community to serve an adequate patronage group at the most convenient points. Other types, serving larger patronage groups, will appear at strategic outlying retail centers in such numbers as to permit each outlet to survive, including some of the original type-representatives of the center. As a general rule, the smaller the minimum patronage group required to support a given type of store, the smaller the share of such business which will be done at the center.

Of course, the retail center may not expand in extent proportionately to community growth. Nevertheless, the volume of goods and services purveyed there may still increase. Once the city grows beyond a certain size through greater efficiency in the utilization of space, the center usually becomes more productive with very little or no increase in area. Many kinds of stores can greatly increase their volume of sales without need for increased floor space. For example, the stores which lined Madison's capital square in 1921 could probably have tripled the volume of business without any increase in floor space.

As the city grows, however, the more intensive types of retail outlets tend to dominate the central area. For instance, the department store is usually in a multi-story building. Variety stores offer a wide choice of articles in a small space served by many clerks and secure a high rate of turnover. The parasite types, such as the candy store, use a small floor area with high intensity. Conversely, some of the shopping and specialty types, such as furniture stores, which tend to leave the central area are enterprises which require relatively large areas not intensively used.

But intensity in the physical use of space is not the only measure of productivity. Productivity is finally measured by profitability or rent-paying capacity. Among retail types, there is a hierarchy of rent-paying capacities (assuming appropriate sites) measured by the dollar difference between gross income and costs before rent. This balance available for rent is, therefore, affected not only by volume of sales but also by prices, mark-up, and costs of operation (except rent). Thus a retail type, such as a jewelry store or a very fashionable women's dress shop, with a low turn-over, a high sales price, and a wide mark-up, may have a higher rent-paying capacity and a higher productivity than another type, such as a family shoe store, which has a higher turnover and uses the floor area more intensively but has a lower price per sale and a smaller mark-up. If productivity is synonymous with rent-paying capacity, any increase in the proportion of central area space absorbed by the higher rent-paying types may be said to increase the aggregate productivity of the entire central area without expanding its total extent. Such a rise in productivity would be accompanied by a rise in land values and rental income to landlords.

Even in a growing city, therefore, a static or declining central area land coverage is not necessarily a sign of decay. After an optimum size is reached, the typical behavior of central retail areas is to grow in intensity of use rather than in extent. This rule does not bar moderate growth of the whole central area as metropolitan areas expand and as the complexity and variety of economic activities grow. The central area of Chicago is larger than that of Milwaukee, which in turn is larger than that of Madison. But the areal differences among these cities reflect only a fraction of the differences in nighttime population. They also reflect variations in the use of central sites for non-retail purposes, such as offices, and the effects of large daytime populations which support retail trade in the central area.

Measured by changes in shopping goods activities, the Madison data fail to reveal any evidence of central area decline over the period studied. On the contrary, the importance of the shopping goods group of uses increased significantly both in terms of number of outlets and in front feet. There was a steady increase in the front footage devoted to shopping goods outlets. There was also a continuing replacement of less intensive uses with the more intensive uses; of types of land uses with lower rent-paying capacity with types of higher rent-paying capacity; and of non-commercial or non-retail uses, and convenience and specialty goods outlets, with shopping goods outlets. These are indications of healthy growth.

Because the cohesion of central area functions is so strong, disintegration is most unlikely within the foreseeable future. The strength of the central area lies in its unmatched variety or availability. Even the newest, most elaborate one-stop regional shopping center provides only a fraction of the activities and combinations of services which are available in the downtown destination area.

Viewed functionally, developments like regional shopping centers are a natural adaptation of the urban retail structure to metropolitan growth. For decades, every large American city has had regional shopping centers composed of facilities located at major intersections which provide services even more elaborate than the post-war versions. These older regional shopping centers are now buried in the built-up areas of the city; many of them are as congested as the center. Since they originally depended largely on mass transportation, they are not well adapted to the automobile age.

In comparison, the post-war regional center is aesthetically superior and functionally modern. It is built at one time in contrast to the older centers which grew over the years by accretion. Today the serious competition is not between new regional centers and the central area but between new and old regional and neighborhood centers.[12]

Toward increasing the availability of central urban areas, various means of minimizing the costs of movement are basic. Improved parking and traffic control, free ways, added parking space, and street widenings all contribute to increased accessibility and offset, in varying degree, the convenience of outward travel to competing services in regional shopping centers.

But as we devote our energies to making the central area more accessible, we should work even harder to maintain the variety of activities and the concentration of employment which are functional essentials. Positive action and promotion by business groups and downtown property owners' associations could induce new businesses to locate in central spots with some selectivity as to types of activity. A refined type of zoning, such as that based on the packet of functions which Haig proposed, might be developed to better adjust activity to environment and to exclude locationally inappropriate uses from areas where their presence will increase frictions. Every effort should be made to adjust the central structure to social, economic, and technological change so that its physical rigidity of buildings and street patterns will not hamper prompt locational adaptations. In this connection, the use of long-term leases and the erection of special-purpose buildings should be discouraged. The highest degree of flexibility should be maintained to permit the free and constant rearrangement of land uses in patterns which maintain frictions at a minimum in the face of changing conditions.

The urban redevelopment device is a method of accelerating the natural readjustments of the land-use pattern. This plan should be pushed in full confidence that its initial costs will be repaid many times in increased productivity of the urban structure. For areas peripheral to the central business district, the large office-type activity would be a desirable type of reuse. On cleared land outside the congested central area, an establishment like the home office of an insurance company or some other activity with most of its contacts outside the community could enjoy adequate parking and could utilize the converging lines of transport to carry its employees from all parts of the city. Unless these activities can escape the worst of the congestion, the advantages of central location are nullified. The dominance of the central area is basically dependent on the presence of a large daytime population of workers; every effort should be made to preserve and increase this number.

Perhaps we have assumed that the central area is worth preserving without explicitly stating the reasons why. The basic advantage is the efficiency or convenience in the arrangement of land uses which is the source of the cohesion of central functions. To break up and disperse the related constellations of interrelated activities which comprise the center is to increase greatly the time, money, and human energy costs of doing the city's work. Only a web of fast, cheap, and strategically-located mass transport could serve as a substitute for foot travel within a concentrated destination area, and only New York City has anything remotely approaching such transport. We conclude, therefore, that the preservation of the central area is desirable in terms of productivity. It is also most likely by reason of the instinctive human inclination to minimize the disutilities of movement and in light of the calculated efforts to overcome the frictions which growth and the automobile age have created.

CONCLUSION

Many manifestations of urban change are popularly assumed to be unfortunate and destructive. Actually, most of them are natural adaptations to new conditions which move toward higher, not lower, total efficiency. The problems are not ones of size but of imperfect or delayed adaptation, though they are aggravated by size. They are problems of growth and problems of physical rigidities in a milieu of social and technological mutation. With all its problems, the modern city is more efficient and more productive than its forebears.

Collective efforts to raise urban efficiency through planning, land-use control, taxation, improvements in traffic, transport, and parking, urban redevelopment, and metropolitan integration should be directed toward the facilitation of land-use changes which enhance *total* efficiency, the discouragement of changes which diminish it, the reduction of *total* costs of friction, and the equitable distribution of those costs which must be borne.

FOOTNOTES TO CHAPTER 7

1. R. M. Haig, *Major Economic Factors in Metropolitan Growth and Arrangement* (New York: The Regional Plan of New York and Its Environs, 1928), I. Chapters 1 and 2 previously appeared in *The Quarterly Journal of Economics*, XL (February and May, 1926).

2. The quotations from Haig on pages 126–140 are taken from *Major Economic Factors* in the following order: pp. 21, 22, 37, 38, 39, 44, 44, 20, 19, and 43.

3. R. U. Ratcliff, *Urban Land Economics* (New York: McGraw-Hill, 1949), p. 375.

4. *Ibid.*, p. 372.

5. C. Woodbury (ed.), *The Future of Cities and Urban Redevelopment* (Chicago: University of Chicago Press, 1953), p. 286.

6. R. U. Ratcliff, "The Problem of Retail Site Selection," *Michigan Business Studies*, IX, No. 1 (1939).

7. Ratcliff, *Urban Land Economics*, Ch. 4.

8. J. D. Carroll, Jr., "The Relation of Homes to Work Places and the Spatial Pattern of Cities," *Social Forces*, XXX, No. 3 (November, 1952).

9. M. D. Mills, "Decentralization," *Mass Transportation*, July, 1953.

10. According to Larry Smith, in cities under 250,000 population, 70 per cent of retail business is done at the center; in cities from 250,000 to 500,000, 50 per cent; and in cities from 500,000 to 1,000,000, only 40 per cent. See *Business Action for Better Cities*, A Report on the Businessmen's Conference on Urban Problems, June 23 and 24, 1952 (The Chamber of Commerce of the United States), p. 46.

11. R. U. Ratcliff, *The Madison Central Area* (Madison: Bureau of Business Research and Service of the University of Wisconsin, 1953).

12. *Local Shopping Districts in San Francisco* (San Francisco: San Francisco Department of City Planning, 1952), p. 30.

8

Commentaries

By **Harold M. Mayer,** *Professor of Geography, University of Chicago*

Professor Florence has demonstrated that the metropolis is a phenomenon distinctive in many ways from other urban concentrations. It exists primarily to satisfy economic and social needs which cannot be served so adequately by smaller concentrations. Despite certain metropolitan drawbacks, a considerable economic and social loss would occur if our largest urban areas were dispersed as a result of defense planning or other considerations.

Mark Jefferson, the great geographer, pointed out some time ago that most regions and countries have one urban agglomeration which is much larger than all others.[1] Having established its primacy, this city tends to draw to it the intellectual, economic, and commonly the political leadership of its surrounding region. The multiplicity of metropolitan attractions, in fact, may produce a cumulative effect which results in further growth.

By studying the advantages and disadvantages of metropolitan agglomerations, conclusions presumably may be reached which might apply to smaller communities. In addition to size, other important aspects of metropolitanism are accessibility, variety, transportation and land use, and artificial restraints upon freedom of residential choice.

ACCESSIBILITY

In pre-mechanized civilizations, the area served by any urban center was limited by the degree of accessibility between city and hinterland. About a century ago, von Thünen presented a generalized description of the concentrically-arranged service areas of an *isolated state*.[2] This community consisted of a large town situated in the midst of a fruitful plain. The plain itself eventually ended in a wilderness, so that the state had no commercial intercourse with any other city.

Within the isolated community, the town served as the focus of concentric hinterlands whose extent varied with the weight and bulk of the goods to be transported from them to the center. The activities in the hinterland were localized in direct relation to the bulk of goods handled and the frequency of communications required. Even in von Thünen's isolated state, therefore, transportation assumed a dominant role in both the functions and forms of urban development.

Although cities carried on special functions in pre-mechanized ages, they had relatively few opportunities to develop characteristics distinct from one another. The main exception was the metropolis. It was generally favored by good access, usually by water, to a vast hinterland. Indeed, the metropolis existed as a distinct type of city even in the ancient world. All roads lead to Rome.

Today the economic base of many industrial and commercial cities depends upon the physical handling of large volumes of goods. But in spite of the availability of highway, railway, and air transport, these communities still tend to locate on navigable waters. Other metropolitan functions, such as financial and professional services or the origination and communication of ideas, do not depend directly upon the handling of bulk goods and need not be tied so closely to water routes. Hence capital cities are more likely to be found inland at locations central to the countries which they serve and central to routes of internal rather than external communication.

Because accessibility is essential for a metropolis, all large cities are transport centers of major importance. There is a striking analogy between the accessibility of a metropolis to its hinterlands and the balance between site rentals and transport costs for any given location within the metropolis (as developed by Professor Ratcliff). The metropolis is the central business district of its region.

Professor Florence noted that the largest countries tend to have more than one metropolis in order to reduce the time and costs of access to metropolitan activities by all parts of the nation. This tendency indicates that accessibility is an indispensable prerequisite to metropolitanism.

VARIETY

The variety of activities and opportunities within a metropolis depends upon relative accessibility. For in order to carry on any given function, the metropolis must be accessible to a hinterland which is large enough to provide adequate support for the activity. The facilitation of access by mechanized transport has been directly responsible for the proliferation of the metropolis in modern times.

As a metropolitan advantage, variety cannot be measured entirely in economic terms. Professor Florence has pointed out that only the metropolis has a sufficient variety of specialization so that a satisfactory number of congenial persons with mutual interests can be found. Likewise, only the metropolis offers a sufficient variety of persons with diverse and complementary interests to provide a stimulating cross-fertilization of ideas.

In its variety, the metropolis affords a wider selection of economic opportunities to the individual than any other form of human settlement. The metropolitan labor market provides a greater number and diversity of job opportunities without the disadvantage of changing one's residence with every change of employment. Conversely, the metropolitan dweller normally has a wide choice of residential environments, including different houses, dwelling types, and neighborhoods. He is relatively free to seek new residential environments without the necessity of changing his employment each time he changes his residence.

The employer, on the other hand, has the widest possible choice from among a large labor force. He can expand, contract, change the direction of his effort, or even relocate without the dire consequences to the community that would follow with a less varied and smaller labor force.

Transportation and Land Use

If the accessibility and variety of a metropolis are to be maximized, other aspects of metropolitan development and planning should receive more attention in the future than in the past. The first aspect (mentioned by Professor Ratcliff) is a reduction of the friction of movement within the metropolis and a consequent reduction of the monopoly position of certain sites which capitalize upon undesirable congestion.

Professor Ratcliff points out that improvements in local transportation and consequent reductions in its costs tend to even out differences in site rentals. This tendency implies a broadening of the choices among alternative sites for business as well as for residence.

The nature, location, and extent of future local transportation facilities are inextricably related to the present and future patterns of land use. Problems of land use and transportation must be studied together and solutions must be planned on a metropolitan basis. The obstacles to such comprehensive metropolitan planning are well known. They include inadequate knowledge of the interrelationships of land use and transportation, obsolete areal jurisdictions of overlapping and often competing local governments, and conflicts relative to the desirable degree of public participation in such metropolitan activities as redevelopment, housing, expressway and transit operation, and the provision of parking facilities.

Research into these aspects of metropolitan development is meager in proportion to the magnitude of the problems involved. Official planning agencies apparently are not sufficiently competent to deal with them. This is the case partly because of the pressures of day-to-day routine tasks imposed upon the agencies but mainly because few planning boards are legally authorized to investigate metropolitan problems as such. Likewise, unofficial metropolitan planning agencies are often subject to the pressures of the groups which contribute their financial support and are rarely able to conduct research on the scale which the questions require. Only the great metropolitan universities can be sufficiently objective and comprehensive in their research upon metropolitan problems. They are the only organizations which are free from artificial limitations upon the areal extent of their investigations and

which are sufficiently detached to be able to view the metropolis in relation
to its regional, national, and world-wide functions.

ARTIFICIAL RESTRAINTS UPON FREEDOM OF RESIDENTIAL CHOICE

Restrictions upon freedom of choice of residential locations within the
metropolis are of two general types. The first restriction is related to the
separation of places of work and residence. It is inherent in the nature of the
metropolis itself. The second is expressed through zoning and deed restrictions
and the operation of the housing market. It is the result of specific action by
individuals and groups within the metropolitan area.

Separation of Places of Work and Residence

Advances in transport technology have greatly facilitated access among cities
and between cities and their hinterlands. Access among the various portions
of a built-up metropolitan area, however, has not been comparably improved.
The problem is especially acute in the metropolitan areas. For the larger
the urban agglomeration, the greater the total number of travel miles per
capita involved in the daily journey to work. Hence the greater the dependence
upon mass transport.

The automobile has merely aggravated the problem, and cannot be relied
on as the chief means of urban transport. For it produces traffic at rush hours
in the concentrated centers of employment; its speed of movement is slow
in congested areas; its cost of parking (where space is available) is high; and
its flexibility makes available for development ever-expanding areas on the
metropolitan periphery at greater and greater distances from the center.

No wonder, then, that the riding habit on mass transit is higher in metropolitan areas than in smaller cities. But mass transit routes are so oriented that
they primarily serve the central business districts. In fact, the traffic density to
and from other areas of employment would be insufficient to support adequate
high-speed mass transit. The worker employed in the central business district
thus has the greatest freedom of choice among the residential locations within
the metropolitan area. For him, all locations are accessible by relatively good
transit, either directly or by means of feeder lines with good connections.

A person employed in other parts of the metropolitan area, however, does
not enjoy comparable transit facilities or residential mobility. He does not
have complete freedom of choice among all neighborhoods in the metropolis
where housing is within his means. For in many cases the costs in time,
money, and effort of the journey to work become disproportionate.

An individual working outside the central business district often must
commute by automobile, and the expenses of automobile operation and maintenance, including insurance and garaging, is greater in metropolitan areas
than anywhere else. In fact, it constitutes a sizable item in the high cost of
metropolitan living.

Furthermore, the worker employed in an outlying establishment is faced with the problem of the high cost (or impossibility) of finding garage space if he wishes to live in a dense multi-family apartment development which many persons prefer. And he usually cannot live in a residential area so located as to involve travel through the central business district on the way to work because of the time-consuming congestion involved in passing through the downtown district.

Considerable research is required in order to solve the problem of how to provide adequate transportation to points within the metropolitan area other than the central business district. Research on attitudes toward automobile ownership in the metropolis, as they pertain to choice of residential location, would also be fruitful. The entire subject of work-residence relationships in the metropolis, especially as they affect choice of residence and employment and hence the housing and labor markets, is only now beginning to be studied and should receive much more concentrated attention.

Zoning and Deed Restrictions and the Housing Market

Heretofore we have generally assumed that it was desirable to concentrate upon a limited range of housing types and costs in any given neighborhood. But within some metropolitan areas, this assumption has given rise to serious problems. Take, for example, the case of an upper-income suburb of large homes which attracts many influential persons partly because of its excellent school system. This suburb may now be threatened by an acute shortage of school personnel because potential teachers cannot afford either to live in the community or to expend the time and cost of commuting from elsewhere in the metropolitan area. Research on attitudes concerning a greater diversity of neighborhood development, and methods of achieving it, is needed.

Another restriction upon freedom of residential choice arises from the fact that individual neighborhoods tend to be developed within a relatively limited period of time. As a result, block obsolescence develops and all buildings eventually become obsolete within the same short period of time. If the location of the neighborhood is otherwise desirable, an individual may have to choose between a deteriorated and obsolete house or a new one beyond his means. Research is required on methods of achieving a gradual development and redevelopment of residential areas in order to broaden the freedom of choice of housing types within such areas.

Other restrictions upon freedom of choice arise from the attitudes toward racial and other minority groups, and the restricted housing supply available to these groups. The provision of housing and appropriate community facilities for young as well as old unattached persons has received virtually no attention. Indeed, we do not clearly understand what facilities they require. Meeting the needs of young attached persons seeking careers in the metropolis, and of elderly persons living alone or in couples, is becoming more important, especially in the large metropolitan areas where both groups are forming rapidly increasing proportions of the total population.

CONCLUSION

This discussion has tried to set forth a few implications of the chapters by Professor Ratcliff and particularly Professor Florence in terms of the problems related to the present and future maintenance of metropolitan advantages. Accessibility and variety, which are perhaps the two outstanding metropolitan advantages, give rise to a richer and fuller kind of living than is possible anywhere else. If these advantages are to be preserved in the face of threats to the metropolis and the kind of living which it provides, much basic research will be required and new planning solutions tried. Herein is the challenge to the metropolitan university.

By **Larry Smith,** *President, Larry Smith & Company, Real Estate Consultants, Seattle*

These comments pertain mainly to the position of the investor in commercial real estate and the position of the retail store. From this viewpoint, it seems evident that, as Professors Florence and Ratcliff indicate, a metropolitan concentration of population today provides a net-plus to the geographical area or country in which it is located. Furthermore, the manifestations of change in the distribution of urban activities are chiefly natural adaptations to new conditions which move toward higher, not lower, total efficiency. Finally, the modern city is more efficient than its forebears. Collective efforts to raise urban efficiency should be directed toward encouraging land-use changes which will enhance total efficiency.

As Professor Ratcliff adds, the central business district appears to be a permanent institution which cannot be replaced by the development of similar suburban facilities. In other words, the efficiency and contribution of the central business district are based upon the assemblage in one central location of many functions which can serve the entire city most effectively by being situated in a single district.

For business organizations and investors in our larger cities, six of the concepts mentioned in the chapters by Professors Florence and Ratcliff are of particular interest. These are the cost of dispersion, modern shopping centers, equalization of costs, the hierarchy of values, the distribution of the tax burden, and the allocation of parking charges. In addition to these specific concepts several more general questions are suggested by Professors Florence and Ratcliff. These questions pertain to the location and preplanning of metropolises and the future form of central business districts.

THE COST OF DISPERSION

The cost of dispersion is not necessarily the same for various members of the business community. In a period of rapid growth, for instance, one segment of the community may move to a new location which is more advantageous to its operations. But its dispersal may at the same time be disadvantageous or costly to other parties.

As an example, take the recent campaign by certain Southern states to attract industries from New England. In many cases, this move is urged on the basis of temporary "fractional" advantages, such as tax benefits or free sites, which in the long run might not be sufficient to justify a move. In that event, the movement of New England industries to the South in search of presumably better locations may eventually harm the industries as well as New England itself.

On the other hand, if the fractional advantages are merely the trigger which sets in motion a transfer which is basically logical, then this objection would not be valid. Whatever the case, the remedy available to the New England states is not merely a criticism of the Southern states for offering fractional advantages. It also includes an investigation and promotion of the real advantages which New England offers various industries best suited to its own location.

Modern Shopping Centers

Shopping centers are logical adaptations to the automobile age of older suburban developments located at the intersection of public transportation lines. In this sense, they should prove to be sound real estate investments if they are related to the growth of population and the needs of the suburban community. Beyond that point, however, they may encourage an excessive diffusion of retail facilities which is not justified by increased advantages to the retailer, consumer, or the metropolis itself. Here, again, the cost of dispersion might not be the same for every member of the community.

Considering our population growth in the last five years and the predicted growth in the next ten or fifteen years, the justifiable number of modern shopping centers is probably several hundred. This is particularly true if shopping centers are defined to include neighborhood groupings of stores headed by a supermarket as well as regional centers serving a more extensive population with typical drug, variety, junior department stores, and similar merchandising units.

From community to community, the justifiable number of centers varies greatly. Before the development of modern shopping centers in Detroit, Michigan, there were approximately 250 nuclei in suburban areas. Of these, 60 were large enough to include drug, variety, a limited amount of apparel, and banking and similar service functions. About 30 of the 60 were of major consequence; each had a total retail floor area of more than 100,000 square feet. The number and profitability of the pre-automobile age shopping centers are indications of the normal need of the suburban community for such facilities.

However, few shopping centers in the past have accommodated branch department stores and retailing facilities comparable to those found in the downtown district. This is probably a logical expression of the limited opportunity for the development of that particular type of shopping center in the United States today and over the next ten years.

Nevertheless, many modern shopping centers are being promoted despite the lack of either a suitable market or a well-designed layout. Some of them have already proved to be unsatisfactory investments. Others now in operation or in the planning stage can be expected to have the same experience. The result is likely to be a setback in the normal development of similar suburban facilities. For entrepreneurs, retailers, and insurance companies and other financing agencies may turn their back on all such developments because of the unsatisfactory experience with a few poorly located and poorly developed units.

These facts imply that a diffusion of facilities throughout metropolitan areas is continuing to take place in the United States. In the future, this diffusion will probably be evidenced less by the smoothness which Professor Ratcliff suggests than by the imperfections and lags which he also emphasizes. It will undoubtedly be spurred by entrepreneurs seeking profit to the detriment of sound investment and sound retailing. Such a movement will be followed by setbacks inhibiting the normal forces of diffusion even at a time when the disadvantages of the existing pattern persist beyond the point where diffusion of facilities would be justified.

EQUALIZATION OF COSTS

At certain times, costs may vary among various parts of the country, or between one part of a metropolitan area and another. But within a limited length of time, it is reasonable to assume that these costs will tend to be equalized and the temporary benefits of any local cost advantages will disappear.

One case in point is the improvement in communication during the last few decades. As late as 1935, there were relatively wide discrepancies in the costs of construction within distances of 100 or 150 miles; labor in specialized trades failed to move freely from one local area to another. Today improved transportation has wiped out many of these differentials. Even on a national basis, total costs of labor, as distinct from hourly wages, have tended to equalize among different areas.

Another illustration is the price of land used for shopping centers. One of the incentives in such projects has been the fact that raw land has been bought at relatively low prices and has risen substantially in value after it was improved with retail stores. However, experience in many projects has shown that this appreciation in value is not so great as it might seem. For the cost to the entrepreneur of installing on the raw land the necessary improvements and utilities (which are normally provided at the expense of the municipality in central business districts or in established suburban areas) has almost entirely absorbed the apparent differential between the low cost of the raw land and its value after development.

In the same fashion, many of the factors creating favorable cost differentials for suburban retail stores today may disappear within the next few years.

Favorable wage, delivery, publicity, or other costs may vanish if continued suburban population growth tends to bring about cost levels characteristic of the central business area. It behooves both investors and retailers, therefore, to make certain that new investments in suburban areas are based upon strong, permanent, natural advantages rather than upon artificial cost conditions which may disappear at any time.

HIERARCHY OF VALUES

Both Professors Florence and Ratcliff referred to the natural hierarchy of values in the central business district. They pointed out that governmental and institutional functions, retailing, and office and other high-type business uses are likely to be justified in areas of high land values, and are likely to create those values. There is a fertile field for study in determining the effect of population growth, the need for these types of facilities, and their influence on property values.

A great body of information is now at hand concerning the extent of certain types of land use required in communities of varying population and economic background. But few data exist concerning the types of activities appropriate for such land-use revisions as the redevelopment of slum areas or the relocation of freight classification yards on the outskirts of the community, with a resulting availability of substantial land areas in the central business district.

DISTRIBUTION OF THE TAX BURDEN

Certain new shopping centers have evidently been planned to minimize expenditures by the land owner for parking and traffic controls, or for utilities and other facilities normally provided by the municipality. Other regional-type shopping centers have been supplied by their owners with extensive systems of deceleration lanes, traffic control units, parking lots, sidewalks, road systems, sewage disposal plants, water mains, and similar facilities which would otherwise be furnished by the community at large.

In some cases, the assessed valuation of the larger projects has been based upon the total expenditure by the landlord, having regard to the normal equalization of assessed valuations. As a result, the landlord who develops his property efficiently and thereby relieves the community of a large capital investment is penalized not only by the additional capital investment involved but also by the increased amount of taxes he must pay when his assessment is related to the total expenditure for improvements in the project. In view of these facts, assessments should be so equalized that the tax burden will not be unduly severe on the property owner who plans to develop his project in such a way as to provide the greatest net benefit to the community.

ALLOCATION OF PARKING CHARGES

Professor Ratcliff has stated that streets and terminal parking lots are two-way and benefit individuals and businesses at both ends. Thus he concludes that they should rightly be a general charge on the community.

Nevertheless, the cost of parking as a terminal facility is closely related to the problem of the public transportation system. The consumer or employee who uses public transportation facilities is at least as important to the health of the central business district as the owner of a private automobile who drives downtown. The presumption that the driver may be a more profitable customer for the downtown stores has apparently not been satisfactorily proven.

It does seem obvious, however, that the per capita cost of providing facilities for the user of the public transportation system is much less than the cost of furnishing street and parking facilities for the movement of a single individual who ties up 200 or 300 square feet of land or garage space during the time he shops. Consequently, there appears to be as much justification for subsidizing the public transportation system as for providing free street and parking facilities for the user of private transportation vehicles.

The parking problem, in other words, must be related to the need of maintaining and improving the public transportation system so that it offers facilities comparable in attractiveness and comfort to the convenience of the parkway and the supervised parking lot. This problem is the concern not only of the persons using the transportation system but also of the owners and renters of property located within the entire central business district.

THE LOCATION OF NEW METROPOLISES

Can we recognize in advance the probable location of a new metropolis which may serve areas where rapid population growth is now occurring? Professor Florence lists eight cities in our country with metropolitan areas in excess of two million persons. They are New York, Chicago, Philadelphia, Los Angeles, Detroit, Boston, San Francisco, and Pittsburgh. In all, the eight areas serve four major Census regions—the northeastern, middle-Atlantic, east north-central, and the Pacific Coast states. In 1950, the four regions contained more than 84 million inhabitants.

Yet five other major Census regions and two-thirds of our land area are not now adjacent to a metropolis. In 1950, the population of these regions was about 66 million persons, or roughly the total population of the United States in 1895. By 1975, the estimated population of the five regions will approximate 90 million—greater than the 1950 population of the four regions now served by our largest metropolitan areas. This anticipated rate of growth also exceeds the expected average growth of the remaining four regions.

In view of these considerations, it seems reasonable to expect that twenty years from now, up to six additional cities may qualify as metropolises serving one or more of the five major Census regions. From a business standpoint, it would be extremely interesting to identify the factors contributing toward the development of these cities to the point where they serve as true metropolitan areas for their surrounding regions.

Preplanning the Metropolis

Can we identify the disadvantages or negatives of a metropolis and eliminate their influence as a metropolitan area expands or as a moderate-sized city grows to metropolitan stature?

The problems of a major city in the United States are relatively easy to point out. They include traffic, parking, public transportation, general municipal finance, zoning, building codes, off-street parking and delivery zones, smoke and noise control, and so on. But they are not so easy to correct. A great psychological problem exists in inducing any government of a growing city to plan and spend in advance to avoid these disadvantages at a time when its revenues are totally committed to meeting the present increasing need for schools, fire protection, streets, sidewalks, and other facilities.

It is nevertheless true that one million dollars spent today in creating conditions which will avoid the need to make expensive corrective measures in the future could easily save an expenditure of possibly ten or twenty million dollars at a later date. With an anticipated population increase in the United States of approximately 50 million persons from 1950 to 1975, the growth of certain cities toward metropolitan status should be capable of prediction. In view of the short term, the benefits to be derived from anticipating future needs would be so imminent and so predictable that energetic measures should be undertaken toward this end.

The Future Form of Central Business Districts

What will be the form of the central business districts of our metropolitan areas thirty years from now? It appears that there are three possible alternatives; none of them is necessarily exclusive. One alternative is that the future form of the central business district may be based upon a rehabilitation of public transportation. A second is that its form may be based upon the provision of sufficient terminal facilities for parking. A third alternative is that the physical form of our downtown areas may be entirely new, although the functions of the central business districts may remain substantially the same or may be decentralized to some extent.

Any solution of these problems should at least involve a consideration of the possibility of planning on a regional basis, probably with assistance from the federal government. There is also the possibility of revitalizing the mass transportation system of the country as a necessary complement to expressway planning. Finally, zoning, assessment, and tax authority may be used to direct the location, size, and specifications of new commercial and industrial developments.

Conclusion

The universities of the world—like the one whose two hundredth anniversary is being honored—have been extremely helpful in analyzing such prob-

lems. They have pointed out many of the influences which bear upon our daily
lives as well as the values which are worth preserving and the dangers which
threaten these values. It seems certain that the universities will continue to
provide leadership in this direction. Each day, the problems call for more
urgent solution in view of our rapid population growth which is now estimated
to carry us to more than two hundred million persons in the next twenty years.

FOOTNOTES TO CHAPTER 8

1. Mark Jefferson, "The Law of the Primate City," *Geographical Review*, XXIX
(April, 1939), 226–232.
2. J. H. von Thünen, *Der Isolierte Staat* (The Isolated State), 1863.

PART FOUR
The Influence of the Metropolis on Concepts, Rules, and Institutions Relating to Property

INTRODUCTION

The metropolis represents a change in the scale of life. It magnifies many problems encountered in smaller communities as well as creates others of its own. With its millions of inhabitants, the metropolis emphasizes the need to control individual actions in the interest of community welfare. Conversely, it also underlines the need to protect the individual against the unreasonable acts of his neighbor or government. In both cases, the goal is to provide a fuller life for all.

Are existing legal powers adequate to accomplish this goal through allocating, developing, and planning the use of community and individual resources? The answer to this question is not simple. Some people believe that existing legal powers are adequate but not enforced vigorously enough. Others maintain that many new controls are desirable. The entire question deserves a detailed inquiry into recent developments in the law of property as well as the impact of the metropolis upon land law. These are the subjects of the chapters by Mr. Reeve and Professor McDougal.

One modern tendency in the law of property is toward an increase in the number and scope of public legal powers in metropolitan areas. As a result, individual freedom of action progressively diminishes, although the welfare of the community itself may be enhanced. What are the merits and dangers of public intervention? How does it affect traditional ways of getting things done, no matter whether skyscrapers, highways, or atomic defense is involved? What does it do to men's expectations and plans?

All these aspects are related to the reciprocal influence of the metropolis upon the law and of the law upon life in the metropolis. Here the political effects of rent control, the economic effects of zoning, and the social effects of slum clearance are most clearly revealed. In order to make the most of the metropolis, all of our legal measures must be clearly defined, assessed, and implemented or altered accordingly.

9

Recent Developments in the Law of Property

HAROLD L. REEVE
Senior Vice President
Chicago Title and Trust Company

This chapter is designed to survey the law of property and furnish some background information for limited conclusions. It purports to state a point of view concerning certain broad legal principles affecting property which have been shaped by the pressures of the metropolis. These principles have influenced the development of the law of property and may further affect the field under inquiry.

The volume of federal and state statutes, municipal ordinances, reported judicial opinions, administrative rulings, and legal literature pertaining to the subject is too vast to permit detailed analysis. Consequently, this inquiry is conducted on a sampling basis. Emphasis is placed on examples of obvious character.[1]

Forces Considered

The concepts, rules, and institutions relating to property are shaped by the same kinds of forces and pressures which fashion other aspects of the law. And they are as fluid. The law grows and changes and adapts itself to new situations primarily because people insist that their wishes must be accommodated. When they want to do something badly enough, ways for doing it ultimately develop. If established and accepted patterns of legal action are available, they are used. If not, over a period of time some adaptation occurs.

The methods used to accomplish changes in the law vary markedly. Ordinarily a persistent need results in a new statute or local ordinance which authorizes the desired action. Witness, for example, the enactment of zoning and community conservation acts and a host of federal acts in the field of housing. Sometimes actions which have already been taken—even though they had no statutory foundation or were questionable under existing doctrines—are ratified by legislative enactment. These actions may, in fact, furnish the basis for a statute which solemnly embodies the debatable procedure as though it always had been accepted. Other times, judicial action may approve what had formerly been frowned on, or judicial legislation may change the course of the law. This happened when the United States Supreme Court redetermined the powers of the federal government by adopting new concepts of the interstate commerce and general welfare clauses of the Constitution.

Frequently the desired end is accomplished by contract or custom independent of legislation or litigation. What people actually do in their everyday activities concerning real estate titles, for instance, is as much a factor of change as a statute or judicial decree. And sometimes legal means which are not precisely adapted to the purposes are used to accomplish a given end. Although far from ideal, these means may escape challenge and ultimately attain the respectability of age and custom.

Fields of Law Involved

Throughout this chapter *institution* is employed in its ordinary meaning of a practice, law, or custom which is a material and persistent element in the life or culture of an organized group. *Property* signifies the sum of all the rights and powers incident to the ownership of real estate.[2]

With these definitions in mind, the question may be considered whether or not there has been a discernible influence of the metropolis on the concepts, rules, and institutions relating to property. Although the growth of cities has been paralleled by a relentless evolution of the law, no inevitable relationship between the two processes necessarily exists. On the other hand, it would seem probable that the aggregation of people in cities has exerted some kind of influence upon the law of property. In analyzing this influence, various fields of law are involved.

Vast areas of legislation and legal doctrine are applicable to both agrarian and urban societies and are not exclusively attributable to the influence of either. The fields of criminal law, taxation, judicial procedure, descent and distribution of property, the laws concerning marriage and divorce, adoption of children, wills, and deeds and mortgages, the laws of banking, corporations, negotiable instruments and commercial transactions, motor vehicles and educational institutions, and many other activities apply equally to city and country communities. They owe their present status to factors other than urban conditions.

But other legal fields predominantly concern either rural activities or city problems. The laws applicable to drainage, water rights, control of noxious weeds, farm fences, agriculture, and horticulture do not suggest that urban problems have shaped their present form. On the other hand, the words slum clearance, zoning, building codes, private restrictive agreements, city planning, rent control, air rights, cooperative apartments, and many aspects of the law of landlord and tenant call to mind the confusions, antagonistic interests, and pressures which build up in a metropolis. These confusions, interests, and pressures shape the permitted actions of its people. They become reflected in the legislative acts of its officials, the actions of public agencies which make its decisions, and the judgments of the courts which decide its controversies.

Legal Areas Illustrating Metropolitan Influences

Illustrations of the influence of the metropolis may be found in statute books as well as court decisions. They include the police power in an urban society; the types of statutes and municipal ordinances which have evolved in populous communities; social controls of land use in cities as demonstrated by zoning laws and conservation acts; the maze of statutes and institutions which spring from the federal government in the area of housing, slum clearance, and the alphabetical agencies concerned with realty; and some phases of the law of landlord and tenant.

Other illustrations of metropolitan influences have developed from business practices and local customs. They comprise such everyday affairs as the techniques devised for using air rights and for holding and conveying real estate titles involved in syndicate and other group operations; the philosophical problems connected with the legal relationships incident to cooperative apartments; the course of private restrictive agreements; and the practical efforts which are being made to find realistic title standards which will facilitate rather than hinder the marketing of city real estate and the making of mortgage loans.

THE POLICE POWER IN AN URBAN SOCIETY

Under a constitutional form of government, urban life requires a constant adjustment between an individual's rights and the limitation that the public welfare takes precedence over an individual's right to exercise uncontrolled freedom of action. When large masses of people live and work in densely populated urban areas, this adjustment creates acute and delicate problems. Not the least of these problems is found in the pressures exerted upon the legal concept of the police power of the state.

The Traditional Doctrine

The United States Supreme Court outlined the traditional doctrine in 1876 as follows:

> When one becomes a member of society, he necessarily parts with some rights or privileges which, as an individual not affected by his relations to others, he might retain. "A body politic," as aptly defined in the preamble of the Constitution of Massachusetts, "is a social compact by which the whole people covenants with each citizen, and each citizen with the whole people, that all shall be governed by certain laws for the common good." This does not confer power upon the whole people to control rights which are purely and exclusively private . . . but it does authorize the establishment of laws requiring each citizen to so conduct himself, and so use his own property, as not necessarily to injure another. This is the very essence of government, and has found expression in the maxim *"sic utere tuo ut alienum non laedas."* From this source come the police powers.[8]

In applying these principles to changing circumstances, the courts have developed the fundamental doctrine that the police power extends to the protection of the lives, limbs, health, comfort, and quiet of all persons and the protection of all property within the state. Moreover, the police power may be exercised in the interest of public morals and safety and for the promotion of the general welfare.

The authority of the states to enact laws reasonably necessary to promote the public health, morals, safety, and general welfare comprehends a wide range of judgment and discretion in determining what matters are sufficiently important to be subject to state regulation and administration. For the limitations of the federal constitution do not deny to the states the power to establish all regulations reasonably necessary to advance and secure the health, morals, safety, and general welfare of the community.[4]

In exercising the police power, no compensation is paid by the state or collectible by a property owner because of limitations imposed upon the free use of his property where those limitations are within the police power. Section I of the Fourteenth Amendment to the federal constitution prohibits the taking of property without just compensation. But it does not prohibit the exercise of the police powers. Even in the face of a great financial loss, the police power is upheld. Private loss will not be permitted to impede a proper exercise of that power, because the well-being of the people is more important.[5]

The Essence of the Doctrine

The police power involves two conflicting concepts. One is that the state has power to make regulations to promote the health, peace, morals, education, and good order of the people even though in so doing individual rights have to be sacrificed to the common good. The other is that individual rights and freedom of action are so basic and important that a legislative act whose effect would deprive a citizen of property rights cannot be sustained in the courts under the police power unless the public health, comfort, safety, or welfare demanded such enactment, and unless there is some logical connection between the object to be accomplished by the legislation and the means prescribed to accomplish that end.[6]

Among the cases decided by courts of last resort, those which involve the police power originate more often than not in problems created by the crowding of urban living. Even in the days of maximum individual free action, privately-owned buildings which were a menace to public health or which were unsafe and constituted a fire hazard could be demolished by the state under the police power without compensation to the owner. The doctrine went so far as to permit a private residence to be destroyed without compensation in order to prevent a general conflagration. It also allowed the destruction of property to prevent flood damage to adjoining property.[7]

Earlier legal decisions emphasized the basic concept that an owner of property has the constitutional right to make any use of it he desires, so long as he does not endanger or threaten the safety, health, comfort, or general welfare of the public. The desirable end was individual freedom of action, not prohibition of free choice. Thus the line was clearly drawn against municipal regulations like those prohibiting the location of a retail store in a residence area. It was also drawn against regulations prohibiting the location of a store in a residential zone without the frontage consents of a majority of the property owners on both sides of the street in the block in which the store was to be located or against regulations based upon aesthetic considerations.[8]

The Elasticity of the Doctrine

The most notable aspect of the legal concept of police power has been its ability to change and grow and adapt itself to new conditions. Over the years, the courts have refused to compress the police power into a limited and rigid definition. They have kept it flexible and poised to meet changing conditions which from generation to generation require new regulation or different application of an old principle to new facts.[9]

This elasticity has been sustained primarily by the courts. In passing upon the constitutionality of legislative acts, the courts have shifted the line between the permissible and the forbidden to accommodate prevailing social, political, and economic ideas. They have done this through recourse to the convenient and fluid concepts of public welfare or public good and general prosperity. According to Mr. Justice Cardozo, "property, like liberty, though immune under the Constitution from destruction, is not immune from regulation essential for the common good. What that regulation shall be, every generation must work out for itself."[10]

Recent generations have worked out regulations in the light of the fact that most people are city dwellers. As a New Jersey court stated in 1938:

> While the police power is not variable in either quality or quantity, it is coincident with the requirements of the general public welfare arising from changing conditions—social, economic, or otherwise. The complexities of modern community life necessarily impose a greater demand upon this reserve power for such reasonable supervision and regulation as may be essential for the common good and welfare. . . . They have placed reciprocal restrictions upon individual rights; and the authority may be directed to the reasonable accommodation of relative rights and duties dictated by the common interest. To borrow the language of Mr. Justice Holmes, "it may be put forth in aid of what is sanctioned by usage, or held by the prevailing morality or strong and preponderant opinion to be greatly and immediately necessary to the public welfare." . . . [For] "circumstances may so change in time or so differ in space as to clothe with such an interest what at other times or in other places would be a matter of purely private concern."[11]

The changes which have taken place in the factual background against which the concept of police power must now be applied were ably summarized many years ago.

> The rapid development of American cities has caused much concern to those interested in the welfare of the American people. The city planning

and zoning movement, which has had a phenomenal growth in the last decade, is the result of apprehension for the future of our congested and badly organized municipalities.

A great number of problems have been created by this concentration of population. Sewage disposal, traffic congestion, housing conditions, race segregation, public recreation, and the like have become absorbing topics. Municipal and state governments have engaged in paternalistic enterprises which would have been regarded as socialistic a generation ago. Clinics, housing bureaus, sanitary departments, museums, libraries, municipal universities and trade schools, employment agencies, community centers, civic operas, and so forth are but a few of the recent governmental activities.

Life has ceased to be home life but has become apartment life. Meals are now eaten at cafeterias, and we sleep on beds that disappear behind the door to furnish more of the room that has become so precious. There was a time when a man's affairs were his own; his house was his own; his liberty and his property were the things most dear to him. His yard and his house were spacious and isolated. If he wanted water, he dug a well or went to the town pump; his lights were furnished by a kerosene lamp that any one might own.

In the city, today, we are forced into co-operation with our neighbors whether we desire it or not. We cannot dig our well in the city; the water would become impure. We cannot throw the dish water out of the window; a neighbor's complaint would result. We must own small parts of a water system, a sewer system, and a light system. We may have our home in a co-operative apartment house. We live among people, and this association with people determines whether our lives are livable or not.

The law has taken cognizance of the changing conditions in city life. A great deal of legislation has been concerned with the public health, safety, and morals. The sense of smell is protected, as well as our sense of hearing. And everywhere we find laws passed under the police power of the state which are designed to promote the comfort and general welfare of the citizens. . . .[12]

LEGISLATION RESULTING FROM URBAN PRESSURES

The Common Law

The influence of the metropolis on the concepts, rules, and institutions affecting property primarily manifests itself through the enactment of legislation. The Congress, General Assemblies of the States, and lesser legislative bodies all are responsive to the problems of their constituents, most of whom now live in cities.

Back of legislation enacted to meet current pressures lies a great body of nonstatutory law which has accumulated through generations of nonurban people whose customs and ideas still have a positive influence upon the law as it affects the whole economy. Throughout the country, except in a few areas which have Spanish or French background, the common law of England was adopted and still exists as the basis of existing state jurisprudence. It was the everyday law of an agrarian society—a system of elementary rules and general judicial declarations of principles. These rules and principles continually expanded with the progress of society, adapting themselves to the gradual changes of trade, commerce, arts, inventions, and the exigencies and usages of the country.[13] This development continues unabated.

Many states have adopted by statute the fourth year of the reign of James the First as the date when the common law of England was transplanted into their basic law. That year began March 24, 1606, and ended March 23, 1607. It was the period during which the first territorial government was established in America. The original statute fixing that date was passed by the general convention of the colony of Virginia in May, 1776. From Virginia it spread through most of the country as the territories and states adopted the legal background of their ancestors. However, not all of the states have taken the same date as the start of their individual jurisprudence.[14]

By constitutional provision, New York takes as its legal background "such parts of the common law, and of the acts of the legislature of the colony of New York, as together did form the law of the said colony, on the nineteenth day of April, one thousand seven hundred seventy-five, and the resolutions of the congress of said colony, and of the convention of the State of New York in force on the twentieth day of April, one thousand seven hundred seventy-seven, which have not since expired, or been repealed or altered." Florida patriotically fixed July 4, 1776, as the date of which "the common and statute laws of England which are of a general and not a local nature" were accepted as the foundation of State law.[15]

But all of the common law states have used some date between the fourth year of the reign of James the First and the signing of the Declaration of Independence as the time of their adoption of the common law. Yet even in 1776, there was no urban population worthy of the term as it is used today. Early American colonial society, to which the common law was transplanted and adapted, essentially was an agrarian society.[16] The body of the law had developed to meet the needs of a small, predominantly rural, society. It seems to furnish a suitable background against which to view the major influences attributable to the increasing urbanization of our population.

Growth of Urban Areas and Laws, 1790 to 1950

According to the first decennial census of the United States, only 200,000 out of almost 4 million persons lived in urban areas in 1790. In other words, approximately 5 out of every 100 persons resided in urban territory. By 1950, more than 96 million out of a total of about 150 million persons lived in urban areas, or 64 per cent of the entire population. In the 160-year period, therefore, almost two-thirds of the inhabitants of our country have come to reside in urban areas.

Paralleling urban growth, a tremendous amount of legislation has been enacted. Some of it illustrates the effect of the metropolis upon the property rights and interests of the people in our cities. Under earlier constitutional theories which prevailed from the late 1700's until the early 1900's, such legislation was chiefly the product of state action. More recently, under constitutional theories of much broader and more flexible patterns, a vast number of federal statutes have invaded areas theretofore thought to be sacred to the states. In addition, there has always been an even greater and overwhelming quantity of local laws. These local laws have been passed by thousands of lesser legislative bodies which owe their existence to the desire of groups who live together to be self-governing in local matters. This is the case even though local groups now depend upon a great central government with vast taxing powers for security and welfare and protection from economic and social ills.

As urban centers continue to multiply and grow, their problems become more complex and the volume of federal, state, and local legislative enactments continues to increase. As the Lord High Chancellor of Great Britain remarked in 1953, "the truth of the matter lies in this that the greater the complexity of modern life, the greater the need of regulation."[17]

The Pattern of Statutory Law

Among the various state statutes, those which reflect influences of the metropolis form a common pattern. By their subject matter, they are of two general types. One is the creation of (and grant of power to) lesser and local municipal corporations, such as cities, villages, towns, housing authorities, redevelopment corporations, park districts, school authorities, planning boards, and similar bodies. The other is the establishment of general rules of law and overriding limitations, primarily resulting from an exercise of some phase of the police power, or relating to the creation and conveyance of rights of property.

An analysis of state statutory enactments indicates that the more important kinds of legislation fall into a pattern somewhat like that given in Table 14.

Municipal Ordinances

The states have generally delegated a great variety of local powers to their cities and other urban municipalities. In turn, cities and villages, pursuant to the powers granted, have legislated upon innumerable aspects of property law. Building codes, sanitary requirements, fire prevention procedures, requirements as to streets and open spaces for public use, mechanics for obtaining public improvements at the expense of the realty favorably affected, paving, drainage, water supply, sewers, and a multitude of other requirements are reflected in such ordinances. Municipal legislation in particular has the effect of subordinating the right of an individual to do as he pleases to the will of the community in which he lives.

As the pressures generated by the ever-increasing number of persons living in the same limited area rise, so do the laws and ordinances. Consequently, a person who acquires ownership of a lot in a city may be compelled against his will and judgment to install (or at least to pay the cost of installing) sidewalks, pavement, and water and sewer connections. When he builds a house, he may be obliged to submit his plans and specifications to city officials, secure a

TYPES OF STATE LEGISLATION

DELEGATION OF LOCAL POWER

Private Corporations Having A Public Character

Housing Corporations
Neighborhood Redevelopment Corporations
Street Railroad Corporations

Primary Municipal Corporations

Cities
Villages

POWERS

Regulations Affecting Private Property

Building Construction Standards
Bulk and Location of Buildings
Health Regulations
Safety Regulations
Business Use Regulations
Nuisance Abatement
Building Destruction and Removal
Specialized Land-Use Regulations
Subdivision Development Regulations

Direct Governmental Activity

Planning and Coordinating City Development
Slum Rehabilitation and Redevelopment
Industrial Buildings Development for Private Enterprise
Alteration of City Boundaries
Acquisition and Disposal of Real Property
Provision and Regulation of Public Ways
Provision and Regulation of Public Utilities
Local Improvements by Special Assessments
Taxation

Creation of Ancillary Municipal Corporations

Land Clearance Commission
Housing Authorities
Conservation Authorities

Other Municipal Corporations

Drainage Districts
Mosquito Abatement Districts
Park Districts
Public Health Districts
School Districts
Sanitary Districts
Transit Authorities

GENERAL STATUTES

Regulation

Health
Safety
Landlord and Tenant
Public Nuisances
Eminent Domain Procedures

Participation

Assistance and Cooperation in the Fields of Housing, Land Clearance and Redevelopment

Property Interests

Actions
Administration of Estates
Conveyances
Exemptions
Highways
Interests of Husband and Wife
Mortgages
Statute of Frauds
Surveys
Wills

173

permit to build on his own land, and conform to endless city requirements concerning the structure. An analysis of the city ordinances of New York is shown in Table 15.

The Volume and Burdens of Controls

Any given piece of city realty is subject to multiple controls and regulations. These are found in statutes, ordinances, rules, and regulations of many overlapping public bodies within whose jurisdiction the property lies. As metropolitan areas grow in size and complexity, the number of public bodies increases to meet the specific problems which result. For all public bodies have a tendency to meet specific problems by exerting their legislative powers and enacting laws of broad enough scope to encompass the known problems and all related problems which the law makers can foresee. Fig. 2 indicates a number

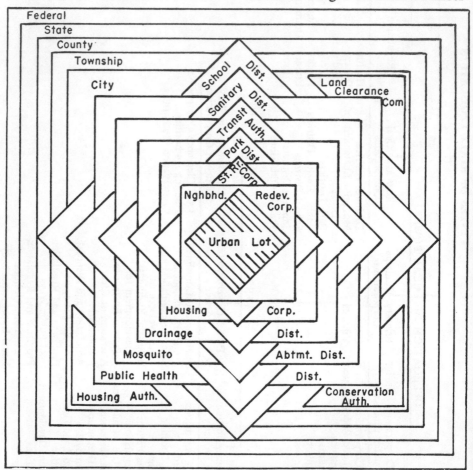

FIG. 2. THE MAZE OF POLITICAL AND CORPORATE ENTITIES HAVING POWER TO AFFECT AN URBAN LOT.

Table 15

NEW YORK CITY ORDINANCES DIRECTLY AFFECTING CITY REALTY

ORDINANCES

CLASSIFICATION OF BUILDINGS

By Occupancy

By Type of Construction

CONSTRUCTION REGULATIONS

Means of Egress
Materials, Loads and Stresses
Workmanship
Excavations
Foundations
Masonry Construction
Reinforced Concrete Construction
Iron and Steel Construction
Wood Construction
Glass Veneer
Fire Resistive Materials
Heating Appliances, Combustion
  and Chimneys
Elevators
Plumbing and Gas Piping
Sprinkler Systems
Standpipe Systems
Boilers
Signs
Ventilation
Precautions during Building
  Operations

MISCELLANEOUS REGULATIONS

Restrictions as to Location
Fire Limits
Restrictions as to Height and Area
Restrictions on Projections and
  Construction beyond the
  Building Line and within the
  Curb Line
Rent Control
Nuisances
Repairs of Buildings
Drainage
Paving of Yards and Cellars
No Discrimination or Segregation
  in City Assisted Housing
City Planning Commission
Zoning
Federal and Post-War Public
  Works and Slum Clearance
  Projects

of the sources from which regulatory measures emanate and the kinds of public bodies which may have jurisdiction over a single piece of land.

These bodies may impose many (sometimes overlapping) restrictions and limitations upon a given piece of realty which falls within their jurisdiction. Many of them have powers of eminent domain. All of the public bodies are supported from taxes. Through powers to zone and regulate the details of building, cities, villages, and towns have many more direct influences on realty within their jurisdiction than do other bodies. Some have very limited powers, others much broader powers. But all are illustrations of what happens when land becomes part of a metropolitan area. Typical examples of the burdens which may be imposed by them are shown in Fig. 3.

Zoning

Possibly the most spectacular present-day influence of the metropolis upon the concepts, rules, and institutions relating to property is found in the aspect

Fig. 3. Burdens Imposed by Public Bodies on an Urban Lot.

of the police power known as zoning. Within the last generation, practically every sizable city and village has enacted zoning ordinances.

Comprehensive zoning of a whole city is intended to control the destiny of every parcel of land within its jurisdiction. Through this device, the metropolis seeks to limit by districts the character of buildings which may be erected, prescribe the areas of land which may be built upon, require observance of height limits, setbacks, building lines, and other details.[18]

This exercise of social judgment and compulsion has slight regard for the wishes of an individual landowner. It is a clear exercise of the power of a large group, intent on serving what is conceived to be the general welfare. It is in sharp contrast to a simpler social setting which would have cherished and protected the right of the individual to use his land to suit his own convenience, provided he did not affirmatively harm his neighbors. Modern zoning regulation has required the application of old principles to new facts. It has shifted the line between the permissible and the forbidden within what was formerly a field of free action.[19]

The Background

Zoning has been practiced for many years in European cities. There is some disagreement as to when it was first put in use. One author fixes the date as 1810, under a decree of Napoleon Bonaparte. Another fixes the date as 1853, in Paris. In England, the first official zoning law was the Town Planning Act, which combined zoning and planning, and was passed in 1909.[20]

Although the initial date for the United States is not certain, it is clear that as settlements grew from hamlets into cities, problems of congestion and safety became more pronounced. The attempts to solve such problems, however, are products of the twentieth century. Los Angeles apparently experimented first in this field in 1909, and the city of New York enacted the first Comprehensive Zoning Ordinance in 1916.[21] Following these starts, many ordinances were adopted, although there has been a considerable time lag between the creation of a metropolitan need for zoning and the finding of a workable legal answer to that need.

In the field of zoning, the states generally have adopted enabling acts, giving their municipalities appropriate power to enact local ordinances by which the lands and buildings of the entire municipality are controlled. Pursuant to the grant of such power, a large number of municipalities in the United States have enacted comprehensive zoning ordinances.[22]

Early zoning efforts resulted in considerable litigation, and at first many zoning ordinances were held to be invalid. A typical example of the reasoning of the courts occurred in 1925 in a case in which the zoning ordinance of Baltimore was ruled invalid. The court said:

> We have reached the conclusion, therefore, that so much of the ordinance as attempts to regulate and restrict the use of property in Baltimore city is void: First, because it deprives property owners of rights and privileges pro-

tected by the Constitution of the state; second, because such deprivation is not justified by any consideration for the public welfare, security, health, or morals apparent in the ordinance itself; and, third, because it does not require that the restrictions shall in fact be based upon any such consideration. But in reaching this conclusion we do not hold that the use of property in Baltimore city may not be regulated or restricted where such regulation or restriction is based upon such consideration.[23]

Despite early setbacks, however, the fundamental legal principles involved in zoning were finally settled in 1926 by the United States Supreme Court in the well-known case of *Village of Euclid* v. *Ambler Realty Company*.[24] In subsequent years, the principles of zoning and the legal foundation for comprehensive zoning ordinances have been established in so many cases that zoning is no longer subject to question. The *Euclid* case has been followed by the courts of last resort in most of the states. All the states, except New Mexico and Vermont, have cases either citing it with approval or following the principles there laid down.

After the fundamental principle of zoning was clearly established, there was a good deal of litigation to test the question of whether or not specific zoning ordinances were unreasonable as applied to specific property and therefore void. Many decisions have held that municipal ordinances were unreasonable and invalid as applied to the facts of particular situations.[25] But so far there does not seem to be any general feeling that the power of the courts has been misused to exercise judicial control of zoning in this manner.

Nonconforming Situations

Cities like New York, Chicago, and Los Angeles grew to large size before effective efforts were made to control their growth and development through the exercise of the police power. Much of their growth took place before there was public acceptance of the ideas of city planning and comprehensive zoning. When zoning ordinances went into effect, therefore, they were applied to situations which had accumulated over the years. And they necessarily had a prospective rather than a retroactive effect.

As a consequence, the amortization of nonconforming uses is one of the most serious problems in zoning regulations. Generally, buildings which do not conform, and uses which exist when an ordinance becomes effective, are permitted to continue. The theory has been that lawfully-erected buildings and nonconforming uses should be allowed to continue because "zoning seeks to stabilize and protect and not to destroy."[26] As a concession to existing conditions, nonconforming uses and buildings are tolerated but are not allowed to multiply.

When a nonconforming use or building is abandoned, it usually may not be reinstated. Some zoning ordinances allow rebuilding in case of destruction; others permit rebuilding only in cases of partial destruction. Generally, they do not permit an owner to tear down a nonconforming building and then erect a new nonconforming building in its place. Thus zoning depends somewhat upon the promise that time will correct past mistakes and result in greater uniformity of development.

Recent Developments and Problems

No comprehensive zoning ordinances can remain static. Urban conditions change in spite of diligent efforts to maintain the status quo. Neighborhoods alter. Buildings grow old and unfashionable. People move to new areas and new houses which contain new equipment.

To keep zoning ordinances sufficiently flexible to meet changing conditions and at the same time maintain maximum benefits from past efforts, two chief remedies are used. One is in the form of general amendments to the ordinance as they may be required. The other is in the form of specific amendments, usually made after notice and hearing before a board of appeals, relating to specific realty which suffers undue hardship from the application of the ordinance.[27]

Among recent developments in municipal zoning which are designed to meet changing conditions has been the creation of buffer zones and requirements for off-street automobile parking in connection with densely-occupied buildings. An off-street parking ordinance came before the Illinois Supreme Court in 1953. While it was ineffectual to accomplish the particular end sought because its application was too limited, the ordinance sheds some light on future developments which probably will take place in many communities.[28]

A section of the Municipal Code of Chicago required apartment buildings to provide off-street automobile parking facilities on the lot where the apartment building was maintained, at the ratio of one automobile for every three apartments. But the Code did not apply to large rooming houses or hotels. The Supreme Court of Illinois affirmed the decision of the Circuit Court that the section of the Code was invalid because it created an unlawful classification, discriminatory in its nature. The court held that differences in kind between apartment buildings and other structures did not warrant the distinction created. However, the court did state that relieving congestion in the streets is a proper legislative purpose although it was not properly accomplished by this ordinance.

Among various zoning problems still to be solved is the question of the legislative designation of private persons as proper plaintiffs in suit to enjoin zoning violations. Some cases have held that a violation of a zoning ordinance may be enjoined at the suit of a private party who can show special damage, even though there is no statute which makes express provisions for such an action by a private party. Other decisions, however, have adopted a contrary view. Some legislation is now being enacted to clarify this situation.[29]

Another problem is the administrative question which arises out of the constant pressure of individuals who seek to profit by securing a preferred classification of their holdings regardless of its effect upon the over-all situation. A third problem arises from the fact that every large metropolitan area is now composed of a number of communities which gradually have been annexed to the original city as it expanded. So far, no clear solution has indicated how to effect uniform controls of realty located in the different jurisdictions which constitute parts of the same metropolitan area. Several alternatives exist. They include regional planning, the formation of new governmental entities like the Port of New York Authority,[30] or joint action based upon unity of purpose and ideas without a single adequate compulsory entity.

New concepts of social compulsion similar to zoning have been observed in the attempted use of the legal powers of the state requiring property owners to maintain their buildings adequately so that slum-like decay and deterioration are prevented. In 1953, the General Assembly of Illinois adopted a statute, called the Urban Community Conservation Act, aimed at those ends. In broad outline, the act seeks to bring about effective and preventive cooperation between property owners and city officials in districts which are deteriorating but still have salvage possibilities before they become actual slums. The mechanics for accomplishing these purposes involve definition of the affected area, initiation of specific plans by conservation boards working with local community councils, and final judgment and ultimate power largely vested in the city council and the courts.[31]

GOVERNMENTAL ACTIVITIES

During the financial and real estate collapse of the early 1930's, federal and state governments took remedial measures aimed at many aspects of various problems. The resulting legislation was of two general types. One was a variety of emergency stopgap measures. The other encompassed long-range plans and activities in the fields of housing and real estate finance.

Despite the number and complexity of these acts, they follow a fairly simple pattern. Through governmental grant, subsidy, insurance, or active participation, federal acts have sought to provide housing and to protect individuals and lending agencies against financial disaster. In the main, state acts sought to conform to the pattern of federal acts in whatever manner was essential to permit the states and their municipalities to qualify for grants of federal aid. The states also set up the necessary entities to implement the program embodied in federal legislation. In addition, they passed mortgage moratoria laws, acts limiting the recovery of deficiency judgments against mortgagors, and similar measures to temper the storm of economic distress.

In the depression period, there were numerous legislative, executive, and judicial governmental efforts to forestall the epidemic of mortgage foreclosures, stimulate employment, strengthen existing institutions, create new agencies of real estate finance, change fundamental concepts concerning mortgage lending, and employ various aspects of the public welfare idea, including housing, slum clearance, and neighborhood redevelopment. Throughout all these efforts ran one consistent idea—that the general welfare must be served, and that whatever aided the general welfare, as it was then conceived to be, was appropriate and therefore legal.

The Concept of General Welfare

Of all legal concepts, the idea of general welfare has probably exerted the greatest influence upon the urban portion of our population. It has affected the relations of the city inhabitant with the government and increased the power of the government to reach into his daily life and control his actions.

In the depths of the depression, the United States Supreme Court showed the way toward liberalizing the concept of general welfare by resolving a constitutional argument which was as old as the federal constitution. In the case in point, the Court held that the Agricultural Adjustment Act of 1933 was unconstitutional. This decision of a pre-New Deal Court laid the foundation for changing the life of the nation. It said:

> The clause [of the federal constitution] thought to authorize the legislation, —the first,—confers upon the Congress power "to lay and collect Taxes, Duties, Imposts and Excises, to pay the Debts and provide for the common Defence and general Welfare of the United States . . ." . . . The Government concedes that the phrase "to provide for the general welfare" qualifies the power "to lay and collect taxes." The view that the clause grants power to provide for the general welfare, independently of the taxing power, has never been authoritatively accepted. Mr. Justice Story points out that if it were adopted "it is obvious that under color of the generality of the words, to 'provide for the common defence and general welfare,' the government of the United States is, in reality, a government of general and unlimited powers, notwithstanding the subsequent enumeration of specific powers." The true construction undoubtedly is that the only thing granted is the power to tax for the purpose of providing funds for payment of the nation's debts and making provision for the general welfare. . . .
>
> Since the foundation of the Nation sharp differences of opinion have persisted as to the true interpretation of the phrase. Madison asserted it amounted to no more than a reference to the other powers enumerated in the subsequent clauses of the same section; that, as the United States is a government of limited and enumerated powers, the grant of power to tax and spend for the general national welfare must be confined to the enumerated legislative fields committed to the Congress. In this view the phrase is mere tautology, for taxation and appropriation are or may be necessary incidents of the exercise of any of the enumerated legislative powers. Hamilton, on the other hand, maintained the clause confers a power separate and distinct from those later enumerated, is not restricted in meaning by the grant of them, and Congress consequently has a substantive power to tax and to appropriate, limited only by the requirement that it shall be exercised to provide for the general welfare of the United States. Each contention has had the support of those whose views are entitled to weight. This court has noticed the question, but has never found it necessary to decide which is the true construction. Mr. Justice Story, in his Commentaries, espouses the Hamiltonian position. We shall not review the writings of public men and commentators or discuss the legislative practice. Study of all these leads us to

conclude that the reading advocated by Mr. Justice Story is the correct one. While, therefore, the power to tax is not unlimited, its confines are set in the clause which confers it, and not in those of section 8 which bestow and define the legislative powers of the Congress. It results that the power of Congress to authorize expenditure of public moneys for public purposes is not limited by the direct grants of legislative power found in the Constitution.[32]

With such a concept of the general welfare, legal theories and precedents of earlier times became of little importance except as they indicated areas of inevitable change. More than ever before, the words of the legal prophet were true: "Hardly a rule of today but may be matched by its opposite of yesterday."[33]

The Federal Program

In the depression and urban atmosphere, political and social measures were geared largely to the voting power and needs of city workers. Obviously, many of the governmental agencies were created as a result of public demand for and reliance upon bigger and better government aid in the property field. Numerous agencies dealt primarily with urban realty. Their essential function, in fact, was to help to provide housing for the private individual in the metropolis. Subsequently, federal activities have become an accepted factor in the world of city realty.

With respect to realty, federal legislation created a program of power and aid of many kinds. There was federal aid to individuals, mortgage borrowers, and mortgage lenders. In most of the large cities, there was federal aid to state housing bodies and local public agencies created to aid in slum clearance and formed by cooperation with the state. Everywhere, there was federal participation in real estate transactions which theretofore the federal government had not participated in. The federal legislation gave rise to a highly complex series of inter-governmental efforts to shelter the people through public housing or private enterprise and to bring about neighborhood redevelopment by governmental cooperation with private capital.

To carry out the federal programs, governmental agencies generally operated by pouring government money or government credit into threatened areas. Some, like the Home Owners' Loan Corporation, the Reconstruction Finance Corporation, and later the Veterans' Administration, put the government directly into business contact with its citizens in connection with·their individual financial investments and obligations on mortgage loans. Some, like the Federal Housing Administration and the Federal Home Loan Bank System, employed the concept of governmental insurance. They offered both incentive and protection. They also set technical standards of performance which in many ways changed the thinking and habits and business fashions of the time. One of the most dramatic of these changes brought about public acceptance of government-insured, long-term amortized loans on urban real estate, with the principal of the mortgage being a high percentage of the value of the security. In a surprisingly short period of time, home loans of this type practically superseded what had been considered to be conservative, small percentage, fixed-term loans, which would be continued indefinitely.

As a result of these complicated legislative efforts, the Veterans' Administration, Reconstruction Finance Corporation, Federal National Mortgage Association, Community Facilities Service, Home Loan Bank Board, and a host of other legislatively-created entities function in the field of urban real estate. Some of their activities are frankly paternalistic, presumably protecting the mortgage borrower from his own ignorance or bad judgment and against the traditional money lender. Other activities seek to protect mortgage pools or investors against loss in the event of another economic collapse.

A large segment of governmental activity was dedicated primarily to the task of providing living quarters for private individuals in the cities of the nation. It took the form of assistance to a buyer in the private enterprise market, insurance of mortgage debt, public housing for people who allegedly could not afford housing offered by private enterprise, clearance of slums and redevelopment of blighted areas, control of rents according to the interests of tenants, and temporary emergency housing for war workers. Most of these areas had formerly been considered to be an individual's own responsibility. The remedies devised were typical of the political atmosphere in which they were born. They were the start of a program which developed to unprecedented proportions in a few years and whose limits cannot yet be defined.

The emergencies of World War II came upon a people considerably conditioned to governmental supervision and control. The war called forth more governmental activity than the nation ever had seen or the founding fathers could have envisioned. In addition to the ideas which by then had become commonplace, the war was characterized by further federal regulations and controls which affected the daily life of every individual. Rent control became an economic, social, and political factor. War agencies sprang into being. Existing federal programs were stepped up. There was direct building activity by the federal government to meet the housing needs of the military and industrial forces. Individual freedom of action came to an all time low. These measures had their greatest application in urban centers, for the cities carried the burden of industrial mobilization.

Table 16 shows the channels which federal governmental legislation has taken in its effort to accomplish these purposes. It also indicates the extent to which the federal government has furnished the initiative and set the pattern for every type of activity in the field of housing.

Some State Legislation

With respect to the policy of placing public housing and slum clearance in the hands of local public agencies, state legislatures have provided the necessary legislation. This legislation can be divided into two classes. The first is

Table 16

FIVE CHANNELS OF FEDERAL LEGISLATION IN THE FIELD OF HOUSING

I	II	IV
Financial Operations to Assist an Individual to Purchase a House Offered by Private Enterprise	Direct Subsidy by Way of Public Housing and Slum Clearance to Aid in Housing Private Individuals who Cannot Afford to Rent or Purchase a House Offered by Private Enterprise	Temporary Alleviation of Housing Shortages (stopgap housing)
Federal Home Loan Bank Act (1932) (a) Federal Home Loan Bank System (1932) (b) Federal Home Loan Bank Board (1932)	Emergency Relief and Construction Act (1932)	Lanham Act (1940) (utilization of wartime structures for temporary veterans' housing) Housing Act of 1950 (college housing)
Reconstruction Finance Corporation Act (1932) (a) RFC Mortgage Company (1935) (b) Prefabricated Housing Activity (Housing Act of 1948)	National Industrial Recovery Act (1933) (Housing Division of PWA) U. S. Housing Act of 1937 Housing Act of 1949	**V** Rent Control
Home Owners' Loan Act (1933) (a) HOLC (1933) (b) Federal Savings and Loan Associations (1933)	**III** Provision of Housing during Wartime	Emergency Price Control Act of 1942 Housing and Rent Act of 1947 Housing and Rent Act of 1953
National Housing Act of 1934 (a) FHA (1934) (b) Federal Savings and Loan Insurance Corporation (1934) (c) Federal National Mortgage Association (1938)	Lanham Act (1940) Defense Homes Corporation (RFC 1940) FHA (modified for wartime activity) Defense Housing and Community Facilities and Services Act of 1951	
Servicemen's Readjustment Act (1944)		
Veterans' Emergency Housing Act (1946)		
Housing Act of 1948		
Housing Act of 1950		
Defense Production Act (1950)		
Housing Amendments of 1953		

designed to carry out the federal program of financial assistance. The second is intended to solve related problems independent of federal aid. The latter class of legislation has often adopted some of the federal concepts. However, it is ordinarily characterized by predominantly local financing.

Thirty-five states, four territories, and the District of Columbia have enacted legislation authorizing local public agencies to undertake slum clearance and urban redevelopment projects. The general pattern of these statutes is to authorize the municipality, the local public housing authority, a separate redevelopment agency, or some combination of these bodies to acquire land in slum areas through exercise of the right of eminent domain. The public body is also authorized to clear the land by razing structures, construct streets and utilities, and make the land available for redevelopment by private enterprise in accordance with redevelopment plans approved by the municipality at its fair value or use value.[34] Generally, this value is less than the cost of acquisition.

As an illustration of the legislative activities of one state pertaining to housing and slum clearance, Table 17 shows the two classes of legislation enacted by the Illinois General Assembly.

Table 17
ILLINOIS HOUSING AND SLUM CLEARANCE LEGISLATION
LEGISLATION

Illinois Legislation Designed to Carry Out the Federal Program of Financial Assistance.		Illinois Legislation Designed to Solve Related Problems Independent of Federal Aid.	
Housing Authorities Act	(1934)	Housing Cooperation Law	(1937)
State Housing Act	(1933)	Neighborhood Redevelopment Corporation Act	(1941)
Blighted Areas Redevelopment Act	(1947)		
Act for Rehousing of Persons in Redevelopment Project Areas	(1947)	Blighted Vacant Areas Development Act	(1949)
		Housing Development and Construction Act (Replaced State Contribution Act—1945)	(1947)

PRIVATE RESTRICTIONS

The field of privately-imposed limitations upon the use and improvement of urban realty probably reflects most clearly the evolutionary character of the concepts and rules which are influenced by city living. With the crowding together of masses of people in a limited living area, neighborhoods are likely to change for the worse if they are not controlled by some means. If a desired atmosphere is to be preserved for long, measures are needed to stabilize conditions and limit the use of realty involved. Frequently, private restrictions are taken to supplement public acts which are aimed at these ends.[35]

Legal Basis for Private Restrictions

Generally, an owner of land who desires to control, protect, or improve an area which he is marketing may impose any restrictions he sees fit, provided such restrictions are not against public policy. Reasonable conditions imposed by appropriate legal methods become binding upon successive owners for a reasonable period of time.[36]

On the whole, legal machinery to achieve the imposition of effective private restrictions has its basis in the function of courts of equity to prevent fraud and unfair dealing. Practical enforcement rests upon the equitable doctrine of notice. In other words, a person who takes land with notice of a restriction upon it will not in equity and good conscience be permitted to act in violation of its terms.

Such restrictions do not depend for their existence upon legislative authority, which may reflect long-range community objectives as opposed to individual current thinking or unacceptable urban standards. An owner may create certain private restrictions by complying with the provisions of statutes, which set forth the requirements and procedures for platting and subdividing lands. But most restrictions do not depend upon a statute or municipal ordinance to give them vitality. They are created by individual arrangements.

So far, the imposition of reasonable restrictions is uncontrolled by public authority. However, there is some sentiment to the effect that the private limitations commonly placed upon realty may fall into an area where public control and supervision are desirable.[37] To date such a program has not received statutory sanction.

Where restrictions imposed by zoning laws differ from restrictions imposed by private covenants, neither overrules the other, but the property is subject to the burden of both.[38]

Methods Used to Create Restrictions

Frequently restrictions of the type under consideration originate in an agreement of some kind. More often than not, this agreement is embodied in and reflected by a deed of conveyance. It constitutes a covenant, which, because it affects the enjoyment of the land, thereby runs with the land. As such, it passes with the conveyance of title and becomes binding upon successive owners.[39] Ordinary restrictive covenants permit or prohibit specified uses without attempting to impose a penalty of defeating the title in case of violation.

In addition to occurring in deeds, real covenants running with the land may be found in a lease or in an agreement apart from a lease or deed. Or the limitations may arise out of equitable restrictions or equitable servitudes. In the famous case of *Tulk* v. *Moxhay,* an English court laid down the principle in 1848 that where an owner of land enters into a contract that he will use or abstain from using his land in a particular way or manner, equity will enforce the agreement against any purchaser or possessor with notice who attempts to use the land in violation of its terms, irrespective of whether the agreement creates a valid covenant running with the land at law or not.[40]

Generally, any agreement which fails to satisfy the formal requirements concerning a covenant running with the land at law may create an equitable restriction if it comes under this principle. Common practical examples are furnished by an agreement by implication, or one resulting from a general building plan or scheme.

Restrictions may also be produced by methods which contain at least a continuing threat that violation will result in loss of title. This may be done by the ancient device of an estate upon condition subsequent, created in a deed or will. Such restrictions depend for their vitality and enforcement upon a right of re-entry for condition broken. Or they may owe their origin to another estate, subject to a special limitation created in a deed or will, which depends for effective enforcement upon the possibility of reverter.[41] Sometimes restrictions arise out of an estate subject to an executory limitation created in a will or deed.

Practical Operations

In laying out urban communities or in selling lots or houses, subdividers have customarily imposed many restrictions upon the property in addition to socially-imposed limitations, such as zoning, which may exist. The most common restrictions upon city realty relate to the improvement of the land and the character, location, size, and use of buildings.

Restrictions aimed at controlling the use to which realty may be put by successive owners include limitations as to the type of buildings which may be erected; prohibitions against erection or occupancy for business or public purposes; prohibitions against certain businesses or trades; or limitations on the sale or occupancy to persons of a stated race, color, or creed.

Other restrictions are aimed at controlling a uniform or otherwise acceptable type of improvement. These include provisions defining the size or shape of buildings, the number of families to be accommodated, or the materials used; limiting the height of buildings; setting minimum cost standards; imposing an obligation to build or maintain a fence, or not to do so; and prohibiting embankments or buildings disconnected from the main building. Still other restrictions may contain specific provisions to control the location of buildings by establishing buildings lines. Such restrictions are frequently shown upon the plat of the subdivision.

From a review of cases which have been decided by courts of last resort, the experience of subdividers and purchasers of closely-built realty discloses a need for taking steps designed to preserve the values and appearances of neighborhoods. To accomplish such control, wholesalers of realty and individual owners have followed the practice of imposing restrictions of various kinds upon neighborhoods in which they operate. In doing so, they have employed established legal principles of long standing, and their efforts generally have been effective in many areas for substantial periods of time. But private restrictions have never been a complete or satisfactory solution to the problem of preserving the status quo. Ultimately, other pressures become apparent which cause many of these efforts to give way to the superior forces of evolutionary legal change.

The Shortcomings of Restrictions

As generally used, privately-imposed restrictions are far from an adequate substitute for over-all city planning. They are an individualistic approach to the problem of preserving a desired condition for a limited time in a limited area. They lack the compulsion of a public law enforced by public officials who may impose a rigid pattern of integrated supervision upon everyone concerned.

Restrictions are neither self-policing nor self-enforcing. They exist and their effect persists only so long as they are conformed to. When violations begin, some private person must bring suit at his own expense to enjoin the violation or enforce other rights. Otherwise the violation will go unchallenged and additional violations of the same or an aggravated kind will occur. Once a breakdown goes unchallenged, courts refuse to enforce restrictive covenants, basing their action upon the principle of equitable estoppel or abandonment.[42] They also refuse to enforce an equitable restriction when a neighborhood changes or when circumstances become so altered that enforcement is undesirable.

Moreover, changed urban conditions frequently cause possibilities of reverter and rights of entry to become unwanted and inflexible burdens upon land and titles. In order to permit some measure of control over these technical interests and make them responsive to the changes which inevitably occur in city neighborhoods, a number of legislatures have passed remedial statutes. In general, such statutes take one of two forms. One form seeks to limit the duration of the interest to a given period of time.[43] The other seeks to bar actions to enforce the interest unless the action is commenced with fair promptness after a right of action comes into existence.[44]

Race Restrictions

The race restriction is probably the most controversial of all private restrictions. It clearly portrays an effect of the metropolis upon the legal concepts and rules of law relating to property. During the last generation, there has been a great influx of colored people into crowded industrial areas which theretofore had been predominantly white. This influx, and the entry of many Asiatics into the western cities, have intensified many of the latent difficulties of race relations which often exist in rural as well as urban areas.

Until the late 1940's, race restrictions applicable to realty generally were considered to be an effective means of preserving neighborhoods for white occupancy and ownership. In many cities over a long period of time, owners in some sections customarily covenanted that they would not sell or lease to Negroes. Sellers often inserted into deeds of conveyance provisions designed to limit the sale of realty and its occupancy to members of the white race.

But within a comparatively short period of time, attacks upon the principles involved produced notable changes in the application of legal doctrines which at one time seemed settled. In 1948, the cases of *Shelley* v. *Kraemer* and *McGhee* v. *Sipes* were decided together before the United States Supreme Court.[45] At that time, the Court ruled that "we hold that in granting judicial enforcement of the restrictive agreements [against use or occupancy of property by Negroes or non-Caucasians] in these cases, the States have denied petitioners the equal protection of the laws and that, therefore, the action of the State courts [sustaining the restrictions] cannot stand." The Court's ruling in the *Shelley* case was cited in 1953 in *Barrows* v. *Jackson*.[46] Then the Court held that a racial restrictive covenant could not be enforced at law by a suit for damages against a co-covenantor who allegedly broke the covenant.

Other examples involving racial problems further illustrate the change which has recently occurred in judicial attitudes toward a constitutional principle inherent in the sale and conveyance of real estate. There have been numerous cases in the fields of education, transportation, public eating places, recreational areas, and public housing.[47]

But constitutional provisions, statutory enactments, court rulings, or administrative regulations do not wipe out racial prejudice by themselves. In the metropolis, efforts are still being made to find effective ways to accomplish racial segregation which recent court decisions have condemned. Since the case of *Shelley* v. *Kraemer*, "realty men had devised at least two ways of barring Negroes from new white neighborhoods without resorting to covenants. Under one plan, used in Washington and elsewhere, developers require home buyers to guarantee them exclusive listing of the house if it is ever offered for resale. Another dodge is a neighborhood club. By limiting sales in a tract to club members, the members can exclude anyone they choose.

"Both systems work most effectively in new developments. The nation's chief battle over segregation was being fought out in older neighborhoods. And there, though segregation was dying hard, bit by little bit the evidence grew that it was dying."[48]

COMMERCIALLY ACCEPTABLE URBAN REAL ESTATE TITLES

There is no uniform standard as to what constitutes a commercially acceptable real estate title. In each area, the problem is a local matter based upon historical developments of local or sectional character. In all cases, however, there is the question of demonstrating that a title to realty is adequate so that a purchaser will pay his money for it or a mortgage lender will accept it as security.

Methods Used to Determine Acceptability

Among different cities in the United States, one of four methods is generally used to determine what an acceptable title is. These methods include searching records, abstracts of title, title insurance, and the Torrens System.

The oldest method is a direct search of the public records by lawyers. Once the records are searched, the lawyers judge the results and give opinions as to the quality of the title. This system continues to be common to many of the rural and smaller urban areas of the eastern states. Where it is employed, the examining lawyers makes their own investigations and furnish their clients with opinions of title. The lawyers, in effect, perform what in other areas is done by a combination of the abstracter and title examiner.

In much of the country, abstracts of title are used as the chief method of determining whether or not a title is acceptable. An abstract is usually prepared by an abstracting company engaged in that business. The function of the abstract is to reflect all matters of public record which may affect the title to the property involved. An examining lawyer then examines the abstract and renders his opinion, limiting it to the quality of title revealed by the abstract.

A third method of determining the acceptability of a title is title insurance. In some areas, the willingness of a title insurance company to insure title has become the test of its acceptability. The Supreme Court of California stated in 1948 that "title insurance is a contract to indemnify against loss through defects in the title or against liens or encumbrances that may affect the title at the time when the policy is issued. . . . It is a reasonable method by which a vendee may determine the merchantability of the vendor's title . . ."[49]

This method is ordinarily used in most of the large cities throughout the country. Other jurisdictions employ title insurance as one of several methods to determine whether a title is acceptable. Or they may use title insurance when a title is sound but technically unmerchantable so that a sale or mortgage could not be consummated in the absence of a policy acceptable to the parties and their counsel.

A fourth method is to furnish a Torrens certificate which reflects the character of the vendor's title. The availability of the Torrens System is limited to a small proportion of the transactions which occur in about one per cent of the counties of the United States. These counties are located in a few states which have adopted legislation authorizing its use.

The Test of Acceptability

The test of what constitutes an acceptable title has been in a process of commercial evolution paralleling the growth of urban areas in which most real estate transactions take place. In practical effect, the earlier idea of an acceptable title involved the concept of a substantially flawless title perfectly connected by a chain of conveyances from the original sovereign to the present owner. Every element of the chain of title was disclosed by the public record, and none presented a substantial question.

The later idea of an acceptable title concerns a title which, despite some imperfections, is sufficiently sound so that a purchaser may buy it with reasonable confidence in his ability to enjoy fully the usual rights of ownership, and in his ability to satisfy a subsequent purchaser or mortgage lender that he, in turn, will acquire adequate rights. As a practical matter, buyers, sellers, and mortgage lenders have increasingly come to require some means of accomplishing their desired ends quickly with reasonable safety but without concern for unnecessary technical perfection.[50]

What makes a title acceptable? According to a general rule, unless a contract for the sale of real estate provides otherwise, the seller ordinarily must convey to the purchaser a marketable title. Such a title may also be called a merchantable or good title.[51]

The essence of the rule of marketable title is that when a real estate sales contract, by express terms or legal effect, requires the purchaser to convey a marketable title, the contract purchaser cannot be compelled against his wish to accept a doubtful title which may reasonably and fairly be questioned or which has defects which would materially impair its marketable quality. In other words, a marketable title is a substantially flawless title of such high quality that a court of equity will force it upon an unwilling contract purchaser.

The original concept of a marketable title was that it must be fairly deducible from the record and be supported by a connected chain of transfers, each of which was adequate and adequately demonstrated by the record. In later years a number of factors have influenced legal and public opinion concerning the suitability of the test of traditional marketability. The country has grown older, some sections have developed techniques for judging titles which differ from those formerly used, the volume of real estate transfers has increased, and real estate title chains have lengthened to cover long periods of time between the original grant and the present.

As a result, many questions have been reconsidered, such as the period of time to be covered by a title search, the weight to be given to many kinds of imperfections of differing degrees, and the kind of evidence of title which proves locally satisfactory to those persons who put their funds into real estate and who are concerned with the unquestioned right of possession and ability to dispose of their realty and have its title freely accepted by purchasers and mortgagees. Consequently, the original pure doctrine of merchantable title deducible from the record, like many other principles of law, has yielded somewhat to the pressures of commercial development and local practices.[52]

Under the marketable title rule, an examining lawyer always has taken a most conservative view with regard to even minor imperfections which render a title less than perfect of record. For his own protection against subsequent examiners, he must raise every minor imperfection and insist upon its elimination, by litigation, if necessary. Otherwise he could expect that one day an irate client would confront him with the circumstance that a subsequent examiner for a prospective purchaser refused to permit consummation of a sale unless and until the imperfection was removed, or, worse still, rejected the proffered title because of it, even though it had little merit.

The necessity of raising unessential imperfections as objections is a serious burden which brings lawyers into disrepute with their clients and causes them much inconvenience and trouble. More important, it causes their clients delay, vexation, and the expenditure of what they consider to be uncalled-for sums of money for attorneys' fees and court costs in litigation required to eliminate objections which may hold no real threat but which will in turn be raised by every subsequent examiner for his own protection rather than that of his client. In an urban economy, where business men are accustomed to the directness, simplicity, and assurance of conducting large commercial and credit transactions according to the customs of the Stock Exchange and the banking world, these practices have developed a demand for principles and procedures more analogous to those applicable to personalty.

The Remedies Evolved

To facilitate real estate transactions and meet the difficulties inherent in the full re-examination of title upon every sale or mortgage of land, four types of remedy have been evolved. They include legislation, agreements among title examiners as to common procedures and attitudes toward title objections, contract provisions for an insurable title, and title registration under the Torrens System.

Legislation: Some phases of the problem of what constitutes an acceptable title to real estate are reflected in legislation of fairly recent origin. In 1945, Michigan adopted a Marketable Record Title Act. In substance, it provides that an owner in possession "who has an unbroken chain of title of record for forty years, shall at the end of such period be deemed to have a marketable record title to such interest . . ." Whether or not such a conclusion is judicial opinion or is within the realm of the legislative branch of the state government remains to be seen. In addition to its Marketable Record Title Act, Michigan has many other acts designed to simplify title examinations. Similar marketable title acts may be found in Illinois, Indiana, Iowa, Minnesota, Nebraska, North and South Dakota, and Wisconsin.[53]

In Vermont, statutes concerning investments by savings banks, trust companies, and insurance companies have been amended to recognize title insurance as the equivalent of marketable title. The statute requires such real estate mortgage investments to "be supported by either evidence satisfactory to the bank that the title is marketable or a mortgagee's title insurance policy. . . ."[54]

Kentucky and Vermont have amended their statutes to indicate that title insurance is an acceptable means of overcoming defects in a title. Kentucky's insurance statute requires loans to be secured by mortgages on "fee simple, unencumbered, improved real property." Effective September 1, 1950, the statute was amended to provide that a number of elements which normally would cause unmarketability, such as easements, joint driveways, or current taxes, are not to be considered as prior liens or encumbrances. In this category, it includes "restrictions or conditions as to building, use and occupancy if there is not a right of re-entry or forfeiture for violation, or if there is protection against any such right of re-entry or forfeiture through a policy of title insurance."[55]

Vermont has the simplest test. By amendment passed in 1947, insurance company mortgages must be supported either by satisfactory evidence that the title is marketable or by a "mortgagee's title insurance policy." This requirement may be omitted only if the principal of the loan is less than $1,000.[56]

Many states now have amended their statutes of limitation to give them greater efficacy in eliminating old claims or interests. These statutes are grounded on the theory that certainty and marketability outweigh the giving of undue protection to the legally disabled. Federal governmental agencies dealing with real estate mortgages, however, do not use marketable title as a test of acceptable title but have based their operations on titles which are locally acceptable.[57]

Agreements among title examiners: In some parts of the country, agreements have been made among lawyers who are members of the state or local Bar Associations as to what shall be considered proper objections to a title. As a consequence, a number of Bar Associations have developed so-called Rules for Title Examination, which in effect are codes of agreed practices concerning title defects. Some of these codes, as in Connecticut, are state-wide, elaborate, and formal. Others are only county-wide in application. Their purpose is to excuse lawyers from liability for not raising every objection which might interfere with strict marketability. They are based upon the idea that if there is a uniform and common course of not raising inconsequential objections, nobody will be hurt. Because of the unofficial character and differences of legal views regarding the codes, not all lawyers are willing to rely upon them. Lack of unanimous agreement renders them largely ineffective.

In Iowa, the Supreme Court recently decided a marketable title case on the authority of a standard set up by the Title Standards Committee of the Iowa State Bar. South Dakota has done likewise. In Nebraska, the Supreme Court set aside its first opinion in a case, granting a rehearing, and reversed its earlier ruling to achieve the result indicated by one of these title standards.[58]

Contract provisions for an insurable, as distinguished from a marketable, title: In many sections of the country, by common custom among lawyers, their clients, and real estate brokers, contracts for the sale of real estate have generally become silent on the question of marketability. They substitute in its stead the willingness of a named title insurance or guarantee company to issue its insurance policy, either in the first instance or as a cure for objections which may be raised by the purchaser's attorney upon the examination of an abstract of title. Such contract provisions have become common in cities within the states of California, Illinois, New Jersey, New York, Pennsylvania, and Washington.[59]

By this practice, a sound title which is subject to defects which prevent it from being technically marketable is nevertheless made commercially acceptable. As a matter of commercial usage, a title of this quality can be readily sold to a reasonably prudent purchaser, or mortgaged to a person of a reasonable prudence as security for the loan of money. Many titles which do not meet the test of true legal marketability nevertheless are sound in spite of the defects which render them technically unmarketable. Being sound, they are defensible and insurable. So long as they are protected by a suitable title policy, they are saleable and acceptable to purchasers and lenders. In effect, contract provisions of this type make insurability the final test in the community of the acceptability of title. Such an arrangement obviates questions associated with marketability which heretofore have plagued lawyers, real estate men, and sellers.[60]

One of the important results of this practice is to broaden the base for lending transactions and sales of real estate by making it possible for mortgage lenders safely to accept as collateral, or for purchasers to accept without concern, perfect titles and marketable titles as well as titles which are subject to defects which render them technically unmarketable, provided they still are sound, defensible, and insurable.

Title registration under the Torrens System: A peculiarly urban effort to make titles more attractive is furnished by the Torrens System. Between 1897 and 1917, nineteen states adopted statutes authorizing the registration of land under the Torrens System and one additional state adopted a constitutional amendment authorizing such legislation but never went further. No other state has adopted a Torrens act since 1917. Four states subsequently repealed their Torrens statutes, four made negligible use of them, and five more very slight use.

In the United States, there are 3,072 counties. In only 33 counties—located in the states of California, Illinois, Massachusetts, Minnesota, and Ohio—has the Torrens System ever become a factor in establishing or evidencing an acceptable title to real estate. Even so, it was used in only a minor proportion of the possible cases.[61]

LEASES, LAND TRUSTS, AIR RIGHTS, AND COOPERATIVE APARTMENTS

Among various techniques employed in the joint use of land and in the establishment and conveyance of joint rights in realty are included leases, land trusts, air rights, and cooperative apartments.

Leases

Like other phases of the law, the legal relationship between landlord and tenant has felt the pressure of city living. In every sizable city, many people come under its direct influence. As a result, the traditional autocracy of the landlord has been modified over the years by principles of law responsive to the needs of tenants who inhabit city apartment houses and do business in rented stores, factories, and offices.

In the area of state legislation, this modification has been accomplished by statutes covering many aspects of the problem. Some of these statutes concern the creation and termination of the landlord-tenant relationship, the necessity of written leases, and requirements for the giving of notices in advance of the date of termination. Other statutes pertain to rent control, evictions, prohibition of the exclusion of children in rented residential accommodations, and special treatment of leases which involve the granting of rent concessions. Municipal legislation has chiefly emphasized laws concerning practical items like the obligation to keep rented buildings repaired and in safe and healthful condition.

The judicial area has dealt with problems of commercial frustration, where premises were leased for limited specified purposes and governmental acts or regulations and restrictions have prohibited or seriously interfered with such use. Decisions have been concerned with tenancies of uncertain duration, constructive eviction, assignments of leases, renewals, extensions, trade fixtures, options, subletting of the demised premises, destruction of (or serious damage to) leased buildings and buildings in which leased premises are located, the effect of condemnation of leased premises, and the relative rights of mortgagee and lessee upon foreclosure of a mortgage upon the leased realty.[62]

Agreements between landlord and tenant have kept pace with other urban commercial developments. Rentals frequently are agreed upon according to formulae. They may be related to some percentage of the lessee's sales or profits. Or they may be adjustable through escalator clauses or through provisions for periodic adjustments to accord with future valuations of the premises.

Long-term leases with payment of ground rents and construction of buildings by the tenant have become common in the larger cities. Where this device is used, numerous complicated legal relationships result. In a large project, property rights become split up and diversely held. Different individuals or groups may own the fee, mortgages on the fee, the basic leasehold, corporate shares in different corporations which hold various interests, leases from the basic lessee to the tenants of a building which is constructed on the land by the lessee, subleases by the tenants, and frequently a mortgage on the leasehold estate.

Sale of the underlying fee or sale of the building by the basic lessee involves intricate, technical, and coordinated legal procedures. There have to be necessary conveyances of rights under the parent lease, assignments of rights under the building leases, transfers of corporate shares, the giving of notices and holding of required meetings of directors and shareholders of the various corporate entities involved, the preparation of new mortgages and the paying off and releasing of old mortgages, the examination and clearing of titles, and the securing of satisfactory evidence of title.

These larger metropolitan real estate deals have become so complicated that the sale and conveyance of buildings like the Empire State Building and the Chrysler-Graybar group of buildings receive wide comment in the public press. Even the weekly picture magazines emphasize the money involved, the great number of documents required, and the diverse interests which are affected and are represented by counsel.

Land Trusts

A distinctively urban solution of some of the problems of holding title to city realty is found in land trusts. They have become popular within fairly recent times. The creation of a land trust, its operation, and the ultimate conveyance of the realty involved employ the use of settled principles of contract law and of trust law. Generally, title to realty is vested in a corporate trustee under the terms of a deed in trust and an unrecorded trust agreement. Actual management and control of the realty so held is enjoyed by undisclosed beneficiaries of the trust.

Among other things, the deed in trust and trust agreement provide powers to the trustee which, insofar as third persons are concerned, are adequate to enable it to do all of those things which an owner holding title in his own name normally could do. In addition, they provide that the trustee will deal with the title to the real estate only upon the direction of persons named in the agreement, whose names are not disclosed by the public record.

Under the arrangement, both the legal and equitable titles to the realty are vested in the trustee.[63] The rights and conveniences of ownership are exercised by the beneficiary of the trust, whose interest likewise is not disclosed of record. The beneficiary of such a trust may be an individual. Or the beneficiaries may be a group of persons interested in one building, a syndicate marketing a subdivision by means of installment sales, an unincorporated professional group which lacks legal capacity to hold title to realty, or builders of many small homes.

The vesting of title in the trustee affords convenience and protection both in the holding of title and in the execution of deeds to individual purchasers. Frequently, the trust arrangement vests in a manager for the beneficiaries the authority to direct the trustee concerning the execution of deeds, contracts, or mortgages which may be required from time to time. Management of the realty, collection of rents, collections of installments due under sales contracts, payment of taxes and insurance, and all such matters are reserved to the beneficiaries of the trust.[64]

Under carefully prepared forms of deed in trust and trust agreement, the interest of the beneficiary is specifically provided to be personalty which may be assigned with less formality than is required in the execution of a deed.[65] By its terms, a mortgage of realty so held may limit recovery to the realty pledged, without personal liability being assumed by any of the parties to the transaction.

In connection with city realty in particular, such an arrangement frequently affords the advantages of privacy of ownership, escape from problems which arise under some forms of multiple ownership when one interested person dies, simplicity in the holding and conveyance of title, and freedom from some risks inherent in other types of joint ownership and control which arise out of human problems like divorce, litigation, judgments, and disagreements which might provoke partition suits.

Air Rights

An interesting development of the joint utilization of land occurs with respect to air rights. One owner may use most of the surface of the land. At the same time, another owner may have sufficient rights in the same tract to allow the construction of a foundation for a building which occupies the air above the land. Ordinarily, this joint utilization is accomplished by a conveyance of air rights as well as rights in the underlying land which will permit the construction and maintenance of the building.

The use of air rights seems to be most common in cases where city land is used by a railroad. Frequently, a building may be constructed over the railroad right-of-way with foundation supports located between existing tracks. By so doing, the surface use of the railroad is substantially uninterfered with, and the bulk of the building occupying the air space lies above a suitable level to permit uninterrupted rail operations. In New York, railroads run under Park Avenue. In Chicago, the Merchandise Mart, the Daily News Building, and the Prudential Building have all been built by utilizing air rights.

Familiar legal principles and devices permit such a solution. The owner of the land retains rights of ownership and occupancy needed to permit his desired operations. He conveys other rights which will permit the construction and maintenance of a foundation and supporting pillars to a given level. Above this level, a building can be erected to rest upon the foundation below.[66]

In the law of real property, it is a general principle that the owner of the fee simple estate in land also owns the space above it. This principle was originally expressed in the maxim, *cujus est solum ejus est usque ad coelum* (he who owns the soil or surface of the ground owns, or has an exclusive right to, everything which is upon or above it to an indefinite height).[67]

But aerial navigation has brought about essential modifications of this broadly stated generality, and further modifications are inevitable. As airplanes increase in speed, size, and importance, airports have to be enlarged. In addition to the actual airports which they use, modern airplanes require a longer approach to runways, particularly when they approach for instrument landings in bad weather. In the approach area, high buildings, smokestacks, radio towers and similar objects can be the cause of serious accidents which affect the airplane, its passengers, and persons within crowded metropolitan areas beneath the traffic pattern. Tragic examples occur all too often. Legislation concerning the means and extent of federal control of the use of lands adjoining airports therefore seems certain.[68]

In modern times it has become settled law that the air space, excluding the immediate reaches above the land, is part of the public domain. This modification has not extinguished the right of the owner of urban land not subject to the problems of air commerce to exercise a dominant right of occupancy for purposes incident to his use and enjoyment of the surface and that portion of the air space which he may reasonably expect to use and occupy.[69]

Within physical limitations, the surface owner may build to any height he desires. He may also sell this air space to other persons to build on while he retains the ownership and use of the surface. It has long been established that one may own a house, or only one room of a house, in fee without owning the land.[70]

In 1787, an English court pointed out how the metropolis had already adopted the idea of multiple use of the same area:

> Now, it seems to me, that the construction of all deeds must be made with a reference to their subject-matter. And it may be necessary to put a different construction on leases made in populous cities, from that on those made in the country. We know that in London different persons have several freeholds over the same spot; different parts of the same house are let out to different people. That is the case in the Inns of Court.[71]

The recognition of the value of air space on the real estate market has led New Jersey to enact a statute which states in part:

> Estates, rights and interests in areas above the surface of the ground, whether or not contiguous thereto, may be validly created in persons or corporations other than the owner or owners of the land below such areas, and shall be deemed to be estates, rights and interests in lands.[72]

Illinois also has a statute allowing railroads to sell or lease real estate at, above, or below the surface of the ground, providing there is no impairment of the railroad's operations. The Illinois act is a reflection of the procedures actually used in accomplishing effective use of air rights. In effect it gave legislative approval to what was being done in the area of conveyances of air rights.[73]

In conveying air rights, the land and the air above it are commonly subdivided into lots or parcels capable of ascertainment and conveyance. The situation generally requires three types of identifiable lots. One is a cylindrical lot in which a caisson will be sunk; the second is a prism lot sufficient to accommodate a steel pillar running between the caisson and the building proper; and the third is the air lot above some specified level to which the pillars will reach. Figs. 4 and 5 indicate how this is done.

As shown in Fig. 4, the land area involved is subdivided into circular, or caisson, lots. The center of each lot is the intersection of two range lines which are expressly created to locate the caisson lots. The first range line in each

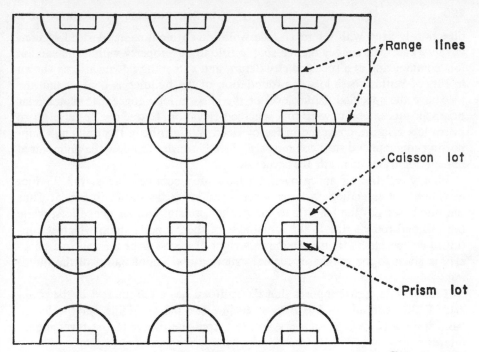

FIG. 4. IDENTIFICATION OF CAISSON AND PRISM LOTS FOR THE CONVEYANCE OF AIR RIGHTS.

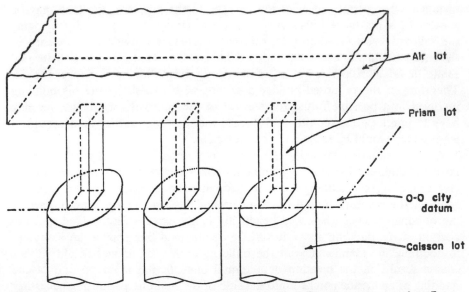

FIG. 5. LAND AND AIR SPACE CONVEYED IN FEE SIMPLE FOR AN AIR LOT.

direction is fixed with reference to a well-known monument. A deed of conveyance can then convey the fee simple title to all property within the caisson lots commencing at a specified city datum and extending downward, as shown in Fig. 5. Within these lots, the foundation of the building is constructed.

Above the specified datum level of the caisson lots, concentric rectangular prism air lots extend upward to a specified elevation, frequently 23 feet. These prism lots also are conveyed in fee by deed. Within them, the building's supporting concrete and steel columns are placed in order to allow the unimpaired passage of trains beneath the structure.

Finally, all the air space over the land area commencing at the 23 foot elevation and extending upwards is conveyed in fee, as shown in Fig. 5. Thus the purchaser has the fee title to the caisson, prism, and air space lots, while the railroad retains title to the remainder of the property upon which it continues to operate its trains. An express right of access over the railroad property is given to the purchaser for construction and maintenance of the building.

This technique presupposes that the railroad has a fee interest in the property. If the railroad has less than a fee interest, the air rights may be leased from it, or a conveyance may be secured from the owner of the reversionary interest.

Another method of accomplishing the same end is to have the entire property conveyed except the space below a designated height, and excepting from the exception the right to place supports and pillars within the excepted space.

Every situation of this general type, of course, is unique and involves technical engineering and legal problems of potentially serious character. For instance, when a railroad owns the fee title to the property, the land may be subject to a mortgage either specifically describing it or generally pledging the railroad's assets. Frequently, railroad mortgages provide for a release of the mortgage in the event the railroad has sold or contracted to sell its real estate or other property, but not if it merely grants a lease or an easement. Therefore, if the proposed builder does not wish to risk having his building involved in a possible future foreclosure of the railroad's mortgage, he may have to purchase the fee title and release the mortgage rather than acquire a lease which would be subject to the mortgage.

Another situation involving air rights may arise when a city exercises its power of eminent domain in widening narrow streets to accommodate modern city traffic or in extending a street through a large building. Here again a solution sometimes is found by condemning the land and whatever part of the building reaches a specfied height above the street. Or the land and the portion of the building above it may be condemned but granted an easement to continue the maintenance of the building above the agreed height. Either course results in the creation of a tunnel beneath the main portion of the building or an arcade notched into the side of the building permitting necessary traffic at the street level and the existence of the building above that level.

Cooperative Apartments

Many factors contribute to the idea of cooperative ownership of an apartment house. High rents paid for rented accommodations, inability to find rentable space in a time of shortage, less capital expended for the purchase of an apartment than for a house, more space or a better address for the same investment, space in a newer building which can be acquired only on the basis of cooperative ownership, and even the distinction of a substantial tie to socially-acceptable neighbors—all furnish the impetus for ownership of a cooperative apartment.

Unfortunately, many participants do not appreciate the implications of the responsibility they assume when they enter the cooperative relationship. There are duties of mutual control, recurrent operating decisions, and variations in maintenance expense. Nor do they realize the problems which may confront them when they try to sell their interest. For the market is more limited and the transfer methods are not so well organized as they are for more conventional properties.

Cooperative apartments are typically urban. But the idea, which has become identified with the modern metropolis, can be traced back to ancient times and diverse places.[74] In the United States, the first cooperative apartment house was created in New York City in 1870. The first building expressly erected for such apartments was located in the same city in the early 1880's.

Until World War I, cooperative developments proceeded spasmodically. Then an era of scarce housing and high rents favored the multiplication of cooperative projects. The cooperative movement continued until the depression of the 1930's which brought widespread failures. Thereafter, it lay dormant until World War II, when a new generation of housing seekers revived the idea again.

The legal means of organizing a cooperative apartment project is not fixed or prescribed in detail in the statute books. Ordinarily, a development is accomplished through one of three legal structures. It may involve fee simple ownership, a trust, or a corporate entity.

In the first case, each tenant-owner ordinarily has the title to his apartment conveyed to him in fee, with entrances, stairways, halls, and public rooms along with rights of support controlled by cross-easements. Methods of management and the apportionment of maintenance and operating expenses are usually determined by contractual agreements. The resulting property rights cannot be technically defined or charted with any degree of certainty. This form of legal structure provides the least flexibility in management and operation. It is said to be used less frequently than the other two methods.

Under the second method, legal title to the realty is placed in a trustee— usually a corporate one. The purposes and provisions of the project are set forth in a declaration of trust. Certificates of beneficial interest, entitling the holder to an apartment and the use of common facilities, are issued by the trustee to the tenant-owners, accompanied in some instances by leases. A Board of Governors or Executive Committee is selected by the tenant-owners among their members to advise the trustee in its management of the project. The trust arrangement generally provides adequate powers so that the trustee may mortgage the trust property, or terminate the trust and sell the realty, upon the request of a given proportion of the owners of beneficial interests. The trust form is more flexible than the fee form and is used to a greater extent. But it is not so common as the corporate form.

In using a corporate form of cooperative ownership, incorporation ordinarily may be effected under a number of different statutes, a general incorporation act, a nonprofit corporation statute, a special cooperative statute, an urban redevelopment law, or a limited dividend housing act. The stock certificates usually contain provisions restricting subleasing and the transferability of the stock. The certificates provide for the assessment of costs, give the corporation a prior lien on the stock, and contain additional standard provisions found in corporate certificates. As specified in the bylaws, a holder of the requisite amount of stock generally receives a proprietary lease which entitles him to an apartment. Here again, provisions governing rights under the lease in the advent of the lessee's death, diminution in the lessee's shares of stock, assigning of the lease or subletting, or requirements for an annual assessment and house rules are joined in the proprietary lease with other provisions common to long-term leases.

The trust or corporate form of project may operate under a 100 per cent plan or a semi-cooperative plan. In the 100 per cent plan, every apartment is occupied by a tenant-owner. In the semi-cooperative plan, some of the apartments are rented out to third parties and the proceeds are applied to the expenses of the project.

A majority of the court-of-last-resort cases involving cooperative projects deal with problems concerning the corporate type of operation. In some of these cases, questions have arisen as to the extent, quality, and legal character of the interest held by a tenant-owner of a cooperative apartment. In discussing the question, some of the courts have expressly refused to give the interest a name. Others have used designations ranging from tenancy through equitable title. The type of interests peculiar to the cooperative apartment concept apparently do not fit precisely into any of the ancient legal categories.

So far, the courts have not agreed upon the technical legal relationships which are involved, although they seem to have no difficulty in deciding the cases before them. Depending upon the case and the appropriate decisions, the courts have supported their opinions by different processes of reasoning.

In 1922, a New York court stated that "the stockholders are in effect regarded as the owners of the rooms occupied or to be occupied by them . . ." But in 1939, the court held that "the relationship between the tenant-owners in the present case is in effect a partnership for the mutual benefit of the cooperative owners expressed in corporate terms." In 1945, the court coined the phrases owner-lessee and landlord-lessor.[75] In 1951, the court said:

> It is true that the object of cooperatives "so far as practical, is to constitute the persons to whom space in the building is assigned as the owners of such space" . . . and that the stockholders [in] a cooperative, in effect, have title to each respective apartment. It is not true, however, that the space or apartment to which title is held by a cooperative shareholder becomes a house rather than an apartment because of the peculiar nature of this type of ownership. There are many similarities between the ownership of a house and that of stock in a cooperative apartment, but the differences between the two types of housing accommodations are essential and obvious.[76]

While the other courts fail to agree about the kind of interest acquired by a purchaser of a cooperative apartment,[77] they still continue to adapt the law to the actions of persons who buy, sell, and utilize property rights of this nature without recourse to technical objections aimed at defeating the obvious intention of the cooperative apartment owner.

Conclusion

The influence of the metropolis upon the concepts, rules, and institutions relating to property is not unique. It follows a historical pattern of evolutionary adaptation of the law in response to pressures of self-interest of the majority of the people who live in urban areas. This metropolitan influence is reflected primarily in legislative and judicial processes at national, state, and local levels. It is evidenced by the use or alteration of concepts, rules, and institutions found in an agrarian society as well as the creation and development of new ones applicable chiefly to an urban environment.

As a result of the United States Supreme Court's interpretations of the general welfare and commerce clauses of the federal constitution, the federal government has exercised hitherto unused powers affecting the concepts and institutions relating to property. So have the states and their municipalities. In addition to legislative bodies and courts, public administrative agencies have played an unprecedented part in developing rules and imposing controls which affect urban realty. Consequently, the influence of the metropolis has brought about the intervention of the government into areas formerly occupied solely by private business and individual free action.

As long as urban population increases, these influences probably will continue and intensify. Over the long run, there will be a further lessening of free choices by the individual property owner and a greater measure of social control and governmental participation in matters relating to property. The process of change will doubtless continue to proceed at a gradual but uneven rate. Its progress will depend upon the social climate of the times. In the words of Mr. Justice Cardozo, "this work of modification is gradual. It goes on inch by inch. Its effects must be measured by decades and even centuries. Thus measured, they are seen to have behind them the power and the pressure of the moving glacier."[78]

FOOTNOTES TO CHAPTER 9

1. Charles G. Dalton and Edward H. Snyder assisted in the research and in the preparation of some of the charts and compilations.

2. See Llewellyn, "Law and the Social Sciences—Especially Sociology," 62 *Harvard Law Rev.* 1286. Also American Law Institute, *Restatement of the Law of Property*, I, p. 3 and E. M. Fisher, *Urban Real Estate Markets: Characteristics and Financing* (New York: National Bureau of Economic Research, 1951), p. 1.

3. Munn v. Illinois (1876), 94 U.S. 113, 124, 125.

4. People v. City of Chicago (1952), 413 Ill. 83, 108 N.E. 2d 16, 21.

5. See C. B. & Q. Railway v. Drainage Comm'rs (1906), 200 U.S. 561, 591, 594. Also Hadacheck v. Los Angeles (1915), 239 U.S. 394, 410 and Donoghue v. Stevenson (1932), A.C. 562, 580, per Lord Atkin.

6. See People v. Rosehill Cemetery (1929), 334 Ill. 555, 562, 166 N.E. 112, 114. Also People v. City of Chicago (1913), 261, Ill. 16, 20, 21, 103 N.E. 609, 49 L.R.A.N.S. 438.

7. For public health, see Sings v. City of Joliet (1908), 237 Ill. 300, 309, 86 N.E. 663, 665 and Miller v. Schoene (1928), 276 U.S. 272, 279, 280. For fire, New England Trust Co. v. City of Boston (1938), 300 Mass. 321, 15 N.E. 2d 255. For general conflagration, Page v. Town of Warrenton (1913), 210 Fed. 431, 433. For floods, Aitken v. Village of Wells River (1898), 70 Vt. 308, 40 Atl. 829, 830, 41 L.R.A. 566, 67 Ann. St. Rep. 672.

8. For freedom of action, see Scott v. Frazier (1919), 258 Fed. 669, 678; People v. City of Chicago, note 6 supra; Spann v. City of Dallas (1921), 111 Tex. 350, 235 S.W. 513, 19 A.L.R. 1387, 1392. For retail store in residence area, see Fitzhugh v. City of Jackson (1923), 132 Miss. 585, 97 So. 190–194 and Spann v. City of Dallas. For frontage consents, see People v. City of Chicago, note 6 supra. For aesthetic considerations, Bjork v. Safford (1929), 333 Ill. 355, 359, 164 N.E. 699.

9. For ability to change, see People v. City of Chicago, note 4 supra; Herrin v. Arnold (1938) 183 Okla. 392, 82 Pac. 2d 977, 979, 119 A.L.R. 1471; Leonard v. State (1919), 100 Ohio St. 456, 127 N.E. 464, 465; and People v. Rosehill Cemetery, note 6 supra. For application of old principles to new facts, Jacobson v. Massachusetts (1905), 197 U.S. 11; Sligh v. Kirkwood (1915), 237 U.S. 52; Cusack Co. v. City of Chicago (1917), 242 U.S. 526; and Powell, "The Supreme Court and the State Police Power, 1922–1930," 17 *Va. Law Rev.* 529.

10. For line between permissible and forbidden, see People ex. rel Brixton Operating Corp. v. La Fetra (1920), 185 N.Y.S. 632, 113 Misc. Rep. 527 affirmed 186 N.Y.S. 58, 194 App. Div. 523, which is affirmed 130 N.E. 601, 230 N.Y. 429, 16 A.L.R. 152; also Pettis v. Alpha Alpha Chapter of Phi Beta Pi (1927), 115 Neb. 525, 213 N.W. 835, 838. For fluid concepts, see Bacon v. Walker (1907), 204 U.S. 311, 317, 318; Walls v. Midland Carbon Co. (1920), 254 U.S. 300, 314; C. B. & Q. Railway v. Drainage Comm'rs, note 5 supra; Chicago & Alton Railroad Co. v. Tranbarger (1915), 238 U.S. 67, 77, 35 S. Ct. 678, 59 L. Ed. 1204; State v. Perley (1917), 173 N.C. 783, 92 S.E. 504, affirmed in Ferley v. State of North Carolina, 39 S. Ct. 357, 249 U.S. 510, 63 L. Ed. 735; City of Portland v. Public Service Commission (1918), 89 Oreg. 325, 173 Pac. 1178, 1180; and State v. J. M. Seney Co. (1919), 134 Md. 437, 107 Atl. 189, 193. Quotation from B. N. Cardozo, *The Nature of the Judicial Process* (New Haven: Yale University Press, 1922), p. 87.

11. Mansfield & Swett Inc. v. Town of West Orange (1938), 120 N.J.L. 145, 198, Atl. 225, 232.

12. N. F. Baker, *Legal Aspects of Zoning* (Chicago: The University of Chicago Press, 1927), pp. 1–2.

13. For basis of existing state jurisprudence, see Penny v. Little (1841), 4. Ill. 301. For usages of the country, Kreitz v. Behrensmeyer (1894), 149 Ill. 496, 502, 36 N.E. 983.

14. For the year 1606, see Ill. Rev. Stat., 1951, Ch. 28, Sec. 1 and Ind. Ann. Stat. (Burns 1933), Secs, 1–101. For colony of Virginia, 9 Hen. St. 127; Bulpit v. Matthews (1893), 145 Ill. 345, 34 N.E. 525, 22 L.R.A. 55.

15. N. Y. Const. (1938), Art. I, Sec. 14; Fla. Stat. Ann., Sec. 2.01; 1 *American Law of Property* 56.

16. Simes, "Historical Background of the Law of Property," 1 *American Law of Property,* Part 1, Ch. III.

17. Address by Lord Simonds, Lord High Chancellor of Great Britain at the Annual Meeting of the American Bar Association, Boston, Mass., August 27, 1953.

18. Zoning ordinances are detailed and broad in scope. Due to the fact that many cities enacted ordinances at about the same time, zoning laws conform to a general pattern and usually consist of two parts. One part is composed of detailed use and volume district maps which depict the entire city, block by block, and indicate by suitable symbols the use and volume districts applicable to each tract. The other part is made up of definitions and specifications of actions that are permitted and prohibited.

19. City of Aurora v. Burns (1925), 319 Ill. 84, 93–94, 149 N.E. 784; Goldman v. Crowther, City Inspector of Buildings, et al. (1925), 147 Md. 282, 128 Atl. 50, 57, 38 A.L.R. 1455.

20. See J. Metzenbaum, *The Law of Zoning* (New York: Baker, Voorhis, and Co., 1930) and E. C. Yokley, *Zoning Law and Practices* (Charlottesville, Va.: Miohio Co., 1948).

21. For twentieth century, see Women's Kansas City St. Andrew Soc. v. Kansas City, Mo. (1932), 58 Fed. 2d 593, 599. For Los Angeles, see E. M. Bassett, *Zoning* (New York: Russell Sage Foundation, 1936) p. 13. For New York, Metzenbaum, note 20 supra, p. 17.

22. For municipality control, see Casner and Leach, "Legislation Restricting the Use of Land and Constitutional Limitations Thereon," *Cases on Property* (Rev. Temp. Ed. 1948), Ch. 1, Part VII. For comprehensive zoning ordinances, see Fisher, "Economic Aspects of Zoning, Blighted Areas and Rehabilitation Laws," *American Economic Review Supplement,* XXXII, No. 1 (March, 1942), p. 331.

23. Goldman v. Crowther, City Inspector of Buildings, et al. (1925), 147 Md. 282, 128 Atl. 50, 60, 38 A.L.R. 1455.

24. Euclid v. Ambler Realty Co. (1926), 272 U.S. 365, 47 S. Ct. 114, 71 L. Ed. 303, 54 A.L.R. 1016

25. See Euclid v. Ambler, note 24 supra, at 272 U.S. 397; 2700 Irving Park Bldg. Corp. v. City of Chicago (1946), 395 Ill. 138, 69 N.E. 2d 827; De Mott Homes at Salem, Inc. v. Margate City (1948), 136 N.J.L. 330, 56 Atl. 2d 423, affirmed 136 N.J.L. 639, 57 Atl. 2d 388; O'Connor v. City of Moscow (1949), 69 Ida. 37, 202 Pac. 2d 401; Polk v. Axton (1948), 306 Ky. 498, 208 S.W. 2d 497; Cassel v. Mayor and City Council of Baltimore (1950), 195 Md. 348, 73 Atl. 2d 486; People ex rel. Joseph Lumber Co. v. City of Chicago (1949), 402

Ill. 321, 83 N.E. 2d 592; Galt v. Cook County (1950), 405 Ill. 396, 91 N.E. 2d
395; The People ex rel. The Trust Company of Chicago v. The Village of Skokie
(1951), 408 Ill. 397, 97 N.E. 2d 310; and Hitchman v. Oakland Tp. (1951), 329
Mich. 331, 45 N.W. 2d 306.

26. Bassett, note 21 supra, p. 105

27. Ordinarily, state statutes contain specific provisions concerning variations,
the creation of Boards of Appeals, administrative review of questioned decisions,
and judicial review of final administrative decisions. See Ill. Rev. Stat., 1953, Ch.
24, Sec. 73–3, 4, 5, 6.01, and 8.

28. For buffer zones, see Evanston Best & Co., Inc. v. Goodman (1938), 369
Ill. 207, 16 N.E. 2d 131. For off-street parking, Ronda Realty Corp. v. Lawton
(1953), 414 Ill. 313, Ill N.E. 2d 310.

29. For other decisions, see Annotation, 129 *A. Law R.* 885 and 54 *A. Law R.*
366. For legislation, Ill. Rev. Stat., 1951, Ch. 24, par. 73–9 and House Bill 609,
1953 Session, Ill. Rev. Stat., 1953, Ch. 24, Sec. 73–9.

30. See Chicago Regional Port District Act (1951), amended 1953, Senate Bill
158, Ill. Rev. Stat., 1953, Ch. 19, Sec. 154. It creates "a political subdivision, body
politic and municipal corporation" embracing lands located in Cook and DuPage
Counties, Illinois.

31. Ill. Senate Bill 524, 1953 Session, approved July 13, 1953, Ill. Rev. Stat.,
1953, Ch. 67½, Secs., 91.8–91.16.

32. United States v. Butler (1935), 297 U.S. 1, 63–68. For other significant
cases, see United States v. Darby Lumber Co. (1941), 61 S. Ct. 451, 312 U.S.
100; United States v. South-Eastern Underwriters Ass'n (1944), 64 S. Ct. 1162,
322 U.S. 533; Santa Cruz Packing Co. v. National Labor Relations Board (1938),
58 S. Ct. 656, 303 U.S. 453; National Labor Relations Board v. Jones & Laughlin
Steel Corp. (1937), 57 S. Ct. 615, 301 U.S. 1, and U.S. v. Wrightwood Dairy Co.
(1942), 62 S. Ct. 523, 315 U.S. 110.

33. Cited from Cardozo, note 10 supra, p. 26.

34. Municipality authorization is the case in Colorado, Connecticut, Delaware,
Indiana (Indianapolis only), Kentucky, Maryland (Baltimore only), Michigan,
Missouri, New York, Ohio, Texas (San Antonio only by local charter), West
Virginia, and Wisconsin. Public housing authority authorization is the case in
Alabama, Alaska, Arkansas, Delaware, Florida, Georgia, Illinois, Kentucky, Louis-
iana, Massachusetts, Missouri, Nebraska (Omaha only), New Hampshire, New
Jersey, Minnesota, Oregon, Puerto Rico, South Carolina, South Dakota, Tennessee,
Virgin Islands, Virginia, and West Virginia. Redevelopment agency authorization
is the case in California, Delaware, District of Columbia, Hawaii, Illinois, Ken-
tucky, Maine, Massachusetts, Missouri, New Jersey, North Carolina (in cities of
25,000 or over), Pennsylvania, Rhode Island, and West Virginia. For fair or use
value, see Report of the American Bar Association Section of Real Property,
Probate and Trust Law, Committee on Planning, Rebuilding and Developing Communities, *Proceedings,* 1952, pp. 43–44. The decisions have been published in
"Summaries of Slum Clearance and Public Housing Decisions" (Washington, D.C.:
Division of Law of the Federal Housing and Home Finance Agency, October
1949) and First Supplement, July 1, 1951, thereto.

35. See Ascher, "The Role of Covenants as a Tool of Urban Redevelopment,"
American Bar Association Section of Real Property, Probate, and Trust Law, *Pro-
ceedings,* September, 1951; also "Private Covenants in Urban Redevelopment," in
C. Woodbury (ed.), *Urban Redevelopment: Problems and Practices* (Chicago:

University of Chicago Press, 1953). See also C. E. Clark, *Real Covenants and Other Interests which "Run with the Land"* (2d ed.; Chicago: Callaghan, 1947), and Hays v. St. Paul M. E. Church (1902), 196 Ill. 633.

36. For public policy, see G. W. Thompson, *Commentaries on the Modern Law of Real Property* (Indianapolis: Bobbs-Merrill, 1939–41), IV, Sec. 3360; Brandenburg v. Country Club Building Corp. (1928), 332 Ill. 136, 163 N.E. 440; Dixon v. Van Sweringen Co. (1929), 121 Ohio St. 56, 166 N.E. 887; Fitzsimmons v. South Realty Corp. (1932), 162 Md. 108, 159 Atl. 111; Anderson v. Marshall-Malaise Lumber Co. (1935), 66 N.D. 216, 263 N.W. 721; Onachita Home Site & Realty Co. v. Collie (1938), 189 La. 521, 179 So. 841; Grant v. Craigie (1940), 292 Mich. 658, 291 N.W. 44; Pappas v. Eighty Hundred Realty Co. (1940), 138 S.W. 2d 762; Andrews v. Metropolitan Bldg. Co. (1942), 349 Mo. 927, 163 S.W. 2d 1024; Sheets v. Dillon (1942), 221 N.C. 426, 20 S.E. 2d 344; Lion's Head Lake v. Brzezinski (1945), 23 N.J. Misc. 290, 43 Atl. 2d 729; Housing Authority of Gallatin County v. Church of God (1948), 401 Ill. 100, 81 N.E. 2d 500; and Spencer v. Poole (1950), 207 Ga. 155, 60 S.E. 2d 371. For reasonable period of time, see Barton v. Moline Properties (1935), 121 Fla. 683, 164 S. 551, 103 A.L.R. 725; Whitmarsh v. Richmond (1941), 179 Md. 523, 20 Atl. 2d 161; and Norris v. Williams (1947), 189 Md. 73, 54 Atl. 2d 331.

37. See McDougal, 58 *Yale Law J.* 500 ff., a review of the book by Clark, note 35 supra.

38. See Gordon v. Caldwell (1924), 235 Ill. App. 170, 54 A.L.R. 843n; Vorenberg v. Bunnell (1926), 257 Mass. 399, 153 N.E. 884, 48 A.L.R. 1431; Ludgate v. Somerville (1927), 121 Oreg. 643, 256 Pac. 1043, 54 A.L.R. 837; Dolan v. Brown (1930), 338 Ill. 412, 170 N.E. 425, 4 A.L.R. 2d 1176n; Magnolia Petroleum Co. v. Drauver (1938), 183 Okla. 579, 83 Pac. 2d 840, 119 A.L.R. 1112; Strauss v. Ginzberg (1944), 218 Minn. 57, 15 N.W. 2d 130, 155 A.L.R. 1000; Ault et al. v. Shipley (1949), 189 Va. 69, 52 S.E. 2d 56; City of Richlawn v. McMakin (1950), 313 Ky. 265, 230 S.W. 2d 902; Faubian v. Busch (1951), 240 S.W. 2d 361. Also Hecke, "Zoning Ordinances and Restrictions in Deeds," 37 *Yale Law J.* 407 and Dilts, "Municipal Corporations—Zoning—Abrogation of Private Restrictive Covenants by Zoning Regulations," 48 *Mich. Law Rev.* 103 (1949).

39. In general, see *American Law of Property*, II, 336, 364; Clark, note 35 supra, p. 157; A. Dunham, *Modern Real Estate Transactions* (Brooklyn: The Foundation Press, 1952), p. 6; C. P. Berry, *Digest of the Law of Restrictions on the Use of Real Property* (Chicago: G. I. Jones, 1915), p. 27; *Restatement of the Law of Property*, I (1936), Sec. 24; H. T. Tiffany, *A Treatise on the Modern Law of Real Property* (Chicago: Callaghan, 1940), I. See also Natural Products Co. v. Dolese & Shepard Co. (1923), 309 Ill. 230, 140 N.E. 840.

40. Tulk v. Moxhay, 2 Phil. 774, 41 Eng. Rep. 1143 (Ch. 1848); 2 *American Law of Property* 402.

41. See R. D. Niles (ed.), *1948 Annual Survey of American Law* (New York: New York University School of Law, 1949), p. 703. Also L. M. Simes, *The Law of Future Interests* (St. Paul: West Publishing Company, 1936), I, p. 24, n. 75.

42. Loud v. Pendergast (1910), 206 Mass. 122, 92 N.E. 40; Ocean City Land Co. v. Weber (1914), 83 N.J. Eq. 476, 91 Atl. 600 affirmed in (1915), 84 N.J. Eq. 505, 94 Atl. 1102; Bryant v. Whitney (1918), 178 Cal. 640, 174 Pac. 32; Gage v. Schavoir (1924), 100 Conn. 652, 124 Atl. 535; Schwartz v. Holycross (1925), 83 Ind. App. 658, 149 N.E. 699; Brandenburg v. The Country Club Bldg. Corp. (1928), 332 Ill. 136, 163 N.E. 440; Tindolph v. Schoenfeld Bros. (1930), 157 Wash. 605, 289 Pac. 530; Nashua Hospital Ass'n v. Gage (1932), 85 N.H.

335, 159 Atl. 137; Matthews Real Estate Co. v. National Printing and Engraving Co. (1932), 330 Mo. 190, 48 S.W. 2d 911; Oliver v. Marbut (1938), 22 Tenn. App. 405, 123 S.W. 2d 859; Rich v. Isbey (1939), 291 Mich. 119, 288 N.W. 353; and Edwards v. Wiseman (1941), 198 La. 382, 3 So. 2d 661.

43. See Ill. Rev. Stat. (1951), Ch. 30, Secs. 37b ff. Also Niles, note 41 supra, p. 703.

44. See Ill. Rev. Stat. (1953), Ch. 83, Secs. 1, 1(a), (b), and (c). For other states, see Colo. Stat. Ann. (Supp. 1951), Ch. 40, Sec. 154; Ind. Stat. Ann. (1951), Sec. 2–628; Mass. Ann. Laws (Supp. 1951), Ch. 184, Sec. 23; Mich. Stat. Ann. (1937), Sec. 26.46; Minn. Stat. Ann. (1947), Sec. 500.20; and Wis. Stat. (1951), Sec. 230.46.

45. Shelley v. Kraemer and McGhee v. Sipes (1948), 334 U.S. 1, 68 S. Ct. 836, 92 L. Ed. 1161. For an earlier case in which the same problem was decided in an opposite manner, see Corrigan v. Buckley (1926), 271 U.S. 323.

46. Barrows v. Jackson (1953), 346 U.S. 249, 73 S. Ct. 1031.

47. For education, see Gong Lum v. Rice (1927), 275 U.S. 78; Missouri ex rel. Gaines v. Canada, Registrar of the University of Missouri (1938), 305 U.S. 337; Sipuel v. Board of Regents of the University of Oklahoma (1948), 332 U.S. 631; Sweatt v. Painter (1950), 339 U.S. 629, rehearing denied 340 U.S. 846, No. 44; McLaurin v. Oklahoma State Regents for Higher Education (1950), 339 U.S. 637; and 21 United States Law Week, 3307. For transportation, see Hall v. DeCuir (1877), 95 U.S. 485; Louisville, New Orleans and Texas R'y Co. v. Mississippi (1890), 133 U.S. 587; Plessy v. Ferguson (1896), 163 U.S. 537; Chesapeake and Ohio R'y Co. v. Kentucky (1900), 179 U.S. 388; Chiles v. Chesapeake & Ohio R'y (1910), 218 U.S. 71; McCabe v. A.T. & S.F. Ry. Co. (1914), 235 U.S. 151; South Covington & R'y. Co. v. Kentucky (1920), 252 U.S. 399; Mitchell v. United States (1941), 313 U.S. 80; Morgan v. Virginia (1946), 328 U.S. 373. For public eating places, see District of Columbia v. Thompson Co. (1953), 346 U.S. 100; Henderson v. United States (1950), 339 U.S. 816; Powell v. Utz (1949), 87 F. Supp. 811; Nash v. Air Terminal Services, Inc. (1949), 85 F. Supp. 545; For recreational areas, see Valle v. Stengel (1949), 176 Fed. 2d 697; Rice v. Arnold (1950), 45 So. 2d 195; Sweeney v. City of Louisville (1951), 102 F. Supp. 525, affirmed 202 Fed. 2d 275; Williams v. Kansas City, Mo. (1952), 104 F. Supp. 848; and Hayes v. Crutcher (1952), 108 Fed Supp. 582. For public housing, see Seawell v. MacWithey (1949), 63 Atl. 2d 542; Dorsey v. Stuyvesant Town Corporation (1947), 190 Misc. 187, 74 N.Y.S. 2d 220, affirmed 274 App. Div. 992, 85 N.Y.S. 2d 313.

48. *House and Home,* IV, No. 1 (July, 1953), 39.

49. King v. Stanley (1948), 32 Cal. 2d 584, 590, 197 P. 2d 321.

50. See Basye, "Streamlining Conveyancing Procedure," 47 *Mich. Law Rev.* 935 (1949).

51. See Ogg. v. Herman, 227 P. 476, 71 Mont. 10; Irving v. Campbell, 24 N.E. 821, 121 N.Y. 353, 8 L.R.A. 620; Moore v. Williams, 22 N.E. 233, 115 N.Y. 586, 5 L.R.A. 654, 12 Am. St. Rep. 944; and Emmens v. St. John, 29 N.Y.S. 655, 79 Hun. 102.

52. Report of the Committee on Acceptable Titles to Real Property, American Bar Association Section of Real Property, Probate and Trust Law, *Proceedings,* September, 1952, p. 27.

53. For recent legislation, see Payne, "Increasing Land Marketability Through Uniform Title Standards," 39 *Va. Law Rev.* 1 (1953). For Marketable Record

Title Act, see Mich. 1945 Sess. Laws, p. 267, as amended in 1947 Sess. Laws, p. 156, Mich. Stat. Ann., Sec. 26.1271. See also Aigler, "Clearance of Land Titles—A Statutory Step, 44 *Mich. Law Rev.* 45 (1945). For judicial or legislative realm, see Aigler, "Constitutionality of Marketable Title Acts," 50 *Mich. Law Rev.* 185 (1951). For other Michigan acts, see Mich. Stat. 26.595, 596; 26.527, 26.581, and so on. For other states, see summary by Basye in Appendix C to the Report of the Committee on Acceptable Titles to Real Estate of the American Bar Association's Section of Real Property, Probate and Trust Law, August, 1953.

54. Vt. Stat. 1947, Sec. 8754.

55. Ky. Rev. Stat., Sec. 304.433.

56. Vt. Stat. 1947, Sec. 8754.

57. The Home Owners' Loan Corporation made no requirement that titles should be marketable. The Federal Housing Administration's attitude is reflected in Sec. 8 of Article VI of its "Regulations for Mutual Mortgage Insurance" and Sec. 5 of Article V of the "Regulations for War Housing Insurance" under Section 603. For the Veterans' Administration, see Reg. Sec. 36.4325 (b), 36.4350 (a), and 36.4320 (h) (5) of Title III Servicemen's Readj. Act of 1944.

58. For Iowa, see Siedel v. Snider (1950), 241 Ia. 1227, 44 N.W. 2d 687. For South Dakota, see Grand Lodge v. Fischer (1945), 70 S. Dak. 562, 21 N.W. 2d 213. For Nebraska, Campagna v. H.O.L.C. (1941), 140 Neb. 572, 300 N.W. 894, reversed on rehearing (1942), 141 Neb. 429, 3 N.W. 2d 750.

59. See LaCourse v. Kiesel (1951), 366 Pa. 385, 77 Atl. 2d 877; Butler v. Santosus (1948), 62 York 31; Brinn v. Mennen Co. (1949), 5 N.J. Sup. 582, 68 Atl. 2d 879; and Hebb v. Severson (1948), 32 Wash. 2d 159, 201 Pac. 2d 156.

60. See Wilson v. Pacific Coast Title Ins. Co. (1951), 106 Cal. A. 2d 599, 235 Pac. 2d 431; Hocking v. Title Ins. & Trust Co. (1951), 37 Cal. 2d 644, 234 Pac. 2d 625; Foehrenbach v. German-Am. T. & T. Co., 217 Pa. St. 331, 66 Atl. 561; and King v. Stanley (1948), 32 Cal. 2d 584, 197 Pac. 2d 321.

61. See R. R. Powell, *Registration of Title to Land in the State of New York* (New York: The New York Law Society, 1938), p. 54. Also the Report of the American Bar Association Real Property, Probate and Trust Law Section's Committee on Acceptable Titles to Real Property, as of Aug. 1953.

62. For cases of commercial frustration, see Colonial Operating Corp. v. Hannan Sales & Service, Inc. (1942), 34 N.Y.S. 2d 116 (1943), 39 N.Y.S. 2d 217; Signal Land Corp. v. Loecher (1942), 35 N.Y.S. 2d 25; Schantz v. Am. Auto Sup. Co., Inc. (1942), 36 N.Y.S. 2d 747; Byrnes v. Balcom (1942), 38 N.Y.S. 2d 801; First Nat'l. Bk. of New Rochelle v. Fairchester Oil Co. (1943), 45 N.Y.S. 2d 532; Megan v. Updike Grain Corp. (1938), 94 Fed. 2d 551; Johnson v. Reeves (1910), 133 Ga. 822, 66 S.E. 1081; Heart v. E. Tenn. Brg. Co. (1908), 121 Tenn. 69, 113 S.W. 364; and Houston Ice & Brewing Co. v. Keenan (1905), 99 Tex. 79, 88 S.W. 197. In England, a statute was enacted defining the rights of landlord and tenant where leased premises were destroyed or damaged by enemy action. See Landlord and Tenant (War Damage) Act, 1939, 2 & 3 Geo. VI, c. 72 and Comment, 52 *Yale Law J.* 130 (1942). For a discussion of significant decisions during only one year, see *1949 Annual Survey of American Law* (New York: New York University School of Law, 1950), p. 759 ff.

63. Aronson v. Olsen (1932), 348 Ill. 26.

64. Beilin v. Krenn & Dato, Inc. (1932), 350 Ill. 284; Drexel State Bank v. O'Donnell (1931), 344 Ill. 173; and Crawford Corp. v. Woodlawn Bank (1943), 382 Ill. 354.

65. Duncanson v. Lill (1926), 322 Ill. 528; Whitaker v. Scherrer (1924), 313 Ill. 473; Sweesy v. Hoy (1927), 324 Ill. 319; The People v. Village of Lombard (1925), 319 Ill. 56; C.N.S. & M.R.R. Co. v. Chicago Title & Trust Co. (1928), 328 Ill. 610; Chicago Title & Trust Co. v. Illinois Merchants Trust Co. (1928), 329 Ill. 334.

66. See Bell, "Air Rights," 23 *Ill. Law Rev.* 250 (1928) and Barnhill, "The Creation of Estates in Airspace," 25 *Rocky Mtn. Law Rev.* 354 (1953).

67. For the general principle, see Corbett v. Hill, (1870), 9 L.R. Eq. Cases 671; Wood County Petroleum Co. v. West Virginia Transportation Co. (1886), 28 W. Va. 210; Murphy v. Bolger, et al. (1888), 60 Vt. 723; Metropolitan West Side Elevated Railroad Co. v. Springer (1897), 171 Ill. 170; Murray v. Heabron (1947), 74 N.E. 2d 648; and Piper, et al. v. Ekern, Atty. Gen. (1923), 180 Wis. 586, 194 N.W. 159. See also "The Air Space as Corporeal Realty," 29 *Harvard Law Rev.* 525 (1916). For the maxim, see Baten's Case, 9 Coke's Rpts. 54 (b) (1611); Fay v. Prentice (1845), 1 C.B. 827; Corbett v. Hill (1874), 9 L.R. Eq. Cases 671; Ellis v. Loftus (1874), L.R. 10, C.P. 10. Also Bouve, "The Private Ownership of Air Space," 1 *Air Law Rev.* 232 (April, 1930).

68. For modifications, see Markby, "Airspace Rights and Liabilities As Affected by Aircraft Operation," 26 *Notre Dame Lawyer* 629 (1951); Pickering v. Rudd (1815), 4 Camp. 219; Ball, "The Vertical Extent of Ownership in Land," 76 *U. of Pa. Law Rev.* 631 (1928); and Hinman v. Pacific Air Transport (1936), 84 F. 2d 755. For federal control, see S. 3129, 82d Cong., 2d Sess. Also "Federal Control of Land to Protect Airport Approaches," 48 *Northwestern U. Law Rev.* 343 (July-Aug., 1953).

69. For public domain, see United States v. Causby (1946), 328 U.S. 256; The Air Commerce Act of 1926, 49 U.S.C.A., Secs. 171 ff.; Talcott and Jones, "Airspace Rights of the Subadjacent Landowner," 2 *Ark. Law Rev.* 448 (1948). For airspace reasonably used and occupied, see Swetland v. Curtiss Airports Corp., 55 F. 2d 201, 83 A.L.R. 319, modifying 41 F. 2d 929 (1932); United States v. Causby, cited above; Eubank, "The Doctrine of the Airspace Zone of Effective Possession," 12 *Boston U. Law Rev.* 414 (1932). For airspace ownership under civil law jurisdiction, see Eatman, "Ownership of Airspace in Louisiana," 8 *Louisiana Law Rev.* 118 (1947); Elliott, "Law of the Air," 6 *Indiana Law J.* 165 (1930); and Mace, "Ownership of Airspace," 17 *U. of Cincinnati Law Rev.* 343 (1948).

70. Loring v. Bacon (1808), 4 Mass. 575; Cheesborough v. Green (1834), 10 Conn. 318; Proprietors of the South Congregational Meetinghouse in Lowell v. City of Lowell (1840), 1 Met. 541; Rhodes v. McCormack (1857), 4 Iowa 383; McConnel v. Kibbe (1864), 33 Ill. 175 and 43 Ill. 12 (1867); Ottumwa Lodge, etc. v. Lewis (1871), 34 Iowa 67; Badger Lumber Co. v. Stepp, et al. (1900), 157 Mo. 366, 57 S.W. 1059; Madison v. Madison, et al. (1904), 206 Ill. 534, 69 N.E. 625; Townes, et al. v. Cox (1931), 162 Tenn. 624, 39 S.W. 2d 749; "Real Property-Air Rights-Condemnation Proceedings," 24 *N.Y.U. Law Quar.* 443 (1949).

71. Doe on the Demise of Freeland v. Burt (1787), 1 T.R. 701.

72. N.J.S.A. 46: 3–19 ff. See also 52 *Harvard Law Rev.* 335 (1938).

73. Ill. Rev. Stat., 1951, Ch. 114, Sec. 174a (1927). See City of Chicago v. Sexton (1951), 408 Ill. 351, 97 N.E. 2d 287 and comment, 30 *Chicago-Kent Law Rev.* 76 (1951).

74. The following discussion is based upon numerous articles and books, including: 32 *Architectural Forum* 240 (1920); 33 *Architectural Forum* 31, 55, 111, 187 (1920); 37 *Architectural Forum* 17, 219 (1922); 53 *Architectural Forum* 313, 370 (1927); 88 *Architectural Forum* 93 (1948); 89 *Architectural Forum* 14, 16

(1948); Castle, "Cooperative Apartments in Southern California," *National Real Estate Journal* (July 26, 1926), and "Legal Phases of Cooperative Building," 62 *Southern Cal. Law Rev.* 1 (1928); Chicago Real Estate Board, "Standard Forms and Methods of Operation for 100 Per Cent Cooperative Apartment Projects" (1928); Claar, "Cooperative Apartment Homes as an Investment," pamphlet published by Northwestern University School of Commerce, 1924; M. L. Colean, *American Housing* (New York: The Twentieth Century Fund, 1944), p. 234; Curtis, "Why Cooperative Apartments Are In Demand," 2 *Annals of Real Estate Practice* 20 (1927); Elliman, "Cooperative Ownership," 2 *Annals of Real Estate Practice* 3 (1927); Flamm, "Housing Cooperatives," *Lawyers Guild Review*, VI, No. 5 (1946); Marks and Marks, "Coercive Aspects of Housing Cooperatives," 62 *Ill. Law Rev.* 728 (Jan.-Feb., 1948); N. W. MacChesney, *The Principles of Real Estate Law* (New York: Macmillan, 1927), Ch. 8; "Nonprofit Housing Projects in the United States," U.S. Dept. of Labor Bulletin 896 (1947); Note, 61 *Harvard Law Rev.* 1407 (1948); Ross, *Planning and Projecting a Cooperative Apartment Plan of Ownership* (National Assn. of Real Estate Boards, 1949); Stockbridge, "Own Your Own Flat," 8 *Annals of Real Estate Practice* 7 (1926); and Yourman, "Some Legal Aspects of Cooperative Housing," 12 *Law and Contemporary Problems* 126 (1947).

75. 542 Morris Park Ave. Corporation v. Wilkins et al. (1922), 197 N.Y.S. 625, 627; Tompkins v. Hale (1939), 15 N.Y.S. 2d 854, 857; Curtis v. LeMay (1945), 60 N.Y.S. 2d 768, 770. See also Smith v. Feigin (1947), 75 N.Y.S. 2d, 204.

76. Danforth v. McGoldrick (1951), 109 N.Y.S. 2d 387, 389. See also Flamman v. McGoldrick (1952), 110 N.Y.S. 2d 477 and Application of Massey (1952), 112 N.Y.S. 2d 677.

77. See In re Pitts Estate (1933), 218 Cal. 184, 22 P. 2d 694; Ten Winkel v. Anglo Cal. Sec. Co. (1937), 74 P. 2d 317; Chelten Ave. Bldg. Corp. v. Mayer (1934), 172 A. 675; Mayer v. Chelten Ave. Bldg. Corp. (1936), 183 A. 773; Tudor Arms Apartments, et al. v. Shaffer, et al. (1948), 191 Md. 342, 62 A. 2d 346; Kenny v. Thompson (1949), 338 Ill. App. 248, 87 N.E. 2d 229; Hicks v. Bigelow (1947), 55 A. 2d 924; Glennon v. Butler (1949), 66 A. 2d 519; 1915 6th St. Coop. Ass'n. v. Pinkett (1915), 85. A. 2d 58; Valois, Inc. v. Thorne (1952), 86 A. 2d 530; Stafford Owners, Inc. v. United States (1930), 39 F. 2d 743; Moses, et al. v. Buss, et al. (1934), 72 F. 2d 1005; and Abbot, et al. v. Barlove, et al. (1948), 81 F. Sup. 532.

78. B. N. Cardozo, *The Nature of the Judicial Process* (New Haven: Yale University Press, 1922), p. 25.

10

The Impact of the Metropolis upon Land Law

MYRES S. McDOUGAL
William K. Townsend Professor of Law
Yale University

The material in this chapter is restricted mainly to a consideration of the impact of the modern American metropolis upon certain aspects of land law. It includes a discussion of the conception of property, the metropolis as a community, the possible impacts of the metropolis upon property, a hypothesis about the impact of the modern American metropolis upon land law, trends toward rationalization in land law, and future perspectives. The framework and method of inquiry suggested here may possibly be adaptable to comparative studies through different times and across nation-state boundaries.[1]

THE CONCEPTION OF PROPERTY

Property is customarily defined in terms of legally protected interests with respect to resources. The Restatement of Property uses the word property to "denote legal relations between persons with respect to a thing." The relevant *legal relations* are called rights, privileges, powers, immunities, and interests. A *thing* includes not only physical objects but also intangibles.[2]

Similarly, Noyes writes that "property is any protected right or bundle or rights (interest or thing) with direct or indirect regard to any external object (i.e. other than the person himself) which is material or quasi-material (i.e. a protected process) and which the then and there organization of society permits to be made the object of that form of control, either private or public, which is connoted by the legal concepts of occupying, possessing or using."[3]

Although definitions of this type are accurate, they are incomplete and ambiguous. A detailed examination would reveal that they—and all the supporting concepts and rules commonly labeled the law of property—purport to describe, predict, and prescribe the responses of official decision-makers to competing claims for the control and use of resources. To make these definitions and rules more meaningful, therefore, an observer must locate both the decision-makers and the competing claimants in the total social process of people applying institutions to resources for the production of values. He must also distinguish among the descriptive, predictive, and prescriptive functions of such words.[4]

For any particular community, therefore, the important initial questions are: What people, make what claims, to what resources, in pursuit of what values? What, in detail, are the specific practices by which people allocate, plan, develop, and employ resources in the production, distribution, and consumption of values?

Questions of legal policy may next be raised. How is community coercion organized and applied for regulating and policing claims and practices with respect to resources? Who are the decision-makers and what is their authority? Among other variables, what is the role of the concepts and rules labeled property law in influencing decision? What variables are likely to be important in the future and how can they be manipulated to secure decisions more in accord with community values?[5]

The conception of property recommended here, consequently, includes the traditional notion of legally protected interests with respect to resources. But it also extends this notion to the whole pattern of actions and flow of decisions by which community coercion is organized and applied in regulating and policing claims and practices with respect to resources. From this perspective, the concepts and rules commonly called the law of property are only one of many variables that may affect decision-making. By themselves, they are not adequate intellectual tools for describing, predicting, or prescribing decisions. For this task, a new theory is needed which will subsume traditional concepts and rules but escape their ambiguities.[6]

THE METROPOLIS AS A COMMUNITY

Emphasizing the notion of community, a metropolis may be defined as a group of people, with an identifiable resource base, pursuing certain common values, by various institutions.[7] The people may be in constant flux and the resource base may be continually changing at its peripheries. But the values and the institutional structures of a metropolitan community remain reasonably distinct.

In large urban communities, people demand the greatest possible efficiency in the management of their physical environment.

> They are demanding . . . a physical environment of appropriate efficiency to exploit to the utmost the potentialities of their resources and skills for the fullest production of all their values—wealth (in terms of a high standard of living), enlightenment, congenial personal relationships, the preservation and transmission of their moral and cultural patterns, the wide sharing of respect throughout the community, and a democratic diffusion of participation in the making of important decisions. They are demanding an efficiency in their institutions for land use planning and development and for the provision of public services which will make the most economical use of their financial resources and free more of their resources for pursuit of other values.[8]

Toward these ends, the distinctive institutions of a metropolitan community are designed to process its physical environment. In addition, they are intended to supply the values and services demanded by the members of the community. By categories, the institutions may be classified in terms of basic community components, such as habitation, servicing, productive, and governmental.

Habitation components are institutions which directly affect the formation of character values and the transmission of cultural inheritance. They include homes, neighborhood units, and systems and centers of recreation, health, welfare, education, and so on. Servicing components comprise public utilities and services. Productive components supply real income and include systems of manufacturing and processing goods and services for exchange with other communities. Governmental components include institutions by which community coercion is organized and applied for community purposes.[9]

Each component depends upon the others for its proper functioning. Thus a community-wide interdependence exists with respect to all values sought there. This interdependence, in fact, extends beyond the community and embraces the surrounding region as well as the entire country. At each level of areal or geographic organization, there are distinctive aggregations of people with characteristic value demands, identifications, and expectations as well as distinctive institutions and interdependences. The functioning of the larger communities affects the lesser communities which they enfold. At the same time, the functioning of the lesser communities affects the greater communities which they constitute.[10]

IMPACTS OF THE METROPOLIS UPON PROPERTY

The impacts of the metropolitan community upon property must be observed in their effects upon the perspectives and operations of the decision-makers who create and apply property policies. It is assumed that the decision-makers act to maximize all their values. It is also assumed that they acquire their values through interactions with the groups in which they operate and with which they identify themselves.[11]

Even in metropolitan communities, the decision-makers who create and apply property policies are not located exclusively in local governmental structures. They are also commonly found at state, regional, national, and perhaps even international government levels. Because of the contemporary dominance of metropolitan perspectives over all our life, it is probably safe to assume that such perspectives exert an influence upon decision-making at all levels.[12]

But the focus of this inquiry is more limited. It is generally confined to the impact of the distinctive perspectives of the metropolitan community upon the flow of governmental decisions about land use, including the regulation and performance of functions of allocation, planning, and development.

The hypothesis advanced here is that distinctively-metropolitan perspectives have fostered trends toward the rationalization and technicalization of policies.[13]

In the latter part of the nineteenth century, the heritage of property prescriptions and institutions available to American decision-makers was still largely a body of English law. It originated in a country of aristocratic family dynasties under an agricultural economy. At that time, lingering deference to the mysteries of seisin continued to affect decisions about estates and interests in land; competition between Courts of Chancery and Courts of Common Law created an artificial distinction between equitable and legal interests; the community maintained no recording system but honored primitive and formal modes of conveyancing; generalized notions of freedom of contract and private volition in the management of landed wealth had not developed; and direct governmental intervention in land-use planning and the provision of public services was at a minimum.[14]

Upon this heritage has fallen the impact of modern metropolitan perspectives, with their intense demands for efficiency in land use and their increasing recognition of interdependences in land use. That impact has been expressed in two different but interrelated trends. The first trend has been toward the de-development of a body of land law prescription which gives the utmost possible effect to private agreements between parties and to unilateral expressions of intent about land transactions. The second trend has been toward the direct use of governmental powers in planning and controlling land use and in remoulding and developing the physical environment, with appropriate facilities and services, for community purposes.

These trends exemplify the continuous process by which decision-makers reassess, redefine, and re-create their inherited doctrines and practices for the richer achievement of contemporary values. To trace such trends over recent decades, a detailed study would be required of the expression of metropolitan perspectives in legislative debates and reports, judicial opinions, executive pronouncements, party platforms, pressure group appeals, and so on.[15] For present purposes, however, emphasis will be placed only upon the origins of metropolitan perspectives and the increasing flow of decisions illustrative of rationality and technicalization.

The importance of the trends toward rationality and technicalization rests in their implications for the future. They provide legal tools which have been well tested in many communities. If an appropriate public opinion can be created, these tools are reasonably adequate to resolve many of the land-use problems confronting our metropolitan communities.

TRENDS TOWARD RATIONALIZATION IN LAND LAW

Trends toward rationalization may be observed in each of three functions which a community performs in processing its physical environment for production and consumption purposes. The three functions include the allocation, planning, and development of land use.[16]

The Allocation of Land Use

Policies by which communities allocate land uses among different claimants include (1) the provision and application of a body of prescriptions for regulating private agreements and expressions of intent about land use, and (2) practices of direct community intervention, by eminent domain or other powers, to shift use from one claimant to another.

For effective policies concerning private agreements or intents, community officials must perform functions like the following:[17]

Securing intent: Making certain that there is a final expression of agreement or intent, or some sequence of behavior, which should be regarded as raising expectations in others that a commitment has been made.

Fixing policy limits: Determining whether the purposes and probable consequences of agreements and expressions of intent are compatible with over-all community policies.

Enforcement: The use of community coercion to make certain that the expectations created by agreement or expression of intent actually are honored, or that appropriate redress is made. This is the role of traditional remedies in damages, injunction, specific performance, imprisonment, and so on.

Protecting against third parties: Preventing third parties from interfering with promised expectations or from taking the benefits of agreements or intents without appropriate assumption of burdens. The recording statutes are relevant here.

Honoring transfer of benefits: Protecting promisees, under appropriate conditions, in the transfer of the benefits of agreements and intents.

Construction or interpretation: Establishing the relations of the parties with respect to problems which they did not foresee or foresaw only vaguely.

Termination: Putting an end to the effects of an agreement or intent when it has served its purposes or when, though lawful in the beginning, it has since become inimical to community policy.

Subjection to community claims: Imposing appropriate community burdens in the form of exercises of the police power, tax power, eminent domain, and so on.

Trends toward rationality and technicalization can possibly be observed in the performance of each of these functions. The trends have arisen through the creation and application of policies pertaining to private agreements and intents in allocating land uses. They may be illustrated by reference to vendor and purchaser agreements; leases or landlord and tenant relationships; expressions of deadhand control; and allocation by public acquisition.

VENDOR AND PURCHASER AGREEMENTS. Land transfer has not yet become as expeditious, cheap, and secure as it might be made by a few appropriate changes in the maintenance of the public books about land interests.[18] Nevertheless, there have been various developments in the direction of rationality.

Because vendors have difficulty in establishing the validity of their claims under our present system of records, in most communities transfer is still effected by a ceremony requiring both a contract and a deed. However, after purchasers get a contract, they are now given practically the same protection that a deed later confirms. Moreover, almost any informal statement which contains all the essentials of intent has come to suffice as a deed. The result is that today a vendor may transfer whatever interest he has with ease and simplicity. The formal modes of conveyancing inherited from England have long been invoked only to sustain intents which might otherwise be defeated by a failure to comply with special statutory requirements.[19]

Further illustrations of increasing rationality are suggested by the protection afforded purchasers against economic duress in time stipulations as well as in land contracts designed to be substitutes for mortgages; by the increased use of tract indexes in public recording systems and in the plants of private title companies; by the development of the doctrine that the vendor does not have to establish an absolutely good title but merely a marketable one; by the formulation of doctrines of equitable conversion to effect an appropriate balance of benefits and burdens between vendor and vendee in the interval between contract and deed; by the statutory reform of traditional remedies for establishing claims to and protecting interests in land; and by the improvement of statutes of limitation for alleviating some of the inadequacies of anachronistic recording systems.[20]

Similar developments might be noted in policies with respect to mortgages. The trends in doctrines and practices concerning rights to possession, claims to profits and income, foreclosure, redemption, and so on, continue to seek a balance between perfecting the mortgage as a security device and protecting the mortgagor against economic duress.[21]

LEASE AGREEMENTS—LANDLORD AND TENANT RELATIONSHIPS. In recent decades, the conception of the lease agreement has gradually changed. It was formerly thought to be a conveyance which creates an estate—a conception originated in agricultural England when contract law was still primitive. Recently the lease agreement has been called a simple contract which is subject to contract doctrines and remedies.[22]

This change has been attributed to new social factors which with the "growth of cities and the employment of leases for urban properties have stifled the background of this field of law from one predominantly agrarian to one predominantly urban." In considerable measure, the change has been effected by the parties through introducing into leases specific clauses designed to regulate by intention (rather than by judicial derivations from estate) their relationships concerning relevant problems. This practice of introducing specific clauses has become so common that the law of estates for years is now said to have "a predominantly contractual ingredient."[23]

Other notable developments include the invention of the doctrine of constructive eviction to permit lessees deprived of the substantial enjoyment of the premises to terminate their liability for rent by vacating the premises within a reasonable time after interference; some expansion of the notion that covenants in leases are mutual or dependent, as contrasted with the older notion of independent covenants; statutory imposition of duties upon lessees to maintain the repair of premises; statutes permitting lessees to terminate their liabilities by surrendering the premises upon accidental destruction thereof; and the gradual imposition of tort liability upon lessors for concealed defects, negligence, misfeasance in making repairs, or failure to perform agreements or statutory duties.

Additional developments comprise statutes and decisions outlawing exculpatory clauses by which lessors seek to immunize themselves from tort liability; one line of decisions imposing upon lessors a duty to deliver effective possession of premises; the use of tests in terms of the intention of the parties in determining whether benefits and burdens of covenants extend to successors of the original parties; similar tests in terms of the intention of the parties and the damage to their interests in determining whether a lessee can remove fixtures; legislation protecting lessees with respect to rents during times of emergency; tax advantages encouraging long-term leases as instruments of urban land development; expansion of doctrines of anticipatory breach to protect lessors in their claims for rent; and the improvement of remedies for the lessor's recovery of possession of the premises.[24]

ALLOCATION BY DEADHAND VOLITION. Within limits, community policies honor and protect expressions by which donors seek to project their control into the future, even into periods after their death. The objectives for which donors seek such control include wealth effects as well as effects on other private and public values. The transferors and transferees themselves may differ greatly in wealth and institutional position. Hence they vary in their capacity to affect community values.[25]

The methods by which community coercion is brought to bear upon efforts to secure deadhand control include doctrines and practices about taxation, condemnation, agreements, and corporations. They also include a vast body of doctrines and practices commonly known as the law of trusts and of possessory estates and future interests. The law of trusts and possessory estates and future interests comprises an elaborate and technical superstructure.[26]

All such doctrines and practices are supposed to guide and limit community officials in their decision-making concerning the eight functions (securing intent, fixing policy limits, enforcement, protecting against third parties, honoring transfer of benefits, construction, termination, and subjection to community claims) which must be performed with respect to any agreement or expression of intent.

But it should be recalled there that these dichotomies, categorizations, and prescriptions had their origin in an agricultural country of family dynasties, competing courts, and primitive modes of conveyancing. One may reasonably wonder, therefore, how much guidance they can offer for decisions in a modern metropolitan society where wealth is largely in the form of liquid claims and demands for efficiency in land use are most intense.

As a matter of fact, a study of the decisions through recent decades would probably reveal trends toward uniformities in the eight types of functions indicated above. These trends would be in terms of policies applicable to each of the eight functions as well as in terms of relevant factual probabilities concerning future interests. They would not be in terms of the supposed dictates of the traditional dichotomies, categorizations, and prescriptions.

The result of the study would show that the traditional superstructure has become largely meaningless save for the purpose of stimulating or rationalizing an occasional harsh or impolitic decision. The one striking exception to these trends is the continued immunization from the application of the rule against perpetuities of interests reserved in the grantor and his successors. But vigorous proposals are already being made to remedy this evil.[27]

Other developments include the increasing enactment of statutes authorizing highly discretionary judicial sale, mortgage, and lease of land subject to future interests; statutes enhancing the powers of trustees to sell, mortgage, and lease when settlor granted powers are inadequate; judicial decisions implying special powers in trustees to cope with exigencies unforeseen by settlors exercising deadhand control; the imposition of the rule against perpetuities time restriction on restraints upon trustees' powers to alienate; the elaboration of numerous constructional preferences designed to mitigate the impact of rights of entry and possibilities of reverter upon the alienability and development of land; and the application of the perpetuities time limit to options in gross which fetter the alienability and development of land.[28]

ALLOCATION BY PUBLIC ACQUISITION. Direct community intervention in the allocation of resources by shifting use from one claimant to another is commonly effected through exercises of the powers of eminent domain, taxation, and spending. The most important limitations upon such intervention are requirements of public use for exercises of the eminent domain power and of public purpose for exercises of the taxing and spending powers.

In the middle of the nineteenth century, the perspectives of an agricultural, laissez-faire economy were dominant. At that time, the courts rendered many decisions greatly restrictive of community powers. They also elaborated tests of propriety in terms of physical use by public officials or by the public generally; of natural monopoly and the breakdown of competition; of the necessity of services for community existence, and so on.[29]

Toward the end of the century, however, the growth of industrialism and the rapid movement to cities confronted the courts with a whole flood of new community interventions. Demands were insistent that these interventions should be sustained as appropriate exercises of public power. The result has been a transformation of the earlier restrictive criteria into broader considerations of the degree of public advantage. There has also been an enormous flow of decisions sustaining exercises of community powers for promotion or operation of activities and enterprises like waterworks, electric light plants, ferries and wharves, gasoline filling stations, tourist camps, public golf courses, fairgrounds, opera houses, markets, airports, and so on.[30]

Among significant recent developments are decisions sustaining exercise of the necessary powers in the public housing program; decisions sanctioning the exercise by municipalities of powers to buy, sell, lease, and operate factories in promoting their economic development; a decision by the Supreme Court of the United States sustaining the TVA in what amounted to an exercise of the power of excess condemnation; and state court decisions sustaining the exercise of the powers necessary to carry out the new nation-wide program of urban redevelopment.[31]

Most symptomatic of the probable future expansibility of the concepts of public use and public purpose is perhaps a decision handed down in 1953 by the Supreme Court of Illinois. It authorizes the inclusion of vacant, undeveloped, suburban land within an urban redevelopment project. Citing a legislative declaration that "there existed in many communities of the State, areas of predominantly open land which are unmarketable for housing or other economic purposes because of 'obsolete platting, diversity of ownership, deterioration of structures on site improvements, or taxes or special assessment delinquencies [sic] usually exceeding the fair value of the land,'" the court concluded:

> The purpose and use to which the vacant blighted property is to be taken is both a public purpose and a public use, since the taking tends to alleviate a housing shortage, is an essential aid and adjunct to slum clearance, removes hazards to health, safety, welfare and morals of the community by developing the area, and eliminates factors impairing and arresting sound community growth.[32]

The Planning of Land Use

Land use is determined within our communities by doctrines of nuisance, by private agreements, and by public powers and controls. The impact of metropolitan perspectives may be observed upon all three of these methods.

BY DOCTRINES OF NUISANCE. Our metropolitan communities are characterized by a mixture of intensive land uses without a physical plan to mitigate their interference with each other. This situation has increased the importance of the traditional judicial zoning[33] of land uses through a retroactive application of doctrines of nuisance.

One source-book annotation, published in 1934, lists the following industries as having disturbed the peace, quiet, beauty, and safety of urban dwellers to a degree sufficient to cause them to ask the courts for redress: aeroplane engine shop, asphalt plant, automobile accessories factory, bakery, cement block plant, cotton gin, dye works, electric plant, ice-cream factory, ice plant, iron or steel works, laundry, lighting system, machine shop, mortar manufacturing plant, oil refinery, pottery, printing establishment, quarries and rock crushers, rubber factory, saw mill, shoe factory, stone-cutting plant, wire and metal products factory, woodworking plant, and miscellaneous.[34]

Confronted with this complicated situation, courts and commentators today prescribe a body of doctrine which explicitly confers upon the courts the widest discretion in resolving particular cases. Thus the Restatement of Torts frames its rules in terms of reasonableness. It generalizes that substantial and intentional invasions of "another's interest in the use and enjoyment of land" are unreasonable unless "the utility of the actor's conduct outweighs the gravity of the harm."[35]

Operating with such flexible rules, courts may reach whatever decision they deem best for balancing the equities between the parties or for determining the community's land-use patterns in any particular case. But it should be emphasized that the courts enter the case only after damage has been done. So long as conditions have not changed substantially, the courts decide only between the two parties. Moreover, they do not have the staffs or technical aids necessary for an efficient and continuous performance of planning functions. The only technical standards at their command are these elusive tort doctrines.

BY PRIVATE AGREEMENTS. The objectives of private agreements or intents to plan land uses may be confined to securing efficient uses for purposes which the community honors. But they may also include more questionable designs, such as thwarting basic community values by provisions that resources shall be locked up from beneficial use or that occupancy shall be reserved to specified races or groups.

In policing these agreements and intents, decision-makers still purport to apply the structure of doctrines inherited from pre-metropolitan days. This structure begins with an alleged distinction between estates or possessory interests and non-possessory interests or rights in the land of another. It makes questionable distinctions between legal and equitable restraints or servitudes, and among such legal interests as easements, profits a prendre, licenses, leases, and so on. All these terms refer confusingly to facts, official responses to facts, and relevant policies.[36]

It may be recalled that this structure of doctrines had its origins in a non-industrialized, rural economy which exhibited no great interdependences of land use. Moreover, as previously suggested, a study of the decisions in recent decades would probably reveal trends away from the imperatives of these traditional doctrines and toward policies uniquely relevant to the functions and agreements in context.[37]

Particular developments include decisions concerning requirements with respect to seals, writing, and other formalities with a flexibility designed to secure the reasonable expectations of parties; decisions dispensing with requirements of strict necessity and considering a variety of relevant factors in implying interests from parties' agreements; and decisions by the United States Supreme Court outlawing agreements designed to achieve racial discrimination in land occupancy. Other developments comprise an extension of

the recording acts to apply uniformly to all land planning agreements; a definition of touch and concern, as a traditional test for determining the enforce-
ability of legal covenants against successors of the original promisor, in terms
that make it essentially tautological and functionless; a definition of privity of
estate, as another such test, in terms which insure its universal presence;
the development, through the application of requirements of notice, of equitable doctrines of servitudes adequate to remedy surviving archaisms with respect to legal interests; and decisions permitting affirmative burdens in agreements to be enforced against successors to promisors.[38]

Still other developments include the definition of touch and concern in a way
to permit a flexible implication of the transfer of benefits to successors of
promisees; decisions sustaining the transferability of easements in gross; the
development of a flexible concept of building schemes to effect a wide reci-
procity in the benefits of agreements in residential developments; increasing
acceptance of the runability of both benefits and burdens in party-wall agreements; the application of a doctrine of normal evolution of uses for the
adaptation of old agreements to changing needs; the development of highly
discretionary doctrines for the judicial termination of agreements when conditions so change that continued enforcement is unfair or against community
interests; decisions designed to promote alienability by freeing covenantors
from the burdens of promises after the sale of their interests in the burdened
land; and legislative measures for termination which are designed to mitigate
the impact of ancient agreements upon contemporary uses.[39]

Despite all these trends toward rationalization in prescription, however,
private agreements are still limited instruments for community land-use
planning. Without power to coerce dissenters to join, such agreements seldom
account for all relevant interdependences. Lacking a comprehensive community plan, the permanence or stability in arrangement toward which such
agreements aspire is commonly illusory. The effective role of private agreement can scarcely extend beyond reinforcing and augmenting public standards
and controls within the context of total community planning.[40]

By PUBLIC POWERS AND CONTROLS. During recent decades, conspicuous
trends toward the rationalization of land-use planning policies appear in new
community interventions through public powers and controls. Such trends may
be illustrated by the development of techniques to secure and maintain comprehensive community design, maintain the quality of development, and
establish planning powers in areas of efficient size.

Techniques for securing comprehensive community design: An over-all
plan for physical design should anticipate and guide the community's growth
or change. To interrelate basic community components effectively, the plan
should secure the most appropriate ordering of major physical contours, including the location of business centers, industries, residential areas, public
buildings, public utilities, streets and other arteries of circulation, and so on.[41]

Within recent decades, most of our states have enacted legislation which confers upon urban communities numerous necessary powers. These powers pertain to the establishment of commissions or agencies for the continuous performance of this general planning function. They also pertain to the translation of planning recommendations into legal prescriptions for regulating private and public land use. Fortunately, the courts have uniformly sustained this legislation. The result is that today we have numerous models of statutes and procedures for comprehensive planning which are well tested for both constitutionality and effectiveness in action.[42]

Qualitative controls are now being proposed and achieved through the imposition on private subdividers of such requirements as conditions governing the recording of transfers. Extensions of municipal services to unapproved subdivisions are prohibited, and permits are refused for structures which are not properly accessible from planned streets.[43]

For the first time, the Housing Act of 1949 contains an official national recognition of the need for comprehensive metropolitan community planning. This act provides that contracts for financial aid shall require that the redevelopment plan conforms to a general plan for the development of the locality as a whole. It also specifies that in extending financial assistance, the federal administration shall encourage planning on a unified metropolitan or regional basis.[44]

Techniques for maintaining community design: The most important control which has been developed for maintaining community design is zoning, or the areal segregation or districting of uses. Every state in the country now offers legislation conferring upon municipalities various powers to zone land uses. Thirty-one states confer certain powers upon counties.[45]

In the famous *Village of Euclid* v. *Amber Realty Company* case, the United States Supreme Court sustained in principle the constitutionality of zoning. But the Court made it clear that any particular zoning ordinance might be declared unconstitutional as applied to a specific plot. In fact, this power to declare particular applications of zoning ordinances unconstitutional has been exercised occasionally by the state courts.[46]

On the whole, the courts have increasingly accepted broad conceptions of public welfare (rather than nuisance) as a justification for zoning. As a result, constitutional assaults upon zoning appear to be decreasingly successful. Some of the more recent cases invalidating zoning ordinances have involved rather arbitrary ordinances devised on the spur of the moment to forestall specific undesired developments. However, one recent case applies the test of the highest and best use to the property owner to invalidate an ordinance.[47]

The most difficult zoning problem has been the management of nonconforming uses. If permitted to continue, a nonconforming use is a sore spot which infects its area. It also increases the probability that the courts will declare invalid any applications of an ordinance to other properties, thereby augmenting the spread of nonconformity and blight. One common form of legislation meets this problem by prohibiting expansion, rebuilding when more

than a given percentage of a structure has been destroyed, or revival of a
discontinued use. A more effective type of statute authorizes the amortization
of nonconforming uses over a limited period of time. For the most part, recent
state amortization statutes apply only to counties, where the problem is not so
acute. Several cities have also adopted ordinances[48] of this type.

The trend of decision suggests that amortization provisions will probably
meet a reasonably favorable reception from the courts. The theory that a nonconforming use may be immediately eliminated as a nuisance per se, however,
has only occasionally found judicial acceptance. Most courts concede that any
given nonconforming use may be a nuisance, but require a specific showing as
to the particular enterprise. Where the investment is unsubstantial, the New
York Court of Appeals has allowed the immediate prohibition of raising
pigeons and maintaining parking lots as nonconforming uses. Where investment is substantial, as in the case of a well-constructed building, it is still
doubtful whether courts will approve less than a plan for amortization spread
over a reasonable number of years. The Fifth Circuit has upheld the application of a ten-year amortization ordinance to gasoline filling stations.[49]

Another difficult problem concerns the use of zoning ordinances in undeveloped areas. Some courts have stricken down these ordinances as unreasonable with respect to particular property owners. Other courts have
sustained carefully drafted plans, and the trend of decision appears hopeful.[50]

Perhaps the most significant recent judicial developments are the new concepts of regionalism and ordered mixed uses. The New Jersey Supreme Court
has embraced the regional concept to uphold the exclusion of heavy industry
from a small residential township. In its opinion, the Court pointed to the
availability of industrial sites nearby. The Maryland Supreme Court has approved the zoning of a part of a county against the charge that the ordinance
did not meet the statutory requirements of comprehensiveness. The New York
Court of Appeals upheld an ordinance creating a floating zone which allowed
the construction of garden apartments on any plot of ten acres or more when
approved. The decision thereby enabled a single-residence community to open
its gates to younger families whose economic development did not yet permit
the purchase of single homes. Against the charge of "spot zoning," the Connecticut Court of Errors and Appeals has upheld a Bridgeport plan for locating
small local business centers in residential communities.[51]

Another development indicates that aesthetics has achieved an increasing
acceptance as a legitimate ground for zoning. Though few courts have as yet
openly embraced the concept, recognition is sometimes phrased in terms of the
effect of unsightly structures upon neighboring property values which would
reduce tax returns. Billboard restrictions are also obtaining more sympathetic
judicial reception. A few courts, unwilling to stand on aesthetic grounds, have
reasoned that the success of billboard advertising depends on the fact that it
can be seen from the street and since the street is a public way, the state or
municipality may impose reasonable regulation.[52]

Other recent developments concern efforts to specify minimum standards for the height of buildings, the floor space or cubic content of homes, and the size of plot. Thus far, the courts have taken a cautious view of minimum height restrictions, which they regard with some justification as snob zoning or illegitimate attempts to maximize returns on taxes. With respect to minimum floor space or volume, even the Supreme Court of Michigan, which has stricken down certain specific restrictions, recognizes a reasonable relationship between the size of a home and the health of its occupants. In the much discussed *Wayne Township* case, the Supreme Court of New Jersey rested its approval of such restrictions in part upon expert testimony as to the effects of a small house upon the psychological health of its occupants. It has been severely questioned, however, whether such considerations justify the effective exclusion of an economic class from a whole township, as in the *Wayne Township* case. With respect to minimum plot restrictions, several courts have approved graduated scales for different sections of a township, upon grounds of relationship to health, aesthetics, and property values.[53]

Techniques for maintaining the quality of development: Under the conditions of intense metropolitan occupancy, communities have developed a considerable variety of techniques for policing the quality of development. Their techniques range from early tenement and multiple-dwelling regulation through building codes to more recent requirements about the compulsory repair, vacation, and demolition of buildings.[54]

The courts have accepted broad interpretations of nuisance regulation and police power urged upon them in support of these techniques. In doing so, they have confined themselves to protecting property owners against particular arbitrary actions by elaborating and applying technical prescriptions with respect to notice, hearing, the necessity of findings, modes of enforcement, appeal, review, personal liability of officers, and so on.[55]

Although some of the techniques for maintaining the quality of development may be unwise, there appear to be no constitutional or other legal reasons to preclude our communities from adopting the best existing models in regulation and procedures, including new techniques in appraisal.[56] Here, as in the case of so many other problems of the public control of land use, legality has been made to depend upon reasonableness and the degree of its proof.

Techniques for establishing planning powers in areas of efficient size: The principal obstacle to effective planning in metropolitan communities in the United States today is their almost universal division into numerous governmental units. These units disrupt natural interdependences and preclude integrated administration. A pre-eminent authority upon local government has recently asserted that no metropolitan area in our country is now "organized to prepare, adopt, and execute plans for the whole community."[57] The result is tremendous inefficiency and failures in the performance of public planning and services, with an attendant defeat of basic community values. It is also the slow economic death of the indispensable central city core of many of our metropolitan communities, as the suburbs draw the blood of such centers without contributing to their regeneration.[58]

For coping with this obstacle, a variety of legal instruments has been developed and tested within recent decades.[59] Some of these instruments, such as the extraterritorial exercise of central city powers, intergovernmental agreements, and special authorities performing special limited functions, are obviously stopgap measures designed for limited purposes and subject to many disadvantages. When procedures are adequate, however, other instruments, such as the extension of boundaries of municipal corporations to include previously unincorporated territory, the joining of two or more municipalities into a single governmental unit, and city-county consolidation, can be effectively employed in merging the disconnected parts of a community into a healthy whole.

Unfortunately, it appears that procedures for such methods are adequate only in Virginia, which has a system based on judicial determination, and in Texas and Missouri, which offer simple procedures through amendment of home-rule charters.[60] Elsewhere procedures are commonly based upon the consent of the majority of potential annexees. It remains for the state legislatures to take advantage of the wide constitutional limits in establishing more effective procedures.

The Development of Land Use

For securing specific developments in land use, communities still rely principally upon private enterprise operating within the bounds of federal, state, and local law. But some notable recent trends include the increasing employment of government ownership for the provision of facilities and services, and the increasing use of community powers to stimulate private enterprise to appropriate development.

PUBLIC OWNERSHIP AS AN INSTRUMENT OF DEVELOPMENT POLICIES. As indicated previously, the concepts of public purpose and public use have in recent decades been defined in highly expansible terms. Today they offer very little constitutional hazard to communities which seek to operate public utilities and services or other enterprises.

In fact, a tremendous flow of decisions has sustained our communities in the provision and operation of such traditional public utilities as water, sewerage, light, transportation, communication, and so on. It has also upheld communities in the acquisition and maintenance of a variety of health, educational, and recreational facilities, and most recently in the provision of low-rent housing, factory sites and facilities, and recleared sites for development in accordance with community plan.[61] In the light of these recent decisions, most of the earlier, more restrictive decisions would appear to be of doubtful future persuasiveness.

Furthermore, legally-acceptable proposals are now being made for still more extensive use of public ownership of land as an instrument of comprehensive community planning and development policies.[62]

Extensive municipal land ownership is promising not only for replanning developed urban areas, but also as a reserve for future needs and as a means of controlling private property uses. Thus blighted sections and premature subdivisions could be acquired by the municipality for replatting and title-clearing, and either retained for development at public expense or resold with restrictive convenants to control future use. Assembly of large reserves of undeveloped land, both simpler and cheaper than rehabilitation, would permit full control of future growth and withdraw property from disruptive exploitation.

With such reserves, greenbelts could be established to restrict the size and disorderly expansion of new developments, to prevent inharmonious encroachments upon homogeneous communities or to provide breathing spaces and recreational areas for congested sections. Further, such land reserves would serve as a source of future low-cost housing sites, thus eliminating much of the present obstruction caused by prohibitive land prices. And speculation in land could be substantially governed by disposal of cheap municipal real estate at strategic intervals. No control short of public ownership will be strong enough to achieve such a thorough-going regulation of urban land-use patterns and policies.[63]

COMMUNITY STIMULATION OF PRIVATE DEVELOPMENT. Trends toward increasing community stimulation of private development may be clearly observed in certain manipulations of credit and tax policies. They may also be noticed in the contemporary nation-wide urban redevelopment program which builds upon a variety of community powers invoked at different levels of government.

The manipulation of credit policies: Since the beginning of the economic depression of the 1930's, an enormous revolution has occurred in national credit policies with respect to land purchase, development, and ownership. Competent authorities have estimated that the impact of this revolution has removed practically all risks from builders and lenders in their land-use development operations.[64] The assumption of risk by the federal government obviously confers a high degree of control upon federal officials in determining the quantity and location of developments, the specific character of particular developments, and the types of public and private ownership.

The manipulation of tax policies: Students of economics have long recognized that the general real property tax is regressive. It tends to deter improvement and encourage continued exploitation of outmoded facilities. A trend toward counteracting these effects can be observed in the increasing use of various exemptions and concessions to secure desired housing and industrial developments. It may also be seen in the deliberate differentiation in a few communities of the burden on site value from the burden on improvements through the so-called graded tax.[65]

Recent observations have also indicated that the administration of the federal income tax has discernible effects upon the quantity and character of land-use development. As a result, such administration offers potentialities for guiding and stimulating developments.[66]

The contemporary urban redevelopment program: The program of urban redevelopment inaugurated under the Housing Act of 1949 represents the most comprehensive attack ever made on community slums, blight, and planlessness.[67] It would be too much to expect that this program in urban redevelopment will arrest the long-term trend toward the decentralization of our cities. Properly managed, however, it can be used to guide and promote processes of reorientation in land use which are already well under way. By the joinder of federal funds and municipal powers of land assembly, for the first time our cities are given an opportunity to enlarge and reorder their traffic facilities, to substitute modern centers of living for slums and blight, and to sponsor appropriate new commercial and industrial developments. It is to be hoped that the dispensing of federal funds can be managed so as to encourage the execution of such operations on a metropolitan or regional basis. With a few exceptions, this urban redevelopment program so far is successfully meeting its constitutional tests.[68]

FUTURE PERSPECTIVES

Today the problems inherited by our cities from their horse-and-buggy days are dwarfed in significance by the desirability of achieving the greatest possible security against atomic and bacteriological warfare. In this matter, professional planners disagree whether requirements for survival coincide with requirements for optimum living.[69] Whatever the case, one fact seems reasonably clear. If our contemporary metropolitan communities are to cope successfully with either the newer problems of achieving maximum security against attack or the older problems of arresting the decay and increasingly rapid death of their basic components, they must develop new programs in land-use allocation, planning, and development.

Has the total impact of the above-mentioned trends toward rationalization and technicalization in the land law created a body of concepts, rules, and institutions adequate to sustain and implement the necessary new programs? The answer seems to be clearly in the affirmative. Existing prescriptions and procedures are not, of course, everywhere adequate. But a comprehensive documentation of the trends discussed in this chapter would probably establish that all important constitutional issues have been resolved in ways which promise their continued favorable future resolution. It would also indicate that appropriate models in prescriptions and procedures, relating to the performance of every specific functional task necessary to the success of the required new programs, have been tested in many different communities.[70] In our present crises, therefore, the difficult problem that confronts us is not the invention of new legal alternatives. It is rather the problem of creating a consensus of opinion in our national community which will demand a more effective use of the legal alternatives now available.[71]

The task of creating a national consensus which will demand a more effective use of community powers in allocating, planning, and developing land use for both survival and a better life is one of enlightenment. Its performance will require a clarification of the fundamental values that people seek from their communities; a deepening of their consciousness of the conditions of interdependence under which they must seek such values; and an increase in their understanding of available alternatives for securing their values under recognizable conditions.

Great institutions of learning, such as the one whose bicentennial we are celebrating, are appropriately dedicated to performing these tasks. In the planning and building of his communities, man has "a right to knowledge." It is among the functions of great universities both to provide him with that knowledge and to encourage "his free use thereof."

FOOTNOTES TO CHAPTER 10

1. For various countries, see United Nations Secretariat, "Current Information on Urban Land Policies," ST/SCA/9 (April 15, 1952). For English developments, see C. M. Haar, *Land Planning Law in a Free Society* (Cambridge: Harvard University Press, 1951). For Russian developments, see J. N. Hazard, *Law and Social Change in the U.S.S.R.* (Toronto: Carswell Co., 1953).

2. 1 *Restatement of the Law of Property* (1936) 3 ff.

3. C. R. Noyes, *The Institution of Property* (New York: Longmans, Green, 1936), p. 436.

4. For ambiguous definition, see Pittsburgh Athletic Club v. KOV Broadcasting Co. (1938), 24 F. Supp. 490. For distinguishing among functions of words, see M. S. McDougal and D. Haber, *Property, Wealth, Land: Allocation, Planning and Development* (Charlottesville, Va.: Michie Casebook Corp., 1948), p. 28.

5. See R. R. Powell, *The Law of Real Property* (New York: Matthew Bender, 1949), I, Ch. 2 and Leach, "Property Law Taught in Two Packages," *J. Leg. Ed.* 28 (1948).

6. See McDougal and Haber, note 4 supra.

7. See M. S. McDougal and M. E. H. Rotival, *The Case for Regional Planning With Special Reference to New England* (New Haven: Yale University Press, 1947), Ch. 3; R. M. MacIver, *Community* (London: Macmillan, 1914), *Society* (New York: Farrar & Rinehart, 1937), Ch. 8, and *The Web of Government* (New York: Macmillan, 1947); Goodman and Goodman, *Communitas: Means of Livelihood and Ways of Life* (Chicago: University of Chicago Press, 1947), reviewed by Riesman, "Utopian Thought and Community Planning," 57 *Yale Law J.* 173 (1947); and Wirth, "Urbanism as a Way of Life," 44 *Am. J. Soc.* 1 (1938) at 18.

8. McDougal, "Planning and Development for Metropolitan Communities," *1950 American Planning and Civic Annual*, 94, 95. Cf. C. Woodbury (ed.), *The Future of Cities and Urban Redevelopment* (Chicago: University of Chicago Press, 1953), p. 718 ff.

9. See McDougal and Rotival, note 7 supra. The word *productive* used here refers to industrial and agricultural enterprises.

10. For values sought, see McDougal and Haber, note 4 supra, Ch. 6; M. L. Colean, *Renewing Our Cities* (New York: Twentieth Century Fund, 1953), Ch. 2; N. S. B. Gras, *An Introduction to Economic History* (New York: Harper, 1922), p. 187; and B. Hackett, *Man, Society, and Environment* (London: P. Marshall, 1950),

p. 4. For functioning of lesser and greater communities, see McDougal and Haber, note 4 supra.

11. See Lasswell and McDougal, "Legal Education and Public Policy: Professional Training in the Public Interest," 52 *Yale Law J.* 203 (1943); H. D. Lasswell, *Power and Personality* (New York: W. W. Norton, 1948); and Lasswell and A. Kaplan, *Power and Society* (New Haven: Yale University Press, 1950).

12. See Wirth, note 7 supra. Also Angell, "The Moral Integration of American Cities," 57 *Am. J. Soc.* 1 (1951). The most intensive inquiry would look to the structure of effective controls over the apportionment of resources. Within any given metropolis, what individuals, located in what value and institutional positions, actually make what effective decisions as to how resources are to be allocated, planned, and developed? The difficulties in obtaining answers to such questions need no emphasis.

13. See Wirth, note 7 supra, at 12. Also M. F. Millikan (ed.), *Income Stabilization for a Developing Democracy* (New Haven: Yale University Press, 1953), p. 45.

14. For an outline of real property law origins, see W. S. Holdsworth, *An Historical Introduction to the Land Law* (Oxford: The Clarendon Press, 1927).

15. For contemporary values, see *ibid.*, p. 3. Also R. R. Powell, *The Law of Real Property* (New York: Matthew Bender, 1950), II, p. 182. The point made with respect to leases may be generalized to apply to the whole flow of decisions with which we are concerned. For an indication of what a detailed study would require, see citations in note 11 supra. Illustrations of how metropolitan perspectives may permeate official utterances can be found in New York City Housing Authority v. Muller (1936), 270 N.Y. 333, 339, 1 N.E. 2d 153, 154; Duffcon Concrete Products v. Borough of Cresskill (1949), 1 N.J. 509, 513, 64 A 2d 347, 349; and the declaration of national policy in the Federal Housing Act of 1949, 63 Stat. 414.

16. Acknowledgment is made to the Michie Casebook Corporation for permission to adapt in this section a few sentences in paraphrase and quotation from McDougal and Haber, note 4 supra. The writer is also indebted to Russell C. Dilks and Richard W. Funk, third year students in the Yale Law School, for suggestions with respect to some of the illustrations in this section.

17. Adapted from McDougal, "The Comparative Study of Law for Policy Purposes: Value Clarification as an Instrument of Democratic World Order," 61 *Yale Law J.* 915, 936 (1952).

18. Such changes would include a shift from alphabetical indexes to tract indexes and the making of the public records more conclusive. See Payne, "Increasing Land Marketability Through Uniform Title Standards," 39 *Va. Law Rev.* 1 (1953) and Basye, "Streamlining Conveyancing Procedure," 47 *Mich. Law Rev.* 935, 1097 (1949).

19. For both a contract and a deed, see McDougal, "Title Registration and Land Law Reform: A Reply," 8 *U. Chi. Law Rev.* 63 (1940). For a deed later confirms, see 3 *American Law of Property* (1952) 5, 173; A. Dunham, *Modern Real Estate Transactions* (Brooklyn: The Foundation Press, 1952), p. 442; and A. L. Corbin, *Corbin on Contracts* (St Paul: West Publishing Co., 1950), V. p. 637. To suffice as a deed, see 3 *American Law of Property* 222, 279; M. Handler, *Cases and Materials on Vendor and Purchaser* (St. Paul: West Publishing Co., 1933), p. 514. For statutory requirements, see Rood, "The Statute of Uses and the Modern Deed," 4 *Mich. Law Rev.* 109 (1905).

20. For mortgages, see McDougal and Haber, note 4 supra, p. 136. For title companies, see Dunham, note 19 supra, pp. 791, 904; D. D. Gage, *Land Title Assuring Agencies in the United States* (San Francisco: The Recorder Printing and Publishing Company, 1937); and R. R. Powell, *Registration of Title to Land in the State of New York* (New York: The New York Law Society, 1938). For marketable title, see 3 *American Law of Property* 123; 4 *American Law of Property* 670; Handler, note 19 supra, p. 181. For contract and deed, 3 *American Law of Property* 62 and Handler, note 19 supra, p. 312. For interests in land, see McDougal and Haber, note 4 supra, p. 181. For recording systems, Basye, note 18 supra and 3 *American Law of Property* 755.

21. R. R. Powell, *The Law of Property* (New York: Matthew Bender, 1952), III, Ch. 36; 4 *American Law of Property* 31; Dunham, note 19 supra, p. 353; and E. M. Fisher, *Urban Real Estate Markets: Characteristics and Financing* (New York: National Bureau of Economic Research, 1951), p. 17.

22. Bennett, "The Modern Lease," 16 *Tex. Law Rev.* 47 (1937).

23. Powell, note 15 supra, pp. 181 and 182.

24. The illustrations in the last two paragraphs are taken from Powell, note 15 supra, Ch. 16; 1 *American Law of Property*, Part 3; A. C. Jacobs, *Cases on Landlord and Tenant* (2d ed.; St. Paul: West Publishing Co., 1941); McDougal and Haber, note 4 supra, Ch. 4; Niles, "Intention Test in the Law of Fixtures," 12 *N.Y.U. Law Q. Rev.* 66 (1934); and Stone, "A Primer for Rent," 13 *Tulane Law Rev.* 329 (1939).

25. See McDougal and Haber, note 4 supra, Ch. 3 and Lynn, *The Rule Against Perpetuities as an Instrument of Community Policy* (J.S.D. Thesis, 1952, Yale Law School Library).

26. This superstructure may be observed in any standard treatise or casebook upon future interests and trusts and in the *Restatement of Property* and *The Restatement of Trusts*.

27. For impolitic decision, this suggestion is based largely upon unpublished studies made by the writer and some of his students over a period of years. But it is believed that it can be substantiated by a critical reading of the standard texts. Some documentation appears in Lynn, note 25 supra, and McDougal, "Future Interests Restated: Traditional versus Clarification and Reform," 55 *Harvard Law Rev.* 1077 (1942). To remedy this evil, see Leach, "Perpetuities in Perspective: Ending the Rule's Reign of Terror," 65 *Harvard Law Rev.* 721, 739 (1952).

28. For future interests, see Report of the Law Revision Commission of New York (1935), p. 349 and Powell, "The Liquidity of Land in New York," 25 *Col. Law Rev.* 989 (1925). Powers are inadequate, see W. B. Leach, *Cases and Materials on the Law of Future Interests* (2d ed.; Chicago: The Foundation Press, 1940), p. 803. Deadhand control, A. W. Scott, *The Law of Trusts* (Boston: Little, Brown and Co., 1939), II, Sec. 167 and Brunswick, "The Court Moves the Dead Hand: The Power of a Court of Equity to Alter, Vary, or Modify the Express Terms of a Trust in an Emergency," 15 *Chi.–Kent Law Rev.* 24 (1936). For powers to alienate, see Leach, cited in this note, p. 830 and 12 *Corn. Law Q.* 549 (1927). For reverter and development of land, see Williams, "Restrictions on the Use of Land—Conditions Subsequent and Determinable Fees," 27 *Tex. Law Rev.* 157 (1948). For options in gross and development of land, see Leach, cited in this note, p. 914.

29. See McAllister, "Public Purpose in Taxation," 18 *Calif. Law Rev.* 137, 241 (1930) and Nichols, "The Meaning of Public Use in the Law of Eminent Domain," 20 *B.U. Law Rev.* 615 (1940).

30. Comments, 52 *Yale Law J.* 634 and 58 *Yale Law J.* 599 (1949).

31. For housing program, see Hill, "Recent Slum Clearance and Urban Redevelopment Laws," 9 *Wash. & Lee Law Rev.* 173, 184 (1952); McDougal and Mueller, "Public Purpose in Public Housing: An Anachronism Reburied," 52 *Yale Law J.* 2 (1942). For economic development, see Note, 47 *Yale Law J.* 1412 (1938) and People of Puerto Rico v. Eastern Sugar Associates (1946), 156 Fed. 2d 316. For excess condemnation, see United States ex rel. Tennessee Valley Authority v. Welch (1946), 327 U.S. 546, 66 S. Ct. 715. For urban redevelopment, see Hill, cited in this note, and Mandelker, "Public Purpose in Urban Redevelopment," 28 *Tul. Law Rev.* 96 (1953).

32. State ex rel. Gutknecht v. City of Chicago (1953), 414 Ill. 600, 111 N.E. 2d 626, 630, 635. Cf. Robbins and Yankauer," Eminent Domain in Acquiring Subdivision and Open Land in Redevelopment Programs: A Question of Public Use," in C. Woodbury (ed.), *Urban Redevelopment: Problems and Practices* (Chicago: University of Chicago Press, 1953).

33. W. L. Prosser, *Handbook of the Law of Torts* (St. Paul: West Publishing Co., 1941), p. 585.

34. 90 A.L.R. 1207 (1934). See also McDougal and Haber, note 4 supra, Ch. 6.

35. *Restatement of Torts* (1939), Sec. 826.

36. This structure may be observed in any standard treatise or casebook. See 2 *American Law of Property* (1952) Pts. 8 and 9; 5 *Restatement of Property* (1944).

37. This suggestion is again based largely upon unpublished studies, but it is believed that the materials collected in McDougal and Haber, note 4 supra, Ch. 8 offer substantial confirmation. See also McDougal, Review, 58 *Yale Law J.* 500 (1948).

38. For parties, see the series of articles by Conard, "The Requirement of a Sealed Instrument for Conveying Easements," 26 *Iowa Law Rev.* 41 (1940); "Words Which Will Create an Easement," 6 *Mo. Law Rev.* 245 (1941); "Easements, Licenses, and the Statute of Frauds," 15 *Temple Law Q.* 222 (1941); "An Analysis of Licenses in Land," 42 *Col. Law Rev.* 807 (1942); and "Unwritten Agreements for the Use of Land," 14 *Rocky Mt. Law Rev.* 153, 294 (1942). For agreements, see 2 *American Law of Property* 255 and 5 *Restatement of Property*, Sec. 476. For land occupancy, see Shelley v. Kraemer (1948), 334 U.S. 1 and Hurd v. Hodge (1948), 334 U.S. 24; Abrams, "Bias in the Use of Governmental Regulatory Powers," 20 *U. of Chi. Law Rev.* 414, 420 (1952) and "The Segregation Threat in Housing," 7 *Commentary* 123 (1949); also 57 *Yale Law J.* 426 (1948). For planning agreements, see C. E. Clark, *Real Covenants and Other Interests Which "Run With the Land"* (2d ed.; Chicago: Callaghan, 1947), p. 183. For references to functionless, presence, and interests, see *ibid.*, pp. 97, 111, and 170, 180. See also Neponsit Property Owners' Ass'n. v. Emigrant Industrial Savings Bank (1938), 278 N.Y. 248, 15 N.E. 2d 793. For promisors, see 2 *American Law of Property* (1952) 437.

39. For promisees, see 165 Broadway Building, Inc. v. City Investing Company and the City of New York (1941), 120 F. 2d 813. For easements in gross, see 2 *American Law of Property* 291. For residential developments, see McDougal and Haber, note 4 supra, p. 666ff. For party wall agreements, see 2 *American Law of Property* 296. For changing needs, see 5 *Restatement of Property* 479. For community interests, 2 *American Law of Property* 444 and Clark, note 38 supra, p. 184. For burdened land, Note, 21 *Corn Law Q.* 482. For contemporary uses, Clark, note 38 supra, Ch. 8.

40. See Ascher, "Private Convents in Urban Development," in Woodbury (ed.), note 32 supra.

41. See *Local Planning Administration* (2d ed.; Chicago: The International City Managers' Association, 1948); R. V. N. Black, *Planning for the Small American City* (Chicago: Public Administration Service, 1938); G. W. Breese and D. E. Whiteman (eds.), *An Approach to Urban Planning* (Princeton: Princeton University Press, 1953); and S. Spielvogel, *Selected Bibliography on City and Regional Planning* (Washington, D.C.: Scarecrow Press, 1951).

42. For public land use, see R. A. Walker, *The Planning Function in Urban Government* (2d ed.; Chicago: University of Chicago Press, 1950) and *Comparative Digest of State Planning Laws* (Washington, D.C.: Housing and Home Finance Agency, 1951). For legislation, see Mansfield & Swett, Inc. v. Town of West Orange (1938), 120 N.J.L. 145, 198 Atl. 225. For action, see the New Jersey statutes: 40 N.J. Stat. Ann. 27–1 to 27–11, 55–1 to 55–21; 52 N.J. Stat. Ann. 21–1 to 21–11 (1940, 1952 Supp.); 52 N.J. Stat. Ann. 27c (1952 Supp.).

43. See Note, 65 Harvard Law Rev. 1226 (1952); Melli, *Subdivision Control in Wisconsin* (Law in Action Research Report No. 1, University of Wisconsin Law School, 1953); and McDougal and Haber, note 4 supra, p. 790.

44. 63 Stat. 413, 417 (1949) S. 105(a); 42 U.S.C. (Supp. 1950), Sec. 1451.

45. *Comparative Digest of Municipal and County Zoning Enabling Statutes* (Washington, D.C.: Housing and Home Finance Agency, 1952); Aigle, "A New Kind of Zoning," 95 *Architectural Forum* 176 (July 1951); Williams, "Land Use and Zoning," in Breese and Whiteman (eds.), note 41 supra; Harrison, Ballard & Allen, *The Plan for Rezoning the City of New York* (1950); and Note, 50 *Col. Law Rev.* 202 (1950).

46. Village of Euclid v. Amber Realty Co. (1926), 272 U.S. 365, 47 S.Ct. 114. For state courts, see E. M. Bassett, *Zoning* (New York: Russell Sage Foundation, 1940).

47. For decreasingly successful, this statement is based on a sampling of scattered cases. For undesired developments, see People ex rel. Trust Co. of Chicago v. Village of Skokie (1951), 408 Ill. 397, 97 N.E. 2d 310. For ordinance invalidation, see People ex rel. Joseph Lumber Co. v. City of Chicago (1949), 402 Ill. 321, 83 N.E. 2d 592.

48. For nonconforming uses, see Comments, (1951) *Wis. Law Rev.* 685 and 102 *U. Pa. Law Rev.* 91 (1953). For blight, see Reschke v. Village of Winnetka (1936), 363 Ill. 478, 2 N.E. 2d 718. For discontinued use, see Comment, (1951) *Wis. Law Rev.* 698–702. For period of time, see Comment, 9 *U. of Chi. Law Rev.* 477 (1942). For not so acute and adopted ordinances, see Comment, (1951) *Wis. Law Rev.* 691.

49. For judicial acceptance, see State ex rel. Dema Realty Co. v. McDonald (1929), 168 La. 172, 121 So. 613 and State ex. rel. Dema Realty Co. v. Jacoby (1929), 168 La. 752, 123 So. 314. For particular enterprise, see City of Miami Beach v. Daoud (1942), 149 Fla. 514, 6 So. 2d 847. For nonconforming uses, see People v. Miller (1952), 304 N.Y. 105, 106 N.E. 2d 34 and People v. Kesbec (1939), 281 N.Y. 785, 24 N.E. 2d 476. For number of years, see Jones v. Los Angeles (1930), 211 Cal. 304, 295 Pac. 14. For gasoline filling stations, see Standard Oil Co. v. City of Tallahassee (1950), 183 F. 2d 410.

50. For property owners, see Arverne Bay Construction Co. v. Thatcher (1938), 278 N.Y. 222, 15 N.E. 2d 587. For hopeful trends, see West Bros. Brick Co. v. City of Alexandria (1937), 169 Va. 271, 192 S.E. 881 and Reps, "The Zoning of Undeveloped Areas," 3 *Syracuse Law Rev.* 292 (1952).

51. For nearby industrial sites, see Duffcon Concrete Products v. Borough of Cresskill (1949), 1 N.J. 509, 64 A. 2d 347. For comprehensiveness, see County Com'rs of Anne Arundel County v. Ward (1946), 186 Md. 330, 46 A. 2d 684. For single homes, see Rodgers v. Village of Tarrytown (1951), 302 N.Y. 115, 96 N.E. 2d 731. For residential communities, see Bartram v. Zoning Commission of City of Bridgeport (1949), 136 Conn. 89, 68 A. 2d 308.

52. For ground for zoning, see City of New Orleans v. Levy (1953), 273 La. 14, 64 So. 2d 798; Sayre, "Aesthetics and Property Values: Does Zoning Promote the Public Welfare?" 35 *A.B.A.J.* 471 (1949); and Bartley, "Legal Problems in Florida Municipal Zoning," 6 *U. Fla. Law Rev.* 355, 376 (1953). For tax returns, see Dunlap v. City of Woodstock (1950), 405 Ill. 410, 91 N.E. 2d 434. For judicial reception, see Comment, 35 *Marq. Law Rev.* 365 (1952) and McDougal and Haber, note 4 supra, p. 789. For regulation, see Wilson, "Billboards and the Right to be Seen from the Highway," 20 *Geo. Law J.* 723 (1942); Comment, 42 *Mich. Law Rev.* 128 (1943); Kelbro, Inc. v. Myrick (1943), 113 Vt. 64, 30 A. 2d 527; United Advertising Corp. v. Borough of Raritan (1952), 11 N.J. 144, 93 A. 2d 362; and Criterion Service v. City of East Cleveland (1949), 88 N.E. 2d 300.

53. For size of plot, see Comment, 60 *Yale Law J.* 506 (1951). For returns on taxes, see 122 Main Street Corp. v. City of Brockton (1949), 323 Mass. 646, 84 N.E. 2d 13; Brookdale Homes v. Johnson (1940), 123 N.J.L. 602, 10 A. 2d 477, affirmed without opinion, 126 N.J.L. 516, 19 A. 2d 868 (1941). For health of occupants, see Senefsky v. City of Huntington Woods (1943), 307 Mich. 728, 12 N.W. 2d 387, 390 and McClory, "The Undersized House: A Municipal Problem," 27 *Chi.–Kent. Law Rev.* 142 (1949). For Wayne Township case, Lionshead Lake v. Wayne Tp. (1952), 10 N.J. 165, 89 A. 2d 693; Haar, "Zoning for Minimum Standards: The Wayne Township Case," 66 *Harvard Law Rev.* 1051 (1953); 21 *Geo. Wash. Law Rev.* 500 (1953). For property values, see Flora Realty & Investment Co. v. City of Ladue (1952), 362 Mo. 1025, 246 S.W. 2d 771 and Fischer v. Bedminster Tp. (1952), 11 N.J. 194, 93 A. 2d 378.

54. Slayton, "Urban Redevelopment Short of Clearance: Rehabilitation, Reconditioning, Conservation and Code Enforcement in Local Programs," in Woodbury (ed.), note 32 supra; also "The Improvement of Local Housing Regulation Under the Law," 32 *Am. J. of Pub. Health* 1263 (1942).

55. Rhyne, *Demolition, Vacation or Repair of Substandard Buildings* (National Institute of Municipal Law Officers, 1945); Miner, "Constitutional Aspects of Housing," 39 *Ill. Law Rev.* 305 (1945); Comment, 29 *Ind. Law J.* 109 (1953); W. Ebenstein, *The Law of Public Housing* (Madison: University of Wisconsin Press, 1940); and McDougal and Haber, note 4 supra, p. 952 ff.

56. Twichell, "Measuring the Quality of Housing in Planning and Urban Redevelopment," in Woodbury (ed.), note 32 supra.

57. Jones, "Local Government Organization in Metropolitan Areas: Its Relation to Urban Redevelopment," in Woodbury (ed.), note 8 supra, pp. 479, 484, 534. Today the only effective metropolitan-wide planning is made by "private" public utility companies.

58. Wright, "Are Suburbs Necessary?" 35 *Minn. Law Rev.* 341 (1951).

59. Reviewed in Jones, note 57 supra, and in McDougal and Haber, note 4 supra, p. 751 ff.

60. Jones, note 57 supra, pp. 560, 562; Note, 36 *Va. Law Rev.* 971 (1950); and Comment, 19 *U. of Kan. City Law Rev.* 186 (1951).

61. J. B. Fordham, *Local Government Law* (Brooklyn: The Foundation Press,

1949), pp. 719–836; Katzenbach, "Financing Public Improvements," in McDougal and Haber, note 4 supra, p. 928.

62. National Resources Committee, *Our Cities* (1937), p. 77.

63. Comment, 52 *Yale Law J.* 634, 637 (1943).

64. For purchase, development, and ownership, see C. Abrams, *Revolution in Land* (New York: Harper, 1939) and *The Future of Housing* (New York: Harper, 1946); M. L. Colean, *The Impact of Government on Real Estate Finance in the United States* (New York: National Bureau of Economic Research, 1950); R. J. Saulnier, *Urban Mortgage Lending by Life Insurance Companies* (New York: National Bureau of Economic Research, 1950); C. Behrens, *Commercial Bank Activities in Urban Mortgage Financing* (New York: National Bureau of Economic Research, 1952); and Fisher, note 21 supra. For development operations, see Abrams, *The Future of Housing,* p. 232 and Robinson and Weinstein, "The Federal Government and Housing," 1952 *Wisc. Law Rev.* 581, 587.

65. Comment, 57 *Yale Law J.* 219 (1947).

66. See Colean, note 64 supra, p. 136; Haar and Rodwin, "Urban Land Problems and Policies in the United States," in United Nations Secretariat, note 1 supra, pp. 189, 202.

67. See Hill, "Recent Slum Clearance and Urban Redevelopment Laws," 9 *Wash. and Lee Law Rev.* 173 (1952); Robinson and Weinstein, note 64 supra; Brown, "Urban Redevelopment," 29 *B. U. Law Rev.* 318 (1949); and Comments, 44 *Ill. Law Rev.* 685 (1949) and 54 *Yale Law J.* 116 (1945).

68. See Mandelker, "Public Purpose in Urban Redevelopment," 28 *Tul. Law Rev.* 96 (1953) and Fordham, "The Challenge of Contemporary Urban Problems," 6 *U. Fla. Law Rev.* 275 (1953).

69. For bacteriological warfare, see Woodbury (ed.), note 8 supra, p. 166. For optimum living, see Monson, "City Planning in Project East River," 9 *Bull. Atomic Scientists,* 265, 266 (1953); Associated Universities, "Reduction of Vulnerability," Part V of *Report of Project East River* (1952); Colean, note 10 supra, p. 33.

70. See Monson, note 69 supra, p. 267 and Comment, "Federal Control of Land to Protect Airport Approaches," 48 *Northwestern U. Law Rev.* 343 (1953).

71. Planners sometimes blame the law for difficulties resulting from a whole configuration of factors. See A. B. Gallion, *The Urban Pattern* (New York: Van Nostrand, 1950), pp. 166, 167, 170. An overemphasis on the role of legal factors, among many other relevant variables, may be a form of escapism.

11

Commentaries

By **Charles M. Haar,** *Assistant Professor of Law, Harvard University*

The unifying thread running through the papers by McDougal and Reeve is a common recognition of one predominating factor—change. Strangely, this factor has not been sufficiently stressed in the field of property. Of all the segments of law, property is regarded as being most precedent-bound. "A page of history is worth a volume of logic." So Mr. Justice Holmes explained an obscure antiquity in the field of property law.

In one respect, adherence to the past is a valid function of the law of property. Certainty is often considered to be more necessary for performing the organized activities of society than justice. It is essential in carrying out the reasonable expectation of the people.

Nevertheless, the institution of property is subject to constant alteration. Society's direct contact with the property is via the police power, and the sole check upon the exercise of this power is reasonableness, a limitation as vague as it is broad. It can mean anything which the mores of society, as recognized by the courts, will accept.

Out of past changes in ideas and methods, Professor McDougal draws his major conclusion: rationalization and technicalization of land law policies. He uses this language as a self-defined description not calling for further exposition. Yet the recognition that even the oak of property law will bend in the wind[1] may lead to an improper identification of change with progress. Hence, there seems to be some ambiguity in the McDougal thesis.

As used by Professor McDougal, rationalization ordinarily refers to a use of reason in formulating policies. It is applied intelligence in the choice of goals, priorities, and means. On closer scrutiny, however, what Professor McDougal means by rationalization or rationality turns out to be a current tendency of the law to give a greater share of the products of society to certain classes and groups with which he sympathizes. If this legal tendency exists, rationalization seems an inappropriate label. Instead, the tendency may be ascribed to the force of political pressure in achieving some type of distributive justice which may or may not increase production or lead more effectively to selected ends.

236

Although the two tendencies are not antithetical, they do not necessarily coincide.

THE CONCEPT OF RATIONALIZATION

Let us examine several applications of the thesis of an increased rationalization in property law over the centuries.[2] In general, there are public aspects in the field of land control and regulation, private relationships between individuals, and also other applications.

Public Aspects of Rationalization in Land Control and Regulation

This field has recently experienced a marked expansion and change in scope of activities. New notions of the general welfare have made startling advances, although their soundness is still being tested.

But many problems remain to be solved. Consider the serious questions regarding our entire urban redevelopment program—problems of relocating displaced families, race relations in a democracy, and the lack of a consistent redevelopment philosophy.[3] Or take the crucial question of capital investment. Since capital investment entailed by urban redevelopment in the United States would represent approximately ten per cent of the nation's total capital requirements, is it desirable or possible to concentrate redevelopment within relatively short time periods?[4] Is the write-down of land costs the most rational way to achieve redevelopment of our cities?

With respect to aesthetics, Professor McDougal considers that its assimilation into the scope of the police power is a further sign of rationalization. But a persuasive case can be made that irrational results come from the legislative imposition of tastes and notions upon others. Most architects shy away from this kind of enforced control. For one thing, there is no one standard on which most people would agree. For another, few things could so restrict innovation and experimentation in building. The Fifth Avenue Association of New York, although fortunately not yet implemented by sanction of law, may object vociferously when a Syrian merchant who sells towels three-for-a-dollar moves into Tiffany's former store. Here is an illustration of the impact of the metropolis—an attempt to control land use because of sheer propinquity. In its control of quality, it resembles more the medieval guild, although at a higher price.

In discussing the rationalization of a land-use program, there is no need to emphasize the difficulties caused by irrationalities of our local government boundary systems. They preclude many types of regional planning which alone make sense in particular situations. Moreover, the present form of financing cities through real estate taxes undercuts much that planners are trying to achieve.

This brief survey, therefore, does not necessarily suggest that the development of property law has been characterized by rationalization and technicalization. Many administrative problems inherent in land planning are still unsolved. Consider, for example, the complicated administrative machinery, the enforcement and formulation of standards, the discretionary problems and their uniform application to those similarly situated, the selection and education of local officials, and the impact of local building inspectors and boards of appeals.

Relationships between Private Individuals with Respect to Property[5]

Here many of Professor McDougal's analogies are apt illustrations of his thesis of rationalism. But others do not seem to bear him out. How can we account for the relative nonuse of a land registration system? Again, are problems of equitable conversion being worked out more rationally today? The determination of whether the seller or buyer will bear the loss of an intervening fire depends more on the lawyer and bargaining power than upon rational equity. In land contracts, is the protection given to purchasers against economic duress in time stipulations a manifestation of increased rationality or of increased political power? While there is a strong case for rent control regulation during an inflationary period, is it rational in the sense of being the procedure best adapted to achieve the end desired? In this case, the dominant drive seems to be the political pressure of people who would not otherwise have a roof over their heads.

Take the case of the lease, which has developed from a conception of a feudal estate to one of contract. Is this progress? Many of the factors which Professor McDougal lists as showing rationality in leasehold arrangements are self-contradictory. Some expedite eviction, others retard it.[6]

One alleged sign of rationality is the increased willingness of the law to emphasize the sovereignty of individual intentions by permitting the owner to dispose of his property as he wishes. In many cases, this tendency holds true. But consider the case of the spendthrift trust. The trust is designed to carry out the grantor's desires to deal with his property as he wishes even though the present owner's intention is frustrated. But if a spendthrift trust is not permitted, the grantor's intentions are frustrated while the present owner's intentions are fulfilled. Whose intention, ownership, and control should be given full force and effect? Which one represents progress when it is favored? Different determinations may be made, of course, depending on whether the object of the beneficiary's bounty is a dashing blonde or a national cancer research institute.

Further Applications

The entire concept of rationalization—or rather humanitarian social welfare —needs further clarification. A sense of conflict of interests and their resolutions is needed. The role of various pressure groups and economic interests which culminated in the Statute of Uses in 1536 is now clear. But what of the other pressure groups and influences which distorted some objective type of rationality in the Federal Housing Act of 1949? There is also the whole range of problems associated with the reformee taking over the reform association. Consider, for example, the case of the Federal Housing Administration and the various charges made in its concern for the builder rather than for the home owner.

The law of property has evolved by constant struggle and compromises over the bundle of rights and privileges the law will protect. Yet just because a program is now being advanced by planners does not mean that it is rational. The identification of rationalism with oughtism becomes overpowering in Professor McDougal's case once it is in the interest of the dispossessed or minority groups.

No obstacle now exists to using the powers of the state for regulating property rights in order to achieve goals considered acceptable by contemporary mores. Perhaps a heritage of the nineteen thirties is the belief that any judicial validation of the exercise of legislative power is a liberal advance. But hurdling legal barriers should not be equated with desirability or rationality. Rather, the challenge has passed from the field of constitutionality to the field of achieving a rational and coordinated approach to land-use planning.[7] Here the struggle between interests, individuals, and groups—which is Professor McDougal's important insight into the processes of the law of property—must be carefully traced and evaluated.

The Influence of the Metropolis

Assuming that some rationalization has taken place, is it attributable to the factor of metropolitanism which Professor McDougal stresses? Is increased rationalism in property law truly due to the growth of cities? Rather than being the product of metropolitanism, it may be more the result of scientific thought and method. These, in turn, may be products of metropolitanism, but the metropolis may be a concomitant rather than a causal factor. The significance of scientific thought and method may be independent of the metropolis, and certainly their interaction with the metropolis requires considerably more attention.[8]

But why are we concerned solely with the influence of the metropolis on property? What about the influence of property upon the metropolis? Have the rules of property shaped the location of cities, the distribution and development of industries, or the activities of their citizens which in turn determine the nature of cities? Are there not three rather than two factors—the law of property, economic forces, and the metropolis—which interact upon each other? The investigation to be pursued then involves, first, the interrelation between market forces which gives rise to the city and its further continuance. Secondly, it pertains to the various types of property laws, and lastly to the nature of the urban center.[9]

If we concentrate on the metropolis in the United States, is there no differentiation among individual cities and metropolitan areas in their impact on the rules, concepts, and institutions of property? Is the law of property of every city, region, and state alike? Professor McDougal has apparently developed a model metropolitan law of property against which further investigation in different metropolitan areas should be made to test the variances as well as the original validity of the initial model.

In attempting to delimit the subject in question, there are at least two methods of procedure. One, chosen by McDougal and Reeve, consists of analyzing substantive problems in the field of property raised by the growth of cities. These problems include land-use regulations, and multiple-dwelling, zoning, subdivision, and urban redevelopment laws.

But are the problems created by the sheer existence of the metropolis a proper focus of attention? Will not any type of organized living—whether a Howard Green Belt system, an English satellite New Town system, or a Frank Lloyd Wright Broadacre development—create special problems which would call for a readaptation of existing property concepts, rules, and institutions? Hence, the particular drive of the metropolis in shaping property concepts should be isolated along with the adaptation which features the impact of metropolitanism. For instance, is there anything unique about the spatial arrangement of population and industry which can be attributed to changing property concepts?

In both chapters, there is nothing incompatible with the title, "The Influence of the *Nation* on the Rules and Concepts and Institutions Relating to Property." What is uniquely metropolitan about the influences therein described? Or, for that matter, what would be inconsistent in entitling this section, "The Influence of the Twentieth Century?" Take the airplane and its forceful impact on the ancient rules of property. Is that a phenomenon of urbanism? Or can changing technology more properly take the credit?

In talking about the impact of metropolitanism, let us try to isolate the non-metropolitan factors. By understanding what something is not, perhaps we will understand what it is. Suppose we look to the farmer.[10] Is he subject to less regulation in his property rights than the urban dweller? In farm areas, perhaps there is as much control and restriction on the individual's freedom, or at least as much individual freedom within a coordinated society, as in cities.

Mr. Reeve's diagram (Fig. 3) which illustrates the burden placed upon the individual lot in the metropolis is indeed striking. Yet an examination of the land-use controls in the agricultural regions of this country also reveals an extensive use of the police power. Recall, for instance, the irrigation district, the soil conservation district, and the ancient mill laws. Where the need has arisen, farmers have treated property rights with as little ceremony as have city dwellers. In short, this whole concept of land-use control is not particularly unique to the urban agglomeration.

True, within the metropolis numerous human actions and transactions occur. The pressure of concentration of people in small areas, and the pressure of competing uses for a relatively limited supply of land, is primarily a reemphasis of land-use problems existing in other societies. Since the opportunities for collision are far more frequent in the urban than in the rural environment, there may be greater need for rules of social organization in urban areas so that society may proceed with its basic activities.

In other words, the law or the underlying principle of regulation may be similar in both the rural and the urban states. Yet urban society reflects the greatest changes. Its impact on all the rural states may have brought about a seemingly uniform change in the older rural law, although the details and manifestations of this apparent process are still obscure.

By sheer number of actions and transactions, an effective demand may arise for circuses as well as for bread, museums, and libraries, or a new type of public utility like open space. This demand may foster a different relationship between the citizenry and government. It may give rise to a greater willingness to use any device, including the supposedly dread hand of government, where other methods of solving pressing needs have failed. By virtue of attitude, it may lead to a greater acceptance and demand for more governmental activity and more governmental regulation.

LAND AND POWER

Historically regarded, land is no longer the hallmark of power as it was in the early feudal times. Nor is it the primary source of wealth, as in eighteenth century England. The landlord-tenant relation no longer is close, with each person bound to the other. Instead of oaths of loyalty or fealty, a different type of swearing is prevalent in the metropolis today. Dominance of non-home ownership in the central cities precludes land from representing any longer an individual's extension of personality. Land has even lost its social status, as evidenced by the great mobility of our population which prevents attachment to any site.

Thus an entirely different scale has evolved with respect to city land. In contrast to quarter sections which form the common media of conveyancing throughout the western United States, in the city there is litigation over two inches of space. Real estate trusts and investment companies buy and sell buildings predominantly for income tax purposes.

Land is far from the castle which Blackstone said could not be invaded even in the public welfare. No longer are our statutes similar to Quia Emptores of 1290 which is by, of, and for the great lords. Legislation is now passed and construed to help the dispossessed and to increase the purchasing power of groups who otherwise could not afford certain types of housing accommodations.

This situation does not necessarily mean a rationalization of the kind which Professor McDougal suggests. To achieve a redistribution of resources, for instance, our present type of public housing program may be less effective than another. New plans and new controls may be more desirable. First, however, the axioms of this reform movement must be re-examined. In the future, there will be problems of potential abuse regarding the new concepts of property rights. There will also be a need to explore the impact of proposed reforms on individual cases.

CONCLUSION

Over the years, the law of property has taken on both advantageous and disadvantageous characteristics of constitutional law. The trend in the law of property indicates a change from certainty to what may be termed inchoateness. It has occurred as property has developed from a field technically called private law into one of public law.

The change from a law primarily governing property relations between individuals to one where the basic interests of society converge (as in eminent domain and police power cases) has important consequences. Precedent and predictability are largely gone. They are replaced by the somewhat hazy field of constitutional generalities, value judgments, countervailing forces, and lack of predictability.[11]

A legal armory is still available for planning purposes, as well as for the rational use of our land resources. But granted this power, how should it be applied? How do we work out an efficient and fair organization of society in dealing with property concepts? Actually, slogans of rationalization and technicalization may be desirable in order to supply an emotional stimulus for the changes greatly needed in our urban environment. However, the slogans should be recognized for what they are and for the confusion in policy formulation they may often engender. In the future, the efforts and energies of the legal profession must be devoted to analyzing what a public use is in a borderline case, and to determining where the general welfare lies in a particular situation.

By **Russell D. Niles,** *Dean, School of Law, New York University*

Among other things, the influence of the metropolis on real property has resulted in a flight from individual ownership of realty and a consequent preference for renting in metropolitan areas. Along with these trends has come a recognition of the important role played by the public in property law.

THE FLIGHT FROM INDIVIDUAL OWNERSHIP

The average metropolitan resident has shifted from ownership of real property to ownership of stocks, bonds, and other kinds of participations. One reason for the flight from realty ownership is that conveyancing practice has not been sufficiently modernized. Although Professor McDougal points out that deeds have now been fairly well simplified, many other conveyancing problems still exist.

Conveyancing Problems

As an illustration, take the case of the block of land on Washington Square in New York, acquired by New York University for its law school building. In

1948, New York University bought the land from Columbia University. Columbia had held it for about thirty years and had previously acquired it from a Mr. Eno, who had assembled the block some twenty years earlier. The houses standing there were more than one hundred years old.

Yet New York University was stalled off a whole year in consummating the transaction. A special proceeding had to be instituted because the mortgage lender was concerned about the status of several small gores, or triangular strips of land, which measured one to two inches wide and ran through the block. No one, except the insurance company which was to lend the mortgage money, had any question about the quality of the title. Nevertheless, plans were delayed for twelve months in order to perfect a title that nobody but the mortgagee doubted.

A little later, New York University bought another parcel of land (premises on Washington Square West known as Holley Hotel and the Holley Chambers) for a residence hall. In 1820—about the time that Aaron Burr was a neighboring owner—the parcel had been conveyed subject to a slaughterhouse condition. In other words, the conveyance specified that if anyone used the property for a slaughterhouse, glue factory, or similar purpose, the grantor could re-enter for condition broken.

That was 130 years before New York University acquired the fee. Although the condition was never repeated in the chain of conveyance, it continued in effect over almost the entire period. Fortunately for New York University, the previous purchaser spent more than $15,000 to secure a release of the slaughterhouse condition from the heirs of the various remote grantors.

These examples illustrate the fact that we still have a long way to go in making real property titles readily transferable. Because the value of property is so great, some way must be found to absorb, institutionalize, or spread the risk involved. Only then will title law and conveyancing practice remotely approach the situation now prevailing with respect to the transfer of securities. Thanks to insurance indemnity policies and regulated institutions with large resources and high ethical standards, transfer risks have been largely eliminated, and securities can be traded easily and quickly.

The solution to our conveyancing problems may lie in the concept of the insurable (rather than marketable) title, as discussed by Mr. Reeve. If so, it may evolve either through the use of the Torrens System, through title intervention by the government, or through the growth of reputable title insurance companies.

The Rule against Perpetuities

In New York and nearby states, bills are now pending to revise and modernize the rule against perpetuities. Unfortunately, these efforts seem to be typical of the mistakes often made in the field of property. Attention is being paid to the wrong thing, since the rule against perpetuities is now almost completely obsolete.

This rule developed at a time when the fee tail and the legal life estate were commonplace. The great passion of families was to retain large landed estates for generations. At present, however, the fee tail has nearly disappeared and the legal life estate is chiefly a dead letter. Although sound in policy, the rule against perpetuities is no longer an issue.

The question today pertains not to entailed estates but to various types of protective trusts. Take, for instance, the case of the Roosevelt family. When Franklin D. Roosevelt was arranging his affairs before his death, he did not entail Hyde Park. Actually, he did not wish to preserve his estate in the family and was probably glad to be able to donate it to the public. In placing the estate under a protective trust, he was astutely following a contemporary tradition of not only the great families but even families of moderate means.

It would be a mistake, therefore, to overhaul the ancient rule against perpetuities and try to adapt it to modern conditions. Instead, we should start afresh with a consideration of the problems of spendthrift or permitted protective trusts and go on from there.

THE METROPOLITAN PREFERENCE FOR RENTING

As Professor McDougal indicated, in England the law of landlord and tenant developed largely under a system of absentee landlordism. The tenant was really the owner for a term, and he assumed the risks of ownership. He did not expect the landlord to protect him against undesirable neighbors, furnish heat, remove garbage, receive parcels, or open his carriage door.

Today most tenants do not think of themselves as owners for a term. They look forward to being treated like the clients of a large department store, on the theory that the customer is always right. Thus the recent law relating to landlord and tenant, as Professor McDougal suggests, has shown an important trend away from the law of property to the law of contracts.

But in New York City, at least, the law has gone one step farther. It has changed from property to contract to status, and the implications of the trend are only dimly being seen. Under controls governing rents, eviction, and other items, the metropolitan lessee now has the status of a statutory tenant. Indeed, he may never have stood in privity with his statutory landlord at any time. Today many tenants in New York are more likely to talk over their housing problems with someone at the so-called Temporary Rent Commission than with their landlord.

In fact, the actual terms of a tenant's lease may be quite different from the original lease. A case in New York in 1953 pertained to a tenant who had signed a lease authorizing the landlord to install automatic elevators.[12] Although the lease did not mention the subject, the tenant successfully claimed that if the landlord did not install automatic elevators, he had to add a doorman. The Supreme Court in New York upheld that contention.

Similar cases suggest that the status of metropolitan tenants is a matter of politics. Considering the number of voters who are tenants as opposed to the number who are landlords, the situation could be extremely dangerous. But the implications are not necessarily bad. In the case of rent control, for example, the law of landlord and tenant seems to have been influenced by political considerations for the better.

Other worthwhile statutory changes in the law have resulted through political intervention at times when the courts could not act effectively. In the tenement house laws, the burden of repair has been shifted to the landlord. It undoubtedly belongs there, since the average New York tenant is totally unacquainted with any plumbers, plasterers, or masons.

The law of constructive eviction itself developed out of political expediency. In a famous New York case in 1826, a landlord owned two adjoining houses. He leased one to a tenant. In complaining later that the second house had been let to a person who was using it as a place of prostitution, the first tenant asked the landlord to clean up the situation. But the landlord said in effect, "It's not my problem. You can go to the police. You can sue to abate the nuisance. You're the owner for the term."

The tenant replied, "No decent person could live here. The risk is really yours." So the tenant moved out. The New York Courts sustained the landlord, of course, because the common law clearly supported such a decision. Then the case came before the highest court at the time, where elected senators sat. They said, "Why, this is an outrage!" and the burden was shifted again to the landlord in a manner contrary to the basic common law.[13]

These examples are not necessarily intended either to censure or applaud government intervention. They are merely designed to suggest that at least for the foreseeable future, the status of tenants in New York will be under the protection of the politicians.

THE ROLE OF THE PUBLIC

During recent years, the teaching profession has been largely at fault in failing to recognize that the law of property has changed. Many teachers were trained in the idea that property—and especially real property—was almost entirely a bilateral affair. There were grantors and grantees, landlords and tenants, and little more.

Today the law of property is three-dimensional, as Professor McDougal has mentioned. Every transaction involves the public as well as two private parties. Teachers have generally been slow to realize this fact. Even when rent control was widespread in the nineteen forties, a treatise published at the time on the law of landlord and tenant included only one footnote on the subject of rent control. The role of the public in property law had not ruffled the academic surface at all.

In our present era of public control and planning, it is hoped that changes will be made with a strong awareness of our historical protection of individualism. When it comes to designing an entire city for future generations, planners would do well to think of the college campus. A college community probably offers the best possible collection of people who are reasonable and tolerant of the views and beliefs of others. But when a master plan is evolved for the physical development of the campus, what happens? Under the stress of actual life, the pressure of donors, the caprice of legislatures, the exigencies of depressions, the demands of returning veterans, the cycles of the birth rate, and the changes in administration, the master plan is soon a shambles.

This does not mean that we should not aspire to a better use of our precious metropolitan land. It does suggest, however, that in doing so, we should have the humility and caution that training in the ancient law of property is likely to give.

FOOTNOTES TO CHAPTER 11

1. Has the law of property been less yielding than the law of contracts or torts? If so, in what way? Would a contrast among them delineate more clearly the impact of the metropolis on the rules, concepts, and institutions of property?

2. The difficulty of generalizing over so long a period of time, over so many diverse jurisdictions, and over so many cross-eddies emphasizes the need for a careful delimitation of the problem. Consider the case of increased marketability of title. Underlying the legal superstructure pertaining to title is the corollary that a servitude ceases when its purpose can no longer be effectively accomplished. Thus where urban land changes from commercial to residential or industrial use, a servitude formerly applicable to commercial uses should become unenforceable. Yet the Uniform Reverter Acts, which in their quest for title marketability seek to undo restrictions on title, may make it impossible to maintain a plan for a desirable subdivision. In fact, the same device which is "progressive" in one case may be "regressive" in another situation. This whole conflict between planning enforcement and marketability has recently flared up in states as diverse as Massachusetts, New Jersey, and Wisconsin. There conveyancers have attempted to repeal some of the planning attempts to control, on the ground that title has been affected too severely. Such countervailing forces, which Professor McDougal's framework so admirably sets up, defy generalization.

3. See the articles by Bauer and Churchill in C. Woodbury (ed.), *The Future of Cities and Urban Redevelopment* (Chicago: University of Chicago Press, 1953).

4. See L. Grebler, "Urban Redevelopment as an Outlet for Capital Investment," *Land Economics*, XXIX, No. 4 (November, 1953), 358–361.

5. One of Professor McDougal's great achievements in the field of property throughout the years has been his emphasis upon the presence of society in many activities which at first glance seem purely "private" transactions between two individuals alone.

6. The development of printed legal forms clearly reflects the impact of the metropolis. They represent a "counter-revolution" by landlords against "liberal" statutes and decisions which favor tenants. The printed forms are said to do everything to the tenants but require them to stand up and salute whenever the landlord enters the room.

7. This is a long-range view of a probable trend. Here the cosmic eye of the law professor should be distinguished from the worm's eye view of the hard-working practitioner, who has the job of pushing the constitutionality of a particular case.

8. Speaking of rationalism, it should be clear that the ancient feudal law of property was rational for its age. Technical rules grew up to meet certain needs of

feudal society. Land law was based on providing administrative, governmental, financial, and military functions in a society in which they would otherwise have been absent.

9. In a study of the impact of the metropolis upon property, the expansion of personal property, negotiability, the law merchant, and commerce should all be emphasized as well as land. Since the papers by McDougal and Reeve concentrate on realty, the attention given to land may be justified. But the importance of personalty should be kept in mind as a possible redress of balance.

10. Perhaps one approach which may help to delimit the problem is a study of a typical day of a country lawyer and of a city lawyer. This might reveal the different type of activities and the different relations of property which their respective clients come into contact with.

11. In this sense, law may be rational even though the result is undesirable. To the extent that law can predict that a certain result will necessarily flow from a certain sequence of events, it becomes rational.

12. In re Jerlan Holding Corporation v. Joseph McGoldrick as State Rent Administrator (1953), 281App.Div. 545, 120 N.Y. Supp. 2d 761.

13. Dyett v. Pendelton (1826), 8 Cowen 727 (Court of Errors of the State of New York), and Pendleton v. Dyett (1825), 4 Cowen 581 (Supreme Court in the State of New York).

PART FIVE

The Influence of Science and Technology on the Metropolis

INTRODUCTION

The metropolis, among other things, is a product of modern science and technology. Recent developments in communication, transportation, sanitation, and similar fields have all contributed toward larger and more complex urban agglomerations. At the same time, they have made it easier to disperse our metropolitan areas. The dichotomic aspects of these contributions are highlighted by the harnessing of atomic energy. It can be used indifferently to supply our communities with power or to blow them up.

Other scientific advances have brought about a progressive decline in urban death rates, especially in infant mortality. It is questionable, however, whether it makes sense to speak of the ability of cities to renew themselves biologically. To what extent can biological measures be applied significantly to political units? When should they be employed only within reference to a whole demographic region of a nation?

The suburban trend has been made possible by better methods of communication and transportation. But its implications for the future are uncertain. Just because everyone seems to be running in the same direction does not necessarily imply that the goal is correct. Suburbanization may be desirable in face of possible future warfare. It may be undesirable in terms of man's possible inability to adjust to the new conditions and tensions which suburban commuting imposes.

Can the scientific advances which have led to atomic energy devise a form of the metropolis which is relatively immune to damage from atomic bombs? It may be foolish to incorporate the latest scientific and industrial improvements in our growing metropolitan areas if they thereby become more likely to be bombed in event of war. Whatever the case, the future use of atomic energy—for isotopes, power, or war—is now primarily a political rather than a technological question. It is largely a matter of federal policy decided behind closed doors.

Possibly the ultimate answer to our scientific and technological problems rests in our minds. Our only salvation may reside in a spiritual consideration of human values. If further technical improvements are realized in communication and transportation, urban populations may travel extensively and spread over the face of the earth. When the whole world has become one metropolis, perhaps a new world-wide community spirit will allow us to concentrate exclusively on the peaceful uses of atomic energy for the benefit of all mankind.

12

The Effects of Scientific Progress on Metropolitan Communities

A. V. HILL

Professor Emeritus of Biophysics
University College, London

About seventeen cities in the world have more than two million inhabitants. Twenty-seven others have one to two millions. Their total population is sixty to seventy millions, or approximately 2½ per cent of the population of the earth in 1954. Proportionately, their importance is much greater than the number of their people. They contain many of the principal treasure houses in the world and many of the best examples of how people live and work together. Their influence is outstanding in intellectual, religious, artistic, and civic activities, science and engineering, social, legal, and political development, industry, and world trade and intercourse. The influence of these great cities is largely derived from the special opportunities they offer to people of outstanding ability who are born and bred outside them. Most great urban areas come under the category of the metropolis—the mother city.

It might be said that the word metropolis has outgrown the maternal metaphor and today merely refers to an urban region of more than a certain size. Detroit, for example, has nearly two million people. Is it therefore a metropolis? A mother city of what—automobiles? Or should the biological metaphor now be dropped? If metropolis is used merely as a measure of size, however, is not the English language being robbed of a pleasant word for an important idea?

London, for instance, is an enormous built-up area with about one-sixth of all the inhabitants of the United Kingdom. But it is something more, as the London soldier revealed when he was asked by Canadian soldiers where he came from. Replying "London," they inquired, "London, Ontario?" To which he retorted scornfully, with Cockney impudence, "London, the whole bloody world."

That is the real sense of metropolis. It implies a relationship of affection,

253

tradition, and pride as well as of common interest. Despite their size, many comparatively small cities qualify for metropolitan status because communities throughout the world look to them with affection and interest.

SCIENTIFIC AND TECHNOLOGICAL DEVELOPMENTS AND CITY LIFE

The chief characteristic of the mother city is the wide variety of its activities and interests, and their connections with the world outside. These aspects can be considered from various social, economic, political, or religious viewpoints. With regard to science and technology, the hour-to-hour activities of a modern city depend on many achievements based on discovery and invention in engineering, telecommunications, medicine and surgery, hygiene and microbiology, metallurgy and chemistry, agriculture (by which 10 per cent of the population today can feed the remaining 90 per cent), food preservation and water supply, drainage, and all the scientific control by which normal needs are met and emergencies anticipated.

There is a very long history behind all these achievements, starting perhaps with the invention of fire, the use of wheels and the domestication of animals, down to present-day nuclear power and biological control. Rather than explain how the whole pattern of life in a modern city depends from moment to moment on established technical methods, it were better to speculate on how changing techniques based on new discovery may fundamentally alter the conditions, or even the possibility, of city life in the next fifty years.

Birth and Death Controls

Suppose for example, that family planning became easy by the oral administration of a harmless drug. Whether we like it or not, this might come with no more warning than the discoveries of insulin and penicillin. Suppose further that it were practicable by simple means to arrange beforehand whether the intended baby should be a boy or girl. What would the effect be? Would the ratio of the sexes remain about unity, or would there be more men than women, or vice versa? And would far fewer children be born than now, so that the population would become a rapidly aging one?

As a matter of fact, the population is already aging, because sulpha drugs and antibiotics have removed some of the chief killing diseases of the elderly. Suppose that other killing diseases, particularly cancer and disorders of the heart and circulation, were brought under control. As a result, physical and mental efficiency as well as the longevity of the older group would increase, particularly if such diseases as rheumatism, arthritis, and arteriosclerosis were controlled. Then older people could continue to do the world's work efficiently, if the younger ones would let them! But it is scarcely likely that increased efficiency would fully compensate for the fall in the death rate. For one characteristic of old age, as much as incapacity, is lack of ambition and desire.

If all this happened—as it well may, for intense effort is being devoted to these things—and if far fewer children were born, the problem of providing for the aged would greatly increase the social and economic burden which the younger would have to bear. We cannot be sure that these discoveries will be made or when. But the trend is obvious and there can be little doubt of the extent of the impact they would make on social, economic, and political life. Remember that old people have votes, which will tend to exert a continually increasing political pressure as their numbers rise. All this will affect the life of the whole population. It will particularly influence the life of people in cities, for that is where its impact will be first felt.

Power Supply

The future of industrial civilization, and consequently of large cities, is completely dependent on an adequate supply of power. The available fuel resources of the world, taken all together, may last a good many centuries, although the most convenient of them, oil, will endure for a much shorter time. The exploitation of known sources of power, particularly water power, will continue. In some countries like Brazil, immense reserves are still available. Other sources of power from sunlight, tides, winds, and nuclear energy will be tried out.

In the meantime the more convenient reserves of stored energy, in coal and oil, will gradually be used up. The remainder will become increasingly difficult to exploit and transport unless power can be developed directly from underground coal and transferred electrically over long distances to where it is needed. In the United States, the problem of power is not likely to be acute for several decades, at least. But many countries are entirely without oil and coal; others, such as India, have very little oil, and their moderate amount of coal is located hundreds or thousands of miles from where much of it is wanted.

Granted reasonably stable world conditions and facilities for exchange and transport, there is no immediate emergency. Without being unduly optimistic, one may expect new sources of power gradually to become available. The future of industrial civilization will depend absolutely on that. Meanwhile, we shall continue to use up our reserves of stored energy and, more important, our stored chemicals. Our great grandchildren may well look back on us as reckless spendthrifts for the way we have wasted valuable chemical materials, the basis of chemical engineering, merely for producing calories which we then use very inefficiently. But there is little yet we can do about it, except to husband what we have and press on with scientific invention and the technical development of new resources.

The possibility exists of obtaining electric power directly from sunlight by enormous photocells, with a high quantum efficiency. The expense of the photocells would be equally enormous, but not much more than that of inefficiently producing power from steam generated by reflectors of sunlight. In the winds and tides, an enormous amount of power is potentially available. But the apparatus for collecting it would be of vast size and the amount of machinery and space needed for 100,000 kilowatts—the output of a medium generating station—would be prohibitive. Moreover, the supply would be intermittent, depending on weather, time of day, and other variable factors.

Unfortunately, no convenient and economical method of storing electric energy on a large scale has yet been developed. That invention, if it could be made, would have vast economic importance. Imagine the improvement of transport, and of many other social and industrial activities, if electric power could be stored in a form as light and convenient as fuel. Instead of going to the gas station, one might just connect up for a few seconds to the power mains. There is no practical approach to this problem as yet, nor may there ever be. Still, television was unthinkable fifty years ago.

As a source of power, the most likely substitute for chemical fuel in the future is nuclear energy, the internal energy of the atom. The technical problem itself is already some distance along the way to solution, at least in principle. But the economics of large-scale power production depends on a number of technical questions which research and experience alone can decide. It depends upon the supply of fissile material, the possibility of breeder reactions for producing more, the disposal of radio-active products, the behavior of metals subjected to long-term neutron bombardment, the cost of the plant, and the remote possibility of using the energy directly instead of through the wasteful intermediary of heat and steam.

In spite of these uncertainties, it is a reasonably good guess that in fifty years electric power will be generated to a considerable extent from nuclear fission. Such a state of affairs could have a vast influence on the development of industry, and indirectly of agriculture, particularly in large regions where fuel supplies of the present kind are difficult to transport and short in supply. This may mean that large centers of population will grow up in many places in the world where the availability of power is now the limiting factor. Or, it may mean that smaller industrial centers will be preferred, especially in places where water supply provides the limiting factor.

A plentiful supply of power, preferably electric, is essential to the development of modern industrial civilization. At present, the only practical method of obtaining mechanical or electrical energy from chemical or nuclear energy (the internal energy of the molecule or atom) is to turn it first into heat and make it drive a heat engine. As a result, only a fraction of the energy is made available and the greater part is wasted as heat. If other means than the heat engine could be developed for producing electric power more directly and efficiently from atomic energy, the problem of power would be greatly eased.

Or if even a more efficient and inexpensive heat pump could be devised, it might have a vast effect on the amenities of cities. Consider the influence which refrigerators have already exerted. Only a few years ago, refrigerators were a novelty. Today space cooling, or air conditioning, is becoming a necessity in hot countries. A refrigerator is a cold pump, and generally a very inefficient one, but the amount of power required is small in proportion to the value of the result achieved. Its invention and common use have made a major contribution to nutrition, hygiene, and general comfort.

Noise and Dirt

In the city, a great reduction of noise and vibration is not at all beyond the range of invention and technology. Smoke can be greatly diminished by methods and regulations already known. Rather than using individual fires and furnaces, district heating could reduce smoke almost to nothing, perhaps by employing the waste heat of power stations or industrial undertakings.

Dirt is largely a matter of educating the public conscience. Imagine what London would have looked like after the coronation in 1953 if bulky American papers had been available to throw about instead of their slender English counterparts!

Transport

One of the gravest burdens of the large city is transport. The electrification of railways has gone a long way in the greater metropolitan areas, and now the problem lies largely with the highways. If three-dimensional transport through the air could be developed to operate over medium and short distances, highway congestion might be relieved to some extent. It may be, however, that human nature on the whole rather likes crowds and is ready to accept a certain saturation level of delay and inconvenience. If new methods of transport were supplied, people might pour into the cities until the same degree of inconvenience, danger, and delay was achieved. This is a common feature of human behavior. It provides a social and psychological problem as much as an engineering one, and has no simple solution.

Water Supply

One of the primary needs of a metropolitan region is a plentiful supply of water. As the standard of living rises, so does the quantity of water used and wasted. The amount of water available in rivers and lakes, or underground, is not at all unlimited. In many parts of the world, water is the dominating factor both in agriculture and in urban and industrial life.

Near the sea, unlimited salt water is available, but this is useless for most industrial or domestic purposes. According to thermodynamics, the minimum amount of energy required to produce fresh water from the sea is extremely small in principle. For example, a cubic foot of fresh water would need about 60,000 foot pounds, which is the amount of work required to lift the water 1,000 feet. One horsepower could produce 20 tons in a day. That may sound absurd today, because by any known or conceivable method the amount of energy required would be hundreds of times greater. Or if chemical methods were used, the cost of the chemicals on a large scale would be prohibitive. But improvements in invention and technology now being sought may give fresh water from the sea with an expenditure of energy within the range of what is economically profitable. If so, the problem of water supply for industry and urban life might be solved for regions near the coast where fresh water is at present inaccessible.

Modern Warfare

In the present state of scientific and technological development and world politics, the possibility of a major war between great industrial states continues to exist. Judging from World War II, such a struggle would be fought not only between navies, armies, and air forces but also by attacks on industry and the industrial population. Pursued with ruthless ferocity, the war might bring civilization as we know it to an end over large regions of the earth.

The efficient conduct of modern war requires enormous technical development and industrial production, now concentrated more and more in relatively confined regions. According to a report by the American Institute of Planners, more than one-quarter of the manufacturing employment of the United States is assembled in the five largest metropolitan areas. More than one-half is found in the top forty. In the United Kingdom, one-sixth of the whole population lives in London; one-third resides in towns (including London) with populations of more than a quarter of a million.

Apart from "frightfulness" by which the *will* to resist is intended to be broken, major damage to industrial production and transport, obtained possibly by surprise attack, could greatly reduce the *power* to resist whatever happened to the will. In fact, if war is to be regarded as a possibility, the target provided by these enormous industrial areas, together with the possession of a reserve of nuclear weapons and the means to deliver them, might put an almost unbearable temptation in the minds of crazy men like Hitler and the Japanese rulers of 1941.

The future, therefore, of the great metropolitan areas is bound to depend on several factors. First of all, on our assessment of the likelihood of war and of the temptation these targets offer to potential aggressors. Since big cities are not replaceable by small ones on short notice, this assessment must be projected from present data for a long time ahead. Secondly, the future of our cities may be based on our estimate of various technical means of defense against direct military attack or concerted sabotage. Since methods of attack and defense change rapidly with scientific and technical advance, this estimate also must be projected from very imperfect knowledge. Finally, it will rest partly on our appraisal of the cost and profit and loss to civilization and industrial output of abandoning the greater centers and distributing their resources, treasures, and populations elsewhere.

The most likely solution is a compromise between military and other aspects of metropolitan existence, effected by encouraging dispersion and limiting the expansion of existing urban areas. But no major contribution to military security could probably be achieved without a drastic limitation of present freedom and rigorous planning controls.

Unfortunately, there is another possible method of mass attack which, unlike nuclear weapons, does not even have the excuse of destroying industrial war potential. The effectiveness of biological warfare has never yet been tried, but its incidence could only be on populations or possibly on agriculture. It is probable that the potentialities of chemical and bacteriological warfare are as grave as those of nuclear weapons. At any rate, chemical and bacteriological devices are much less susceptible to international control, since the factory required to produce them could be small. In an all-out war, the bacteriological weapon might conceivably be used to finish off built-up areas softened by preliminary bombardment.

In view of such grim possibilities, the argument for dispersal is further strengthened. So is the argument for political settlement and international control. Is man so mad that his passions, fears, ambitions, and parochial selfishness will use scientific discovery and technical development, with all the incomparable gifts they have to offer for human welfare, to reduce all his achievements and treasures to dust and destruction? From such sombre possibilities, we can see that the future well-being of mankind does not depend alone on scientific and technical development and agricultural and industrial expansion, important as these are. It also rests on good will, friendliness, and tolerance, sanity and reasonableness, and the art and craft of statesmanship.

THE CITY AS AN INCUBATOR OF SCIENTIFIC AND TECHNOLOGICAL ADVANCES

Scientific and technical advances, therefore, will play an essential part in the future of our industrial civilization and our cities. But action and reaction are reciprocal, and in many ways our great cities supply both the stimulus and means to promote this knowledge and its application. For example, the stimulus provided by New York City is partly intellectual, as a result of the fact that it furnishes the frequent and familiar contact between learned people of all kinds. It is partly due to the enormous facilities of libraries, museums, galleries, and learned institutions, which only a large community can afford. It is also partly attributable to the impact upon the citizens of the life and industry of a vast and variegated society. Much of this is not found in a smaller center.

From Athens onwards, science and learning have grown up in the larger centers. In England during the last three hundred years, the Royal Society of London has exerted an immense influence on the advance of scientific knowledge and discovery. In the last two hundred years, the British Museum has rendered incomparable service to scholarship, history, and archaeology. The same opportunity has been taken by learned institutions in many of the greater cities of the Old and New Worlds.

But the great cities have provided more than intellectual stimulus and necessary facilities and resources. They have made evident the needs for discovery and technical advance and they have supplied the means to meet them.

Progress in medical knowledge and treatment, for instance, has taken place in large urban centers where the needs of patients are obvious, where a multiplicity of disease occurs, and where public conscience can be stirred to provide the necessary facilities. Had men lived only in small isolated communities, the advance towards modern medicine would have been far slower. The forty greatest cities in the world hold two to three per cent of the world's population. How many times more than two to three per cent of medical knowledge and treatment has been derived from their schools and hospitals?

As in medicine, the same thing is true also in the practical arts and sciences and in industry, transport, and communications. Many applications of these developments have been made a long way from the great cities themselves. But how far would the roads and the great engineering works of imperial Rome have gone without the nucleus of Rome itself? How far would navigation, exploration, and discovery have progressed apart from the energy and enterprise of the great seaports and their companies of merchant venturers? It would be the greatest disaster to the world of learning and discovery if the threat of war caused the great metropolitan centers to dissipate their resources of men and knowledge and abandon their intellectual function in the world.

It were better surely to take the risk. With orderly and peaceful development, the progress of civilization can go on. Somehow in the broad domain between militarism on the one hand and pacifism on the other, friendliness and mutual understanding must bring men together. Here scientific men are offered a peculiar opportunity. For science itself is one of the greatest of all international adventures. Discoveries can be made anywhere and by anyone, and the whole scientific community everywhere profits equally by the work of each. In other words, science can provide a shining and unique example of international friendship and cooperation. In that, perhaps even more than in guiding the way to technical betterment, lies its highest form of service.

13

The Adaptation of Design to the Metropolis

RICHARD J. NEUTRA
Architect, Los Angeles

In recent times, the sciences have perhaps contributed more conspicuously to the development of the metropolis than in ancient or medieval ages. Modern science has not only added comfort to urban life but even appears to have made it possible in its present magnitude. When Herodotus describes Babylon as nearly equalling the size of greater New York and fails to mention rapid transit and subways, or crosstown buses and taxicabs, we are at a loss to picture a megalopis of this kind.

It is only too obvious that the progress of the physical and mechanical sciences during the last five or six generations has contributed to the engineering of what we today call the metropolis. Yet so far, the biological branches of the sciences have only sporadically influenced technical design. Nevertheless, in the coming biotechnic age, as Lewis Mumford has presaged the next to be, criteria to judge design will generally have to be of a well-informed physiological nature.

NEW PLANNING REQUIREMENTS

The Biological Viewpoint

Animal species survive by adjustment to their habitat or else they perish. Our human species may itself perish by its own explosive and insidious inventions. The atom bomb is only the most spectacular of them. Man is a tinkerer, and through the uncoordinated technical avalanches of the Victorian age, the metropolis has become his most gigantic, puzzling tinker-toy. If man is to survive in the city, comprehensive design and systematic redevelopment will have to replace tinkering and profiteering.

But design is not a question of "the bigger the better"—bigger power plants, school systems, hospitals, traffic, or engineering measures. Modern science has overtaken the practical man by emphasizing the minute transactions in organic systems, and specifically in nervous systems. We die not only from the blows from bigger and better sledgehammers. We also are vulnerable to subtle bio-

261

chemical and biophysical actions, arising from the countless irritations of city life. Eight to nine million Americans a year cool their heels in psychiatric waiting rooms and asylums. This technogen pathology can no longer be permitted. Survival of the race calls for plan and design.

In designing our environment, planners must recognize that they ought to act as applied biologists. At least, they should take biological news under advisement and understand that they are not simply dealing with plastics, stainless steel, plate glass, materials, colors, forms, neon tubes, mechanical gears, real estate subdivisions, and highway interchanges. In the last analysis, they are always dealing with human nerves and catering to sensitively-responding human organisms. These organisms are not normally found in an isolated condition, but have grown into a social agglomeration which is a community.

If we take this biological view, magnitudes of large and small take on other values and call for other appraisals than the geometrical or mechanical measures of physics or astrophysics which are indifferent to the capacities of a human being.

Man's Capacity to Assimilate and the Ranges of His Operations

When physiologically observed and understood, size, bigness, or smallness are closely related to man's capacity of assimilation—his range of muscular or sensorial interaction. In other words, whether a dish of food is large or small depends on how much we can digest, or believe we can. Our appetite has its limits and is not of Euclidean or abstract infinity.

Long before man built houses and cities, he was a physiological being concentrically surrounded by specific "ranges." Into these ranges, he can muscularly act by degrees; from them, stimuli reach his senses by degrees and influence his life. These senses and muscles are not independent of each other, but are engaged in a continuously fused operation. Above all, they are thoroughly connected with a brain and, in fact, exert a formative influence on it.

We are surrounded, consequently, not by indifferent space but by specific ranges of our potential acting or sensing. This has very much to do with the community in which a man feels fulfilled, satisfied, or frustrated. If his food is the only food he can assimilate, so his city belongs to him in a similar respect. It would not be his city if it were beyond his ranges of practical biological action.

Practical Biological Facts

In this respect, the word practical is equal to biological. Unfortunately, practical is conceived in contemporary city life only too frequently to be a derivative of the financially economical, the economically promising. But the expression financially economical and promising is in itself quite a composite. Economical has a ring of hard facts clanging metallically against each other. Promising, on the other hand, deals with the pleasantries of imagination. How far, truly, is economics from social psychology, or how close to it? Anything close to psychology is, in turn, closest not to hard facts but to the softly elastic and resilient give-and-take of organic life, and in particular of brain action. These biological facts are now called practical. Obviously, the basic terminology proposed here is different from the parlance of a city council chamber.

Yet such a view is neither novel nor disputable. All events or facts would not exist for us if they were not sensorial, perceptible, and somehow products of our understanding. Biologically speaking, this is an eminently practical picture. In the last analysis, nothing is more practical than to find out whether we organically thrive or wither. This view could be named biological realism.

In a physiological sense, survival is treated as practical, because essentially and originally nothing is more practical. A sewer system, for instance, may not yet be paid off financially, or may be only partly amortized. Yet it may be leaky and superseded, so that it is no longer practical physiologically. The contemporary urban scene is geared to similar advances which are faster than amortizations. In many places, the so-called practical minds of the city fathers, municipal department chiefs, revenue accountants, traffic engineers, redevelopment directors, and in general, voters, taxpayers, and bankers, are untuned to a biological recognition of what is essentially practical and needed. They bewail the abandonment of what has not yet paid off economically.

On the other hand, our cities are often infested with things which *have* paid off a long time ago. In some cases, they seem to be still bringing in handsome financial returns even though they are physiological liabilities. Absentee-owned slums, for instance, may be abandoned to progressive deterioration without upkeep because "rental, as is" provides a lovely yield over "no upkeep and outlay." But biological condemnation of a slum is easy; from this point of view, slums are not at all practical. The statistical search of records of patient admission and medication costs in tax-maintained hospitals, as related to the geographical areas where the patients come from, is only an economically-camouflaged physiological indictment of the slum. It is almost funny that we need a dollar-and-cent proof that it is worth surviving and being well enough for a healthy life.

PLANNING AND DESIGN FOR SURVIVAL

The Planning Process

For a long time, cities both grew and were planned at the same time. Planning generally means to consider known facts, to anticipate further processes of this nature, and to accommodate them by appropriate provisions. The planning and designing process (however described) is intrinsically organic. As such, it has to do with previous growth and conditioning within our nervous system and with simultaneous maturation as essential concomitants. Perhaps we will never quite know what is cause and consequence in these matters.

This sort of planning concerns the anticipated use of modern technical instruments like our unprecedented grading machines which transact equally unprecedented earth movements on a giant scale; our wonderful paving machines which will take care of more than thirty per cent of the area of the new town; our know-how in tunnelling under rivers or downtown sections; our engineering of huge and complex speedway interchanges; our electric signalling of traffic; and the transport of sewage all over the map.

Planning also depends on other technical instruments like mimeographing, blueprinting, and mathematical computing equipment and typewriters which produce eight variously-colored copies of each office memo. Our modern planning presupposes an army of surveying, soil testing, and tabulating crews and a host of other activities. All are endowed with apparatus of which the peaceful Euclidean city planner of Miletus or Alexandria never dreamed. A diversified team of skilled people assembled by an impersonal system of civil service examinations, plus a huge cluster of considerations, is geared to planning as well as to the carefully-anticipated management that goes with it.

The entire process does not confine itself to a planimetric two-dimensional layout. There has already been a pernicious preponderance of mere geometrical architecture and planning. Unfortunately, geometry is pure and indifferent to the exigencies of life. The most natural object of planning is existence in *four* dimensions—in space-time where truly all processes and running events of real life are at home. Metropolitan planning will be safest if geometrical, mechanical, and sociological contributions are weighed in the light of biological realism, and if research on what is biologically bearable underlies all design decisions.

Undoubtedly, planning of a community is hard to accomplish by total anticipation. In most cases, cities undergo a continuous treatment of replanning. This, too, is a justified organic phenomenon. For our brains are not really built to produce thoughts. They are constructed to produce afterthoughts, so to speak, in a continuous chain without beginning or end.

Scientific Observational Methods Suitable for City Planning

In order to fit external circumstances, our thought chains should be swayed by observations so as to be more scientific. In speaking of the active hand science has taken in moulding the metropolis, therefore, we should also talk of the method that science has applied to observation. For example, Professor Detwiler, the renowned physiologist, has expressed doubt that observation can be pure and inactive. He thinks that, when linked with observation, a little active meddling into life processes helps to gauge what happens after the meddling ends. As applied to the living city, organic realism in design can take a leaf from morphology and operative physiology.

"Observational methods alone, without a bit of experimental interference with the observed processes, are bound to remain more or less static," said Samuel R. Detwiler, professor of anatomy at Columbia University, in his outstanding work on neuro-embryology. He maintained that this realization "has gradually transported the embryo into the hands of those who are subjecting living embryos to such alterations . . . in environments as are pertinent to an analytical study of the dynamics of the developing organism." Would it not, then, be interesting to alter also that "post-natal" environment, i.e., the neighborhood, the community in which dwell the infant, the adolescent, and the never quite finished adult?

This physical environment, the neighborhood, the town itself, can be observed as an organism. According to Detwiler there are "many lines of experimental study dealing with the nature of forces underlying the development of normal *architecture* in both central and peripheral systems." Such study will be concerned with the much needed "knowledge of the interacting morphogenetic agencies."

All this may seem rather doctrinaire to the practical planner who is forced to be a politician when he finds himself up to his ears in opportunistic "spot-zoning" to please business interests here and there, or when he has to struggle against the superficial aestheticism of an amateurish lady or gentleman on the planning board. What can the statements quoted above mean to him?

If properly grasped, they can be eye openers. It is indeed possible and fruitful to speak of "morphogenetic agencies" in relation to the physical growth of a human community. We have here a splendidly pointed expression for *form-creating forces*. Science has, in many cases by means of objective observation, established *influences that determine the emergence of forms*, and thus a recognized scientific term signifies a known and fascinating phenomenon. In architecture, the idea is still rather muddled, that is to say, in the architecture of architects, not the "architecture" of embryos and organisms in general of which anatomist Detwiler speaks, and which has been so meticulously investigated by men like him.

"Through studies upon regeneration, and, in recent years, by the methods of surgery on the embryo and penetrating explanation, many interesting and highly significant facts have been made clearer. From these assembled data have emerged various hypotheses regarding the role of agencies underlying normal architecture in the nervous system." If the physiologist does so readily and repeatedly resort to architectural allusions, perhaps the planner may in turn cast his glance on natural prototypes and be well advised to profit from physiological terms. After all, physiology has precedence in studying the interrelations of forms and functions. But on another level, this is also the job of the architect. And so a physiologically minded planner may discover useful hints in terms as well as in certain practical methods of research developed by physiologists. Analogous ideas will indeed suggest themselves to him, while the possibilities inherent in such methods are not likely to come to the mind of one who speaks and thinks of a city in static geometrical terms.

For example, an anatomic-physiological procedure has been developed to study and control flow patterns and dependencies of a conductive system, such as a system of nutritive distribution. This procedure consists of cutting that system once at this, once at that point. The observer then tabulates what happens. This is done while the system is actually functioning, in order to study its degeneration, its devious, interrupted, and abnormal operation under specifically selected conditions.

The traffic system of a city might be similarly cut or blocked here and there for repeated short test durations as part of a well-planned act of research. This should give the planner a chance to observe the resulting difficulties (degeneration) as well as any undirected, spontaneous tendencies toward rerouting (regeneration).

Or, to give another illustration: the method of "staining" is quite commonly used for purposes of physiological observation, especially the staining of a flowing medium when the study concerns the pattern and speed of a living circulation. This method might be borrowed for telling experiments in the field of city planning. For instance, on a certain test day all trucking traffic entering a specified section of a city might be required to display flags of certain prearranged colors, which would designate points of departure or of destination. The measure would make possible a quantitative and qualitative source analysis of particular categories of heavy traffic and their characteristic in mingling with the rest, crowding it, or avoiding it.*

Technical Developments in Locomotion and Communication

Of all the engineered novelties which exert a formative influence on the physical setup of every community, two of the most stunning are locomotion and distant control. To a certain extent, each seems to contradict the other's tendency. Mechanical, powerful, speedy locomotion includes monorail cars, heliocopters, taxicabs, and subways in which we can rush about until stalled in a traffic jam. Distant control comprises telephone and intercommunication systems, television, and so on, which appears to obviate the need to rush about.

Rather than being novel in themselves, both of these technical advantages merely amplify and augment our own physiological endowments. In contrast to rooted plants, we have our indigenous equipment to move from place to place. Confinement becomes most unnatural and opposed to our reflective disposition to travel through the world and change surroundings at will. Yet our cities invest tremendous funds in faster locomotion and fail to provide adequately for the pedestrian's natural and simple delights.

Speedy freeway interchanges are designed with amazing budgets in land and money in order to save a few seconds in making a left-hand turn. On the other hand, funds are lacking to realize a well-landscaped, safe promenade like a schoolwalk which children could take to school without the hazard of being killed or crippled by traffic. In jungle villages, tigers usually remain hundreds of yards away and rarely snatch youngsters from the door of a native hut. But whirlwind traffic death takes its toll in front of many a home in the United States.

The Biological Basis for Planning

Although a city may be huge, it need not be too large if it is well articulated in satisfying the needs of its inhabitants. Atomization or dispersal is not the solution for thickly-populated metropolitan areas. Nor is size or density of habitation itself unnatural. Colonies of bats, bees, and ants give examples to the point. The answer to the problem of size is to match adjustment with sensitive design.

In this planning and redevelopment, a biological bias is needed. "Pleasant

* R. Neutra, *Survival Through Design* (New York: Oxford University Press, 1954), pp. 341–344, with slight modifications by the author.

living" and "comfort" must be physiologically defined; research can cast light on what they consist of, what inner processes are concomitant to them and must be elicited in the inhabitants for their truest benefit. In our age of science, this will be the greatest of all scientific aids which the city dweller can hope for.

But physiological determinants and patterns have evolved so slowly that their readjustment to rushing, industrialized technology cannot take place as fast as new patents are being applied for. City evolution may be much faster than organic evolution in nature. Yet not even today can this evolution, and the capital improvement involved, be speeded up enough to match the velocity of inventiveness, whether in the form of armaments or of equally fatal consumer goods that daily burst into the streets.

We, as no earlier generation, have the scientific know-how to study the organic, the sensorial, the nervous equipment of human beings and their range of capacity to absorb whatever engineering may impose on them. If the city is not to become a man-eater fed only from outer regions, we must honestly and sincerely concentrate on design—not for technical efficiency, production, or commercial gain, but against the thousandfold irritations and damages which now threaten to prove cumulative detriments beyond the bearable. The city of the future may have to rise from the labors of a planning committee under the broad-minded chairmanship of a biologist. This city then will be a happy, compound Design for Survival.

14

Commentaries

By **Harold M. Lewis,** *Consulting Engineer and City Planner, New York*

Dr. Neutra seems to find little satisfaction in contemplating our modern metropolises. Here is a summary of some of his findings along with a few comments.

1. In stating that the city is a gigantic, puzzling tinker-toy, Neutra implies that man has been clumsy and makeshift in its creation. But rather than being a clumsy hodgepodge, the city actually seems to be a complicated machine to whose design and construction many scientists have contributed.

2. According to Neutra, irritations of congestion, noise, and the friction of movement in cities have driven their citizens into psychiatric institutions. Perhaps three wars and a major depression have contributed more to this result than any shortcomings of the scientists. A report by Ralph Linton, formerly Professor of Anthropology at Yale University, suggests still another theory. Editorial comment in the *New York Herald Tribune* of November 17, 1953 said:

> In his report to the New York Academy of Medicine on mental illnesses in primitive cultures, he finds that mental disease exists in all of them; even in those which, unlike our own hectic world, exert a bare minimum of stress and strain on their members. . . .
>
> In reporting that his admittedly limited facts suggest a constitutional basis underlying both neurosis and psychosis, Dr. Linton adds anthropological support to the increasing body of biochemical and other data pointing in the same direction. These include diverse laboratory findings, such as the presence of abnormal quantities of copper in the blood of patients suffering from certain mental diseases and significant differences in hormone and other glandular activity.

3. Neutra accuses the city fathers and their department heads—as well as the average voters, taxpayers, and bankers—of clinging obstinately to outmoded improvements which might better be written off before they are amortized. But poor planning and the resultant misplacing of public works often requires the scrapping of structures which still would be usable if they were in the right place.

4. He deprecates the slum. So do we all, and there are many reasons for its creation. Scientists—as represented by city planners, sociologists, economists, and municipal engineers—are all vitally interested in both slum elimination and prevention.

5. He decries the pernicious preponderance of mere geometrical architecture and planning on the basis that it ignores the biological expression of city growth. If one is going to lay out a city plan, it must include something that can be shown on a map. The chances are that any geometrical pattern will be warped by physical, social, and economic considerations so that it will resemble a study in anatomy rather than the symmetry of a snowflake.

6. For the present technique of city planning, Neutra would substitute the development of a plan based on histology, morphology, and physiology; that is, the study of the growth of organic tissues, the form and structure of animals and plants, and the functions of living organisms. The present writer has himself used the term organic as applying to a functional type of street pattern, which may resemble the cell structure of vegetable or animal tissues.

7. Neutra refers to rapid transit and modern communications through the air in the form of radio and television as opposing or contradictory engineered novelties. He claims that they are really not novel if one analyses the city biologically. But these developments seem to be definite contributions of engineering science The engineer's problem now is to discover various means of controlling the problems which they have often created.

8. He finds that the delights of a pedestrian have been sacrificed to the urges of the speeding automobilist. Yet most of us play both these parts, and our desires depend upon whether we are walking or driving at the moment. Neighborhood planners are very conscious of the need of providing safe and attractive walk-ways for both children and adults. Application of the neighborhood-unit theory of designing residential districts is providing successful solutions.

9. He concludes that the use of the skills and approach of the biologist offers the best solution for planning better cities. But it appears that the professional city planner, now being trained in special departments in many of our universities, will provide the principal solution to this problem rather than the biologist.

CONTRIBUTIONS OF THE PROFESSIONS

The metropolis is the product of science and art, and many professions have contributed to its pattern and design. For example, the *research scientists,* working in either pure or applied science, have laid the technological basis of many of our structures through the development of new materials and new methods of using them.

The *engineering groups*—including civil, mechanical, electrical, and chemical—have made major contributions to the design of the utilities which serve the city. These utilities include the streets and their pavements; facilities for generating power, heat and light; means of communication on the surface, beneath the ground, and through the air; bridges, piers, and the foundations and structural frames of large buildings. In laying out the original street and lot lines, engineer-surveyors did much to determine our city patterns.

The *architects* have given the city its form and silhouette. They have added grace and beauty to our structures, and are taking a leading part in determining the grouping of buildings so as to form elements of an efficient city plan.

The *landscape architects* have laid out our parks and other open spaces. They have done the site planning for large structures—particularly public buildings and modern large-scale housing projects—and have also made a direct contribution in the field of city planning.

City and regional planners, drawn at first from the above professions, are now generally recognized to belong to a separate profession requiring special undergraduate and graduate training. They are assuming the major responsibility for establishing the master plans of our cities. These plans coordinate the use of land, the pattern of communications and other service facilities, and the controls over use of buildings and land through zoning and other procedures.

INFLUENCE OF STEEL-FRAME BUILDINGS

The development of steel-frame buildings made a radical change in the appearance of our business centers and later of our apartment districts. Before such structures were erected, the usual building was two or three stories in height, although there are many examples of old four-story and five-story buildings of brick and timber. With the development of the skyscraper and other smaller multi-story structures, made feasible through freight and passenger elevators, it was possible to substitute vertical transportation for part of the former horizontal transportation in our downtown areas.

In these developments, the engineer and the architect have worked hand-in-hand. The engineer has designed the skeleton and the heavy foundations necessary to take the increased loads. The architect has determined the exteriors, the floor plans, the general relation of the building to the site and—although this was at first often neglected—its relation to adjoining buildings.

Where tall steel-frame buildings crowded upon each other, they created dark chasms between. This condition led to New York City's pioneer Comprehensive Zoning Ordinance, adopted in 1916. The ordinance forced a setback of buildings as they reached successive heights. Today the trend is definitely toward scattered skyscrapers with lower buildings sandwiched in between.

CONCENTRATION VERSUS DECENTRALIZATION

Dr. Neutra points out that opposing or contradictory forces may be created by scientific inventions. For example, they may encourage concentration on the one hand and decentralization on the other. Yet others have worked in both ways by promoting concentration of business and decentralization of residence.

Originally, the size of a city was limited by the distance that a person could conveniently travel on foot or horseback to get from his home to the business center. This radius was expanded successively by the horse car, the cable car, the electrically operated trolley, and the suburban railroads with their loads of commuters. Then came the automobile. It tremendously accelerated urban growth by both increasing the radius of travel and by bringing within urban influence all the open areas formerly located between but not convenient to suburban railroads.

Science and technology have contributed the machinery and power transmission systems for each of these successive steps. The gasoline motor, brought to its present efficiency in the automobile and later the airplane, has been the most *dispersive* factor so far as the distribution of residence is concerned. On the other hand, the electric motor, as developed in our high-speed rapid transit systems, has been the greatest promotor of *centralization* of business through its efficient mass transportation.

Engineers are now in the process of developing the helicopter as a means of travel between home and work. It may greatly increase the possible distance between the two. But let us hope that the engineers will remember the lessons of the automobile and not bring more helicopters to the downtown areas than can be parked there. Just as the early automobiles were called pleasure cars and used primarily for weekend travel, the first intensive use of helicopters, other than for mail or airport taxi service, may be for travel to and from summer homes or vacation resorts rather than for daily commuting to the business area.

CITIZENS ATTITUDES

Most Chambers of Commerce are beginning to see that, as Dr. Neutra points out, bigness is not synonymous with greatness. Today we want better cities, but we can well do without excessive growth. Growth without planning or adequate controls is no longer desirable.

But many citizens unfortunately have little conception of what planning really is. The layman has often accused the city planner of phrasing his reports in jargon and high-sounding theories evolved in an ivory tower. Imagine the reaction of an ordinary city council when it is told that the planning process is simply the application of a study of biological forces developed through the techniques of physiology, histology, and morphogenetic agencies.

Surely we must find some simpler expressions to describe our goals. Among other things, they must include relief of traffic congestion, clearance of slums and blighted areas, and more efficient government—all of which have been discussed previously. Finally, atomic power should be used to enhance the pleasures of urban living rather than to create destructive weapons.

By **Alan Gregg, M.D.,** *Vice President, Rockefeller Foundation, New York*

Why do we have large cities? Why do they seem to meet human needs so effectively that they arouse a common interest, affection, tradition, and pride, as pointed out by Professor Hill?

These questions must be considered in connection with the fact that the number, size, and significance of cities increases as man passes from nomadic through pastoral and agricultural to industrial forms of living. It suggests that the immediate cause of cities is a tendency towards the division of labor. Even among social insects liks bees and ants, division of labor is a constant characteristic.

Grant, as a bare minimum, a tendency toward the division of labor in any scheme of human life, and a cataract of consequences point to city life. For with the division of labor, products accumulate. Accumulation leads to exchange or storage and protection. An excess of food, arrow heads, wampum, hides or feathers, or plows or baskets, calls for distribution and hence movement to or from storage to a place of meeting and barter. First came trails to market centers; then roads to market towns. First grain was stored in huts; then granaries were built in walled towns. As a result of movement to places of meeting, agreements, promises, and institutions were created to facilitate long-term undertakings. Finally, government appeared to provide stability to the institutions so created.

In addition, such meetings offered a choice of persons to be met, amusements, competitions, and leisure. This sequence of events is exemplified in Iceland by the little valley called Thingvallir, located outside the present city of Reykjavik. There the Icelanders foregathered at a yearly fair to trade, play games, hear poetry, make matches, and consummate binding agreements of government. Thingvallir now is the cradle of parliamentary government which was 1,000 years old in 1929.

Here, then, is the complex raison d'être of cities—to provide an easy access to goods, mutual aid in services or protection, and a meeting place with its wider choice of stimulus and pleasure. The metropolis is only an elaboration and magnification of all of these reasons for the city.

THE INCREASING IMPORTANCE OF SUBURBIA

Between 1934 and 1953, the population of the United States increased 25 per cent. During the same period, the suburban population rose 75 per cent. Some 91.5 million persons, or nearly three-fifths of the national population, resided in cities of 50,000 or more inhabitants in 1953. Of that number, approximately 54 million lived on the edges of the inner cities or in the suburbs!*

The true importance of suburbia, however, is not revealed by the data alone. For our suburbs present other significant aspects of metropolitan life in the percentage of their families owning homes, the average number of children

* "Who Are the Suburbanites?" *Fortune,* XLVIII (November, 1953), 231 ff.

per family, the increased birth rate, and the average family income, which is 70 per cent higher than that of the rest of the population. Suburban inhabitants are essentially city folk—from the very same city that grows steadily poorer as its taxpayers leave for the outskirts. The population is usually composed of newcomers who are trying to be provincial but failing to do so. Public education in primary and secondary schools is one of the principal suburban industries, and stores and places of assembly are also beginning to appear.

The Metropolis as a Consumer of Men and Women

Evidence appears to indicate that cities consume not only food imported from rural areas, but also people born and raised in the country. In other words, our metropolises fail to replenish their own populations and are sustained by a flow of young people coming from the countryside and smaller towns. Although big cities provide better medical care and prevention than hamlets, they do not renew the race effectively. Why?

Is the urban population failing to survive modern metropolitan living conditions? Our forebears readily survived some 100,000 years of existence in pre-metropolitan ages, and our own appearance is proof of their success. But in the last 100 years or so, science and technology have radically changed the conditions of living. Instead of eating coarse foods in large amounts and bulk, we now consume concentrated foods which may lack important trace elements found in the larger and more impure bulk. We have become choosey about the parts of animals we eat. Some of our foods lose valuable elements as they are processed—witness polished rice and its resultant beriberi. Metropolitan man steadily overeats, whereas the human race previously survived a long but successful experience with famine as well as feast.

In large cities, we heat and over-heat our houses and so lose less heat from our bodies than we used to. We take much less muscular exercise. With artificial illumination, we reduce the hours of rest and lengthen the period of wakeful stimulation. We increase the number of people we meet, even to the point of reducing the number we can know intimately. In place of fear we experience anxiety. We take on a variety of stimulants, drugs, and chemical consolations in caffeine, nicotine, and alcohol. Sometimes we work to keep up with our machines and sometimes to compete with other people, although that would be unnecessary if the most gifted were not pitted against each other in such numbers. Idleness now produces anxiety, not playfulness.

But as a change from our modern metropolitan style of living, we occasionally take what is called a vacation. While on vacation, we frequently eat coarser food. We consume it a little more irregularly but in larger quantities because we take plenty of muscular exercise and reduce the amount of clothing we wear. We see fewer people more intimately. We deliberately take risks and court danger and perhaps fear but with nothing to worry about. We fool around and play. We get less of the stimulus of light and more of restful sleep. In short, we repeat as many of the conditions as possible which the human race learned to survive over nearly 100,000 years. And we feel fine.

But is our successful survival under an earlier set of conditions strong presumptive evidence of survival under radically new circumstances of modern life in the man-consuming metropolises? The evidence apparently shows that man may have difficulty in surviving this new set of biological demands unless he is more versatile in his capacity to change than he has been in the past.

THE THREAT OF ATOMIC WARFARE

The atomic bomb is the greatest imaginable threat to the large cities. Dispersal is the only certain protection short of human resolution never to use the bomb again. But atomic power has, let us hope, another destiny. What would we feel about the spirit of man if, for example, electricity had been reserved for use only in the electric chair (where its effectiveness is spectacular) and had never been applied to motors, artificial lighting, telegraph, telephone, radio, or television? Even more than electricity, the atomic bomb, all but immeasurable as a destructive weapon, will take the measure of man.

PART SIX
The Impact of the Metropolis
on the Professions

INTRODUCTION

By its very nature, the city encourages a specialization in knowledge and practice among urban activities. The types of specialities which arise and their relationships to each other have an important bearing upon the well-being of the metropolis and the nation.

The impact of metropolitanism upon specialization within traditional professional fields is investigated by Sir Alexander Carr-Saunders. He questions the chance of preserving the integrity of older independent professions in the face of a rise of new salaried professional groups in the metropolis. He believes that the result may lead toward a deterioration in the standing of the established professions which may seriously impair the quality of services rendered by them.

In tracing the role of universities in furthering cooperation among professions, Mr. Young suggests that one means of interprofessional cooperation may be through a greater increase in specialization. A crucial problem is whether newly-emerging institutional forms can lead toward greater interprofessional cooperation. Mr. Young implicitly challenges the prevailing assumption that integration can occur only within a single individual rather than within a single institutional framework.

One consequence of specialization in the metropolis appears to be that a disproportionate number of professional men tend to be found there. Already there is an over-concentration of medical specialists in the great cities. What are the implications of this fact upon the distribution of medical care throughout the country? Will the difference in the general level of medical care between small and large communities steadily grow more apparent? Is a similar tendency evident in other professions so that the small-town citizen may be increasingly deprived of the best professional attention?

As one means of increasing interprofessional cooperation, group practice has developed in the large cities among the legal and medical professions. One of the dangers of group practice, however, comes from the unconscious tendency to control the direction of innovation. In medicine, a whole series of specialty boards have been established to say who is qualified to serve as a medical practitioner and what his training should be. That situation makes for a certain rigidity which may impair the flexibility of training younger men, even though it appears to further interprofessional cooperation.

Moreover, this raises the question of exactly what the functions of each profession ought to be. Should the lawyer, for example, concentrate exclusively on advising his clients what the law is? Or should he also be concerned with the whole structure of formal authority that operates in his community? What are the consequences to his income, and to the welfare of the community, if he chooses one or the other alternative?

The proper functions of the professions raise the further question of what methods should be adopted to train professional personnel. If a specialist concentrates mainly on his own field, there is the danger that he may overlook important peripheral problems that should concern him. Among other things, the social case worker, for instance, works with individuals who need financial help. The economist, on the other hand, is interested in changing existing economic institutions so that fewer people have to ask for financial help. By properly relating the fields of study of both professions, results may be achieved that would not otherwise be considered.

The need for specialists is now so great that a large number of members are being recruited from people educated entirely at the public expense. In England, roughly 80 per cent of the entrants to professions are said to study at universities with the aid of public grants awarded on a selective basis. What implications may this situation have for future educational training and for the public underwriting of professional vocations?

All these questions pertain to the manner by which specialists can be used to best advantage in the metropolis. Since metropolitanism means specialization, specialists must be developed in sufficient numbers and with sufficient skills to meet and solve the problems of modern city life.

15

Metropolitan Conditions and Traditional Professional Relationships

SIR ALEXANDER MORRIS CARR-SAUNDERS
Director, London School of Economics and Political Science

A metropolis has been described by Louis Wirth as a "relatively large, dense and permanent settlement of socially heterogeneous individuals."[1] The heterogeneity of metropolitan populations is also emphasized by Robert E. Park who speaks of the "multiplication of occupations and professions" as one of the most striking aspects of city life.

Within cities, Park points out that the "older social and economic organization of society, which was based on family ties, local associations, on culture, caste, and status" has broken down or been modified. As a substitute, there is "an organization based on occupation and vocational interests. In the city every vocation, even that of a beggar, tends to assume the character of a profession, and the discipline which success in any vocation imposes, together with the associations that it enforces, emphasizes this tendency—the tendency, namely, not merely to specialize, but to rationalize one's occupation and to develop a specific and conscious technique for carrying it on."[2]

Generally speaking, the changes in the professions which have resulted from the impact of metropolitan conditions have been communicated to the whole professional world. Outside metropolitan areas, the professions no longer continue as they were before the rise of the great centers, except in a few instances. At least that is the case in Great Britain where no essential difference exists between the large cities, small towns, and rural areas in matters of professional organization, standards, and practice. This is so because the forces which have produced metropolitan areas have also influenced all the professions. As Wirth says, "What is modern in our civilization is best signalized by the growth of great cities." What is modern in our civilization is also well exhibited by the changes in the outlook and functioning of the professions.

A Definition of Profession

The title of profession is everywhere accorded to the vocations of law, medicine, and the church. They are universally regarded as professions in the fullest sense of the word. The title of learned professions was given to them long ago.

Law, medicine, and the church are generally regarded as professions because they share two characteristics. In the first place, their practice is based upon the theoretical study of a department of learning. Secondly, the individuals who follow them feel bound to follow a certain mode of behavior, and are so regarded by the public. There is a "clear-cut and definite difference on the institutional level [between the professional and business worlds]. The institutional patterns governing the two fields of action are radically different in this respect."[3]

During recent decades, there has been a vast increase in the number of organizations claiming to represent vocations with professional status. Thus the question arises how far such claims are admissible and how far our field of discussion extends.[4] In assessing the validity of these claims, we may fall back on the two attributes of the old established professions of law, medicine, and the church.

One attribute of the older professions is the compulsion to follow a certain mode of conduct which is dictated by the responsible or fiduciary position in which an independent practitioner stands in relation to his client. For law and medicine, this desirable line of conduct has been set out in elaborate ethical codes. Vocations now claiming professional status invariably recognize the obligation to behave in a professional manner. This points to a conviction in the mind of the public that a certain mode of behavior is an indispensable characteristic of a profession.

Another attribute of the older professions is that their practice is founded upon the theoretical study of a department of learning. Among the claimants to rank with the older professions, three groups can be identified according to the nature of these studies.

The first group may be called the *new professions*. Its members undertake fundamental studies upon which their respective arts are founded. Sometimes, the studies are in a department of natural science, as in the case of chemists and engineers. Other times, they are in a branch of social science, as in the case of accountants.

In most instances, the studies of the new professions are specific. But in the senior or administrative branch of the British civil service, they are more general, as is also true of the church among the older professions. The field of study itself is usually but not always new. Architects, for example, have long existed but were recognized only fairly recently as professional workers when their practice was dissociated from business.

Even when the new professions emerged, not all the practitioners were independent workers. Indeed, employment was common from the beginning. Within the civil service, for instance, members have always been salaried. In that respect, there is an obvious difference between the old professions, whose members were originally independent, and the new professions, whose members are ordinarily employed.

The second group—the *semi-professions*—replaces theoretical study by the acquisition of technical skill. The best examples are found among the vocations auxiliary to the medical profession, like nurses, midwives, pharmacists, opticians, and many others. Their skills are acquired only after a lengthy and exact study and an absorption of much precise knowledge. Nearly all the members of the semi-professions are employed.

The third group—the *would-be professions*—requires neither theoretical study nor the acquisition of exact techniques, but rather a familiarity with business structure, administrative practices, and current conventions. In the managerial field alone, there are hospital managers, sales managers, works managers, personnel managers, office managers, export managers, transport managers, and others. Their members are almost all employed.

The would-be professions are particularly encouraged to press their claims to professional status by the non-manual workers who are included within the group. Manual workers, organized in powerful trade unions, are conscious that they perform indispensable work which is visible in the shape of results. By tradition, they are suspicious of non-manual workers who appear to occupy snug places without producing anything obvious. So the non-manual workers feel that they must justify their existence. They must show that they, too, have crafts which turn out indispensable results. In effect, they attempt to demonstrate that they are experts without whose services society cannot get along, and that they are generally not so very far removed from doctors and the fully-recognized professions.

But the non-manual workers exaggerate the degree and quality of their expertness in an attempt to make good their claims. They say little about the ends which they hope to reach by professional recognition; namely, social upgrading and improved remuneration. In practice, their associations act as trade unions in the matter of collective bargaining and in their effort to restrict a particular way of making a living to their members.

Recent Tendencies Reflecting Metropolitan Influences

Insofar as the would-be professions succeed in claiming recognition, the concept of a profession is diluted. In place of the old idea of learned professions to which considerable prestige attached, the public tends to have a vague impression that there are many different kinds of experts, some more highly trained than others, but all of whom are professional persons. Again, insofar as the newcomers improve their economic position, the established professions fear a relative decline in their economic position unless they are similarly active in self-defense.

The movement toward specialization is general. It is as marked in the established professions as elsewhere. Coupled with it is the tendency toward replacing independent practitioners by salaried professional workers.

Generalists versus Specialists

As knowledge is increased through research and investigation, the practice of any art diversifies. Then it becomes difficult or impossible to acquire a competence in all the branches. Practitioners, therefore, tend to devote themselves to one branch. In other words, they specialize. This is pre-eminently the case for professions founded upon the natural sciences which offer the greatest opportunities for research.

The tendency toward specialization is enhanced in another way. A man who specializes is somehow thought to be superior to the man who does not. He also can hope to have an advantage in building up a practice.

The extent to which members of a formerly unified profession remain under its auspices varies greatly. In medicine, they have stayed within the original profession. In engineering, they have formed virtually separate professions of civil, mechanical, electrical, chemical, aeronautical, production, railway, and other kinds of engineers. Whatever the case, the outcome is important because the greater the separation of the branches, the narrower in general is the education preparatory to entering into them.

Fragmentation follows specialization and undermines the position of the general practitioner. The function of a general medical practitioner, for example, increasingly is to serve as a clearinghouse by passing patients to the care of specialist practitioners or of specialist hospitals or other medical institutions. In a recent report by Lewis and Maude on the work of general medical practitioners in Great Britain, Dr. J. S. Collings stated that "the general practitioner of today . . . has ceased either to be, or to follow the ideal of, a family doctor. Most of them have abandoned midwifery and antenatal care to the district nurse and the local authority clinic; they are surrendering the care of children to the school doctors and to the specialist paediatricians, and will probably willingly surrender their 'old chronics' to the new speciality of geriatrics; they thankfully despatch eye cases, without examination but with the regulation green form, to the Supplementary Eye Service; they have abandoned even such elementary 'laboratory work' as blood tests, together with minor surgery such as the removal of a finger nail, sending all such cases to hospitals."[5]

The auxiliary medical profession of nursing is affected in a similar way. Lewis and Maude point out that "there is less nursing (in the old sense) of patients who have to be pulled through crises by the efforts of the nurse; there is more supervision and carrying out of routine treatments—often a mechanical round of medication and injections. When the personal factor is important (as, for example, in the case of old people) it is often difficult to get nurses at all."

So, too, in the field of social work. At the beginning of this century, social workers were engaged in what was called case work. That is, they obtained a general picture of the background and home circumstances of a person in need of help and advised and assisted on the basis of such information. They were in effect general practitioners. In their place, we now find specialist social workers of many kinds, such as probation officers, hospital social workers, psychiatric social workers, and others.

The tendency for the general practitioner to give way to the specialist is almost universal. The only prominent exception is the church, where the priest or minister remains a general practitioner. As a consequence of the trend toward specialization, the professional man no longer takes a comprehensive interest in his client. He feels that he has no general responsibility for those who come under his care, and the personal relationship between practitioner and client is weakened.

Independent versus Salaried Professional Workers

Members of the old professions were originally independent practitioners. They were self-employed and were not hired, salaried, or dismissed by some other persons or corporation. But a certain proportion of members of the new professions have always been employed, and nearly all members of the semi-professions and would-be professions are salaried.

The increase in the number of employed professional workers is due to the rise of large-scale organizations. These organizations need the services of professional men like doctors, lawyers, accountants, chemists, and engineers. Although they can call in independent practitioners for consultation, the tendency is to employ directly any individuals whose services are required.

All modern governments, for instance, set up organizations for recording and advising, and engage the necessary professional staffs. Some governments go further and enter the field of industrial and commercial enterprise and organize public social services. Consequently, the proportion of professional workers who are in independent practice is greatly reduced. In Great Britain, about 10 per cent of lawyers, 40 per cent of the members of one of the leading associations of accountants, and over 50 per cent of registered architects were employed in 1952. According to Lewis and Maude, only some 200 members of the Royal Institute of Chemistry were consultants.

These figures refer to employed professional workers who have no direct dealings with clients. Other employed professional workers continue to render direct services to clients. Social workers and school teachers, for example, have a dual responsibility to the employer as well as the client. But the employer lays down the limits to the service which can be rendered and to some extent determines its kind and quality. As a result, a social worker who is, say, a probation officer is far from free to treat a person committed to his charge in a manner indicated by his professional training and experience.

The same situation is not true of law and medicine where independent practice has hitherto prevailed. When a lawyer or a doctor accepts a salaried private post and ceases to have clients of his own, no problem arises. But the position is very different when the state sets up a service providing free legal aid and advice, or free medical treatment, and invites lawyers and doctors to staff it in return for remuneration from public funds.

In Great Britain, there is a free National Health. Service and a scheme of free legal aid and advice for people whose income is below a certain figure. The legal scheme is in the hands of the legal profession which is able to safeguard the freedom of the lawyer in relation to the clients who obtain his services under the scheme. The National Health Service is not in the hands of the medical profession, and the Minister of Health can dismiss a doctor from the Service. Nevertheless, great care has been taken to leave to the doctor freedom to provide the advice and treatment deemed by him to be best for his patient. While it is not wholly true that the only difference between the doctor under the Service and the doctor in private practice is that in the case of the former the state and not the patient pays the fee, it is not a seriously misleading description. The fact that only 600 out of 20,000 general medical practitioners in Great Britain are entirely outside the Health Service shows how much the traditional form of medical practice has changed under the influence of modern developments.

The Effect Upon the Professions of These Recent Tendencies

Changes within All Professions

The traditional attitude of the professional man is characterized by a sense of responsibility towards his client, and a feeling of pride in service rendered rather than in opportunity for personal profit. The phrase professional pride indicates a code of behavior whose first consideration is the need of the client and the quality of the work. The Hippocratic writings apparently show that this attitude was assumed by medical practitioners in the ancient world. Since medieval times, it has been worked out and embodied in codes. These codes lay down the behavior which is appropriate in the particular circumstances which lawyers and doctors are likely to meet.

Among the guiding principles which have inspired the legal and medical codes, the first general rule of conduct is the obligation to serve the client. The professional man must give his services whenever called upon, and without exercising capricious discrimination on personal or political grounds. He is also obliged to give only the best service and to subordinate all personal considerations to the interest of his client.

The rise of specialists has brought about a subtle change in the traditional relation of practitioner to client. In medicine, the interest in, and the responsibility for, the patient is now restricted. He is not so much a sick person in need of help as an example of a particular type of affliction with which the specialist is concerned. This change is illustrated by the previously-described position of the nursing profession. Here practitioners, now highly skilled in special directions, are scarcely available where the traditional essence of nursing is needed, as in the case of elderly or helpless patients.

Only the general practitioner can carry out the serve-the-client rule in spirit as well as letter. Now even he is being superseded. In the profession of social work, the case worker is being replaced by specialist social workers. Throughout the professional world, specialization has these consequences.

For professional men who are employed and have no clients, the general rule to serve the client has no relevance at all. Nevertheless, it continues to figure prominently in the codes of some professions even when most of the members are salaried. But in the Royal Institute of Chemistry, very few members are in independent practice. As Lewis and Maude indicate, the Institute has abandoned the traditional formulation by specifying that "the predominating characteristic expected of the chemist is loyalty, implying an honest endeavor to give his best services to his employer, and to deal fairly with his colleagues." Since all employees are expected to demonstrate this loyalty, the statement is a tacit acknowledgment that there is little or nothing to distinguish the conduct of a professional worker from that of any other employee.

Actually, the traditional professional rule to serve the client has become irrelevant for an increasing proportion of members of the old, new, semi, and would-be professions. Even for employed professional workers who retain clients, this rule can be fulfilled only in part unless special arrangements are made. The school teacher, for instance, can be devoted to his pupils. But he is limited in what he can do for them, since he must follow his employer's views on the matter or lose his post.

At present, the arrangements under which lawyers and doctors staff the free legal and medical services in Great Britain are generally sufficient to permit freedom in the relations between practitioners and clients. But doctors in the National Health Service are now under reproof for what is called over-prescribing. If limits are set to what doctors may prescribe for their patients, other restrictions will probably follow. Perhaps in time the position of these doctors will become more like that of school teachers.

Another general rule of traditional professional conduct specifies that professional men are allowed to compete with one another only in reputation for ability. This implies that the use of techniques, such as advertising and price-cutting employed in business for competitive purposes, is forbidden. Competition is solely for clients.

For professional workers who are employed, such as school teachers and social workers, the rule has no meaning. Whatever clients they have are allocated to them by their employers. To lawyers and doctors working under the British schemes for the free provision of legal and medical services, however, the rule still applies.

The traditional rules to serve the client and compete only for him are now difficult to carry out or inapplicable for many professional workers. Consequently, it might seem desirable to minimize the importance of these rules. But it is doubtful how long the professional spirit could survive unless a sufficient number of self-employed practitioners continued to follow the traditional codes and thereby served as a reminder of the implications of the professional attitude when free to express itself in independent practice.

Changes within Specific Professions

Under the impact of changing conditions, most professions have encountered difficulties of their own. The church, for instance, has been less influenced by specialization than any other profession. Priests and ministers remain general practitioners. Despite this fact, the standing of the church has declined. Although it formerly was one of the three ancient professions, the church now seems to the public hardly to rank as a profession at all, or at any rate to occupy an isolated position among the professions at large.

The explanation for the situation is not that the functions of the church have altered, but that public views of the functions of a profession have changed. Professional men are increasingly regarded by the public as experts in the advancement of material welfare and bodily well-being. The church, on the other hand, demands self-discipline and standards of conduct that are widely considered to be outmoded in an age of science.

Among architects, the problem is different. Less than a century ago, architects dissociated themselves from business and assumed a fiduciary position in standing between client and builder. At the present time, a minority view in the profession alleges that this position no longer makes sense in a period of increasing technological complexity in building operations. The architect is said to be no longer effective as a leader and might be better placed as a director of a firm of builders or a firm making building components. The fact that such a view is held at all shows how greatly modern changes have altered the position of architects.[6]

CONCLUSION

Under the impact of metropolitan conditions, the concept of a profession has become transformed. No one speaks any more of the learned professions. Professional men were formerly regarded as possessing a broad culture, a wide special competence, and a general understanding of affairs. Consequently, they were influential members of society. A measure of leadership fell into their hands, and much that we value in our society was evolved under the influence of the older professions.

Today, professional men are regarded by the public as experts—persons with high competence in a restricted sphere. Great deference is paid to them while they act within their particular range. Otherwise, they have little prestige. Outside their role, they are thought to have no more claim to be heard than the man in the street.

The change is not so much a transformation as a disintegration of the traditional professional concept. There is hardly any recognition of a professional class whose members possess certain common attributes and also some other kinds of special competence. In its place, the public sees different kinds of experts who have little or nothing in common.

The contemporary attitude of the public towards the professions is based upon an assessment of the present situation which is mainly correct. Preparation for professional life now involves a restricted rather than general study. Modern professional education begins early, extends over many years, but fails to develop character. Universities have become umbrellas to shelter specialized and unrelated schemes of training. A picture of the wholeness of man and the unity of knowledge seldom comes to their students.

Training has taken the place of education. The modern professional man has no comprehensive view of his own field of work and little interest in its place in the scheme of things at large. He is absorbed in restricted problems for which he seeks ad hoc solutions. Unlike the general practitioner of former times, he is no longer able to act as an understanding friend to his clients and to contribute usefully to the discussion of public affairs.

The professional man is becoming one of the numberless experts who work in the service of the common man. The common man is set on a pedestal. The experts seek a way for him out of his troubles and a path to better living. Once the professional man was on top; now he is on tap. As the interests of professional men narrow and as the needs of the common man grow, gaps are discovered and fresh experts appear to fill them. Psychiatrists and other specialists take charge of spheres relinquished by medical men while members of the Institute of Hospital Administrators look after the organizations in which the specialist doctors work. The emergence of specialist administrators is significant. From this source, we get ad hoc management, but we do not get the guidance and leadership we need.

What we really need can be provided only by men of wide education, interests, and experience. Such men were not uncommon in past generations within the ranks of the older professions. Now they are rare. What are the signs of the times? According to Lewis and Maude, "they point to the mounting power of the expert untroubled by conscience, interested only in getting things done; and, for the social repercussions of action, referring to other and separately trained experts." These signs point to the authority possessed by the professional institutions and the universities as the main safeguard against the crumbling away of the professional tradition.

FOOTNOTES TO CHAPTER 15

1. L. Wirth, "Urbanism as a Way of Life," reprinted in P. K. Hatt and A. J. Reiss (eds.), *Reader in Urban Sociology* (Glencoe: The Free Press, 1951), p. 36. A later quotation from Wirth on p. 279 of this chapter is taken from the same source, p. 32. The article by Wirth originally appeared in *The American Journal of Sociology*, XLIV (July, 1938), 1–24.

2. R. E. Park, *Human Communities* (Glencoe: The Free Press, 1952), pp. 14 and 24.

3. T. Parsons, *Essays in Sociological Theory, Pure and Applied* (Glencoe: The Free Press, 1949), p. 196.

4. See M. L. Cogan, "Towards a Definition of Profession," *Harvard Educational Review*, XXIII, No. 1 (1953).

5. R. Lewis and A. Maude, *Professional People* (London: Phoenix House, 1952), p. 180. Later quotations on pp. 282–287 of this chapter are taken from the same source in the following order: pp. 199, 62, 62, and 264.

6. *The Economist*, July 25, 1953, pp. 240–242.

16

Universities and Cooperation among Metropolitan Professions

DONALD YOUNG
General Director
Russell Sage Foundation, New York

Universities have the distinctive obligation to discover and disseminate knowledge. In recent decades, their progress in meeting that obligation has been greatly satisfying. It has been paralleled, however, by an increasing specialization in research and education. Although this trend toward specialization may or may not be avoidable or desirable, it should be properly integrated so that the needs of contemporary urban society can be better served.

Pressures exerted on our universities by the general public and by professional groups are heavily weighted in favor of specialization in education. The public is less reluctant to confess its ignorance and seek professional aid in areas of specialization than in broader fields of human problems which are so complex that it is difficult to frame answerable questions.

Furthermore, the public commonly assumes that the purpose of education is to increase earning power through the acquisition of technical skills. Similar views are widely held by members of the various professions who have done very well within their specialties and consequently have a convincing argument for the present system. A good deal of public and professional sentiment, of course, is critical of the existing degree of disciplinary and professional isolation, but so far it has not been a controlling force.

The advancement of knowledge and its use for the benefit of mankind is the shared responsibility of laymen, professional workers, and universities. But the obligation of leadership rests most heavily on the scholars, scientists, and educators within our institutions of higher learning. The academician has the obvious duty to keep his house in order and to remodel it from time to time in accordance with the changing conditions of research, education, and society. No other professional group is so thoroughly trained to expect and accept change in knowledge and practice.

Yet some persons speak of faculties as being ultra-conservative. Since universities are composed of people, there is naturally a reluctance to incur the inconvenience of change despite the high value given to innovation. Nevertheless, a review of the subject matter, research techniques, and teaching methods found in our universities at the present time shows an eagerness and capacity for rapid adaptation to changing circumstances.

In the metropolis, the need for specialized knowledge and for persons who can use it to benefit others is best recognized. Every community obviously requires the aid of professionally trained specialists. The well-being of villagers and farmers has been extraordinarily advanced by the services of engineers, physicians, lawyers, economists, biologists, and practically all the other specialists. But the most noticeable, most extensive, and most pressing need for the specialized expert is in the metropolis. The rapid growth of the professions in variety, effectiveness, and membership has been associated mainly with the growth of urban civilization.

WHAT A PROFESSION SIGNIFIES

In the United States, the word profession denotes almost all occupations which require more training than those activities vaguely designated as unskilled or semi-skilled. For general purposes, there is no apparent advantage in distinguishing between a business, a trade, a vocation, and a profession. Such a distinction inevitably becomes invidious and is often made without adequate logical basis.

In 1915, Abraham Flexner concluded that social work was not yet a profession because it did not meet fully all of the criteria he established for a profession. Professions, he said, "involve essentially intellectual operations with large individual responsibility; they derive their raw material from science and learning; this material they work up to a practical and definite end; they possess an educationally communicable technique; they tend to self-organization; they are becoming increasingly altruistic in motivation."[1]

This sharp denial of professional status may have served some useful purpose, but it created unprofitable resentment. And social work continued to be regarded as a profession. Certainly, interprofessional cooperation is not facilitated by employing an arbitrary standard to separate professions from lesser occupations.

Occupational specialties may gain or lose professional standing over comparatively brief periods of time. A set of skills accepted as professional when they are first developed may later become so routinized that the individuals who use them are labeled mere technicians. The tendency, however, is to increase the list of professions by subdividing specialties within the established professions and by improving the skills of other occupations. Just when and by what standards an advancing occupation may become a profession is a cause for disagreement. The issue is particularly sensitive when closely cooperating occupations, such as medical practitioners, nurses, and clinical psychologists, or librarians and professors, are involved. Confusion and changes in the relative status of occupations make a definitive classification into professional and nonprofessional impractical for general purposes.

At the present time, the term professional ordinarily includes all occupations requiring a substantial intellectual training, a skill in research or practice, and a sense of social responsibility acknowledged by the specialists as a group and expected of them by the public. Because many members of the older professions do not yet realize how far the process of professionalization has gone in the United States, here is a quotation illustrating how the concept has been extended to business and labor:

> The professional business managers are beginning to accept notions of responsibility that allow labor an important measure of self-government. Similarly the professional labor union administrator is increasingly willing to think of industrial and societal as well as labor problems. Many unions now press for efficiency in work, actively interest themselves in production problems, and find substantial areas of common interest with managerial groups. The professionalization of the industrial workers themselves is of major importance to both developments. As workers advance in educational level, in security of employment and wage, in measure of respect, self-direction, and accountability accorded them in the general community, they become increasingly "professional" and not merely "workers."[2]

From this point on, however, the term profession will be limited to occupations that require several years of academic study usually extending, at least for many leaders, beyond the undergraduate course. Ideally, a profession involves the use of all pertinent knowledge obtained from the entire range of relevant disciplines and accumulated experience for the solution of problems in research or practice.

This notion is in accord with the findings of a study made by Carr-Saunders and Wilson in England that ". . . the application of an intellectual technique to the ordinary business of life, acquired as the result of prolonged and specialized training, is the chief distinguishing characteristic of the professions." It is a flexible concept which allows for indefinite expansion.

> But science advances and techniques multiply. In the long run, technical advance implies an increase in the number of those doing more or less specialized intellectual work relative to the number of those who are engaged in manual labor or in unspecialized intellectual routine. It may be that, while the extension of professionalism upwards and outwards will be fairly rapid, its extension downwards, though gradual and almost imperceptible, will be continuous. Thus, taking the long view, the extension of professionalism over the whole field seems in the end not impossible.[3]

SPECIALIZATION WITHIN PROFESSIONS

Not so long ago, our society was relatively satisfied with a very small number of professions like the ministry, law, medicine, engineering, and teaching. Each of these professions required a great breadth of knowledge and a capacity to work effectively on a wide range of problems. Although Benjamin Franklin perhaps was not a member of any particular profession, he illustrates the breadth of interest, learning, and achievement which one man could realize at the time our nation was founded. He also illustrates a method of inter-professional cooperation in that he diligently communicated with scholars and practitioners of all types and recognized no arbitrary boundaries in learning or practice. Actually, the trend toward professional specialization did not become strong until well toward the close of the nineteenth century. Engineering, for instance, was late in developing specialties other than the ancient distinction between military and civil engineering. The subsequent expansion in the number of distinctive professions paralleled an expansion of human needs and of useful knowledge gained through cumulative experience.

The complexity of modern Western civilization and the concurrent advances in knowledge and skills have taxed men's competence and comprehension within every profession. To keep in the vanguard of his profession, a minister today must follow the current thought and practice in many fields of human relations, from economics and business to psychiatry and social work. Within the ministry, specialization is perhaps a less suitable solution to the problem of staying abreast of the latest developments than in other major professions. For this purpose, social workers have divided themselves into case workers, group workers, and community organization specialists, and have subdivided still further by specializing in such fields as individual and family service, child welfare, court services for children or adults, school social work, mental hygiene service, service with health agencies, and recreation.[4]

Engineering has been divided on such bases as concern with food, tools, transportation, mineral industries, structures and construction, chemical industries, communications, energy, health and human engineering, and urbanization. Within each of these specialties, there are again subdivisions. For example, the members of the American Institute of Mining and Metallurgical Engineers include mining, metallurgical, petroleum, mineral-dressing, and ceramic engineers, and geologists, geophysicists, fuel technologists, metallurgists, and mineral technologists.[5]

This seemingly endless process of professional splintering has dismayed many people. It results from a conflict between the need for precise knowledge and skill to maintain our civilization and the recognition of the fact that mankind's problems are multifaceted and can ultimately be resolved only by a holistic approach. Illness, for instance, has been described as "a state of disturbance in the 'normal' functioning of the total human individual, including both the state of the organism as a biological system and of his personal and social adjustments."[6] The current degree of medical specialization, however, rarely permits a diagnosis and treatment even in rough accordance with this definition. Problems of government, business and industry, agriculture, housing, international relations, education, and so on are similarly inclusive in nature but are usually attacked piecemeal in a similar manner.

THE RESULTING COMPLEXITY OF METROPOLITAN LIFE

Difficulties in Communicating among Individuals

As a result of the increasing amount of specialization within professions, the public is often confused by the great number of relatively isolated, incomprehensible, and inaccessible experts, and covers its confusion by ignoring, condemning, or caricaturing them. At the same time, the general public seems to be overconfident in believing that crises can usually be overcome by the same practically anonymous experts.

Interspecialty incomprehensibility is also a source of confusion and loss of effectiveness. Here indifference, the pressure of time, and the lack of adequate channels of interspecialty communication play an important role, as well as the use of different professional languages which are required for precision in research and practice.

Another source of difficulty is the overlapping of functions. For example, it is a well-known fact that professional counseling on marital problems is offered by ministers, physicians, lawyers, and social workers, as well as by members of the new and growing group of professional marriage counselors. Yet somehow or other, without any discernible rational plan, the activities of the various professions and their numerous subprofessions have supplemented each other in a reasonably workable pattern. The point is not that the cumbersome machine is not working, but that it should be made to work much better.

A positive note may be appropriate here to offset the previous emphasis on the complexity of modern living and the somewhat atomistic means adopted to meet its problems. As Oliver Wendell Holmes, Jr., remarked in a speech made at the turn of the century:

> Until lately the best thing that I was able to think of in favor of civilization, apart from the blind acceptance of the order of the universe, was that it made possible the artist, the poet, the philosopher, and the man of science. But I think that is not the greatest thing. Now I believe that the greatest thing is a matter that comes directly home to all of us. When it is said that we are too much occupied with the means of living to live, I answer that the chief worth of civilization is just that it makes the means of living more complex; that it calls for great and combined intellectual efforts, instead of simple, unco-ordinated ones, in order that the crowd may be fed and clothed and housed and moved from place to place. Because more complex and intense intellectual efforts mean a fuller and richer life. They mean more life. Life is an end in itself, and the only question as to whether it is worth living is whether you have enough of it.[7]

Various Types of Response

The proliferation of professional specialties is, of course, a consequence of the complexity of living that Mr. Justice Holmes considered the chief worth of living. The response to this complexity is often more emotional than intellectual. Many people, for instance, do little more than lament the passing of the less fractionated agrarian patterns of life. A few attempt to retreat to a simpler rural life. Undoubtedly, the back-to-the-farm solution to the problems of specialization has met the needs of an appreciable number of families. But it is not the answer to the urban need for disliked multiple division of labor.[8]

The trend toward living in the suburbs of our metropolitan centers is an outstanding phenomenon that may continue indefinitely. Yet so far there is no lack of demand for large-scale housing projects constantly being built in the heart of New York and other large cities. Furthermore, peripheral residential, business, and industrial communities are an extension of the metropolis rather than a social retreat, and do not materially reduce the need for professional and other specialists.

The yearning for true neighborhoods within the metropolis is another nostalgic response to the complexity of urban civilization. Confronted by an assumed lack of satisfactory interpersonal and intergroup relationship patterns, many people naturally strive to re-create some semblance of the small town or rural neighborhood. Numerous physically convenient and relatively self-sufficient areas now exist within our cities. Presumably, they can be increased considerably in number and social effectiveness. The better-planned housing projects are commonly designed and managed with an eye to community requirements, ranging from convenience in family purchasing to the facilitation of tenant participation in civic affairs.

Except in a physical sense, however, the extent to which such efforts have led to the development of communities is debatable. And they certainly have not reduced the need for all the specialists that society can provide. There is little reason to believe that groups of urban residents will increasingly become neighborhoods in a socio-psychological sense. Propinquity in living, buying, and recreation is not enough to counteract the contrary forces of the metropolis. It is even far from certain that the forces of the metropolis need counteracting in the interest of citizen satisfaction.

The Decline of Generalists

A third lament about the functioning of our complex urban civilization concerns the relative decline of the generalists, typified by Benjamin Franklin and Thomas Jefferson, in comparison with the rise of the specialists. Here the responsibility for the situation is divided about equally between educational institutions and more impersonal social forces. Professional schools are alleged to have gone too far in training narrow specialists and in offering practical courses for students interested in learning how to make money. Educators themselves seem to question their outstanding successes in advancing the physical and biological sciences, and more recently economics and the other social sciences, as fields for research and as knowledge for practical application. It is a rare faculty that is not now debating the possibility of increasing the general education content of the professional curriculum. Precisely what is meant by general education is not always clear. But it is safe to say that those individuals who promote the idea are partly motivated by a concern about interprofessional communication and cooperation.

Such a concern is healthy. For institutions of higher learning should assume leadership in research and in determining the educational requirements of the ideal scientist and professional practitioner. It may be questioned, however, whether the persons who claim that specialization is a primary source of difficulty and suggest turning back the academic clock are in fact facing the problems of education for modern life. Belittling the specialist by assuming that he is a poor citizen without a sufficient moral, social, and cultural education seems odd in a society that could not function without his aid. The specialist may be far from perfect, but his shortcomings are more likely to be bettered by an improved understanding of the specialized roles he must play than by looking backward to a social order which may not be expected to return. Paradoxically, a good part of the answer to professional atomism may lie in more intensive specialization rather than in the reverse.

The contrary view, that specialization narrows perspective and limits integration, is widely held by leaders whose opinions must be respected even in disagreement. A noted theological educator, Henry P. Van Dusen, President of Union Theological Seminary, has stated this opposing view:

> May I attempt to present theological education's challenge to the basic issue of our discussion (of education for professional responsibility), not only as it affects the seminaries but as it affects every type of professional training—the issue between *specialization* and what I may be excused for naming *generalization*.
>
> The divinity schools have a special interest in this issue, for it concerns one of the "great enemies" of religion and the Church in our modern society— specialization. Specialization—the concentration of attention upon some one problem, or phase of a problem, to the neglect of its organic connections and larger setting. Specialization so essential to scientific advance, so fruitful of increased knowledge. Specialization—so stunting to large-mindedness, so fatal to comprehension of the whole truth, that is, the real truth.[9]

The opinion of the present author is that the great enemy is faulty education and practice, not specialization as such.

Yet much specialist training is atomistic, shallow, and without the depth of intellectual content or regard for social responsibilities which are among the essential qualities of a profession. Indeed, the word specialist for many people has the implications of narrowness, lack of depth, and self-centered outlook resulting from a superficial training limited to obviously useful facts, skills, and procedures.

This type of training does not seem to be worthy of a university, although it is not uncommon in our institutions of higher learning. Nor can it be made worthy by adding supplementary materials and courses to supply breadth and depth. These qualities must come rather from an integrated program of professional education which equips the student to probe into the many corners of any problem engaging his professional attention and to realize that he is an inseparable part of the community of men. The man who depends on a relatively fixed body of knowledge and a routinized set of skills may be called a specialist, but he is far from the ideal of university professional education. He is not the type of man referred to here when the word specialist is used.

Efforts to check the continuing growth of professional specialization may be about as successful as past attempts to restrict the use of power machinery. Actually, the introduction of machines which were more efficient than men has been advantageous for society. The basic question always was: what adjustments in the economic and social systems were needed and how could they be effected; not how could a monstrous invention be destroyed. So it is with the development of professional specialization.

TRENDS IN COOPERATION AMONG PROFESSIONS

Fears that increasing specialization will reduce interprofessional cooperation are unwarranted, since the result must inevitably be just the opposite. There are no sharp dividing lines in nature. This fact becomes more self-evident as more is learned about man and his world. For example, the more that has been learned about the details of health and illness, the clearer it has become that a socio-psychosomatic approach is necessary for the understanding and treatment of disease. This requires cooperative effort of medical practitioners, biologists of many varieties, physical scientists, social scientists, social workers, and others. In comparison, consider the professional pattern that prevailed when, in the absence of specialized knowledge, illness was related to magic, sin, phlogiston, or humors; or more recently when disease was considered an entity, with little regard for the whole patient living in a conditioning social environment.

Within the natural sciences, specialization has allegedly gone to ludicrous extremes. Nevertheless, it has obliterated the earlier distinction between physics and chemistry and has also brought these disciplines into the closest collaboration with the biological sciences. In the social sciences, subdisciplinary specialization can claim the major credit for bringing sociology, social psychology, and social anthropology together in such a close working relationship that they are now generally called the behavior sciences. Before long, the behavior aspects of economics and political science may well be integrated with these behavior sciences. Such scientific collaboration automatically leads to increased cooperation in the practicing professions. Professional cooperation similarly requires coordination in research across arbitrary disciplinary lines.

There is a positive relation between the degree of specialization and the use by specialists of discoveries in the sciences and the accumulated knowledge gained from experience in professional practice. The unspecialized social worker of fifty years ago, for instance, could well ignore the generalized social sciences, and had no knowledge of psychiatry. In our time, the list of social work specialties mentioned earlier indicates the extent of change in the direction of collaboration. The offerings in collegiate programs for nursing education show a similar trend,[10] as do the curricula in our leading universities which are designed to prepare students for every learned profession.

Argument has been made that interprofessional collaboration can be greatly advanced by increasing the *number* of interspecialty teams in research and practice. But the problem rather concerns the kinds of measures that can be taken to increase interprofessional *teamwork*. For every profession practices it to some extent. Yet each one also neglects opportunities to extend such practice. No profession in modern society can live by itself, nor does any one try to do so.

Many individuals have set themselves tasks which are so narrowly defined that a minimum of contact, knowledge, and interprofessional cooperation is necessary beyond their specific fields. It would be unfortunate if the need for improved collaboration among the professions suggested that the demand for work of this type has been reduced. For basic research and practice within narrowly-defined fields eventually leads toward an effective interprofessional collaboration.

Interprofessional cooperation has come from pressing internal need rather than from external exhortation. Here several illustrations may be drawn from engineering—a profession traditionally regarded as one of the most narrow and isolated of all. In this case, the professional specialist has been faced time and again with problems that he was not fully equipped to solve. Consequently, he has called for the aid of other specialists. Machines, for example, must be designed so that they may be operated efficiently by men. This requires a knowledge of the physical and psychological capacities and also of the attitudes, values, and behavior patterns of the operators. Such knowledge must be obtained from people like physiologists, psychologists, medical specialists, economists, and sociologists. On other occasions, appeals for help have come to the engineer from other professions, such as public health and city planning. The need for collaboration in similar professional fields has usually been evident several decades before the requisite specialties were developed to the point where effective collaboration was feasible. Rarely is collaboration delayed much beyond the time of practical possibility.

How the Universities Can Promote Interprofessional Cooperation

The inevitable growth of interprofessional cooperation paralleling the extension of specialization does not imply that university faculties should ignore the problem of collaboration and let nature take its course. Specialists who overlook the need and opportunity for collaboration across disciplinary and professional lines are all too numerous. But that is a matter of individual failure rather than of specialization as such. It is also evidence of university failure in educational vision and technique.

Impartial Studies

In planning for future development, members of the professions and professional faculties apparently assume that they are sufficiently familiar with their milieu so that they do not need additional information obtainable through collaboration with specialists. This assumption is evident in the reports of studies sponsored by various professions and made by members of the same professions who show little regard for the fact that their training ordinarily has not prepared them for the task. Contrary results can hardly be expected when studies are conducted by professional associations usually possessing some of the membership advancement characteristics of a guild or trade association.

It is more reasonable to anticipate that impartial studies, which take account of social requirements without undue emphasis on the demands of specific professions, will be conducted increasingly under academic auspices. The universities are best equipped to make objective analyses of current social needs and trends.

Physical Integration

Interprofessional cooperation can also be promoted by insisting upon a maximum amount of physical propinquity of all university elements. This is in contrast to the policy of locating some schools and divisions at a distance because of convenience in practice, as in certain medical schools, or for some other reason, such as the gift of a usable but remote piece of property.

Obviously a medical school must have ready access to patients and good hospital facilities. But how many patients and how large a hospital are required? What are the educational costs of separating a medical school from the core of the university by a distance as great as that from Ithaca to New York City (as in the case of Cornell University) or across the city (as at Johns Hopkins in Baltimore) or even from 116th Street to 168th Street (as in the case of Columbia University in New York)?

How high is the educational price when a school of social work is located primarily with a concern for proximity to social agencies rather than for total academic facilities? Does a research institute gain more than it loses by being situated at a distance from an intellectual center in order to be close to the source of its raw data? The increasing interlocking of disciplines and professions suggests that the costs of physical separation are mounting. What substitutes are available for the stimulus and criticism which come from talking with a colleague from another specialty? What alternatives exist for the comparatively simple access to the techniques, knowledge, and wisdom of related professions to be found on a university campus?

A Cosmopolitan Academic Community

For a metropolitan university, the problem of physical integration is accompanied by the difficulty of developing an academic community which includes members of the faculties of all schools, or even the members of a single school. Faculty clubs, seminars, housing, cultural and recreational activities, and even committees all help. But more consideration and possibly more dollars should be given to welding academic personnel into an academic community. For the distinguishing character of a university is not delineated by its functions of research and teaching. It is to be found rather in the complex of academic values which ideally form the core of a professional subculture within our society.[11] To promote interprofessional cooperation, this subculture should be nurtured as a cluster of academic values and behavior patterns in addition to those prevailing in the community and nation.

In nurturing an integrating academic way of life, an account must be taken of the fact that each profession naturally tends to develop a subculture, with its special language, hierarchy of motivations, sense of responsibility, and code of behavior. Social workers are concerned with legal questions relating to criminal offenses, domestic relations, citizenship, housing, relief, and public assistance. So are lawyers. But the differences between these two professions in fundamental assumptions and educational approaches to matters like individual and social responsibility for legal infractions or professional obligations and procedures in client relations are not now appreciated. Or consider the professional pressure on medical practitioners to avoid public criticism of each other when errors in diagnosis or treatment are made, as contrasted with the obligation of lawyers to attack each other in open court under the prevailing adversary system of justice.

These two examples of differences in patterns of professional standards and behavior illustrate the diversity of existing professional subcultures. They also suggest that the differences have come into existence naturally in response to varying conditions of practice. In some utopian future, the need for professional subcultures may possibly be reduced to a minimum. Meanwhile, it is futile for one group to berate the other for its divergent patterns of behavior.

As Carr-Saunders and Wilson point out, "every profession lives in a world of its own. The language which is spoken by the inhabitants, the landmarks so familiar to them, their customs and conventions can only be learnt by those who reside there. But no man is a citizen of more than one country." Even so, we may hope for some degree of cosmopolitanism. The alternative of provincialism is now accepted as inevitable by far too many specialists. It may be inevitable for a large number, but this does not mean that the specialty as a field must progress in isolation.

Interprofessional Understanding

What can the university do to advance an objective study and discussion of these divergencies and increase interprofessional appreciation of their nature and rationale? Two possible contributions pertain to their research and instructional methods.

RESEARCH METHODS. Several differences in basic orientation are sources of misunderstanding among the professions. One occurs between the professions relying primarily on academic research techniques and others dependent mainly on the clinical approach. The professions obviously rely in varying degrees upon field investigation, the library, the laboratory, and the clinic, and the problem of mutual understanding between them has long been recognized. Abraham Flexner, for example, observed in 1925 that "the clinical sciences cannot be prosecuted in the spirit of the university unless clinical teachers practically identify themselves in respect to income and scale of living with the university rather than with the medical profession."[12]

The difficulty of obtaining mutual understanding by professions is illustrated by the differences in the presuppositions and methods of the psychiatrist and the social psychologist. Both seek almost precisely the same knowledge of human behavior. The one is at home in the clinic; the other is more familiar with academic halls. The one tends to focus on a comparatively small number of individuals; the other, on gathering data about as large a number as possible. One is concerned with learning as much as possible about the whole individual through intensive depth interviews; the other works with fractions of knowledge about each of his subjects. One interprets his data with little reference to statistical techniques; the other runs innumerable correlations in the hope of substantiation or refutation of his hypothesis. One is convinced that no true understanding of behavior can come from procedures that depend on fragments of information about many individuals; the other is happy with actuarial knowledge and does not see how the most complete data about a few individuals can apply to a larger population.

These contrasts are unfair, of course, in that they reflect an academic bias; they are not wholly true for any known pair of individuals. Nevertheless, they do indicate roughly a type of methodological argument that hampers cooperation between two closely-related professions which have been earnestly seeking improved cooperation for many years with some success. Similar difficulties are hampering cooperation between other medical specialists and the social scientists, social workers and sociologists, lawyers and specialists in the behavior sciences, and others. Yet an increasing progress in cooperation indicates that the difficulty will ultimately solve itself. Much can be done within academic walls to hasten its resolution.

INSTRUCTIONAL METHODS. Closely related to differences in emphasis in research methods are variations in emphasis in traditional methods of professional instruction. Education for the law, social work, and medicine stresses the use of the case method. In comparison, courses designed to give the student a command of a universal body of knowledge not specifically related to any given problems do not use the case method. Of course, no profession fails to take advantage of both instructional approaches; neither can be used effectively by itself. Nevertheless, some professions have identified themselves with the one, and some with the other, with the result that an interprofessional barrier has been created. This barrier may be largely a matter of tradition but it reflects a significant difference in orientation.

The presentation of a case to students preparing for any occupation concerned with social behavior and human welfare permits a discussion of the points of view and knowledge of other disciplines. Most specialist teachers may possibly ignore this fact, or give it little more than lip service. Many of them, however, take most seriously their responsibility for helping the student to gain an understanding of the interprofessional ramifications of the cases used in instruction. Problems in business administration involving wages, personnel policy, or marketing admittedly require a knowledge far beyond the pale of economics narrowly defined. Engineering problems may involve matters like economic trends, wages and work incentives, public opinion, sanitation and other health questions, legal problems, and so on. To the extent that university faculties leave the introduction of ancillary professional material only to the consideration of the individual teacher or even to the various professional faculties without the full cooperation of the university staff as a whole, they are missing an excellent opportunity for professional integration.

It is generally assumed that the learned practicing professions work harmoniously with research specialists insofar as an awareness exists of a relevance of specific areas of research to practice. There is, however, a sufficient difference in motivation between the man who is devoted to the extension of knowledge and the man who gives his life to the application of knowledge to problems of practice, to justify a special university effort to improve liaison between the two.

The medical profession is certainly as research-minded as any concerned with alleviating human misery. Yet as recently as the early years of the present century, practice-oriented members of medical school faculties were impatient with the idea that time and money should be devoted to the study of a subject like the chemistry of the blood. Even today, there is a difference of opinion within the medical profession which is traceable in large part to differences in basic motivation about the proper use of patients in research.

Among social workers, there is a tendency to overprotect the client in relation to research. Lawyers similarly tend to be impatient with persons who study the nature of criminal behavior, the socio-psychological factors in the validity of testimony by witnesses, or the process of decision-making. It is quite understandable that practitioners should have difficulty in maintaining a rapport with individuals who devote themselves to trying to advance knowledge. If it is agreed that research and practice in the learned professions are inseparable, the university should do its utmost to maintain such a rapport at the highest possible level.

Rapport between research and practice is perhaps greatest in professions concerned with physical and biological problems. These are the oldest sciences and professions. Over the years, they have developed ways of integrating research and practice which work exceedingly well within the range of the natural sciences and their application. But the pressing problems of the day concern people in relation to each other and to their environment. The social sciences are very young, and an effective means for communicating with the older practicing professions have not yet come into use. Few well-developed channels of communication exist between the practicing professions and the social sciences. Although the best communication prevails between economics and business and government, few people would claim that this is satisfactory.

The findings of research are not ordinarily usable in their original raw form by the professions. They need to be adapted and integrated with the knowledge of previous relevant research and experience with specificity for practical application. Very little attention has been paid so far to the ways in which this adaptation may best be done, or to the training of individuals to do it. There is no social science counterpart to the educational system that brings physical and biological science into practical use for the benefit of mankind. Here is another task in which the university must take leadership.

CONCLUSION

All the tasks that have been suggested as leadership responsibilities for the university, in cooperation with the professions and the lay citizenry, are tasks of study, planning, facilitation, and education. In some way, they will be accomplished because of the pressure of the needs of metropolitan living and as necessary companions of progressive specialization. Specialists must inevitably become increasingly literate in related fields. Frequently, all that is needed is an intelligent respect for other types of specialists and knowledge of when and how to consult them. This may seem simple to accomplish. But to be done properly, it requires the rational use of the great resources of our universities for research, planning, and educational operation.

Universities have helped to create the need for interprofessional cooperation by their success in developing a multitude of specialists in response to the requirements of modern civilization. They also have accomplished more than all other agencies combined toward integration, and they are in the best position to do much more. In pursuing the objective of professional integration, resistance to the charge that professional specialization itself is an evil may be strengthened by recalling that neither wholeness in concept nor cooperation in effort is achieved by neglect of detail.

FOOTNOTES TO CHAPTER 16

1. A. Flexner, "Is Social Work a Profession?" *Proceedings of the National Conference of Charities and Correction* (1915), p. 581.

2. R. M. Williams, Jr., *American Society: A Sociological Interpretation* (New York: Knopf, 1951), pp. 192–193.

3. A. M. Carr-Saunders and P. A. Wilson, *The Professions* (Oxford: The Clarendon Press, 1933), pp. 491 and 493–494. The later quotation on p. 299 of this article is taken from the same source, p. iii.

4. For a list of positions in social work indicating the range of current specialization, see E. V. Hollis and A. L. Taylor, *Social Work Education in the United States* (New York: Columbia University Press, 1951), pp. 60–63.

5. For engineering specialization, see L. R. Lohr (ed.), *Centennial of Engineering* (Chicago: Museum of Science and Industry, 1952), table of contents. For specialties within mining and metallurgical engineering, see A. B. Parsons, "The Role of the American Institute of Mining and Metallurgical Engineers in the Profession," *ibid.*, p. 141.

6. T. Parsons, *The Social System* (Glencoe: The Free Press, 1951), p. 431.

7. Quoted in J. W. Hurst, *The Growth of American Law: The Law Makers* (Boston: Little Brown, 1950), pp. 341–342.

8. In the depression of the early 1930's, there was both an individual and governmental emphasis on migration to the less densely populated areas of the United States as a means of reducing economic distress of the unemployed and improving the long-run relation between population distribution and economic resources. The impracticality of this approach is well documented in C. Goodrich and others, *Migration and Economic Opportunity* (Philadelphia: University of Pennsylvania Press, 1936).

9. H. P. Van Dusen, "Ministers in the Making," *Education for Professional Responsibility,* a report of the proceedings of the Interprofessional Conference on Education for Professional Responsibility, held at Buck Hill Falls, Pennsylvania, April 12–14, 1948, p. 65.

10. See E. L. Brown, *Nursing for the Future* (New York: Russell Sage Foundation, 1948). Also M. Bridgman, *Collegiate Education for Nursing* (New York: Russell Sage Foundation, 1953).

11. See O. Pollack, "The Culture of Psychiatric Social Work," *Journal of Psychiatric Social Work,* XXI, No. 4 (June, 1950).

12. A. Flexner, *Medical Education: A Comparative Study* (New York: Macmillan, 1925), p. 324.

17

Commentaries

By **Thomas Parran, M.D.,** *Dean, Graduate School of Public Health, University of Pittsburgh*

Although Sir Alexander Carr-Saunders and Donald Young selected different points of departure, they do not seem to be far apart in their conclusions. Both agree that the number of professions, semi-professions, and would-be professions is multiplying. Mr. Young implies that a continued fractionation is inevitable and possibly desirable. Sir Alexander is apparently nostalgic for the days when only law, medicine, and the church were dignified by the term profession. He understandably resents the clamor of so many occupations for professional status. Mr. Young, on the other hand, sees no apparent advantage in distinguishing between professional and other occupations.

Sir Alexander has indicated that the members of the old professions were originally independent whereas today this situation no longer generally prevails. But it should be noted that some professions like the clergy were never independent. The clergy has always been bound either by the dogma of the church or by the approval of the congregation. Even in medieval times, physicians were retainers of the lords of the manor or the dukes of the feudal court. Moreover, practically all the advances in the medical sciences have occurred in the universities. Only occasionally does a William Jenner or a William Beaumont produce new knowledge almost singlehandedly. It should be recalled, too, that Beaumont was an army surgeon on a salary.

One of the great recent advances in medical practice seems to be the development of the pattern in which a group of physicians work together. They accept full responsibility for the complete health care of families under their charge and receive an assured income through a prepayment plan. This is the modern equivalent of the old family doctor at his best.

Unfortunately, many of the old family physicians were not of the best. Indeed, medicine was at a low ebb here for 150 years after the first colony was settled. There was no organized medical school. Few doctors were able to study in the medical centers of Great Britain or on the continent. Quacks abounded. Epidemics all but wiped out the early settlers. Even now, we cannot say that the majority of our population receives adequate medical care.

Sir Alexander Carr-Saunders appropriately designated a profession by the criteria that its practitioners must master an organized body of knowledge and follow a self-imposed code of conduct or ethics. But as a matter of fact, some of the semi-professions today master a body of knowledge greater in extent and usefulness for the care of the sick than all of the medical knowledge of a century ago. In addition, they have codes of ethics and possess techniques as exact as those of the brain surgeon.

Does the metropolis—the mother city—have a primary impact upon the professions? Or is the multiplication and fractionation of professions a result of advances in scientific and technical knowledge over a vast area of human affairs? Also is not the metropolis itself a result of this same growth in scientific and technical knowledge? The modern metropolis certainly could not exist except for the great advances in the natural sciences.

MODERN MEDICAL EDUCATION

In attempting to prove his point that salaried doctors may practice poor medicine, Sir Alexander quotes Dr. Collings to good effect. It should be noted, however, that Dr. Collings made an earlier study of general practice in England in 1949 soon after the National Health Service went into effect. In this study, he was led "to write what is indeed a condemnation of general practice in its present form. . . . It soon became obvious that many problems which had existed for years and were inherent in general practice as we know it, were being interpreted as results of the new National Health Service. This is serious."

Responsibility for the lack of standards and other shortcomings which Dr. Collings found among British practitioners must be due to poor medical training and to the inherent nature of their individual practice. The doctor works alone in his surgery or in the patient's home with little or no effective professional control. Add to this the financial incentive, in terms of time saved, to send the patient on to a specialist or hospital, and the result is not surprising.

Sir Alexander says that the more the specialization, the narrower in general is the education preparatory to entering into the professions. In the United States, the universities certainly shelter specialized and unrelated schemes of training. As a result, the student loses the picture of the wholeness of man and the unity of knowledge.

Because of this situation, individuals who are engaged in public health education are challenged by an opportunity to draw together in one faculty representatives from the biological, social, and physical sciences, each searching for the principles which contribute to a common goal. This faculty can explore the dynamics of man's interrelationship with his total environment, and can effectively promote a synthesis of the sciences which constitutes the domain of public health.

Many attempts are currently being made to counteract the atomism which has developed during the past few decades in medical education in the United States. Here are a few of the ways and means:

1. Prior to coming to medical school, the student should have a broad cultural education. In fact, there should be no such thing as pre-medical education.

2. The badly fragmented curriculum in medical schools needs to be put together into a more understandable whole. Walls between the several departments should be broken down.

3. The patient as a whole being—his mental, emotional and physical characteristics, his home, his work, his life, his family—all are basic factors in his health or lack of it. These and other factors should be appraised in a time dimension.

4. The undue preoccupation of medical education with diagnosis and treatment—particularly with the unusual, rare, and baffling medical museum pieces—should be broadened to emphasize prevention and to include rehabilitation.

5. The function of the teaching hospital should be enlarged to embrace many kinds of home care programs.

6. As Mr. Young has stated, medical education is beginning to draw upon the behavior sciences for help in understanding the human beings with which medicine is concerned. It should increase its use of these sciences.

Once these ways and means are adopted, the student will be exposed increasingly to an understanding of life and health prior to the time he begins to specialize. If this trend continues, medicine may recapture its ancient status—of a learned profession. For during the twentieth century, too many medical practitioners have already become only more or less skilled technicians.

By **Reginald Heber Smith,** *Director, The Survey of the Legal Profession, Boston*

Sir Alexander Carr-Saunders and Donald Young both define a profession in terms that apply to the legal profession. As Roscoe Pound has said:

> When we speak of the old recognized professions we mean an organized calling in which men pursue a learned art and are united in the pursuit of it as a public service . . . no less a public service because they may make a livelihood thereby.
> Here, from the professional standpoint there are three essential ideas—organization, learning, and a spirit of public service.[1]

For studying the impact of the metropolis upon the legal profession, this definition lays bare two important facts.

First, for about 75 years of our early history—roughly from the adoption of the Constitution to 1870—the United States had no legal profession. The colonial bar associations disappeared, so that no organization existed. As a consequence of the so-called Jacksonian revolution, standards of legal education were destroyed. Without such standards and organization, the ideal of public service faded. Americans generally were in an acquisitive mood and lawyers followed suit.[2]

Secondly, the rebirth and revival of the legal profession took place in metropolitan centers. This is strange, because lawyers are admitted to the bar of a state rather than a city. Yet the progess of organization was from metropolitan bar associations to state bar associations to the American Bar Association.

LEGAL ORGANIZATION IN BAR ASSOCIATIONS

The oldest bar association is in Philadelphia. The pioneer modern association is The Association of the Bar of the City of New York. It was founded in 1870 for the primary purpose of ousting the corrupt judges of Boss Tweed's regime. Dorman B. Eaton, an outspoken critic of that regime, was feloniously assaulted and left close to death. One of the first acts of the infant Association was to offer a $5,000 reward for the conviction of the criminals.

Seventy-five years later, Chief Justice Stone said that "it [the Association] has sought to promote no individual or Association interest which was not calculated to advance the best interests of the profession and the public."[3] Like other bar associations, the New York City Bar Association interested itself in educational and ethical standards from the start. It should be remembered that this association was formed in 1870 when the city was just approaching metropolitan stature with a population of one million persons.

In the United States, legal aid started in 1876 also in New York City and spread from there to other metropolitan centers. To this day, legal aid is organized on a city, not a state, basis. Metropolitan influences have caused legal aid work to be organized in special offices devoted exclusively to the conduct of the work. They are staffed by salaried lawyers paid by the Legal Aid Society which receives its funds from lawyers and from the community in general. In contrast, the Legal Aid and Assistance Plan in England sends its clients to the regular offices of the solicitors on the panel and not to one central legal aid office.

THE ASSOCIATION OF LAWYERS IN PARTNERSHIPS

Just as the metropolis brought about the organization of the legal profession in bar associations, so it has brought about the association of lawyers in partnerships for the practice of law. Actually, they engage in *group practice,* although the phrase is not commonly employed in the legal profession.

The lawyer who works alone is called a solo practitioner and the word carries no derogatory implication. On the other hand, a group of lawyers must have a number of offices, and that is called a law factory, an intentionally derogatory and damning phrase. In 1952, there were about 120,000 private solo practitioners in the United States and slightly less than 57,000 partners in private firms or employed in firms. Thus 68 per cent of the active practitioners were solos and 32 per cent were in firms.[4]

Specialization within Legal Practice

There has long been a spirited debate on the merits of solo and group practice. On the one hand, it has been said that "the Main Street lawyer is a distinct species in our land. As an individual member of the profession he glories in his independence and his individuality; [he] is the principal guardian of the traditions of our profession and of the best that there is in our civic and social life."[5] On the other hand, "antiquated in organization, in methods of doing business, in methods of getting business, in nose for where services are needed, the bar finds its buggy crowded to the wall."[6]

What have non-lawyers had to say? The sociologist Harry Elmer Barnes notes that "in legal practice this vast volume of law puts the great law firm—the law factory—at a distinct advantage, compared with the single practitioner or small firm, however able."[7] In speaking of medical practice, Dr. Richard C. Cabot remarks that

> . . . the daily companionship and teamwork with others who share the responsibility and contribute the advantage of their slightly different angle of vision, all tend to raise and to maintain high standards of work. The isolation of the private practitioner, on the other hand, makes it harder for him to attain and to keep up such standards.[8]

In lecturing on industrial civilization, Professor Elton Mayo suggested:

> Whether as anthropologists we study a primitive race or as individualists we study some part of the modern complex and chaotic scene, we find, either in the natural wilds or in the modern city, groups of individuals who find their happiness and such sense of personal security as may be in the subordination of an individual to a common interest. The solitary who works alone is always a very unhappy person.[9]

In the teaching profession, James Bryant Conant suggested in his President's Report for 1948 that "the status of a profession derives from the age-old concept of a faculty as an independent entity; the older members of the group are to each other as partners in a modern law firm—they share both responsibility and power." Just as we find group practice of law in metropolitan centers, so we find specialization within the group.

Sir Alexander Carr-Saunders rightly says that "the traditional attitude of the professional man is characterized by a sense of responsibility towards his client, and a feeling of pride in service . . ." But he fears that "the rise of specialists has brought about a subtle change in the traditional relation of practitioner to client." The same fear is reflected in an address by the President of the Association of American Law Schools:

> Abraham Lincoln could practice law in the frontier community of which he was a part without special competence in any field but with a general facility which enabled him to handle all types of cases in an acceptable manner. Today, at least in the larger centers of population, lawyers are becoming specialists whose community of interest is constantly shrinking as their knowledge of particular areas is enhanced.[10]

Bulk and complexity forced specialization. So did big business, big labor, and big government. Consider the United States Steel Company, which operates under federal laws as well as 48 state laws, or the Standard Oil Company, which does business all over the world under many different legal systems. When such a client says, "How do we act so as to obey these laws?" it takes an army of lawyers to find the correct answer.[11]

Advantages of Legal Partnerships

Is it possible that group practice by lawyers using the partnership form of organization may offer a solution to the dilemma of specialization? The partnership form gives each partner both responsibility and authority. The partners have no boss; they are employed by themselves and are responsible to each other. The partnership has both flexibility and durability. The Rawle law offices in Philadelphia are older than the Declaration of Independence.

From the client's point of view, the partnership has the stability and responsibility of a social institution. The liability of partners is unlimited; all the assets of all the partners are placed behind every action of every single partner. A study of brankuptcy court records back through the banking holidays of the early nineteen thirties discloses not a single instance of a law firm going into bankruptcy.[12]

A by-product of the law firm is system—a word cordially hated by most professional men. They should heed the words of Sir William Osler:

> How can you take the greatest possible advantage of your capacities with the least possible strain? By cultivating system. . . . Let me entreat those of you who are here for the first time to lay to heart what I say on this matter.[13]

A by-product of system in the law firm is cost accounting, which means that at the end of a case, the lawyer actually knows what the cost of the work for the client was.[14] This fact adds an essential element in the determination of a fair fee. It enables the lawyer to explain the basis of his charge to the client. That has proved to be reassuring to clients who are apt to believe that the lawyer either guesses or charges what the traffic will bear. Several elements enter into what is a fair fee, but actual cost is an indispensable factor.

LAWYER-CLIENT RELATIONSHIPS

Logically, there is nothing to prevent each lawyer-specialist from being independent, having his own separate office, and practicing solo as many medical specialists do. Depending upon your problem, therefore, you could go to one office for tax advice, a second for a will, a third for litigation, a fourth for title examination, a fifth for a labor negotiation, a sixth for a divorce, a seventh to collect a bill, or an eighth to try to get out of jail.

In a human world, clients needing legal help will have no truck with any such setup. Human beings go to a lawyer because they respect and trust him. They think of him as "their" lawyer. In a well-organized firm, the specialist is a specialist only part of the time. The rest of the time he is a family lawyer.

There need be no mystery about what goes on within the walls of a well-organized law firm. A client goes to the lawyer whom he trusts. The client may have been run over and severely hurt by an automobile and needs to have suit brought. His lawyer is an expert in patents; but he is also a wise and compassionate counselor. First, he takes the burden of worry and responsibility off his client's shoulders by taking them onto his own shoulders. This is literally true; the lawyer feels the weight. He tells the client he shall have the very best help, and this also is true. He does not send the client *out* of his office; he has his partner who is a trial lawyer join them *in* the same office. The client sees strength being mobilized in his behalf.

From then on, the procedure within the office will depend upon the nature of the client. If he or she is frightened or timid, all advice will come through the family lawyer. In most instances the client is happy enough to go direct to the expert assigned to his case. That is better, quicker, and cheaper. But even so, the client never goes outside of the firm's offices, which to him are always the offices of "my" lawyer.

This system gives to the client accurate and skilled legal service at maximum speed and minimum cost. It suits human nature. The client is reassured by the knowledge that his lawyer is always there, always available, always responsible. And the client knows that he will settle the fee with his lawyer.

It is common experience that many of our best friendships are the result of working shoulder to shoulder with other men. Think, then, what it means to work among a group of partners for a lifetime. According to partnership law, it is a matter of "for better or worse, for richer or poorer." In a good firm, it is also "until death do us part."

Within a partnership, the best in the professional spirit merges and blends with the best in the human spirit. The partnership becomes a team. Each member is inspired to do his best. He develops his innate powers to the uttermost. When he errs, he is brought back by hands he trusts. In sorrow, he is sustained by the loyal affection of his associates. All this is good for men as men, and results in finer lawyers. It also produces better service for clients.

By **Dana W. Atchley, M.D.,** *Professor of Clinical Medicine, Columbia-Presbyterian Medical Center, New York*

Although metropolitanism is not the cause of specialization, there is a vast difference between the work of professional men in a small community and in a metropolis.

For a professional man like a doctor, the simplicity of life in a small community enables him to know everybody and to be known by everyone. This opportunity gives the doctor a certain amount of intuitive knowledge which must be obtained in a more self-conscious way in the metropolis. What the small-town doctor does not know by talking with his male friends, his wife picks up at the sewing circle. Thus there is a simplicity and ease of obtaining knowledge about the whole man, and a special discipline for that purpose is not necessary in some senses.

SPECIALIZATION IN LARGE COMMUNITIES

Within a metropolitan community, however, these things have to be done by specialists. Such specialization is necessary and inevitable. Rather than remaining static, as the term fragmentation implies, it evolves. The process of specialization resembles the fragmentation of the acorn growing up into a tree. From the branches other acorns drop, and out of their fragmentation comes new trees. This growth is worthwhile and desirable. The only thing we have to do is to learn how to prune, and in some instances, espalier our trees.

In the medical profession, specialization has two aspects. There is specialization in research and specialization in practice. The former is inevitable because of the growth of knowledge. As knowledge flourishes, new disciplines appear and old ones join in new sub-disciplines. The important point is that the increase in specialization is not fragmentalized but is accomplished in a single institution in a single environment. Therefore, it has the mutuality of interest which is necessary for balance.

A tremendous step forward was taken when research was introduced into the clinical department. In former years, the research departments in at least one medical school were on one side of the street and the clinical departments were on the other. That street was not crossed except when the students went from the second year into the third year of medical school. Otherwise, there was no contact. In fact, there was mutual disrespect from both sides.

At the present time, research is carried on every day in clinical departments. As a matter of fact, we have developed a sort of speciality in the total individual. The internist in medicine is now consciously preoccupied with the total individual. This is true more than ever before. In the past his concern with the total individual was more or less intuitive; now it is self-conscious.

For example, there was once a medical department in the Vanderbilt Clinic of the Columbia-Presbyterian Medical Center composed of little more than a group of men working together. We would see a patient and then send him all over the hospital to one department after another—to gynecology, surgery, and eye, ear, nose, and throat. The patient wandered around and sometimes found his way back to us. But he would be completely lost, and all he might gain would be perhaps a poor knowledge of the building.

About 1948, a so-called group clinic was introduced into the Vanderbilt Clinic. Now the patient comes to the internist who goes over the problem. In the same room or on the same floor are various specialists available to consult with the internist. They come in, give their opinion, and the internist integrates it. In other words, internal medicine is an integrating speciality within the department of clinical medicine.

This integration pertains to the total individual. Offshoots of the interest in the whole person are found in psychosomatic medicine. Any student who takes a history nowadays in the department of internal medicine compiles a description of the social and economic environment of the patient, his home life, and the whole gamut of the individual's contact with his family and his community, as well as his symptoms from head to foot.

The self-conscious approach to the total individual is now a recognized speciality in the practice of medicine. Out of it, we feel that we can espalier our specialities toward coordinating together with the common man.

By **Harry W. Jones,** *Professor of Law, Columbia University*

These comments pertain to interprofessional cooperation as it applies to the field of law in metropolitan practice and also the improvement of legal institutions.

Historically, the lawyer has regarded himself as a kind of professional generalist. His province includes all the actual or potential conflicts of interest which occur in the affairs of men. This is a way of looking at social activity through the spectacles of present or possible future controversy.

There are inevitable overlappings between the lawyer's jurisdictional claims and the day-to-day work of individuals in other professions. Thus far, the interprofessional relations of lawyers have been symbolized by "no trespassing" signs, as in the continuing rear-guard actions by the bar associations against trust companies and accountants. But it is healthier when lawyers think of their interprofessional relations in terms of cooperation rather than the essentially craft union terms of jurisdictional integrity.

The lawyer drawing a will, representing a client in a criminal case, or advising in matters of family relations potentially overlaps with the role of the physician, social worker, psychiatrist, or minister. What, then, is the key to interprofessional cooperation? As Donald Young suggests, it is likely that an effort to achieve effective cooperation *among* specialists offers more promise than any attempt to turn the clock back *from* specialization. But there is one caveat to record. The difficulty is that the specialist is usually the last man in the world to be aware of the interdisciplinary dimensions of the work he is doing.

We could hardly expect the lawyer to make himself an expert in all the areas that touch on his field of action. But he must, as Donald Young says, be "literate" enough in the methods of the related fields to be aware of the extralegal dimensions of his work and to know whom to call on for help. This states one obligation of the university in legal education.

The Improvement of Legal Institutions

It is common knowledge that the methods, institutions, and substantive content of law have not kept pace with modern advances in science, engineering, and medicine. There are, to be sure, many reasons for this developmental lag. Law is more an art than a science. The experimental method is not available to verify bold new legal hypotheses. Moreover, law is not an autonomous discipline; legal improvements, unlike scientific advances, cannot be put into effect until a politically-elected legislature gives the stamp of its approval. It is as if the House of Representatives had the final say on penicillin or on the field theory of physics.

But these difficulties provide no excuse for the lack of interdisciplinary co-operation for law improvement. In other professions like medicine, practice advances by drawing on the discoveries of pure science. Where is the pure science equivalent for law improvement? The social sciences, which should be for law what the natural sciences are for medicine, are incomplete and for the most part tentative in their conclusions. The results of social science investigation are rarely cast in a form that permits them to be used for practical lawmaking needs. Even if there were a mature, ready-to-be-drawn-on body of social science data, lawyer-judges, lawyer-legislators, and lawyer-professors generally would not know how to find it or what to do with it.

Here we begin to pay the price for narrow technical training and narrower professional specialization. If legal specialists stayed within the bounds of their specialties, we would not have to worry about their range of vision. But by virtue of professional prestige or political selection, the successful lawyer-specialist blossoms out repeatedly as a deciding authority on everything. That is what is wrong with any narrowly-educated specialist—there is no guarantee that he will stay specialized.

Again we return to the role of the university. Only there can we hope to find the Benthemite heresy that legal development is too important to be left entirely to the lawyers. Unless the ground is first broken by gains in the social sciences, however, the arts of law cannot be advanced in any way which is comparable to advances in the scientific fields. An effective working technique must be found to marshal the insights and methods of the social sciences to help solve practical legislative problems. Universities must strive toward a broad-gauge legal training by which the lawyer is taught to find his way around in other than legal sources and to invite the cooperation of the other disciplines that study man in society.

What we lack in law is the man who has both the sharpened skills of the specialist and the wholeness of view of the true universalist. There is nothing new about this critical reflection. After all, it was of the law graduates of the University of Paris—the greatest metropolitan university of its time—of whom Rabelais' Pantagruel was talking when he said:

> Besides, the law grew up out of the field of moral and natural philosophy. Then how could these idiots construe it, when by God! they studied less philosophy than the average mule.

The words are characteristically overstated and are not to be taken literally. But if we read "moral philosophy" as including the other professions and the social sciences, there is point in the statement now as then.

FOOTNOTES TO CHAPTER 17

1. R. Pound, "The Professions in the Society of Today," *New York Medicine,* the official publication of the Medical Society of the County of New York, V, No. 19 (October 5, 1949), 21.

2. See R. Pound, *The Lawyer from Antiquity to Modern Times* (St. Paul: West Publishing Co., 1953), p. xxvii; A. T. Vanderbilt, *Men and Measures in the Law* (New York: Knopf, 1949), pp. 111–114; and J. W. Hurst, *The Growth of American Law* (Boston: Little, Brown, 1950), pp. 277 and 336.

3. See A. P. Blaustein, "The Association of the Bar of the City of New York," *The Record,* an official publication of the Association of the Bar of the City of New York, VI, No. 6 (June, 1951), 261, 270.

4. *Second Statistical Report on the Lawyers of the United States* (1952 edition based on the Martindale-Hubbell Law Directory). The over-all statistics for 1952 are: 221,605 lawyers accounted for; 202,037 lawyers with detailed records; 7,471 judges; 19,910 federal, state, county, or city service lawyers; 1,213 law teachers; 11,784 lawyers in private practice, as in law departments of business, banking, or insurance; the balance inactive or retired. These figures are probably the most reliable obtainable anywhere.

5. E. E. Cheatham, *Cases and Materials on the Legal Profession* (Chicago: The Foundation Press, 1938), p. 13.

6. K. Llewellyn, *Law and Contemporary Problems* (winter, 1938), 133.

7. H. E. Barnes, *Social Institutions* (New York: Prentice-Hall, 1946), p. 391.

8. R. C. Cabot, *Adventures on the Borderland of Ethics* (New York: Harper, 1926), p. 53.

9. E. Mayo, *The Political Problem of Industrial Civilization* (Cambridge: Harvard University Graduate School of Business Administration, 1947), p. 21.

10. C. B. Nutting, "Training Lawyers for the Future," *Journal of Legal Education,* VI, No. 1 (1953), 7.

11. See especially R. T. Swaine, "Impact of Big Business on the Profession," *American Bar Association Journal,* XXXV (February, 1949), 89.

12. C. O. Porter, "Lawyer Bankruptcies," *Journal of the National Association of Referees in Bankruptcy,* XXIV, No. 3 (July, 1950). See also *Case and Comment,* LVI, No. 4 (July–August, 1951).

13. W. Osler, *Aequanimitas* (3rd edn.; Philadelphia: The Blakiston Company, 1944), p. 361.

14. R. H. Smith, *Law Office Organization* (Chicago: American Bar Association Journal, 1943), a reprint of four articles from the *Journal* for May, June, July, and August, 1940.

PART SEVEN

The Impact of the Metropolis
on the Spiritual Life of Man

INTRODUCTION

When judging the metropolis, one important criterion to consider is its impact upon the spiritual life of man. For "what is a man profited, if he shall gain the whole world, and lose his own soul?"

In the following chapters, the spiritual life of man is interpreted with the widest sort of connotation. It refers to the aspect of man's life in which he senses and expresses his freedom and transcendence and the ultimate meaning of his existence. In our culture, man's spiritual life has traditionally been focused in religious institutions and ecclesiastical life. But no such restricted meaning of the term is intended here.

Professor Folliet discusses some of the urban influences on Christianity in general, and on Catholicism in large French cities in particular. Professor Casserley examines a number of the spiritual characteristics of the great metropolis. Commentaries by distinguished scholars of the Christian, Jewish, Moslem, and Hindu faiths point to the role of the city in creating and destroying man's spiritual life in various cultures.

18

The Effects of City Life upon Spiritual Life

JOSEPH FOLLIET

Professeur de Sociologie
l'Institut Social des Facultés Catholiques de Lyon

In the Graeco-Roman western world Christianity was at first an urban phenomenon. The countryside long remained pagan, and the French language still bears traces of this persistence. Words like *païen* (pagan) and *paysan* (a rural inhabitant), and the disparaging slang terms *pacant* (boorish) and *péquenot* (peasant-like), are derived from *pagus,* meaning the small country place, as contrasted with *civitas,* the city.[1]

But after the fifth century, A.D., the world, dominated by a land economy,[2] generally became rural, and the ruined or sleepy towns lost their importance. With the development of monasticism and the upbuilding of parishes, Christianity gradually turned into a rural and peasant-like phenomenon, bound by a deep symbiosis to a conception of life which proceeds from daily contact with the soil and the weather.

Nowhere do the traces of that union remain more perceptible than in the European countryside. The countless crosses at the crossroads, the madonnas and the tree and fountain ex-votos, the blessing of cattle, field, or fruits of the earth, the ceremonies of the Rogations instituted by Saint Mamert, Bishop of Vienne in Gaul, the processions through the fields on Corpus Christi day or on Assumption day, the fairs of Saint Martin, Saint Michael, or Saint John, the customs connected with Christmas or Easter, the popular proverbs and sayings —all are tokens of the alliance.[3]

This rural Christianity flowed into the small towns whose rhythms and tastes resembled those of the countryside and whose people were in constant touch with the surrounding areas.[4] In the Paris of the seventeenth and eighteenth centuries, the largest and most urban capital in continental Europe, Monsieur Olier, founder of St. Sulpice, lifted up his heart unto God while beholding the wheatfields which stretched out from the Church of Our Lady of the Fields (Notre Dame des Champs, then rightly named) to suburban Vaugirard. The Parisians, going out for a walk, would watch the Montmartre windmills. They

spent their Sundays under the green arbors of the adjacent hamlet of Por-
cherons, drank goat's milk on the Champs-Elysées, or tasted the unprepossess-
ing wine of nearby Suresnes.

Since the industrial and demographic revolution, however, the European
landscape has become quite urban. Its prominent features are no longer
steeples and elms but factory chimneys and office buildings. Large cities have
multiplied. Ancient towns have extended beyond all measure into such urban
monsters as London, Paris, Berlin, or New York. The rhythms of city life,
regulated according to the mathematical time divisions of the clock, no longer
depend on day, season, or weather. Although the country goes on conditioning
the city, it no longer exerts a determining influence. On the contrary, the
country is influenced more and more by the city. Disappearing cultural peasant
patterns provide subject matter only for museums and folkloric science and art.

Many people consider that this radical change has affected religious life in
an unfortunate manner. Being hostile to urban supremacy, they yearn with
nostalgia for an alliance once again between Christianity and country life. This
accounts for the production of a literature at once rustic, romantic, and archaic
for which France, with its rural traditions, seems to be a natural home. Included here are such poets as Francis Jammes and Louis Mercier, and novelists
like René Bazin, Henri Bordeaux, Joseph de Pesquidoux, Henri Pourrat, and
the Provençaux with the great Frédéric Mistral.[5]

In England, the same nostalgia is expressed by the distributism of Chester-
ton and Father MacNabb; in the United States, by the attempts at a back-to-
the-land movement under the inspiration of Peter Maurin and Dorothy Day;
and in French Canada, by the efforts of some of the French clergy and Catholic laity to maintain rural structures and traditions in an increasingly urbanized
environment.[6]

All these reactions have a psychological and sociological interest. They
underline the relevance of an investigation into the religious consequences of
great urban agglomerations. They remind us that any complete study must
necessarily be dynamic and comparative, confronting the present with the past
and the large city with the village and country.[7]

METHODS OF STUDYING URBAN INFLUENCES

In studying the effects of city life upon spiritual life, a number of techniques
can be used. To begin with, public opinion can be sounded out. This method
has the advantage of producing a few generalizations without taking too many
chances. But it lacks precision and corresponds only to a moment in the
evolution of opinion. To become dynamic, it would have to be employed
periodically so that fluctuations of opinion could be traced.[8]

A methodical inquiry into the practice of religion in a given area would
be capable of more precision. Although such a survey may yield results, it
provides only isolated slices of reality. It registers raw facts yet offers no explanations. Numbers and percentages may try to evoke the soul's secret, but

they fail to reveal it. Thus, a group of people whose religious practice is weak may, in fact, be making significant progress, whereas another group whose practices are more obvious and impressive may actually be starting to decline.

Moreover, this kind of inquiry is valuable only when it deals with an extensive, organized religious group which engages in regular observances. While it is very instructive with regard to Catholic groups, it is less so for Protestant or Jewish ones. That is why any local inquiry, expressed in facts, statistics, and graphs, should be supplemented by religious monographs dealing with districts, parishes, or communities and allowing ample room for historical treatment.

In the same way, the study of religious facts must be related to the social environment. Memoires, collections of documents, biographies, and folklore may contain useful material. It is impossible to study the evolution of religious feeling among the working classes without utilizing documentation of this type, especially the personal confessions of individuals who have renounced religious life and later returned to it from militant unbelief or indifference.[9]

A different approach can be made by analyzing the urban complex as a whole and making notes on religious phenomena with their importance and relation to territorial and social conditions. Or a number of monographs on families could be compared in order to draw some conclusions. The studies of Le Play concerning Parisian workingmen's families have already revealed indications of the religious evolution of the working classes.[10]

In the main, however, no single method can lead toward universal and final conclusions. All relevant methods should be employed and combined together. Thus, we may look forward to the organization of national teams of research workers associated at the international level with similar teams in other countries. We may also anticipate research on religious sociology which will include more than the Christian religion. How has urbanism affected the Moslem or the Jewish faith? What has been its impact upon individuals who are not affiliated with any church or sect but nevertheless hold personal religious convictions and observances of their own? Finally, a study would be welcomed of the religious behavior of adherents of "secular religions," such as political religions of blood, race, class, or state of which Hitlerism and Lenino-Stalinian Bolshevism are the most consistent types.[11]

SPIRITUAL LIFE IN LARGE FRENCH CITIES

Variations among Localities

In studying the spiritual life of large French cities, many variations can be observed among localities. There is an enormous difference, for instance, between the suburbs of Paris or Marseilles, which are very dechristianized, and agglomerations like Lille-Roubaix-Tourcoing, Saint Etienne, or Lyons, where traditional Catholicism is still strong.[12]

In Paris itself, two towns are discernible with different geographical boundaries. One, occupied by the middle class, is relatively religious. In the popular but not proletarian parish of Saint-Lambert-de-Vaugirard, for example, practicing parishioners represent about 25 per cent of the population. This figure suggests a more considerable sphere of influence covering probably one-half the people in the parish. The other Parisian town, inhabited by the working class, is only mildly or not at all religious. Newly-established working-class parishes in the suburban districts of the Department of the Seine or the Seine-et-Oise report that only 2 to 5 per cent of the inhabitants practice their religion regularly. Few of these parishioners are workers or proletarians.[13]

In Lyons, a similar dichotomy is evident. The old "populaires" suburbs of Croix-Rousse, Vaise, or Saint-Just differ considerably from the new proletarian districts of the east, such as Vénissieux or Saint-Fons.

Despite these variations, some constant features are coming to light. Among all large French cities, regular communicants represent only a minority of the population. The proportions fluctuate between a minimum of 2 per cent and a maximum of 30 per cent. In Marseilles, perhaps the most dechristianized large city in France, church attendance on an ordinary Sunday in 1953 equalled about 15 per cent of the population.

The same sort of comparisons should be made for medium-sized and small French towns as well as rural areas. Detailed information, however, is lacking for towns, where religious practice is variable but probably greater than in dechristianized rural areas or in large cities. In the countryside, the practice of religion ranges from almost zero, as in the dechristianized regions of the Avallonais, the Mâconnais, or the Creuse, to almost total fidelity, as in the traditionally-minded regions of Alsace, rural Flanders, or Vendée.

Unfortunately, a comparison of religious trends over time is difficult, because few documents pertain to the past situation. Nevertheless, Gabriel Le Bras has shown that the development of the practice of religion has not proceeded in a straight line, even in the rural France of old. On the contrary, it has taken a sharp and steep curve. A study by Jacques Valdour of the Rue du Faubourg Saint-Antoine in Paris revealed a number of families in which no children had been baptized since the French Revolution. Such a family is described by Lucien Fabre in his curious novel, *Rabevel*.[14] In the memoirs of Martin-Nadaud, a mason from the Creuse who was one of the pioneers of the labor movement and became a minister during the revolution of 1848, religion is given almost no place, although the writer spent his childhood in the country.[15] Thus stereotyped statements concerning the good old times, when the faith of our fathers prevailed, do not harmonize with a complex, changing reality. It would be a mistake to take an idyllic view of the alliance between Catholicism and the French peasantry, which varied in intensity and depth according to time and place.

Finally, Catholic practice should be compared with practices of old established religious groups, such as Judaism and Protestantism, which were minority elements in France. These minority groups apparently were even less active than the Catholic groups, despite claims that religious minorities in large cities tend to exert an influence which is out of proportion to their numbers.

The Practice of the Catholic Religion

Although many variations occur, an important majority of the French people in large cities has been baptized. This is at least a vague sign of a will to belong to the Church.[16] Among the baptized, a minority endeavors to follow the observances dictated by the Church. A smaller minority goes beyond these minimal practices and manifests a vigorous activity. On the other hand, the greater part of the many irregular worshippers declare themselves to be good Catholics, in the belief that God does not ask so much of us and that regular practice is only a legal obligation which can be dispensed with.

With respect to religious practice by Catholics in the larger cities, there is a marked predominance of women over men. This difference is more noticeable in the traditional parishes than in the newer ones, and exceeds the normal numerical superiority of women over men in France. However, religious practice by men has risen since the beginning of the last century. At that time, it was almost non-existent except in a few restricted groups of traditional bourgeoisie or among certain sections of the small middle class.[17]

Within the ranks of the intellectual youth, the practice of the Catholic religion is very important. It is observed almost as much among boys as girls, and sometimes more, as in the great engineering schools. The same situation prevails both in the provinces and in Paris. It happens even that young men, from religiously indifferent or hostile families, discover or deepen their religious faith during their years of study in Paris. One hundred years ago the movement was generally in the other direction.

But religious practice by age groups shows definite differences. These differences confirm the psychological law, imperfectly studied until now, that the male adult is naturally less religious than women, children, adolescents, or old people.[18]

In large French cities, variable religious practices by sex and age contrast sharply with the fixed customs of certain rural areas or small towns. In many villages and towns of the Dauphiné in southeastern France, for instance, it is definitely understood that the men will not return to church after their first communion, except for family or official ceremonies or on the occasion of great feasts. To go to mass on Sunday is approved for women and children but not for men. This attitude still prevailed in many districts of the large cities during the last century. Today it has subsided, especially among the intellectual groups.

By social classes, the distribution of the Catholic faithful follows clear-cut lines. In large cities, parish churches are frequented mainly by men and women belonging to the middle class. The higher bourgeoisie attends smaller places, such as college chapels and oratories of religious orders, except in certain parishes where worldly traditions are deeply rooted and where it is fashionable to be seen at the late masses.

Within the parochial groups, the most stable element is mainly the *salaried* middle class. The same thing pertains to intellectuals, students, and teachers in certain parishes. But the typical French small-business men, like grocers and coffee-house keepers, are much less numerous. Proletarians, in the technical sense of the word used by Goëtz Briefs,[19] are almost totally absent. Within the working classes everything suggests that social pressure is applied against religious practice.

Religious Movements

Although Paris has been the birthplace of certain Catholic religious movements, other large cities have also played important roles. While Marseilles has contributed little to French Catholicism,[20] Lyons and Lille have exerted positive influences. The missionary organization for the Propagation of the Faith was started in Lyons and now extends to the whole world. From Lyons also came the movement of sacerdotal spirituality and parochial apostolate under the Rev. Fr. Chevrier and the priests of the Prado as well as the *Semaines Sociales* whose principles spread throughout France and seventeen other foreign nations. From Lille came the first Christian trade unions and the workers' normal schools in which the first workers' elite were formed.

Paris has always been an important administrative headquarters of social organisms. History indicates that any movement born in the provinces will extend to the whole nation only if part of its administration settles in Paris. That general law of French activity pertains also to religious movements. But in Paris itself, not all parishes with substantial religious activities are located in central districts. Many parishes in "populaires" suburbs are extremely active in all sorts of ways, though they administer smaller resources.

The same tendencies can be observed among the numerous sects within French cities. Because of the cosmopolitan character and large population of Paris, any preacher with a new message can be sure to meet with a certain success there. In Lyons, too, he may find some followers because of the city's ancient tradition of intellectual curiosity and vague mysticism going back to Gnosticism.[21] In these and other large cities, the multiplication of sects may point to the limited appeal of existing religious institutions.[22]

In small towns and the countryside, the sects take root less easily because the individuals who join them call attention to themselves by their behavior. Conformity works against the propagation of a new message. The few sects which remain in the country or in small towns are generally the result of occasional schisms in some established church, or of what is believed to be a greater fidelity toward the past. Vestiges of the Petite Eglise, which was hostile to the Concordat, are still visible in the Lyonnais, Normandy, and Poitou. A few followers of the heretical sect of the Vaudois still subsist in the higher valleys of the French or Italian Alps. The curious post-Jansenistic sect of Fareins can be found in one of the villages of the Dombes region near Lyons.[23]

The infiltration of sects into the countryside and into small towns, however, originates from influences which are found in large cities. The same may be said about spiritualism, which was quite fashionable not so long ago in Paris and especially Lyons. Although it still has many adherents in small towns and country places, spiritualism has recently lost some of its general popularity.

Like spiritualism, secular religions also are indebted to large cities for their origin and growth. The religiosity of communism, for instance, is peculiar to large cities and particularly to their labor-populated suburbs. In Paris, great communist manifestations, such as the annual pilgrimage to the monument of the Confederates in the Père-Lachaise cemetery, are taking on a religious character. In the country and small towns, the social and political aspects of communism are predominant, being mingled with ancient deterministic features of local politics.[24]

But at all times, large towns have played an important part in religious movements. Christianity expanded from cities like Rome and Byzantium and was transmitted in Gaul by Lyons which acted as a turntable for commodities and ideas. From the beginning of the eighteenth to the end of the nineteenth century, the large French towns were mainly anti-religious centers which propagated the rationalism of philosophers, the humanitarianism of Free-masonry, and the anti-clericalism of the French Revolution.[25] Today their role has become more complex. Although the cities still radiate anti-religious practices into the countryside, they also diffuse the revivals of the ancient churches and the religious novelties of the sects. This complexity increases as urban and rural ways mingle together and schools, press, radios, and moving pictures invade the country.

Migrant Populations

Under the influence of the industrial revolution, cities expanded suddenly. "Mushroom town" applies not only to cities in the United States but also to many French towns, the Parisian suburbs, and the Lille-Roubaix-Tourcoing agglomeration.[26] The uprooting of rural populations who migrated to the cities has been a psychological and sociological as well as a geographical phe-nomenon. It was accentuated by the semi-nomadism imposed by difficulties of housing and exigencies of industries in urban areas.

The uprooted rural population generally fell into two categories. Some came from traditionally-religious provinces where religious life developed as a result of social or family pressures, customs, traditions, or clerical influences rather than personal choice. In such a context, religious life could reach genuine heights and depths.[27] Within the city, however, the context faded way, and the individual was no longer exposed to any pressures. Left to himself, he was soon swallowed up by indifference, except for some surviving familiar customs of a folkloric nature. He was importuned by forces opposed to traditional religion and favoring what was then called liberalism.

Other unrooted migrants came from only semi-religious provinces which perhaps had never been fully evangelized. There the exterior ways of Catholicism were only a coating spread over an old foundation of primitive beliefs. In most of these provinces, the events of the French Revolution, the state organization of the clergy, the sale of the Church's property as nationally owned, the influence of the local bourgeoisie which had appropriated church property and was anxious to keep it, the political blunders of the clergy—all aroused anti-clerical feelings and built up an unconquerable antipathy, if not to Christianity at least to the Church and its representatives.[28] On arriving in the large town, uprooted people with such religious feelings had every reason to turn from hostility to indifference.

As a matter of fact, the sudden transition from the country or small towns to the city almost invariably brings about a breakdown of morals. In the former, the framework of familial and village life makes for strict disciplines. In a large town, there is no more supervision, but only an anonymity in which the sense of responsibility dissolves; no more disciplines imposed by a dynamic framework of living forces, but only formal administrative and extrinsic disciplines, such as workshop or police regulations. All this occurred in the atmosphere of the early nineteenth century, with its liberalism and individualism, breakdown of social stratification, exhilaration of new success and disappointment of failure, priority of money and success, and its ferocious "will to arrive," as exemplified by Balzac's Rastignac, Thackeray's Becky Sharp, or Dostoevski's Raskolnikov.

Social Classes

Men are impelled to harmonize in one way or another their religious principles and their day-to-day behavior. So it was that the newly-arrived urban populations in large French towns during the last century set about accommodating their religious thinking to the new value system in which they found themselves. The intellectual atmosphere in Paris in the early part of the nineteenth century was one of the triumphant bourgeoisie, which enjoyed a threefold victory over the aristocracy, the Church, and the absolute monarchy. It was the victory of industry, commerce, and banking over agriculture; the victory of city over village. The ruling bourgeoisie expressed its ideologies in literature, in the arts, in the press, and at school from the primary grades to the university.

Those ideologies were anti-clerical and tended to be either anti-Christian or simply anti-religious. The Protestant and Jewish religious minorities willingly leaned upon the same ideologies in which they saw a guarantee of their liberation. The rising middle and working classes, themselves created by the industrial revolution, were also prone to adopt the bourgeois ideologies, or at least to select aspects of them which seem to meet their own needs.[29]

These general factors influenced all classes, especially the working class, which was the newest of all and the most disinherited and uprooted.[30] In the main, the ideologies fashioned by the working class were characterized by hostility to religion, and were manifested either in a religious indifference or in a channeling of religious feeling into a vague Christianity intermingled with a distrust for the Church, the clergy, and its partisans.

Slowly and incompletely, therefore, the structural features of French Catholicism emerged from their old rural context. The administrative divisions of dioceses and parishes remained on the whole what the Concordat had made them under the First Empire before the industrial revolution. In Paris, church buildings were concentrated at points corresponding to the area of the ancient city, but were more and more widely scattered toward the periphery. A map drawn in 1920 would have pictured the situation before the great building effort under the impulsion of Cardinal Verdier. Many parishes were over-sized and endowed with a theoretical jurisiction over tens of thousands of people so that real contact between the clergy and the faithful was reduced to an impersonal administrative connection. Hence the impression that the Church was only a gigantic piece of machinery.

The mentality of both clergy and faithful did not keep up with the march of events. Generally recruited from the peasant class, most priests remained rural in their gait, vocabulary, speech, and outlook on life.[31] Since the great bulk of the faithful lived in the country, the significant lay and cleric social structures ordinarily sprang from the aristocracy, landed bourgeoisie, or traditional bourgeoisie. All these classes remained tied in some way to the land and its archaic attitudes.

Why was this movement completely reversed at a later time? The answer lies in the fact that within large towns, religion became a matter of individual conviction and will instead of custom and social pressure. Personal choice is clearly observable in the testimonies of people who were so converted. Moreover, in the large towns the vocation to the priesthood or monastic life was no longer the consequence of a family tradition or a mere desire to embrace an honorable career. It was rather the result of personal decision.[32]

For the last few years, the large towns have been exerting less and less anti-religious influence, except among the proletariat. Religious life is most intense today among circles where a taste for criticism and research is normally most developed. In other words, it is most marked among the intellectuals and the scientists, a majority of whom have recently broken away from materialism or from the prejudices of their predecessors. Religious anxiety is also fermenting within the world of arts and belles-lettres, as evidenced by such movements as surrealism or existentialism and by the sudden invasion of religious problems into the French film. The success of writers like Mauriac, Bernanos, Cronin, and Graham Greene and the diffusion of religious books are supplementary indications.[33]

An appreciable proportion of parochial communities or religious movements springs from categories of people which are sociologically rather new and who are not burdened by the mortgages of the past. They consist of salaried middle classes, such as employees, staff workers, technicians, and social workers, whose activities correspond frequently to what the economists after Colin Clark call the second or third sectors, and whose number and importance are continually increasing as a consequence of modern technology. Their newness and relative independence guarantee for them a liberty which is not enjoyed by the business bourgeoisie or the proletariat.

In light of these facts, it is not surprising that the proletarian section of society in our large cities tends to be the least religious group. The more the workers progress away from the proletarian condition, the more accessible they become to religious life. Is it possible, then, to promote religious life among proletarians as long as their condition remains what it now is?

New Religious Liberties

The personalization of the religious phenomenon in large cities points out that religion is more and more related to a concern for the liberty of persons.[34] This means that the metropolitan churchgoer is more critical, more exacting, and more difficult to handle than the churchgoer in a village or a small town. For him an argument based on mere authority or tradition is no longer sufficient as an instrument of persuasion. He asks questions and protests. He frequently passes from crisis to crisis as he progresses spiritually; each crisis destroys a previous equilibrium.[35] He is often anxious, restless, scrupulous, sometimes even somewhat unbalanced. In consequence, he is all the more exacting with his co-religionists and the clergy.[36]

Thus the lay movement, manifested in the Catholic Church of our time and also with its own peculiarities in the Protestant churches in Europe, tends to start from large cities and spreads toward small towns and the country. Meanwhile, a movement of spirituality associated with marriage and the family develops in the city. There everything becomes a decisive act of will power and love performed in the context of the marriage relationship with its characteristically intimate and personal interweaving of two personalities. Finally, regroupings by social categories or special interests are placed in juxtaposition with the old territorial groupings which were regulated by more objective norms.

Through these experiences, new spiritual modes of equilibrium and new types of holiness seek each other. Spiritual itineraries, such as that of Elizabeth Leseur, a Parisian bourgeoise; Fernand Tonnet, a Belgian worker who was cofounder of the J.O.C.; Marius Gonin of Lyons, great social teacher; Pierre Poyet of the Ecole Normale Superieure of Paris; Eugene Duthoit, a professor in Lille; Marguerite Bourcet, a journalist in Paris, and many others all point the way toward new religious experiences. To new conditions, new liberties give new answers.[37]

Are we not witnessing another phenomenon similar to that by which the good news, transmitted by Paul of Tarsus from the Galilean countryside and the towns of Judaea, Galilee and Samaria, reached the great cities of Corinth and Athens, and then Rome, the largest city of the Graeco-Roman civilization, to cast its light upon the world?

FOOTNOTES TO CHAPTER 18

1. On paganism in the countryside, see Henri Dontenville, *La Mythologie Française* (Paris: Payot, 1948) and *Les Dits et Récits de Mythologie Française* (Paris: Payot, 1950). On sorcery, see Henri Pourrat, *Les Sorciers du Canton* (Paris: Gallimard) and M. A. Murray, *The Witch-cult in Western Europe* (Oxford: Clarendon Press, 1951).

2. See Marc Bloch, *La Société Féodale et La Formation des Liens de Dépendance* (Paris: Albin Michel, 1939) and *La Société Féodale: Les Classes et Le Gouvernement des Hommes* (Paris: Albin Michel, 1940).

3. See the series of novels by Henri Pourrat grouped under the title, *Gaspard des Montagnes* (Paris: Albin Michel, 1922), and his *L'Homme à la Bêche* (Paris: Flammarion), *Le Meneur de Loups, La Cité Perdue,* and *Le Trésor Des Contes* (3 vol; Paris: Gallimard). The writings of Goldsmith, Fielding, and Smollett furnish humorous documentaries of the alliance of the Anglican Church in England with the countryside in the eighteenth century. On the evolution of the Anglican Church in relation to industrial and urban phenomena, see M. B. Reckitt, *Maurice to Temple* (London: Faber and Faber, 1947). In Great Britain and the United States, Catholicism is generally urban, while the countryside is ordinarily Anglican or Protestant. This is just the reverse of the situation in continental Europe, and partly explains the psychological differences between Anglo-Saxon Catholics and French Catholics.

4. For over-idealized descriptions of rural Catholicism, see Louis Mercier, *Hélène Sorbiers* (Lyon: Editions du Sud-Est); René Bazin, *Il Etait Quatre Petits Enfants* (Paris: Calmann-Lévy, 1923) and *Magnificat* (Paris: Calmann-Lévy, 1931); Eugène Le Roy, *Jacquou le Croquant* (Paris: Calmann-Lévy, 1912); Jules Renard, *Le Journal* (Paris: Gallimard, 1937); Claude Tillier, *My Uncle Benjamin* (New York: Coventry House, 1941), first French edition published in Paris, 1910; Emile Guillaumin, *The Life of a Simple Man* (London: Selwyn, 1919); and E. Vingtrinier, *La Vie Lyonnaise* (Lyon: Masson).

5. See René Bazin, *La Terre Qui Meurt* (Paris: Calmann-Lévy, 1913) and *Donatienne* (Paris: Calmann-Lévy, 1903); Henry Bordeaux, *La Maison* (Paris: Plon-Nourrit, 1913); Louis Mercier, *Le Poème de la Maison* (Lyon: Editions du Sud-Est) and *Les Voix de la Terre et du Temps* (Paris: Calmann-Lévy); and Frédéric Mistral, *Memoirs of Mistral* (London: E. Arnold, 1907), a translation of *Mémoires et Récits* (Paris: Plon-Nourrit, 1906), and *Le Poème du Rhône* (Paris: Lemerre, 1931). For an extreme example of the nostalgia for country life and religion, see the novels of Pierre l'Ermite, such as *La Grande Amie, Restez Chez Vous, l'Emprise,* and *La Brisure.*

6. The nostalgia for the countryside was not always limited to Catholics and Protestants. For other cases, see the writings of Jean Giono; Daniel Halévy, *Visites Aux Paysans du Centre* (Paris: Grasset, 1922); and E. C. Hughes, *French-Canada in Transition* (Chicago: University of Chicago Press, 1943).

7. See Jacques Valdour, *De la Popinque à Ménilmuche* (Paris: Rousseau); Jean de Vincennes, *Le Bon Dieux Dans le Bled, Parmi Eux,* and *Pauvres Vies* (Paris:

Beauchesne) and *La Mèche Qui Fume Encore* (Editions de Maredsous); Robert Garric, *Belleville* (Paris: Grasset); Gabriel Le Bras, *Introduction à l'Histoire de la Pratique Religieuse en France* (Paris: Presses Universitaires de France), Vol. I (1942) and Vol. II (1945); Godin and Daniel, *France: Pays de Mission?* (Paris: Ed. du Cerf); Y. Daniel, *Aspects de la Pratique Religieuse à Paris* (Paris: Ed. Ouvrières); Chombart de Lauwe, *Paris et l'Agglomération Parisienne* (Paris, 2 vol.); F. Boulard, *Problèmes Missionnaires de la France Rurale*, and *Essor ou Déclin du Clergé Français?* (Paris: Ed. du Cerf) and *La France Est-Elle Encore Catholique?* (Paris: Réalités d'Aujourd'hui); and Voillaume, *Au Coeur des Masses* (Paris: Ed. du Cerf). See also the following journals: *Economie et Humanisme, Masses Ouvrières, Lumen Vitae* (printed in Belgium), *L'Actualité Religieuse, La Documentation Catholique, L'Année Sociologique,* and *Mon Village.*

8. For a criticism of a public opinion poll conducted by the journal, *Réalités,* see the article by Jean Labbens in *Chronique Sociale,* published in Lyons, 1953, no. 1.

9. See D. Hyde, *I Believed: The Autobiography of a Borneo British Communist* (London: Heinemann, 1951); Raymond de Becker, *Le Livre Des Vivants et Des Morts* (Bruxelles: Editions de la Toison d'Or); and Pierre Schaeffer, *Les Enfants de Coeur* (Paris: Editions du Seuil).

10. For notes on religious phenomena, see the articles in *Economie et Humanisme,* "Les Dockers de Marseille," by R. P. Loew and "L'Homme et la Ville," by Michel Quoist. For Parisian families, see Frédéric Le Play, *Ouvriers Européens* (Tours: A. Mame, 1877–1879).

11. For some discussion of the impact of large cities like Paris, New York, or Montreal on Jews suddenly transplanted from the ghettos of central Europe, see the novels by Israël Zangwill. For secular religions, see Jules Monnerot, *Sociology and Psychology of Communism* (Boston: Beacon Press, 1953), originally published in Paris in 1949; Henry Daniel-Rops, *Notre Inquiétude* (Paris: Perrin, 1927); and Pierre-Henri Simon, *Témoins de l'Homme* (Paris: Armand Colin, 1951).

12. See François Goguel-Nyegaard, *Géographie des Elections Françaises de 1870 à 1951* (Paris: Armand Colin, 1951).

13. Godin and Daniel, *France: Pays de Mission?* (Paris: Ed. du Cerf).

14. Lucien Fabre, *Rabevel ou Le Mal Des Ardents* (Paris: Nouvelle Revue Française, 1923).

15. Martin Nadaud, *Mémoires de Léonard, Ancien Garçon Maçon* (Bourganeuf: Impr. de Duboueix).

16. For other signs of religious inclinations, see Joseph Folliet, "De la Captivité Comme Expérience Spirituelle," published in Paris by the Aumônerie Générale des Prisonniers, now called Secours Catholique.

17. See Alfred de Musset, *The Confession of a Child of the Century,* Vol. 8 of *The Complete Works of Alfred de Musset* (New York: E. C. Hill, 1907), French edition originally published in Paris in 1840. Other examples occur in the recollections of Lacordaire, Ozanam, and Père Gratry.

18. Simon Ligier, *La Psychologie de l'Adulte Ouvrier* (Paris: Editions Ouvrières), I.

19. Goëtz Briefs, *Le Prolétariat Industriel* (Paris: Desclée de Brouwer). See also the chapter on the proletariat by Joseph Folliet in *L'Avènement de Prométhée* (Lyon: Chronique Sociale) and "Le Prolétariat," a special issue of the *Chronique Sociale de France.*

20. See J. Duroselle, *Les Débuts du Catholicisme Social en France* (Paris: P.U.F.).

21. See Gascoin, *Les Religions Inconnues* (Paris: Gallimard); Pierre Geyraud, *Les Petites Eglises de Paris* (Paris: Emile Paul, 1937), *Les Sociétés Secrètes de Paris* (Paris: Emile Paul, 1938), *Les Religions Nouvelles de Paris* (Paris: Emile Paul, 1937), and *L'Occultisme à Paris;* Maurice Collinon, *Faux-Prophètes et Sectes d'Aujourd'hui* (Paris: Plon); and "Sectes et Mouvements Religieux," a special number of *Chronique Sociale de France.*

22. See Jules Romains, *Recherche d'une Eglise,* Vol. 7 of *Les Hommes de Bonne Volonté* (Paris: Flammarion, 1934) and André Thérive, *Sans Âme* (Paris: Grasset, 1928).

23. For the Petite Eglise, see C. Latreille, *La Petite Eglise de Lyon* (Lyon: Lardanchat); for the Fareins, see André Billy, *Rue Maudite et Alentour* (Lyon: Ed. Lugdunum).

24. See André Siegfried, *Tableau Politique de la France de l'Ouest Sous le Troisième République* (Paris: Armand Colin, 1913), and Goguel-Nyegaard, *op. cit.,* note 12.

25. See Bernard Faÿ, *La Franc-Maçonnerie et la Révolution Intellectuelle du XVIIIᵒ Siècle* (Paris: Ed. de Cluny, 1935); Berteloot, *La Franc-Maçonnerie et l'Eglise Catholique* (Paris: Ed. du Monde Nouveau); and Roger Priouret, *La Franc-Maçonnerie Sous Les Lys* (Paris: Grasset).

26. See Gravier, *Paris et le Désert Français* (Paris: Ed. du Portulan); Pierre Georges et al., *Etudes sur la Banlieue de Paris* (Paris: Armand Colin, 1950); and the volumes of the Institut d'Etudes Rhodaniennes, published under the direction of M. Allix.

27. See Alphonse de Lamartine, *Le Tailleur de Pierres de Saint-Point* (Paris: Fume, Jouvel, 1877) and *Jocelyn* (Paris: Hachette, 1892); Henri Pourrat, *Gaspard des Montagnes* (Paris: Albin Michel, 1922); Louis Mercier and Frédéric Mistral, *op cit.,* note 5.

28. See André Latreille, *L'Eglise Catholique et la Révolution Française* (Paris: Hachette, 1946); Leflon, *La Crise Révolutionnaire, 1789–1846* (Paris: Bloud et Gay, 1949); and Adrien Dansette, *Histoire Religieuse de la France Contemporaire* (Paris: Flammarion), Vol. I (1948) and Vol. II (1951).

29. See Pierre Joseph Proud'hon, *De la Justice dans la Révolution et dans l'Eglise* (Paris: Marcel Rivière).

30. See Edouard Dolleans, *Histoire du Mouvement Ouvrier* (Paris: Armand Colin), 3 vols. 1950–1953; Jean Montreuil, *Histoire du Mouvement Ouvrier en France des Origines à Nos Jours* (Paris: Aubier, 1946); J. Hours, *Le Mouvement Ouvrier* (Paris: Editions Ouvrières); J. Duroselle, *op. cit.,* note 20; S. Exc. Mgr. Ancel, *La Mentalité Ouvrière* (Lyon: Le Prado); and Henri Rollet, *L'Action Sociale des Catholiques en France* (Paris: Boivin, 1947).

31. Ludovic Halévy, *L'Abbé Constantin* (Paris: C. Lévy, 1904); Jean de la Brète, *Mon Oncle et Mon Curé* (Paris: Plon); Ferdinand Fabre, *L'Abbé Tigrane, Candidat à la Papauté* (Paris: Flammarion, 1913); Octave Mirbeau, *L'Abbé Jules* (Paris: Fasquelles); Louis Pravieux, *Un Vieux Célibataire* (Paris: Plon); Clément Vautel, *Mon Curé Chez les Riches* (Paris: Albin Michel, 1925); and the clerical characters depicted by Flaubert in *Madame Bovary* and Balzac. The tradition still continues in François Mauriac, *Woman of the Pharisees* (New York: Holt, 1946), French edition published in Paris, 1941; Georges Bernanos, *Journal d'un Curé de Campagne* (Paris: Plon, 1947); Henri Queffélec, *Un Recteur de l'Ile de Sein;* Gilbert Cesbron, *Saints in Hell* (New York: Doubleday, 1954); Béatrice Beck, *Léon*

Morin, Prêtre (Paris: Gallimard, 1952); and Daniel Pézeril, *Rue Notre-Dame* (Paris: Ed. du Seuil).

32. For personal testimonies, see George Fonsegrive, *De Taine à Péguy: L'Evolution des Idées dans la France Contemporaire* (Paris: Bloud et Gay, 1917); Julien Laurec, *Le Renouveau Catholique dans les Lettres Françaises* (Paris: Bonne Presse); Don Giovanni Rossi, *Tarqués par Dieu* (Paris: Bonne Presse); and Don Giovanni Barra, *Uomini Nuovi*. For the matter of personal decision, see Boulard, *Essor ou Déclin du Clergé de France?* (Paris: Ed. du Cerf).

33. Among the films are the Journal d'un Curé de Campagne, Dieu a Besoin des Hommes, Monsieur Vincent, Vivere in Pace, Cielo Sulle Palude, Miracle à Milan, and Dieu est Mort. Less serious ones include Don Camillo, Going My Way, and the Sorcier du Ciel. Two of the French religious best sellers are by Henri Daniel-Rops, *Sacred History* (New York: Longmans, Green, 1949), originally published in Paris, and *La Vie de Jésus* (Paris: Fayard, 1948). On surrealism, see Maurice Nadeau, *Histoire du Surréalisme* (Paris: Ed. du Seuil, 1945); and Michel Carrouges, *Le Surréalisme*. On religious anxiety, see Henri Bremond, *L'Inquiétude Religieux* (Paris: Perrin, 1930) and Paul Archambault, *Plaidoyer pour l'Inquiétude* (Paris: Spes).

34. See Folliet, *op. cit.*, note 19.

35. See Roger Martin du Gard, *Jean Barois* (Paris: Gallimard, 1933); Joseph Malègue, *Augustin or le Maître est Là* (Paris: Ed. Spes); Joseph Wilbois, *L'Homme qui Ressuscita d'entre les Vivants* (Paris: Ed. Spes, 1928); and Pierre Schaeffer, *Les Enfants de Coeur* (Paris: Ed. du Seuil).

36. See Y. de Montcheuil, *Problèmes de Vie Spirituelle* (Paris: J.E.C.F.) and *L'Eglise et le Monde Actuel* (Paris: Ed. du Témoignage Chrétien); E. Mounier, *Carnets de Route* (Paris: Ed. du Seuil) and *L'Affrontement Chrétien* (Cahiers du Rhône); Dr. Jouvenroux, *Témoignages sur la Spiritualité Moderne* (Paris: Ed. du Liseron); Lebret et Suayet, *Rajeunir l'Examen de Conscience* (Economie et Humanisme); Joseph Folliet, *Les Chrétiens au Carrefour* and *Présence de l'Eglise* (Lyon: Chronique Social de France).

37. See E. Leseur, *Journal et Pensées de Chaque Jour, Lettres à des Incroyants,* and *Lettres sur la Souffrance* (Paris: de Gigord); Joseph Folliet, *Marius Gonin* (Lyon: Chronique Social de France); Lucienne Ella-Bouet, *Marguerite Bourcet* (Paris: Bloud et Gay); and R. Bessières, *Pierre Poyet* (Paris: Ed. Spes). For a comparison between a rural and an urban curé, see François Trochu, *Le Curé d'Ars* (Lyon: Vitte, 1925) and A. Lestra, *Le Père Chevrier* (Paris: Flammarion).

19

The Children of God in the City of Man

J. V. LANGMEAD CASSERLEY
Professor of Dogmatic Theology
General Theological Seminary, New York

This chapter deals with the impact of characteristic forms of city life upon the spirituality of city residents and upon the modes of behavior through which their spirituality is expressed.

SPIRITUALITY AND IDOLATRY

What is *spirituality?* It is a mistake to use the words spiritual and spirituality only in a favorable sense, or to identify them with the kind of religious behavior which we prefer. For if man is a spiritual being, he always has a spirituality. It may sometimes be evil and perverted. Nevertheless, it remains a spirituality and must be recognized as such. The decay of belief in the existence of evil spirits should not blind us to the reality of evil and perverted forms of spirituality.

Closely related to this error is the tendency to regard total irreligion as the modern alternative to traditional Christian religion. Actually, most forms of irreligion rest upon religious attitudes toward some aspect of the secular world. In other words, the true alternative to religion is not irreligion. It is idolatry—itself a form of spirituality.

What do we mean, then, when we say that man is a spiritual being? There are two answers to this question. In the first place, the term spirit refers to the deeply concealed roots of unity in our human being. Nearly any analysis of the visible phenomena of being human fails to disclose how man succeeds in remaining one being. Perhaps the mind-body problem is the best known example of the way in which all the king's horses and all the king's men cannot put man together again once the philosophers have analyzed him into his constituent parts.

The facts seem to compel us to make a radical distinction between mental and physical behavior. But once we have abstracted and defined mind and body in a satisfactory manner, we cannot find any kind of openness in either one which would render the unity of the two conceivable. Yet in human existence we experience the unity of mind and body just as vividly as we experience their characteristic differences.

So it is that we are compelled in the physical, human, and social sciences to seek an explanation of unity in the midst of diversity in terms of some factor which is not given empirically. The Christian concept of man is a triple analysis into body, mind, and spirit rather than a dual analysis merely into body and mind. Thus it does not raise the body-mind problem which has baffled philosophers since Descartes. With Christian theology, therefore, man's spirituality is the underlying principle which constitutes his unity. In virtue of his spirituality, man is one being.

But man is not only a unity in diversity. His nature seems to commit him to a quest for a similar unity which is expressed through the diversity of the world. At first glance, life may appear to be no more than a continuum of discrete experiences. But in the last analysis, man always sees himself as one being. For him, life is not a mere succession of unrelated experiences. Man relates himself to his world on the assumption that it is also a unity, despite its variety.

There are many ways of describing this assumption of the unity of the world in which we live. The great systems of philosophy do it one way; the sciences in another. Religion—especially the revealed religion of the Hebrew-Christian tradition—generally tends to unify the visible and empirical world in terms of a divine power which transcends it and yet is everywhere involved in its course.

The danger of *idolatry* is inherent in any alternative to the Hebrew-Christian tradition, or in any approach to the problem which falls short of that tradition. Characteristic examples of idolatry are materialism and idealistic humanism which regards human values as the supreme principles of unification and objects of reverence in life. Idols do not have to be unreal or degraded. On the contrary, the most successful and persuasive idols are usually indubitably real, spiritually exalted, or both. Idolatry characteristically selects some element or group of elements in our empirical experience of nature and civilization and attributes to it the divinity which gives unity and meaning to all that is.

Nevertheless, idolatry is just as spiritual as the great religions of which religious people approve. Only a spiritual being can be an idolator. And a spiritual being who does not recognize the living God can scarcely be anything else than an idolator. It is almost inconceivable that any human environment should totally suppress or deprave man's spirituality.

In inspecting any particular form of human culture, we may legitimately ask these questions: What kind of influence does it have upon man's spirituality? Toward what types of spiritual behavior does it ordinarily constrain him?

In discussing such questions, certain aspects of city life will be considered from the point of view of their impact upon the spirituality of the citizens. The aspects include the metropolis as the mother of illusion, the apathy of metro-political man, the clash of the classes, loneliness, and the ethical ambivalence of the great city.

Although these aspects have an influence upon spirituality, they are not decisive or deterministic processes. The forces operative in city life are so numerous that no single one can exercise an absolutely determining influence upon the conduct of any particular person. The fundamental error of all forms of philosophical determinism is the failure to perceive that in a world which includes so many possible sources of determinism, no single one of them can ever be expected to succeed. This fact indicates the possibility and defines the area of our limited freedom.

THE METROPOLIS AS THE MOTHER OF ILLUSION

Spirituality essentially demands and requires attachment to reality. It is the reaction of the whole man to the total reality which surrounds him. Misapprehensions or illusions regarding reality, therefore, are bound to distort spirituality. A spirituality based upon errors in interpreting experience becomes detached from reality and is reduced to feeding upon itself.

Among the various misconceptions fostered by city life is the illusion concerning man's relation to nature and the illusion concerning man's relation to his work.

The Illusion Concerning Man's Relation to Nature

The great city is always a wealthy economic center, usually a political or administrative capital, and often a military stronghold. Outwardly, it appears to be the most powerful form of social existence. It administers its own surrounding countryside and often controls distant food-producing areas through military conquest or investment and economic influence.

The city thinks of itself as an indispensable market of the food producer. Rather than being dependent upon food producers, the city considers that food producers are economically dependent upon it. Yet the great city is actually a by-product of a surplus agriculture. It cannot exist until food producers have learned to support themselves and also to produce additional food supplies which can be used to sustain life in urban areas.

In a time of social and civic collapse—as in Germany at the end of World War II—rural life persists while city dwellers leave their homes and wander through the countryside searching for food. Financially and politically the great city is indeed powerful. Economically and sociologically it is a delicate and fragile thing.

Although city life is as dependent on nature and husbandry as rural life, the day-to-day existence of the great city tends to conceal this fact from its citizens. Urbanites are accustomed to technical industrial and administrative activities in which man seems to be the master who exploits and dominates his materials. They are less familiar with rural activities in which man abdicates any pretence to be the master of nature and instead collaborates with her.

Thus city life provides little opportunity for the citizens to experience the reality of objective nature and the subtleties of their dependence upon it.

> Glory to man in the highest,
> For man is the master of things

is the kind of anthem which can only be sung with simple faith and unquestioning piety in the great cities. There such a worship often appears to be warranted by the facts, although it is actually no more than presumptuous attitudinizing.

The great city tends to assimilate to its own experience and economic practice the rural activities upon which it ultimately depends. People often talk of the agricultural industry. Or they liken the replenishment of the earth to investment, or demand a more technical husbandry, and so on. But urbanism not only comprehends rural life to its categories, it also seeks to subject it to its power. Sometimes rural workers are legally and politically enslaved, or overawed by military force. Other times they are more subtly controlled by economic means, as in any system under which most agricultural workers are constantly in debt to organs of city life which supply them with credit. Sometimes the agriculturalist is himself deluded by the pride and prestige of the great city, and feels that he should ape its methods and attitudes.

Yet in the long run there is nothing so fatal to the life of the city as the means which it adopts to control the areas and activities producing its food. The direction of rural society by an urban mentality slowly destroys the non-urban society upon which the city depends. We can see this tendency clearly in the consequences of financial and economic policies which lead to the erosion of the soil. And we are now getting dark hints from the Soviet Union that the policy of herding the peasants into collective farms, interpreted in urban terms as food factories, is beginning to pay dividends of disaster.

In order to meet its own needs, the city must not only employ cultivators to cultivate the soil. It must also cultivate the cultivators. It must acknowledge its dependence upon and need of a way of life distinct from its own. The city must recognize that it can assimilate this different way of life to its own outlook only at the peril of its own destruction.

Although undesirable, a purely food-producing culture without cities is possible. But a homogeneous urban culture is impossible. Urban culture can only exist in fellowship with and dependence upon rural culture. It must always seek to foster and preserve in health and strength a kind of culture radically distinct from its own. The more the city dwellers have some understanding of and respect for the distinctive values and ways of rural culture, the better for the city.

The normal tendency, however, of city life is in the opposite direction. For the average citizen, the rural area exists to provide cheap food, fresh air, and country sports. At the same time, he views it as a "backward" area which he may aspire to civilize. Because he does not consciously acknowledge his dependence, the city dweller misapprehends it. In consequence, he tends to abuse it and often ends by destroying it altogether.

The Illusion Concerning Man's Relation to His Work

The second characteristic illusion fostered by city life is a by-product of the wages system. Earning a wage is the most normal means of gaining a livelihood in the great city. Most of the citizens earn their living by letting out their time, skill, and energy to people who wish to hire them. This system has the spurious result of making the operative reason in the mind of the worker—his motive for and rationalization of doing what he does—distinct from the real reason for which the work is done. A man employed in a bakery, for example, may believe that he bakes bread for the sake of earning his wage. We know, however, that bread is baked only because people want to eat it. If people did not desire bread, the worker could bake bread seven days a week and never get any wages at all!

Under a wages system, therefore, the subjective reason for engaging in economic processes is never the same as the objective reason for carrying on economic processes. The same thing holds true for citizens who earn their livelihood by engaging in economic enterprise for profit rather than wages. The owner of the bakery who pays the wages of the bakers supposes that all this is done, not because people want bread, but because they are able and willing to pay for it. Thus his subjective reasoning is as remote from reality as that of his employees.

The city, in other words, is a network of economic activities in which each man performs whatever he does for the "wrong" reason. The effect of this mistake is to foster an illusion of independence once again. Each man thinks that he acts as he does for his own sake. Actually, each man does what he does for the sake of others. The fact that doing things for the sake of others is usually regarded as idealistic rather than realistic indicates how far the economic life of the cities is detached from reality.

We are often told that religion or "the churches" are remote from life. This assertion may sometimes be true, because preachers and teachers of religion are not sufficiently interested in life to speak about it in understandable terms. But it may also be true because life itself is remote from reality. We are too apt to assume that life is necessarily the most real of all things. Actually, it is often a passage from illusion to illusion. Some of the illusions, at least, are products of city life which frequently persuade men to ignore their dependence upon nature and misinterpret their dependence upon each other.

THE CHARACTERISTIC APATHY OF METRO-POLITICAL MAN

Apathy refers to a certain inability to do justice to the depth and subtlety of experience. It pertains to an erosion of the inward capacity for response which may cause men to become indifferent to many aspects of their existence. The great city's most obvious way of dealing with this lethargy is to administer

heavy doses of stimulants. Hence the tendency toward the sensational in entertainment and even in the reporting of news.

This tendency does not necessarily imply that city life is itself dramatic or
vivid. The vogue of sensationally advertised sexuality, for instance, does not
mean that the citizens themselves are oversexed. Nor does the popularity of
freak religious sects or sensational preachers indicate that city dwellers are
overreligious. In fact, they point in the opposite direction. Only the jaded
appetite and the worn-out mechanism of response require repeated doses of
artificial stimulation.

Widespread apathy is closely connected with the impersonality of city
life. Although large numbers of persons crowd together in cities, the relationships which bind them together are mostly impersonal. City life emphasizes the
so-called secondary associations which require and evoke no recognition of
personality and individuality in the other man. Normally, we neither see nor
know the people who supply our food, manufacture our clothes, or heat our
apartments. To us, most of them are functional agents—almost things—rather
than known and trusted persons.

The depersonalizing of the personal is the essence of apathy. City life com-
pels us to do it every day, and we are unaware of its implications because we
hardly notice what we are doing. Yet of all kinds of experience, personal intercourse is the most profound and exacting. It calls for subtle and discriminat-
ing powers of response. In a technological civilization, we are apt to discover
that it is easier to manipulate things than to deal with other human beings.

This is perhaps the source of the impatience of so many popular political
judgments. If only men were things, we tell ourselves, we could deal with
these problems much more adequately than we do. So we become impatient
with people because their personality seems to obstruct our own ends. It is
little wonder that techniques of social administration which treat people as
things constantly break down.

Under such circumstances our philosophical, religious, and ethical systems
tend to concentrate upon serene and indifferent patterns of cosmic and spiritual
processes rather than upon substantial personal being. Materialism and
scientific humanism stress the self-sufficient, the admirable and adorable, the
indifference of a remote and self-enclosed reality to human needs and aspirations. Reality is too perfect or complete to concern itself with people
like us.

Nevertheless, reality's indifference may be venerated as the hallmark of its
self-sufficiency and perfection. Many nineteenth century materialists characteristically held a profoundly religious attitude toward the material universe.
The contemplation of its serene processes evoked an admiration akin to the
spirit of worship.

Nor is this attitude by any means dead. It is easy to understand that a mode
of life which tempts us to become indifferent to the personality of each other
will also make us indifferent to personality in our religious and philosophical

thinking. This indifference to personality in life, religion, and philosophy is the quintessence of apathy.

THE CLASH OF THE CLASSES IN THE GREAT CITY

What differences exist among the typical spiritual attitudes of the different classes within a city? To answer this question we must first consider how the various classes are composed.

Important Classes in a Modern City

The important classes in a modern city include the bourgeoisie, the working class, the new middle class, the professional class, and the intelligentsia.

The old middle class or bourgeoisie comprehends all persons engaged in commerce and finance on a more or less independent and responsible basis.

The working class includes the great mass of wage earners, manual laborers, factory employees, and others engaged on a wage basis in distribution and retail trade. The individual members of this class are the weakest and poorest members of the community. But the class itself is usually better organized than the others, and normally consists of the majority of the voters. Where trade unionism is widespread, the working class is usually a well-disciplined, cohesive group. Thus the organization of the least powerful people tends to be the most powerful class. In many great cities, it is the politically dominant class. Yet its mentality is profoundly influenced by the resentments and inferiority complexes characteristic of people who know themselves to be weak.

The new middle class, salaried bureaucracy is becoming rapidly more numerous. In the most highly-developed cities, it may eventually outnumber the working class. It consists of white-collar wage earners engaged in administrative occupations in government, banking, insurance, industry, commerce, and many other bureaucratic enterprises. In the great city of the twentieth century, everything becomes more and more bureaucratic, even the Church. Where a working class succeeds in imposing socialist institutions on the great city, bureaucracy develops even more rapidly and the working class is quickly extinguished.

This new middle class is affiliated economically to the working class, because its members derive their living from the sale of their labor at more or less fixed rates. But in conscious aspiration, it tends to affiliate itself to the old middle class, a social phenomenon which Marx failed to foresee. Although the the city may create socialistic institutions for itself, the powerful bureaucracy which results from urban socialism is the supreme bulwark against any subsequent transition to communism. This bureaucracy is best understood and defined as the new middle class of the twentieth century.

The professional class consists of lawyers, doctors, teachers, clergymen, and so on. It is closely related to the old and new middle classes. But it is distinguished from them by its different mode of livelihood and generally by a more specialized education and higher intelligence. Culturally speaking, this is perhaps the most important group in contemporary urban society and its influence is out of proportion to its numbers.

The *intelligentsia* to some extent overlaps with the professions, but its members are found in all social situations. It is characterized by a certain detachment from class feeling and class loyalty—except perhaps when it occurs in the working classes—and by a prevailingly critical attitude towards existing institutions.

Among the various classes, the greatest contrast prevails between the outlook of the old middle class and that of the working class. Originally, the old middle class created our cities which are monuments to its achievement and relics of its enterprise. Today the old middle class is not numerous; more and more of its members reside outside the city whose activities are the source of their wealth. Their place has been taken by the working class which now tends to dominate the cities established by the old middle class.

The Spirituality of the Various Classes

Formerly an enterprising revolutionary force, the old middle class has become predominantly conservative and even reactionary. Its ideal is the self-sufficient man who creates his own fortune, shoulders his own burdens, pays his own way, and minds his own business. At its best, the bourgeois ethic was essentially a system of personal responsibility. It sometimes added a laudable stress on philanthropy—a conception of richesse oblige which echoed the older aristocratic idea of noblesse oblige. Our country is full of imposing monuments testifying to the extent to which this kind of obligation was fulfilled.

The prevailing spirituality of the old middle class was individualistic and ethical in tone. On the whole, it was not a churchly spirituality, because this group had only a relatively superficial sense of human solidarity. For it, the human race was simply a large number of separate men and women holding more or less contractual and ethical relationships with each other. Humanity was not a real entity in its own right with profound metaphysical significance. The most characteristic forms of such a spirituality are an ethical and dutiful agnosticism or an evangelical Christianity which seeks individual salvation.

The spirituality of the working class is very different. Its experience teaches that man is weak and powerless to help himself. The historic struggle of the working class emphasized the importance of mutual loyalty and mass solidarity. Hence the tendency for mass political movements of the working class to take an anti-democratic direction if political leadership is not wise.

Working class life provides all the requisites for a strong and highly unified church life. In most places, however, the working class has long been remote from the kind of presentation of Christianity so well suited to the needs of the old middle class. As a result, the working class is often detached from any kind of church life whatever. One of the tragic accidents of history is that the working class appears so often to be comparatively irreligious. Perhaps this attitude is due to the fact that much of the leadership of the early working class movements was provided by middle class intelligentsia in revolt against its own origins. On the whole, the more churchly forms of Christianity make the most appeal to the religious instincts of the working class.

But the new middle class is most characteristic of our own time. More than any other group, it probably provides the existentialist philosophers with their theme and the psychoanalysts with their patients. It is the class which experiences individualism as loneliness and spiritual dereliction; the class for which freedom too often becomes a dreadful burden of responsibility; the class which tends to live "inauthentically" and in "bad faith" because its social aspirations consort so poorly with the social and economic basis of its existence. Perched precariously between old middle class and contemporary working class attitudes, it has a tremendous opportunity to work out a great synthesis of the precious elements which are to be found in both of these forms of spirituality. At the moment, it has achieved no more than an uneasy and unintegrated compromise between the two.

The new middle class presents the churches with their most formidable challenge. If the churches can give this new class the necessary leadership and illumination, it can reconcile the individualistic spirituality of the old middle class with the collective spirituality of the working class. Then the churches will not only reintegrate the new middle class and the city life of the future, they will also reintegrate themselves.

Any truly authentic Christian spirituality must necessarily overcome the tension between an individualist spirituality and a collectivist spirituality in a mighty synthesis which reconciles them both in a religion which is personal and at the same time churchly. Only in the context of this spirituality can the new middle class discover the principle of its own integrity and the foundation of its own solidarity.

LONELINESS IN THE GREAT CITY

Urban loneliness is quite distinct from the solitude of the rural worker. It is a loneliness which a man experiences only among a large number of his fellow men in the knowledge that he is not related to any of them on a genuinely personal level. In fact, urban loneliness is not really solitude at all. It is the experience of being outside of rather than away from a group. As such, it is the by-product of the city's tendency to substitute propinquity for community and to expand the range of its associations only on the secondary level.

Many secular and religious urban activities are devoted to alleviating this sense of loneliness. Churches and religious organizations are often valued as community centers where people can become acquainted. Yet the primary purpose of an urban spirituality, and the work of the church in urban areas, cannot be to give back to men what urban life takes away from them. For the replacement of what is lost is not sufficient to consecrate what we have. The real task of spirituality and religion is to consecrate and exalt the values of city life. Spirituality and religion must find some way of giving ultimate meaning to city life by transforming its activities so that they can be dedicated to the greater glory of God.

THE ETHICAL AMBIVALENCE OF THE GREAT CITY

The best and the worst things happen in cities. The metropolis is a center of culture as well as a home of uncultivated masses whose debased standards present a constant threat to our culture. It is the source of law and order and the headquarters of crime; a religious and ecclesiastical center and a place of indifference and impiety. The great city lives in a perpetual state of paradox. In the Bible, side-by-side we find images like Sodom, Gomorrah, and Babylon on the one hand and Zion and the New Jerusalem on the other.

All great cultural and spiritual achievement finds its center and focus in the city. Christianity established its first hold among urban populations in the great cities of the Roman Empire. The word "pagan"—originally meaning "rustic" —bears witness to the difficulty which Christianity experienced in subsequently establishing itself in the countryside.

The city, therefore, offers the most vivid contrast between good and evil, truth and falsehood, beauty and ugliness, and religion and superstition. The city is Armageddon and its denizens are they upon whom the ends of the world are come. To live in a great city is to stand on the edge of the world and participate in the ultimate combat.

In such a context, some people are subjected to the basic antinomies of human experience more sharply than elsewhere. For this reason, the characteristic urban form of religious leadership is prophetic. The gentle pastor, caring for his people, seems to belong naturally to a rural rather than an urban setting. Only the prophetic witness shows the response of vigorous religious forces to the challenge of urbanism. "It cannot be that a prophet should perish out of Jerusalem." The Word of God must be spoken in the great city even though the activity and its consequences may destroy the man who speaks it. The Cure d'Aus for the village. Jeremiah for the city.

The first task of the prophetic form of spirituality is to explain to the people the mystery of where they are and what is happening to them in terms which give these things an ultimate significance. The prophet must interpret city life as epic drama. For him, there are always two cities: the city of God and the city of man. The responsibility of choosing repeatedly between them means that city life is in perpetual spiritual crisis.

But if the prophet sharpens the antagonisms of the city by defining and interpreting them more clearly, he also softens them. He declares war with one breath and then speaks peace with the next. For this prophetic spirituality knows that the conflict within the city is actually the conflict within each citizen. It realizes that any permissible hatred and rejection of what we find in others is at the same time a hatred and rejection of something that we find in ourselves. Thus the great ringing affirmation of the providence of God and His imperative call for personal and social righteousness prepares men for the battle. Then the great healing and wounding concept of original sin reminds us that the victory to be won if the city of man becomes the city of God is the victory of God over all the citizens and not the ephemeral triumph of one particular group of citizens over another.

In the city, whenever men's consciousness of the distinction between good and evil is more lucid than profound, the citizens rise up against each other in wrath and denunciation. This is so because we first learn to recognize sin by discovering it in other people. But once we learn, through the response which our spirituality makes to the ministry of our prophets, to apprehend the distinction between good and evil so profoundly that lucidity itself is inadequate, then we repent together in dust and ashes. For we do not properly recognize the reality of sin and experience its tragedy until we have discovered it in ourselves.

20

Commentaries

By **George N. Shuster**, *President, Hunter College, New York*

Perhaps the most impressive part of the chapters by Professors Folliet and Casserley is their note of cautious optimism. Professor Folliet reports that in France religious inquietude and even spiritual conviction are manifest among intellectuals, especially scientists. He suggests that a new and vigorous religion and spiritual life may emanate from their midst.

Professor Casserley points out that the emerging new middle class presents the Church with its greatest opportunity and most formidable challenge. Through this class, a synthesis may be achieved between the divergent views of social action and ethics as well as a blending of the individualistic and collectivistic approaches to religion.

THE EVILS OF URBAN ANONYMITY

But what one misses is the treatment of a theme over which certain novelists of the nineteenth century brooded deeply and which has assumed a menacing pertinence for us. It concerns the evil which can be spawned in the anonymous pseudo-intellectualism of the cities and may take on form in the world of reality by reason of the suggestibility of the masses.

Dickens, for example, loved the city as a man might love an unpredictable and not always virtuous woman. He was not a romanticist for whom goodness is to be found only in the country. Indeed, many of his most vicious characters are rural bumpkins who seek out the city because its dense crowds can mask their amorality. But who can forget *Barnaby Rudge* and its portrait of the rising tide of venomous and irrational hatred, spreading like a plague from the source of infection—a portrait which is still true to the urban scene today?

Similar are the vast and probing explorations of Dostoevski, especially his *Crime and Punishment, The Idiot,* and *The Possessed.* Dostoevski's apparent gift of prophecy has turned out to be a highly perceptive spiritual sociology. For granted that his evidence was honestly come by, Lenin and Stalin were inevitable. These men offered the crowds of the metropolis the fascinating spectacle of tradition *renverse,* to use a French word for which we have no

344

adequate counterpart. To say, for example, to a people which no longer believes in miracles that one can perform them without difficulty is to capture their attention immediately and also, for some strange reason, to gain their credence.

In the realm thus uncovered by imaginative insight may be found nearly everything one needs to know about such groups as the Jacobins and the Nazis. Adolf Hitler's latest biographers make clear how he suddenly revealed himself on an otherwise insignificant evening. Arising as a stranger to address a meeting, he unburdened himself of a flood of hatred—hatred of anonymity, defeat, civilian life, failure, and Jews—that would not die down until every door in Germany had been sprinkled with blood. Like no one of his kind before him, Hitler studied the nature of mass suggestibility with uncanny ruthlessness and insight. He saw that the emotions bred of urban anonymity are primitive because they are impersonal. If they had been born of the experience of realized human individuality instead, they would have been humanized and personalized.

THE NEED FOR SPIRITUAL COMMUNITY

This being true, it follows that what the city needs is not so much spiritual ideas, learning, or programs of action as spiritual community. Our churches are often huge, and few people who commune in them know one another or even the clergymen in charge. Colleges and universities are haunted, too, by the incubus of size. Many of us are not even slightly acquainted with those who cook and serve our meals, manage our transportation, or minister to us as physicians. Moreover, unions and professional associations tend to be so large and impersonal that they seldom have anything about them which resembles the guild.

Let us, however, stress the word seldom, for assuredly there has been a change. The churches are striving to bring about not merely a greater measure of parish solidarity but also the highest form of unity known to them—the unity of liturgical life. Colleges and universities are eager as never before to build up genuine academic communities and to deal with students as persons. At Camp Tamiment, operated by the Peoples Educational Camp Society in Tamiment, Pennsylvania, and at Unity House, run by the International Ladies Garment Workers Union in Bushkill, Pennsylvania, community centers have been created in the true sense of the term. Of course, much still remains to be done.

But for Jew and Christian, at least, the commitment to the future is apparent. The commandment cannot be fulfilled unless, while worshiping God, man loves his neighbor as he loves himself. Love, however expressed, is the only cement which can bind the citizens of the city together. In its absence, the myths of fascism and communism took root. All this is naturally implicit in what Professor Folliet and Professor Casserley discussed in the preceding chapter.

By **Paul J. Tillich,** *Graduate Professor of Philosophical Theology, Union Theological Seminary, New York*

In speaking of the influence of the metropolis on the spiritual life of man, we can stress either the word spiritual or life. Professors Folliet and Casserley emphasized the latter aspect in describing the impact of the big city on the religious and cultural attitudes of people. But more needs to be said about the spiritual side of urbanism and how the metropolis influences the character of man's spiritual creativity. Although the two aspects cannot be separated, they must be distinguished.

The Metropolis: Centralizing and Inclusive

In doing so, we may take our point of departure from the Greek word *metropolis,* signifying the mother or central city. Everything that exists has the power to be only insofar as it is centered. This is especially true of human personalities and social groups. The power of being, often called vitality, increases in proportion to the degree of diversity which is united at a center. Therefore, man has more power of being than any animal, and a spiritual man has greater vitality than a man with an undeveloped spirituality. In the metropolis, the social group is the center. And the center gives the metropolis its power of being.

There is no necessary conflict between the metropolis and the countryside. The metropolis is present in the remotest hamlet as a focal point to which rural life is partly directed. And the reverse is also true, since the remotest hamlet is present in the metropolis as an element constituting its center. The power of both is rooted in the mutual immanence of the metropolis in the country and of the country in the metropolis.

In applying this ontology of the metropolis to the spiritual life of man, we find that the big city has two functions. It serves in a centralizing capacity and also in an including capacity, and each is dependent upon the other.

The centralized political power of the metropolis can be accompanied, assisted, or replaced by a centralized religious power. The greatest example is the Roman Catholic Church. Rome and the pope belong to each other. The pope is in exile if he is not in the metropolis. At the same time, his sacramental power is real in every village priest in the whole Catholic world.

In the cultural realm, an analogy occurs in the fact that historical periods frequently receive the name of a metropolis from which its characteristic ethos radiated, as in the Alexandrian and Byzantine culture. In discussing the cultural leadership of France during several centuries, for instance, one actually speaks of Paris as the determining center into which everything streamed and from which everything radiated.

A metropolis, therefore, is a center city. It is likewise an including city. It includes everything of which it is the center, and encompasses diversity and freedom of individual creativity and competition. In this connection, the term provincial is revealing. So-called provincial art has not undergone the process of intense competition which occurs in the metropolis. It may be good art, but it cannot be great art. To produce great art, the bearers of the highest spiritual life must first undergo the criticism and the competition provided by the inclusive character of the metropolis.

THE STRANGE AND THE FAMILIAR IN THE METROPOLIS

The anti-provincial experience furnished by the metropolis is typified by encounters with that which is strange. Meeting the strange can have two consequences. It can produce hate against the strange, and usually against the stranger, because its existence threatens the self-certainty of the familiar. Or it can afford the courage to question the familiar. In the metropolis, it is impossible to remove the strange and the stranger, because every neighbor is mostly a stranger. Thus the second alternative of questioning the familiar ordinarily prevails.

There are ways, however, to avoid questioning the familiar. One is to shun the strange. All forms of totalitarianism try to avoid the strange, the problematic, the critical, the rational. To do so, they must deny the metropolitan spirit, equalize everything in city and country, and retain a center which is not the center of anything because everything else is swallowed up by it. Nothing strange—neither questions, criticism, nor competition—is left to the spiritual life, and so it dies.

The only real solution of the spiritual problem of the metropolis is to accept the strange and the questions implied within it. This situation can be compared with the cultural function of travelling. The beginning of classical Greece occurred when the Greeks travelled in war and trade to the Asiatic coasts. They thereby liberated themselves from the traditional gods of soil and blood. The beginning of Western rationalism began when the crusaders went east and met the strange Islamic culture which undercut their Christian self-complacency. Theological orthodoxy began to weaken in the late seventeenth and the early eighteenth centuries, when people started to travel and meet other forms of religious existence. By its nature, the metropolis provides what otherwise could be given only by travelling; namely, the strange.

Since the strange leads to questions and undermines familiar tradition, it serves to elevate reason to ultimate significance. If all traditions are questionable, nothing but reason is left as the way to new spiritual content. There lies the connection between the metropolis and critical rationality—between the metropolis and the intelligentsia as a social group. The importance of the encounter with the strange for all forms of the spiritual life cannot be overestimated. Neither can the social group which experiences and interprets the encounter be underrated. There is no better proof of this fact than the attempts of all totalitarian authorities to keep the strange from their subjects. Books are forbidden and meaningful encounters are prohibited. The big city is sliced into pieces, each of which is observed, purged, and equalized. The mystery of the strange and the critical rationality of men are both removed from the city.

Such terrible developments are sometimes encouraged and precipitated by the critical spirit itself. They are particularly likely to happen when the critical spirit loses an ultimate concern or a spiritual center, like a traveller who does nothing but travel. The freedom of nothingness is the predecessor to the bondage to something very limited. At this point, the relation of spirit with a small *s* and Spirit with a capital *S* becomes decisive.

Without an ultimate concern and symbols which express it, the spiritual life becomes empty. Without priestly tradition and prophetic attack, the critical activity of the intelligentsia paves the way to a situation in which criticism is prohibited, the strange is excluded, and the freedom of the metropolis is lost. The metropolis must preserve the priestly spirit and its traditions, and it must attract the prophetic spirit and its threats. Then alone is its freedom safe.

By **Louis Finkelstein,** *Chancellor and Solomon Schechter Professor of Theology, The Jewish Theological Seminary of America, New York*

One of the most remarkable developments in the history of religion is the sudden emergence of Hebrew literary prophecy some 2,700 years ago. Prophets had dwelt in Israel all the way back to Moses. But up to that time, none except Moses seems to have left any literary monuments. Their memories persist in stories about them, like the biographies of Elijah and Elisha in the Book of Kings, rather than in messages emanating from them.

Yet in the middle of the eighth century B.C., during the reign of Uzziah in Judah and Jeroboam, son of Joash, in Israel, there arose four timeless literary masters—Hosea, Amos, Micah, and Isaiah. Their words became a light to the world, and through them the Word of God became the heritage of mankind.

No complete explanation of this phenomenon can be given. A partial understanding, however, may be found in the development of urban life in Israel and Judea. There is much in the content of the prophecies of Hosea, Amos, Micah, and Isaiah that suggests a concern with the problems of the great urban market place.

The rise of the great cities of Samaria and Jerusalem gave the prophet a chance to repeat his message many times to various groups, and the city crowds contained individuals who were capable of retaining it. There was also an opportunity for the prophet to be surrounded by disciples who made it their business to preserve his words.

For these and other reasons, the phenomenon of literary prophecy is probably associated closely with the emergence of the cities of Jerusalem and perhaps Samaria. This is so even though the population of Jerusalem scarcely exceeded 25,000 persons at that time. Compared with an ordinary hamlet of 15 or so families, a capital city with 5,000 homes might well produce a cultural revolution of no mean proportions.

LITERARY PROPHECY AND URBANISM

Just as the existence of literary prophecy testifies to the spiritual fruitfulness of city life, so its content suggests the perils of urban living. The Mishnah remarks that "community for the righteous is good for them and good for mankind, whereas community for the wicked is evil for them and evil for mankind." The city represents both types of community. In one place, it brings together evil doers, whose united iniquity exceeds the sum of their separate misdeeds, as well as saints, whose continued goodness surpasses the sum of their separate lives.

Perhaps this dichotomy is the most important aspect of urban life. City growth presents man with a continuously increasing cultural and spiritual challenge. Having solved the spiritual problems of cities of 25,000 inhabitants, he finds himself confronted with problems of cities with populations of half a million, and even more than a million.

SPIRITUAL PROBLEMS OF THE FUTURE WORLD CITY

But the city of the future is clearly destined to be more than a locality on the planet. It will be a world city rather than a merely large or overwhelming one. The distance from New York to Los Angeles has become so short that we cannot think of the two metropolises as completely separate social and cultural units. The change from the limited groups of villagers who were addressed by the predecessors of Amos to the groups addressed by the prophet in Samaria is indeed small in comparison to the change from the audiences addressed in the largest halls of our fathers to those reached today on radio and television.

Unquestionably, the spiritual problems of the megalopolis are about to be replaced by those of the world city. On the planetary scene, opportunities for good and evil have multiplied manyfold. So far, the increasing complexity of world-city problems is more evident than the growth in our capacity to solve them. A new super-Samaria is in the making, but where is its super-prophet?

The spiritual problems of the new world city will doubtless demand a new type of cultural leadership in addition to the old. There will always be a need for the man who guides his fellows by means of his own genius. Yet the world is now appearing in which man must learn to deal with human problems on a scale of complexity never before envisaged. It is not enough to invent an electric calculator. We must find a way to discover a better-equipped operator for that calculator. Speed, efficiency, and the solution of immediate, urgent problems are needed. So are profundity, ability to formulate complex issues, and courage to face them.

This is a time, in other words, when we must labor together to discover how to think effectively. A modern Amos will scarcely appear on the scene. Nevertheless, let us strive for a collective Amos grown from the fragments of prophecy distributed in the hearts of us all.

By S. Muhammad Ikram, *Professor in the School of International Affairs,*
Columbia University, New York

These remarks will be confined mainly to the influence of urbanism on
Moslem faith and observance during different periods of Moslem history.

In its origin and development, Islam was something of an urban phenomenon. Mecca, the birthplace of Islam, was the principal city of the Arabian
peninsula. An important commercial center, Mecca also housed the temple of
Ka'ba, the chief religious center and place of pilgrimage in Arabia.

As Islam grew up in Mecca, its new teaching was a challenge and a threat to
the city. Islam's emphasis on the Unity of God and its uncompromising opposition to idol worship was hardly acceptable to the guardians of the temple of
Ka'ba, with its 360 idols, or to the citizens of Mecca whose prosperity largely
depended on pilgrimage to this temple.

Nevertheless, many Islamic usages were more easily adaptable to urban than
rural conditions. Islam encouraged congregational prayer. The Friday prayer
had to be offered in a mosque, which was not normally found in villages. So the
faithful were obliged to journey to the nearest town. This was even more the
rule for the Ir'd prayers, offered on the occasion of principal Moslem celebra-
tions.

By medieval times, religion was full and vigorous in Moslem cities. Arab
travelers and geographers often gave detailed accounts about the religious life
of the cities they visited—the number of mosques, attendance at prayers, observance of the Ramadan fast, and the general attitude of the population. Particularly noteworthy were the descriptions of Ibn Batuta in the fourteenth
century and Eveliya Chebbi, a Turkish traveller who lived in the seventeenth
century.

Modern Islamic Religious Life

By modern times, however, a different religious atmosphere prevailed. The
change in religious life was not a question of mere size. In fact, medieval
Moslem cities like Baghdad were perhaps larger than most modern Moslem
cities. The change concerned more the character of the city. With the introduction of the subway, bus, tramway, and new administrative and economic
arrangements, the city became more closely knit and capable of exercising a far
more potent influence. Out of this new urban character developed what Professor Casserley calls "the characteristic apathy of metro-political man" and
the impersonality of city life.

Another new development related to the effect of so-called Western influences. The industrial revolution, the growth of materialism, and the rise of
modern intellectualism have created vast, complex problems for religious
circles even in the West. Their impact on Moslem urban areas can well be
imagined.

Certain sectors of city population have experienced the Moslem counterpart of the dechristianization of Christian Paris. Interest in religion has decreased. Religious observance in certain circles is at a low ebb. As a result of the influence of modern materialism and an attack from Wahabi Puritanism, Islamic Sufism has lost ground, with a consequent impoverishment of the spiritual life. Of course, counterbalancing influences have also been at work, such as the basic hold of religion on the population, the revivalist movements, and the influence of writers and thinkers like Iqbal.

RELIGIOUS EXPERIENCE IN THE EAST AND IN THE WEST

The interplay of these forces is still in progress and the final outcome is not in sight. Broadly speaking, the picture in Moslem cities follows the same pattern of Christian France, although marked differences occur. In France, for example, religious life is said to be most intense among the intellectuals. In Islam, the trend among Moslem intelligentsia who have received their education at Western universities is toward faith and religion. But no far-reaching change, like that observed in France, is yet evident. As in France, women in Islam are more regular in religious observances than men. Nevertheless, it is doubtful whether the westernized Moslem woman is more religious than the westernized Moslem male.

Perhaps the most important difference between the conditions in France and Moslem countries concerns the working classes and the peasantry. New cities like Karachi have feeble roots in the past, few old religious organizations, and so-called semi-nomad urban inhabitants. There the proletariat shows the beginning of a non-religious atmosphere, especially if the group contains both Moslem and non-Moslem workers, although there is no hostility towards religion. In older cities like Lahore, apathy does not exist at all among the proletariat. In both old and new cities, religion is strong among unorganized labor, which greatly outnumbers organized labor in the East.

Within the countryside, religious life has grown more vigorous in recent years, and the peasantry is more religious than unorganized labor in the city. But the Islamization of rural areas has been slow. The spread of Islamic knowledge has been hampered by the lack of an organized church, the difficulty of communications, and the tardy introduction of printing. Although Islamization is still incomplete, modern developments and revivalist movements have greatly speeded its progress. Observers now find a fervent devotion to religion outside the cities.

Today the rural religious fervor is reacting on the Moslem cities, which are not large or powerful enough to dominate the farm areas. In Eastern countries where democracy has been introduced and where the vast countryside can make itself felt in some proportion to its size, religious forces are gaining in strength. This social phenomenon is responsible for indications of a religious revival in Turkey and for the demand for an Islamic state in Pakistan. It can be seen elsewhere, too, and thus suggests that any religious apathy now existing in some sectors of Moslem cities will eventually be overcome.

By **Swami Nikhilananda,** *Ramakrishna-Vivekananda Center, New York*

From time out of mind, cities have played an important part in the propagation of spiritual ideas. The modern city, however, differs in certain important respects from the city of olden times. The metropolis no longer contains a homogeneous population belonging to the same race or blood and professing the same religious faith. New York City, for instance, is the political, cultural, and industrial center of the New World. As such, it attracts heterogeneous elements from all parts of the earth.

New Factors in Metropolitan Religious Life

The education and culture of urban areas has been tremendously influenced by developments in science, technology, and industry, especially during the past fifty years. The scientific method, based upon experimentation, observation, and verification, dominates the educational system. Technology has helped to create a sensate culture whose chief goal is the enjoyment of material happiness. Industry supplies the big cities with the wherewithal to finance universities, science laboratories, large churches, art galleries, museums, theaters, concert halls, and other centers of cultural activity. All this widens the mental horizon of the city dweller, who soon discovers that goodness or greatness or genius is not the monopoly of any particular race or faith.

At the same time, life in a metropolis moves with speed. The people living in a competitive society sometimes must hurry even to remain where they are. The result is distraction, restlessness, and tension, which are detrimental to spiritual growth. Added to this is the feeling of loneliness which Professor Casserley has pointed out.

The Role of Religion in the Metropolis

All these problems affect the religious life of the metropolis. Religion must solve them in order to promote the spiritual growth of its inhabitants. The part that religion can play in transforming man's lower nature is beyond the scope of any other branch of knowledge. For religion enables man to transcend his limited self and commune with his Creator. In this respect, it has no substitute.

As an antidote for the restlessness of the metropolis, meditation should be emphasized in places of worship and also encouraged as a daily spiritual discipline. It is necessary for everyone—the busy man of the world as well as the hermit. Meditation endows the mind with steadiness of purpose. And though truth may be learned from the scriptures and demonstrated by reason, it is experienced only in the depths of meditation.

The loneliness in city life has been aggravated by an intense emphasis on individualism. We have forgotten men's interdependence. Fear and loneliness result from the consciousness of separateness. Whenever a man regards himself as separate from another, he will be repelled and stricken by fear and loneliness. The cosmic view of life and the idea of men's interdependence must be encouraged both in education and in the teaching of religion.

The solution to some of our most pressing problems may come from an understanding of certain profound religious experiences. The concept of the divine nature of the soul, for instance, can furnish a spiritual basis for democracy and freedom. The idea of the unity of existence can give a spiritual sanction to love of one's neighbors, self-sacrifice, and other ethical virtues. The doctrine of the non-duality of the Godhead can teach men to respect the spiritual ideals of others as they respect their own. Through the realization of the harmony of religions, men can eliminate the religious dissensions which have weakened all faiths.

For the malady of the modern world is a spiritual one. War, political conflict, economic confusion, and moral apathy are but outer symptoms of a deep-seated disease. Science alone cannot change man's lower nature. Intellectual knowledge, if not informed by the spirit, becomes a dangerous weapon in men's hands. Knowledge comes, but wisdom lingers. Free thinking is good, but right thinking better. Ethics, even at its best, is only an enlightened self-interest. The inner voice asks us what it shall avail a man if he gains the whole world but loses his soul. Reason alone cannot give man peace and inner assurance. It creates doubts but cannot resolve them.

Religion, experienced and propagated in an all-inclusive, humanitarian, and rational spirit, is the hope of man's future. If rightly used, the various facilities of the modern city, created through science and technology, can help the prophets and mystics to hasten the advent of the world's unborn soul, for whose sake humanity is patiently enduring its present travail.

PART EIGHT
The Search for the Ideal City

INTRODUCTION

Man has long searched for the ideal city. The forms of his conceptions have varied from generation to generation. They range from Cities of God to man-made Garden Cities. The following chapters discuss how this quest has fared and what its implications may be for the future.

Perhaps too little attention has been paid so far to the fact that the city shelters more than professional people, philosophers, scientists, doctors, and lawyers. Here also congregate world-famous poets and prophets. Although scientists may best define man's problems, only poets and prophets can make men aware of important questions and stir them to action.

Sir George Clark emphasizes the often-overlooked point that each city may be beautiful in its own way. To the loyal New Yorker, there may be nothing lovelier than to drive south through Central Park about midway through a late winter afternoon, just as the lights are coming on in the towers and the black trees can be seen silhouetted against the sky. This is to say that something of the ideal city resides in every community and may be found by a little patient searching.

21

Ideal Cities of the Past and Present

SIR GEORGE CLARK
Provost of Oriel College
University of Oxford

When conditions were ripe, prehistoric cities grew up independently in Egypt, Mesopotamia, the Indus valley, China, and Mexico. Recent conjectures support the idea that the first cities were built by peoples who were acquainted at least with agriculture. Indeed, the book of Genesis reminds us that it was Cain, the tiller of the soil, who builded a city.

Little as we know about the conditions which made cities possible, we know even less about the motives, hopes, and fears which actuated their builders. If written evidence were available, it would probably indicate that every side of human nature was active in creating the first cities, including those aspects which are called idealistic. But no writings exist, for the urban revolution was prehistoric.

CITIES AS THE HIGHEST FORM OF HUMAN ORGANIZATION

Greek and Roman Cities

Passing into the daylight of history, we soon find men imagining the ideal city. To begin with, there were notions that have come down to us from the ancient Greeks and Romans. By derivation, ideal is a Greek word and city is a Latin word. And in the world of antiquity, the city was the highest form of human organization. As Aristotle wrote, it was the most commanding and the most comprehensive of all.[1] The city came into existence in order that men might maintain bare life; it continued in order that they might live well.

In considering what sort of community would be most desirable, therefore, the Greeks were apt to cast their answers in the form of descriptions of the ideal state. These descriptions contained physical as well as social and political specifications. All through the great period of Greek civilization, some new cities were laid out on the rectilinear or gridiron plan, and some old cities were adapted to bring them into conformity with it. The Greeks themselves be-

359

lieved that the plan had an inventor, Hippodamus of Miletus, and that he also wrote about city government. Several modern authorities question this belief but concede that the Greeks showed great skill in adapting the gridiron plan to different sites.[2]

When the Romans conquered all the Greek cities and much of the surrounding Oriental, barbarian world, the city-state ceased to be the highest organization anywhere. A Roman poet, in fact, boasted that Rome itself had made all the world into one city. But the Roman empire was actually an aggregate of cities with their dependent territories. In spite of her supremacy, Rome upheld the civic spirit in the provinces.[3] St. Paul was a Roman citizen, and at the same time, he was also proud of being a citizen of no mean city, Tarsus in Cilicia.

Biblical Cities

The ancient Greek and Roman ideal of the city as the highest form of human organization combined with the conception of the Hebrews. Although the city was also the focus of Jewish tradition, it was not a politically-dominant community, except in the legendary times of David. It was rather a religious center, a Holy City, unique Jerusalem, "the city of our solemnities." Thus the heaven of the early Christians was a city, and the New Testament ends by describing it as an architectural dream.

When the Roman Empire was falling, St. Augustine, the inheritor of both the Greek philosophy and the Christian religion, contrasted the two approaches in his great book, *De Civitate Dei* (The City of God), finished in A.D. 426. By that time, the ancient ideal of the city was disappearing. Indeed, the lineaments of a city can no longer be traced in Augustine's book. Even the title only repeats a phrase of Marcus Aurelius who used it in spite of being a ruler of many cities and a cosmopolitan Stoic.[4]

CITIES AS ORGANS OF THE GREAT SOCIETY

More Recent Cities

After Augustine's time, long centuries followed during which cities fell into ruins. Later still, towns grew up again in an almost wholly rural society. Many of them clustered around the cathedrals of a universal church. The Dutch city of Utrecht, for instance, was planned with the cathedral at the center. Four main streets ran in the form of a cross from the cathedral, and a church was placed at the far end of each street. But no distinctive medieval or Christian plan was widely adopted; where a plan did exist, it was usually rectangular.

As more centuries passed, new worlds were discovered and men's horizons widened. Sir Thomas More's *Utopia* (1516) and Francis Bacon's *New Atlantis* (1627) were not cities but distant islands. The city ceased to be an organism; it was no longer the highest form of human organization. It became "primarily an organ of civilization"—a component of a large and growing society.[5]

Nevertheless, the city sometimes served as the shape in which theorists could embody their aspirations. It was still a token that could be comprehended in a single glance of the imagination, and schemes of reform often used this symbolism. Geometrical street planning, for example, was one of the characteristic ideas of the Renaissance. A Swiss jurist, Hippolytus a Collibus, who was born in 1561 and wrote a book, *De Incrementis Urbium,* praised the Italian cities of Sabloneta and Bozzolo for conforming to a geometrical design.[6] The plan also suited the mathematically-minded seventeenth century as we can see in Philadelphia or Mannheim, or at Noto in Sicily which was rebuilt on a new site after being destroyed in an earthquake in 1693. There is a trace of it in the ideal commonwealth, *Civitas Solis* (The City of the Sun), written in 1643 by the Italian philosopher, Tommaso Campanella.

Another intellectual fashion of the times was a search for an ordered system of universal knowledge. In 1619, the German Protestant theologian and satirical writer, Johann Valentin Andreä, set out his program for the system in a description of the city of Christianopolis.[7] By then, however, the links between political theory and practical city planning were very tenuous. Both Campanella and Andreä knew nothing about surveying or public utilities; the engineers were innocent of Hellenic influences.

It is more impressive than significant that the city metaphor persisted as it did. Although an excellent book by an American scholar was called *The Heavenly City of the Eighteenth Century Philosophers,*[8] the title was intentionally paradoxical. Little remained of the urban component—even less than there was for Walt Whitman in 1855 when he wrote:

> I dream'd in a dream I saw a city invincible to the attacks of the whole of
> the rest of the earth,
> I dream'd that was the new city of Friends . . .[9]

The real legacy of the Greek city-states, therefore, was not to our thought about cities but to our thought about states. Apart from an occasional flash of inspiration, the Athenian ideas about city government proved to be relics of the past. For us, the city is an organ rather than an organism of society.

Modern Cities

In our day, architecture and town planning can properly express common life only by fulfilling two requirements which no one foresaw even dimly in ancient times. These are the requirements of the great society and the democratic ideal. Although the fulfillment of one requirement may be discordant with the other, the shaping of our cities may draw them together into unison.

In our world, every city is a nodal point in a complicated network of rapid and world-wide material and spiritual communications. It is far from being a self-contained community which can shut its gates at nightfall and forget the surrounding world. For the smallest urban grouping gives and receives uninterruptedly by road, rail, water, and airborne traffic, by telegraph, telephone, teleprinter, radio, and television.

While the city is an organ of the great society, it is also an organ of a democratic society. The citizens are no longer a small minority like the slave-owning
Athenians. The good life must be offered to everyone who can make any kind
of livelihood, and the number of breadwinners is greater than ever before. Our
planning, therefore, must provide for the mechanized production line, the
mass relaxations of the baseball stadium and the concert hall, the mass-pro-
duced furniture in prefabricated buildings, and the thousands of architec-
turally-identical homes. How, then, can the visible city still be a real entity?
How can it give breathing space, let alone elbow room, for individuality, creative thought, or imagination?

Less Than Ideal Cities

No easy answer can be learned from the blotted record of the general history
of cities. For many of them were less than ideal. Some served to dominate or
defend; others to trap or debase. Cities like Paris (as Baron Haussmann re-
modelled it for Napoleon III) or Khartoum (as laid out like the town of
Omdurman, opposite it on the west bank of the Nile) were designed to dominate rather than defend. Thus the ancient Greek historian, Polybius, comment-
ing on the function of citadels, noted that they "are regarded as contributing
greatly to the security of the cities in which they stand, and to the protection of
their freedom; but they often turn out to be the origin of slavery and indis-
putable misfortunes."[10]

But instead of being a refuge, the city may be a trap. We have seen the exo-
dus from the doomed cities of 1940 and we feel the uneasiness of the threatened
cities of 1954. Even when the city has not given way before the assault, it has
often been something to defend rather than a defense. There have been tragic
cities from Troy to Warsaw. And there have been cities to be looted in poetry
and story-telling, for Homer as for the Icelandic skalds or the biographers of
Sir Francis Drake.

Again, there is a horror of the city as a place to be abhorred, not idealized.
The protest against the city began long before the industrial revolution when
towns grew up which William Cobbett and William Morris hated—the ten-
tacle-like cities of the Belgian poet, Verhaeren.[11] When William Cowper, with
his eighteenth-century feeling for nature, wrote that God made the country but
man made the town, he was only echoing a Roman writer on agricultural technique.[12] The early Christian monks who retired to the Syrian and Libyan
deserts were not merely seeking solitude. They were consciously repudiating
the tradition of city life.[13] This aversion might be traced back to the beginning
of towns. It is epitomized by the escape of Lot from the cities of the plain.

Idealized Cities

Despite the many less-than-ideal cities, there have also been numerous ideal
cities. Of course, none has ever been perfect. In the world as we understand it,
the ideal cannot be static. We are not designing a city which shall always

remain the same, but a changing and living community in which inventive men can reach towards perfection.

There are many ways in which the ideal comes into being. One is by the process of idealizing something, such as a city, which already exists. Take, for instance, an English city which has been celebrated over the centuries for its beautiful rivers and streets, spires, gardens, and old stone quadrangles, its chimes and choirs. It has been idealized over and over. In poetry, prose, and conversation, it has been credited with fictitious wonders, and its blemishes, slums, prison, and gasworks have been forgotten. Among the volumes of its praises, we encounter something deeper than mere response to beauty, antiquity, or intellect. We find something that we call worship.

There is a famous story which describes the feelings of a young man who had only heard about this city and had seen it but dimly in the distance. Yet he resolved to come and share in its life. "It had been the yearning of his heart to find something to anchor on, to cling to—for some place which he could call admirable."[14] Although his resolve led to tragedy, there was never any disillusion for Jude Fawley. For him, Oxford remained his ideal city.

But why has the city ever been idealized? What makes it kindle the imagination? The city can be idealized because it is the concrete production of human aspirations. It is itself an actualized ideal—a dream come true. Urban life provides satisfactions which cannot be found elsewhere. By living together in cities, men have always dug the wells from which our civilization flowed.

This principle operates so widely that we constantly forget about it. To take one example, urbanization is seldom considered to be one of the causes which has contributed to the great improvement in the expectation of life in Europe and the United States during the twentieth century. But though we may render the leaders of preventive and remedial medicine all the gratitude they deserve, we should also remember how little they could have accomplished without telephones, ambulances, industries which supplied their instruments, or the social organization which produced the doctors themselves. Historians of earlier times often seem to generalize beyond their evidence when they assume that, until the early nineteenth century or later, men always multiplied in the country but were devoured by the unsanitary towns. Today, as well as in some earlier periods, the first purpose of the city is defense not only against human enemies but also against malnutrition, disease, and neglect of the sufferer which is inevitable in inaccessible places.

Misty recollections of poetical writings relating to nature still color much of our thought about cities. We are somewhat surprised that Wordsworth should have chosen Westminster Bridge for his superlative: "Earth has not anything to show more fair." (It is only honest to note that Wordsworth received this impression very early in the morning, and that in the year 1802, the buildings lay "open unto the fields.")

But certainly one element in the praiseworthiness of cities is sheer physical beauty. Long before Wordsworth's time, the Venetian primitives had painted the Grand Canal and the Piazza as subjects which were beautiful in themselves, even when used as backgrounds for figures or processions. Medieval miniaturists in the Netherlands and glass painters in England had carefully studied the huddled roofs and gables of their towns.

The response to the beauty of a city, however, is not simple. For this beauty is viewed, consciously or unconsciously, as symbolic. To look at the walls, gates, and towers is to see the outward and visible expression of civic achievement. Many famous cities have been intentionally designed to intensify the sense of community. What Sir Christopher Wren wrote from a national point of view is even more true from a municipal point of view: "Architecture has its political use; publick buildings being the ornament of a country; it establishes a nation, draws people and commerce; makes the people love their native country, which passion is the original of all great actions in a commonwealth."[15]

So the city halls of the old German, Dutch, and Flemish cities, with their ancillary weigh-houses, piece-halls, and gate-towers, were not bare functional buildings but monuments of civic pride. Today, the proudest of them all, the town hall of Amsterdam, has become a royal residence. Nothing could give such an overwhelming impression of the wealth and power of the city as the central hall of this building, built with freestone from Scotland and ornamented with Carrara marble, rising to a height of one hundred feet. It was always open to the public. Through it, the citizens passed to and fro on their business with the offices and law courts. There were the great burgomasters whose courage and resource saved the city from foreign invaders; there were the financiers who granted or refused the petitions of emperors and kings; there was Rembrandt, at one time planning his great mural paintings which were never completed, at another time finding his way to the commissioners in bankruptcy. High overhead, a dial showed the direction of the wind, reminding everyone of the sails in the harbour outside and the world-wide commerce over which their city ruled.

The Ideal City and Its Citizens

Old Amsterdam and New Amsterdam on Manhattan Island are separated by three centuries of history. But the steel and concrete of our ideal city must still symbolize the common enterprise in which the inhabitants stand or fall together.

Among the city's population, there are generally three attitudes of mind. Some of the citizens are active in the city's behalf. They feel responsibility for it and consciously serve its administrative, business, or cultural life. They are the decision-makers and the artists, writers, thinkers, and educators which strive to make their wares available to all.

Next come the people who participate less positively but still feel a pride and joy in their citizenship. Although self-seekers as well as idealists exist in both groups, the fortunes of the city hinge on the relation of the two groups to a third. This group is composed of people who merely live in, but not for or by, the city and who turn to their own private gain or loss whatever the city proffers to them. The test of city planning in the future is whether or not it can convert the third group to the convictions of the other two.

For the appeal of city planning is no longer to the few. Its instruments include more than city halls and other governmental buildings devoted to limited kinds of public business. They also comprise the airports, railway terminals, hotels, theaters, shops, and other buildings where people come and go. If these structures are appropriately designed, the well-governed city will stand in men's minds as something stable in the whirlpool. Its individuality can become an anchorage for men's individualities within it.

But while we must build for crowds, we must also build so that the individual can hold out against the crowd. Already the modern city displays in museums and galleries its works of art—wonders which once belonged to the decor of exceptional societies, but now enhance the lives of all who enter. Such buildings, and the institutions within them, are ramparts of our civilization. Long may they contribute toward planning our ideal cities not as aggregates of production units and habitation units but as the glory and delight of free men and women.

FOOTNOTES TO CHAPTER 21

1. Aristotle *Politics* i. 1.

2. See A. M. H. Jones, *The Greek City from Alexander to Justinian* (Oxford: Clarendon Press, 1940), p. 214; W. W. Tarn, *Hellenistic Civilization* (London: E. Arnold, 1927), pp. 252 ff.; and Sir John Beazley in the *Cambridge Ancient History*, V (1927), p. 463.

3. As late as A.D. 404, Claudian wrote in his poem, "De Reditu Suo," that "urbem fecisti quod prius orbis erat." The speech by Aelius Aristides, dating from A.D. 154, is well used by M. I. Rostovtzeff in his *Social and Economic History of the Roman Empire* (Oxford: Clarendon Press, 1926), pp. 125 ff., as a statement of the position of free, self-governing cities in the Empire.

4. Marcus Aurelius *Meditations* iv. 23.

5. G. Unwin, *Studies in Economic History* (London: Macmillan, 1927), p. 49.

6. Hippolytus a Collibus, *De Incrementis Urbium* (Frankfort, 1671), pp. 101–109.

7. J. V. Andreä, *Reipublicae Christianopolitanae Descriptio* (1619).

8. C. Becker, *The Heavenly City of the Eighteenth Century Philosophers* (New Haven: Yale University Press, 1932).

9. Walt Whitman, *Leaves of Grass* (1855), "I dream'd in a dream," in the section entitled "Calamus."

10. Polybius *Frag.* ix. 10.

11. Emile Verhaeren, *Les Villes Tentaculaires* (1895).

12. *The Oxford Dictionary of Proverbs* (1935) gives the reference to *De Re Rustica* by Varro (116–27 B.C.).

13. C. N. Cochrane, *Christianity and Classical Culture* (Oxford: Clarendon Press, 1940), p. 269.

14. Thomas Hardy, *Jude the Obscure* (New York: Modern Library, 1923), p. 25. Originally published in 1896.

15. C. Wren, *Parentalia: or Memoires of the Family of the Wrens* (London, 1750), p. 351.

22

Commentaries

By **Steen Eiler Rasmussen,** *Royal Academy of Fine Arts, Copenhagen*

To search for the ideal city today is useless. For all cities are different. Each one has its own spirit, its own problems, and its own pattern of life. As long as the city lives, these aspects continue to change. Thus to look for the ideal city is not only a waste of time but may be seriously detrimental. In fact, the concept is obsolete; there is no such thing.

IDEAL RENAISSANCE CITIES

When we turn to the cities of the Renaissance, it is easy to see why the notion of the ideal city made some sense in those times but not today. In a town, houses were all of the same kind. Although they were not identical, each was a small, self-contained unit with dwellings and workshops under one roof. The contour of the town itself was rigidly shaped by its geometrically-designed fortifications. Throughout the entire period, the need for fortified protection was so great that there was no dividing line between the art and technique of city planning.

By using the laws of applied mathematics, Renaissance cities could be planned with structures which were as geometrically exact as ice crystals. Many excellent books have been written about such town plans. But more volumes ought to be published about the differences between the plans as they were drawn on paper and the towns as they appeared in life after the plans were carried out. For life creates its own patterns inside rigid theoretical systems, and it has beauty which is no less valuable than the geometrical.

Take the case of London. After the great fire of 1666, Sir Christopher Wren designed an ideal plan for London. It is generally regretted that the plan was not carried out. It is less well known, however, that the admired street pattern contained in the plan was designed practically overnight. Only four days after the fire temporarily ceased on September 6, Wren handed his plan to King Charles II. He knew how important it was to be the first to present a plan!

The rebuilding of the city was eventually put in the hands of a committee, of which Wren became a member. The committee eventually rejected Wren's plan. Its action may well have marked the beginning of modern city planning.

Modern City Planning

Today, any concept of the ideal city is wrong, because the town planner must meet his problems without any sort of prejudice about how a city should look. The good city planner is not a quick artist who can design a plan for a metropolis in three or four days. He is more like a doctor or educator who studies human beings and finds out how to guide their development.

The great educator, for example, does not decide in advance that man must be so and so. Instead, he helps each person he works with to utilize his special faculties in a natural way. If the city planner comes with preconceived ideas about how a city ought to be, he may be hindered from properly developing the special qualities and possibilities in each case.

The old city had a conceivable form with clear contours and skyline. Its dominant monuments were the church and the castle. The modern city, on the other hand, has none of these features. All attempts to give it *monumental* artistic effects are against the nature of contemporary urban life. The modern city must express a community spirit which is not subject to the same dominating factors as the old city of absolute monarchy.

The old city was determined by rigid laws pertaining to the outline of its fortifications. The modern city is determined by flexible laws of its interior life. Unlike geometrical rules, these laws are not universal. They vary from place to place. What is right in one place may be wrong in another. The city plan, consequently, is not a finished product. It is rather a long-term working program which allows for all sorts of changes.

In our times, the goal of city planners is to create a physical environment in which the individual can develop himself in the best way, and can benefit the most from being a member of the community. How can this be done if the planner has no recipe for an ideal city? The answer is that the modern city should not be the result of a philosophical construction, but of deep studies of empirical experiments.

Today, both art and science are more experimental than ever, and city planning is an art as well as a science. Sometimes it is carried out by two different teams working together. One group may execute nothing but civic survey work. Its research then forms the basis of the creative planning done by the second group. As the work proceeds, the planners instruct the surveyors what to look for. These instructions are expressed in terms of hypotheses rather than idealizations. The results of the survey are used to modify the planners' hypotheses, and the process is repeated until a suitable plan has evolved.

Consequently, the modern city planner has become an experimenter. His laboratory is the whole world with all its cities. Each new plan he draws up should attempt to remedy mistakes and failures in existing cities. In this sense, the Englishman, Ebenezer Howard, made an important contribution to town

planning. It may be said that his scheme for a garden city was an ideal plan.*
But it was not rigid or fixed. Howard wanted to have his ideas adopted so that
he could watch how people developed when they were given new opportunities.
His aim was to construct only one garden city as an experiment and then study
the results and profit from them.

Unfortunately, Howard's ideas have occasionally been adopted as something complete and finished. In fact, they have been proclaimed as a cure-all
for the ills of society. Long before they were carefully analyzed, the conceptions of a man who believed in freedom and individuality were standardized
into a specific system unsuited to the needs of modern urban life.

Our present duty is not to propagandize any single idea, but to analyze the
results of many experiments and learn from them. To assist us, we have
methods of studying towns which never existed in Ebenezer Howard's time.
No longer should planning be the work of one man or the efforts of one
profession. It should benefit from the endeavors of many professions and many
sciences.

From a world of fixed ideas of ideal cities, therefore, we have come out
to our modern life. In it, positive criticism is expedient to further progress.
For this, we look to the universities to stand for man's right to knowledge
and the free use thereof.

By **Catherine Bauer,** *Lecturer, Department of City and Regional Planning,
University of California* (*Berkeley*)

According to Sir George Clark, the modern city has to fulfill two new requirements. It must be an organ of the great society and also an organ of a
democratic society. These requirements help to explain some of our unre-
solved difficulties.

For the fact that the city is an organ of the great society means that it is
subject to a great many outside forces. Some of them are world-wide in scope,
including population movements, technological developments, and sweeping
political, economic, and social changes. The effects of such forces on our cities
are extremely difficult to control, guide, or even anticipate.

As an organ of democratic society, the modern city poses the universal
dilemma of our times—society versus freedom. The good city must protect
minimum living standards but at the same time provide an environment favorable to creative experiment, freedom of initiative, and maximum consumer
choice. As Sir George put it, "while we must build for crowds, we must also
build so that the individual can hold out against the crowd."

Faced with these complex requirements, is there any point in continuing
the old search for a definite concept of the ideal city? Is there any use in

*Ebenezer Howard, *Garden Cities of Tomorrow* (London: Faber and Faber,
1945). This book first appeared in 1898 under the title *Tomorrow: A Peaceful
Path to Real Reform* and in 1902 under the present title.

seeking for a generalized physical form that would, in theory at least, best satisfy our necessities in terms of modern conditions of urban development?

The answer is yes. It is absolutely necessary to develop *images* of the present-day ideal city. We need a great many images competing with each other for public interest and support.

LARGE-SCALE OPERATIONS AND PUBLIC DECISIONS

Experience during the last twenty years underlines the need for ideal images. The reasons for public housing, slum clearance, rational design, and efficient building methods are as valid now as they ever were. But how have these things fared without the guidance of ideals?

Despite some progress in each field, there are great barrack blocks of public housing which are all too often managed like an old-fashioned orphan asylum or mental institution. There are vast suburban Federal Housing Administration projects with thousands of identical boxes for families who are equally identical in age, income, and race. (In the proud name of neighborhood planning, the developments are frequently set out in military order in random fields quite unrelated to anything else.) There are also expensive slum clearance and redevelopment projects, apparently adding to the congestion and sharpening the race relations problem which is more crucial in the great society than the matter of physical obsolescence.

In short, we have been learning to build for crowds. This was a necessary step. Yet we seem to be farther than ever from building for individuals with their variety of habits, desires, and characteristics.

Unfortunately, there is no simple way to build for the individual. The solution does not lie in passing the responsibility for environmental planning back to the consumers to handle as they see fit. For the tools that shape modern cities are not scaled to their hands. With all our resources, we can provide tailor-made houses in the modern city only for the fortunate few who can afford them.

In fact, machinery for building homes and cities has been revolutionized during the past twenty years by two comparatively new factors that now dominate the whole process. One is large-scale operations in terms of vast housing projects built all at once; huge redevelopment sites, supermarkets, and tremendous networks of highways; transport and utilities interlacing whole regions; and rules and regulations that blanket the city, the state, and even the nation with standards of every description.

The other is the fact that most of the important decisions about the nature of large-scale developments are now publicly made. And public decisions are quite different from the mechanics of the private market. Theoretically, at least, the private market provides some automatic adjustment of supply and demand. Public decisions, on the other hand, must be based primarily on conscious public policy and purpose.

The factors of large-scale developments and public decisions work against the individual citizen so that he must usually take whatever he gets by way of a physical environment. However, to the extent that he loses the power of determination as a consumer, his potential importance as a voter increases. For public decisions are supposed to be his own decisions. But unless he and the other citizens can decide ahead of time what they want and then can develop the necessary policies, his role as a voter will not be very important, either.

Consequently, there must be some more effective process than there now is for helping citizens to decide for themselves about the kind of city they want. Once that is done, they can give suitable instructions to their official representatives and employees.

PUBLIC UNDERSTANDING AND DEBATE

The difference between the modern metropolis and the older town is in some ways analogous to the difference between a modern factory and a handicraft operation. In the latter, it was possible to proceed without a set of exact drawings—whether the general purpose was a shoe or a cathedral—because the final product was gradually built up out of a number of skilled individual decisions. In the factory, however, you have to know ahead exactly what you propose to make and how. Without plans, the machinery will not produce parts that fit together.

In a modern city, powerful machinery is constantly engaged in building vast projects that make continuous and drastic changes in land use and population distribution. Hence there are constant alterations in the entire social, economic, and functional organization of the community. For this reason, it is vital to have some clear-cut image of the over-all result and some public agreement as to the end product. Otherwise, we are likely to get results that nobody anticipated, or a situation in which a few public officials make all the decisions on a piecemeal, ad hoc basis without having previously consulted the public.

But even with an enlightened city plan, the big decisions must be made, the conflicting interests compromised, and the alternative possibilities resolved in advance before the plan is submitted for public approval. Unfortunately, the outcome tends to be either a protective jelling of the status quo, a more or less automatic projection of past trends into the future, or a rather presumptuous crystallization of what the planners happen to think people want or ought to want. Whatever the consequence, the issues and alternatives will be glossed over so that the scheme looks inevitable.

At some point, of course, there does have to be a single comprehensive plan to guide development. But one all-important step is missing in this process of survey, analysis, and plan. For the entire business is carried on by professionals and only the end-result is subject to the approval of the city government, except for any private advance discussions with individuals or departments that may be deemed strategic.

What is missing is public understanding and debate of the big alternatives. In the long run, the issues will undoubtedly have to be compromised in many ways. But before that can be done in any responsible way, they should be publicly posed, with all their long-term implications for family life, business enterprise, social relations, cultural progress, and governmental structure, spread out in the open.

Moreover, the lack of this step tends to keep city planning feeble and ineffective in our nation despite all the money and talent devoted to it. For even if the planners do happen to hit on the right answer, who understands it well enough to back them up? Controversy will rage over certain concrete aspects of the plan that have immediate meaning to one set of interests or another, and the over-all issues will be lost.

In our time, the big alternative confronting modern cities is centralization versus some form of decentralization. Although the forces favoring some form of sub-centralization in large metropolitan areas appear to be overwhelming, there are many potential advantages and disadvantages that must be balanced. In doing so, important decisions have to be taken. They are more likely to be responsibly made if the alternatives are posed in concrete and even dramatic form, designed to stimulate rather than inhibit debate.

That is why we need definite concepts of the ideal city—its size, shape, and socio-economic structure. Not one but several plans are needed in active competition, each presenting the case for a given pattern and the price that must be paid for it. None of these abstract schemes, of course, will ever be built exactly. Compromises must be made. But what is built will profit by the fact that the extreme alternatives have been clarified.

In one country, at least, the alternatives of centralization and decentralization have been publicly debated. They have been discussed in terms of the Utopias of Ebenezer Howard and Lewis Mumford on the one hand, and in terms of the sophisticated modern architect's longing for technocratic urbanity on the other. It is no accident that Great Britain also has the most advanced and positive planning legislation and the best informed citizenry about planning problems and possibilities.

Would that other regions of the world in the process of rapid urbanization might turn up a similar array of ardent and battling Utopians to inform the citizens of the big decisions that still lie ahead.

By **Charles Abrams,** *Professor of Housing, New School for Social Research, New York*

In recent times, the ideal city has been the function mainly of four factors. illusion, amortization, pace, and law. In speaking of the modern ideal city, this commentary will deal not with the world of Plato or the Utopians, nor with the housers and planners, but with the realities of today, their facts, and their present dangers.

CONDITIONING FACTORS IN THE MODERN IDEAL CITY

The factor of *illusion* existed in the Utopias of yesterday as it does in the United States now. It may imply less a realization of the ideal than an idealization of the real. For example, access to home ownership may be essential in an ideal city. Yet an analysis may show that it is not home ownership at all. In Plato's ideal city, the citizens used the words "mine" and "not mine" interchangeably for the same objects of property. This situation may be equally descriptive of a Federal Housing Administration equity in a home at the present time.

Planning, architecture, and the ideal city are all conditioned by *amortization* —by the haste which marks their efforts and by the time the product is meant to last.

The churches of Sir Christopher Wren, the town hall of Amsterdam, or the colleges of Oxford were built to last for centuries. They differ from the dumbbell tenements of the exciting immigrant period in the United States, the hutments of Israel, the *chawls* of India, the mushroom houses of Turkey, the makeshifts of Mexico's squatter parachutists, the *Bidonvilles* of Algiers, or the *barong barongs* of Manila. Any one of these may be the ideal to some people or only way stations toward higher aspirations.

The Ideal City, wherever it may exist, the New Deal City conditioned by experimentation and make-work, or the Ordeal City of the atomic age whose life span is set by the whim of men who control the atoms, must all be measured by the rates of depreciation assigned to them. Each rate ultimately will be set by forces beyond the power of the planner or the philosopher.

The third factor is *pace*. Though earlier cities were built on waterways, the great architect of the eighteenth century was not the technician but the cow. The great ideal in the United States was to have forty acres and a cow. It was the cow around whom homes were planned, just as the cow determines the patterns of the present villages of India. But the cow, alas, no longer counts in our country. Indeed, as one dairy after another in Los Angeles County has been torn up to make way for new subdivisions, the planning commission has made a plea for dairy zoning in a brochure plaintively entitled, "Where Now, Brown Cow."

In the nineteenth century, the great architect was the horse. The distance he could draw a tram to the work places, and the distance and speed a team of horses could pull a fire engine, determined the boundaries of a neighborhood. It was the era of equine city planning, equine streets, equine architecture, and equine industrialization. The age was equine even in its effect on personality, for it slowed human pace to that of the horse whose limitations conditioned man's ideals.

The advent of improved transportation has now freed the individual from the tyranny of sites. It has enabled him to find his utopias in suburbs, in warmer climates or, if he preferred to be on the move, in trailers, furnished rooms, or motels. In the United States, the end of the war saw us cast our swords into T-squares, and as any tourist may observe, our plans have changed from total mobilization to total motelization.

The planner would hardly call this transience ideal. Yet escape may be essential to many people, now that the automobile and easy transportation offer it to them. Escape must be possible from the planned city and the ideal city. It may be more than accident that a planned community like Boulder City has not thrived, while eleven miles away the wicked city of Las Vegas has boomed though it has had no industries except dice, divorce, and dissipation—a far cry from Savonarola's perfect state of purity, sobriety, and justice.

Between 1940 and 1954, three million Negroes moved between non-contiguous states. They did so not because they were dispossessed but because they saw the slums of the cities as their utopias, just as the immigrant had envisioned them in the nineteen hundred and twenties. The same thing holds true with the Puerto Ricans from their hard-pressed little island, and with the Mexicans who wade across the Rio Grande. Perhaps there can be no ideal city. For as long as man strives, the ideal of one will remain the frustration of another.

The ideal in a mobile age can exist only in a society of comparisons—of good, bad, and better environments, of new ideals to seek and discarded ones to flee from. To the New Yorker, the ideal city may be in Connecticut; to the Puerto Rican it may be the environs of Columbia University. In the long run, the ideal city will not be a city of spires but of frontiers. And not until all frontiers are open will the ideal be within reach. For it can never be the ideal of the few or of the excluders against the excluded.

The fourth factor is *law*. The fulfillment of the ideal must depend upon the scope of power. Legal powers to plan the city have been expanded in recent years to such an extent that ample power exists to plan the ideal city. By fathoming the mysteries of fiscal policy, funds have become available to plan many ideal cities.

But although we have learned the new uses of physical power and curbed its excesses, we have not yet learned how to harness political power. The nineteenth century saw government impose upon the individual duties and obligations as well as rights. But in the twentieth century, the frontier of the seeker after the ideal may consist of imposing duties upon government and reharnessing it to the principles of justice and fair dealing.

For who can fail to see that the ideal of a welfare state may also be turned into a business-welfare state where general welfare becomes the residuum of special interests? In this state, the rank and file are only tertiary beneficiaries; the power plant of government becomes the tool of little private governments, each implemented by reinforcements of public power and purse; the rights of minorities are obliterated and other rights are remolded to suit the aesthetic tastes of local majorities; the civil service is sterilized by fear and the government is subordinated from the roles of umpire between competing interests and trustee of constitutional morality to become the pawn of dominant groups.

Ideals are dangerous in the presence of power. They can spark the quest for freedom or smother it under the weight of tyranny. Even the planner's tools have been perverted at one time or another into instruments for oppressing minorities. Zoning has been turned into racial zoning; residential covenants into restrictive covenants; urban redevelopment and slum clearance into devices for evicting minorities; the greenbelt into a device to separate the black belt from the white belt. The powers of taxation, eminent domain, and police have all been used now and then to support biases and interests of local tyrannical majorities. In a world increasingly conscious of caste and status, the democratic ideal may degenerate into the ideal of a hierarchy.

This is not a new process. In the Prussian absolutist state, the philosophers soon found that idealism became the exponent of absolutism. By the same token, we must be careful that the ideal city does not become little more than a house of cards in which *I deal* and *you take*. With every release of public power, therefore, an equivalent citizen interest must arise to put through the reform and also to guard it against perversion.

FREEDOM IN THE IDEAL CITY

The ideal city will be attractive to newcomers and to undesirables. There will invariably be the temptation to keep them out. Yet the essence of freedom includes the freedom to move. When that condition exists, there is always a challenge to the ideal as there is a temptation to preserve it by force or sanctions. Freedom is the essence of the city and must remain so. The freedom to enter it and to live there is its strength and the core of its ideal qualities.

In the long run, the ideal city must facilitate to the fullest extent the power of any individual to realize his desires and fulfill his needs. It must offer entry to all who seek it, and access to a variety of homes all with soundproof walls and untapped wires. It must provide an opportunity to enjoy good health and freedom from the fear of old age, insecurity, and eviction for reasons of destitution or excess income, and it must assure environmental privacy and guarantee political privacy.

With the new age of mobility and transportation, we have been freed from the limitations of space. The fears of the classical economists that land will be in short supply, that the landlord will soon rule the world, or that rent will swallow up all profit, no longer exist.

If we consider Paris as the ideal city, we can put the entire world's population into a similarly designed space not more than 75 miles in diameter. Suppose the victors of World War II had decreed that Germany (which complained of its need for *lebensraum*) must house the world's 2.4 billion people. This could have been done within Germany's present 143,000 square miles at a density of about 25 families to the acre. That would hardly be ideal, but it suggests the new wealth of space in an industrial world.

While we know how to make the most of space that can make cities ideal and beautiful, we have not yet learned the uses and abuses of power. Here lies a new frontier out of which the architect's dreams can be carved. Within it, the ideal can be won with freedom, or freedom can be lost.

By **John E. Burchard**,* *Dean of Humanities and Social Studies, Massachusetts Institute of Technology*

Few people would define a city as ideal even if it managed to handle only one of its problems ideally. Professor Florence would not call a city ideal just because it offered short transport and communication to consumers without congestion, or higher wages without higher living costs. Although every ideal city must be an efficient production and distribution center, economic perfection alone is not sufficient.

Nor would many of us claim that a city was ideal merely because all the citizens believed in a single faith, or because every inhabitant had a warm, safe, private bed at night and a small patch of grass and sun by day. It would not be enough for the city to lie free from the danger of bombing, or to wear architectural diamonds on its avenues.

Yet a definition of the ideal city must be attempted. As a first approximation, we can state one necessary condition: the city must maximize its inherent advantages and minimize its inherent disadvantages.

Some Inherent Advantages of the City

The city is the only place where true diversity can thrive and where specialization can reach its apogee. It is the only place of multiple habitation where anyone who wants to be private can be alone. The opportunity for social mobility is unique to the city. It is the only place from which the waves of change must ultimately reach the country.

If diversity is essential to the healthy growth of a society, then a social institution which promotes diversity must be an admirable one. And, of course, great diversity in occupation and taste is found only in a big city. Only a large population can make it statistically possible to render or enjoy a service which is not generally demanded.

Diversity naturally leads to specialization. Mr. Young has pointed out that the rapid growth of the professions has been associated mainly with the growth of urban civilizations. Professor Florence noted that scientific research is concentrated in cities. Professor Hill remarked that modern medicine would have advanced far more slowly had men lived only in small, isolated communities.

Today a large research enterprise may be decentralized, but not without some risk. For one of the problems of specialization is to keep the boundaries green, and here interspecialist interchange is essential. So Mr. Young indicated that the metropolis offers a better chance for interprofessional collaboration.

* Editor's abridgement of a manuscript read by John E. Burchard at the last session of the First Bicentennial Conference.

Since no single specialist knows what everyone else is doing, he can keep in touch only by being near others and talking with them. Only by this process can professional provincialism be reduced.

Specialization is good for the beneficiaries as well as the practitioners. Mr. Young recalled the words of Mr. Justice Holmes that "more complex and intense intellectual efforts mean a fuller and richer life" for the individuals concerned.

The same richer life is possible for the individual in the city because he can have some privacy. Professor Folliet discussed religious matters. But he might have been talking about anything else when he related how hard it was for individuals in rural communities to adhere to a strange sect. By thus singling themselves out, they were exposed to animosity or disdain, or at least to the laughter of the majority. Anyone who has lived in villages knows the effect which Folliet describes of the incessant and often jealous surveillance by neighbors, the fear of what will be said, and the expressed or tacit imperatives of a conventional opinion which force individuals into a semblance of regularity.

There is no need to plead a case for social mobility. Professor Chevalier has pointed out that it has a much greater chance in cities, Moreover, social mobility seems to become stronger as the urban agglomeration becomes more extensive.

Thus the city offers inherent advantages in the encouragement of diversity, the increase of specialization, the cross-fertilization of specialists, the chance for privacy and off-the-beat originality, and the opportunity for social mobility. The ideal city must maximize all these opportunities.

SOME INHERENT DISADVANTAGES OF THE CITY

On the other side of the coin, the city is dirty, noisy, and pathological. Its anonymity may create political and social apathy, and its congestion may stifle activity. The city encourages a remoteness from nature and hence from reality. It is pointedly vulnerable, especially now that we have learned how to split the atom.

Historically, the city has been a place of physical and moral pathology. Professor Chevalier suggested, however, that these matters may be changing. He found that urbanization is not necessarily synonymous with depopulation; urban states are not inevitably doomed. Moreover, vital statistics are improving in the city. The relative chance of individual survival regardless of economic class has materially improved.

Nevertheless, it is disturbing that the city seems to be more favorable for the young than for the old. This tendency helps the city to be creative, of course, since the young are vigorous. But as more people are getting older all the time, troublesome geriatric questions will be raised with increasing frequency.

Novelists like Dickens, Zola, and Sue gave the city a lurid label of criminality and immorality which it has lived down with difficulty. Since the city naturally develops every specialty, urban immorality is likely to be first-class. But the writers in this book have been most reluctant to impute to the city an immorality greater than that of the country. At most, they have tended to say with Professor Chevalier that the immorality of the city was different.

Much the same things were said about faith. Whatever the historical situation may have been, Professor Folliet noted that the cities, and not the rural districts, have fostered many recrudescences of Catholic faith, notably in the new movements of social action.

Even crime was not accepted as prima facie a product of the city. Professor Chevalier thought it was more a function of the rate of growth of a city than of absolute size, and would change from time to time with the city. Thus, on the whole, the city was not found to be inherently pathological.

Yet the impression still exists that the country is a little bit quieter and cleaner and a little less dangerous than the city. A person is more likely to be mugged in New York City's Central Park than on the common of the small New England town. So even if the evidence is encouraging, it is apparent that the city can do a great deal to improve its record with respect to physical and moral health.

Defects of a more troublesome sort pertain to the anonymity of the city. The very quality which provides desirable privacy may also encourage political or social apathy. Sir George Clark pointed out that the test of city planning is whether it can convert a very large group of city dwellers to a concern with anything beyond their own selfish ends. Mr. Young was skeptical as to whether planned neighborhoods would solve this problem, or even provide anything more than physical community. He suggested that propinquity in living, buying, and recreation may not be enough to counteract the forces of the metropolis. Indeed, Mr. Young added that it is far from certain that the forces of the metropolis need counteracting in the interest of citizen satisfactions.

A more subtle kind of remoteness occurs because the city is estranged from nature. Professor Casserley showed how urban bakers begin to believe that bread is baked because they want to bake it and not because people want to eat it. He also indicated that although the city enormously influences the country, the country can do without the city whereas the city cannot do without the country.

This lack of reality is indirectly related to the vulnerability of the city, especially in the face of nuclear bombs. Apparently, our fear of war is not overwhelming. For Professor Hill stood squarely against decentralization when he said: "It would be the greatest disaster to the world of learning and discovery if the threat of war caused the great metropolitan centers to dissipate their resources of men and knowledge and abandon their intellectual function in the world. It were better surely to take the risk."

This strikes a responsive note, because the city has always been vulnerable. It is vulnerable, for example, to tugboat captains who want to strike. It is vulnerable to two unions who want to control a waterfront. It is vulnerable to other kinds of people with power, not all labor or political.

But in time of social and civic collapse, it is the rough rural life which persists and displays survival power. Professor Casserley added that "financially and politically the great city is indeed powerful. Economically and sociologically it is a delicate and fragile thing." No amount of practical decentralization can spare our culture if everyone feels that the use of atomic bombs is not a very bad thing on the whole. Under such circumstances, it would be better for the city to play its role proudly to the end rather than to decentralize in the time remaining before another war begins. Indeed, in playing it, there is a better chance for a change of heart and hence of true survival.

THE NEED FOR BEAUTY

The ideal city will do what it reasonably can to reduce its vulnerability, to increase its contact with nature, and to improve its chances for moral and physical health, so long as these improvements do not stop it from being a host to diversity, specialization, privacy, and social mobility, which are its only justifications.

All those things are necessary. But after all that has happened, the city still may not be ideal. People are not always happy just because the city is economically efficient or morally strong. Actually, the ideal city must also be a happy, beautiful, and unsuspicious place. There ought to be a good deal of laughter in the ideal city, and it should not be the loud kind that shows a vacancy behind it.

Sir George Clark asserted that one element in the praiseworthiness of the city is sheer physical beauty. But he should have gone even farther. For beauty is an *indispensable* element. While it alone cannot solve all the problems of the city man, beauty will ameliorate his distresses. Does anyone really believe that a poor man will not be happier in Paris than in Shreveport, Louisiana?

In addition to the need for beauty in general, each city must have its own particular beauty. Just as there is need for diversity among people, so there is need for diversity among cities. Some cities are already so delightful that their citizens will not leave them even for wider economic and intellectual opportunities. In the United States, one such city stands on the Pacific Coast, two on the Atlantic Coast, and perhaps one on the Gulf of Mexico. But no more, really. Only these are truly metropolises as yet, for only they are mother cities.

THE HINTERLAND

A city which maximizes its advantages and minimizes its disadvantages, and becomes beautiful and personal, will not be ideal unless it supports the hinterland which in turn invigorates it. By this operation, the city justifies itself.

Professor Folliet indicated that while the provinces may furnish ideas to Paris, these ideas will not be spread through France unless they pass first through Paris. This may not always be the healthiest situation. Yet it prevails nearly everywhere. Even in the United States, which may be too big to have a single metropolis like Paris or London, the same thing tends to occur. In many ways, New York is the clearinghouse for the rest of the country.

INDIVIDUALITY

In searching for an ideal city, we run one great modern risk. It is the decay of individuality. Unfortunately, the periphery of San Francisco is beginning to look more and more like the suburbs of Los Angeles or Sydney or Chicago or Detroit. As this process goes on, San Francisco and every other glorious city may lose its character save as a matter of historical nostalgia.

For as we solve problems of vulnerability, congestion, and all the rest, we are likely to use one solution which has worked in one place and apply it at home as the easiest thing to do. Universal solutions for urban problems presumably do not exist. But if they do and if we apply them, we may as well cease the search for the ideal city; it will no longer have a chance to be found. Our real problem, then, is not to turn Detroit and Los Angeles into Boston and San Francisco, but to prevent Boston and San Francisco from becoming Detroit and Los Angeles.

Obviously, we need something between the laissez faire which produced more Birminghams than Edinburghs and the utter planning which will inevitably produce one kind of a bureaucratic city. Lord Bryce once said in quite a different connection, "A man in crisis in his life can never nerve himself to action or comfort himself under a stroke of fate by reflecting that the angles at the base of an isosceles triangle are equal." So it is for a city.

In solving our problems, we must steer a steady course lest we fail to rediscover the Oxford described by Sir George Clark in quoting Thomas Hardy: "It had been the yearning of his heart to find something to anchor on, to cling to—for some place which he could call admirable."

FREEDOM

Finally, we must remind ourselves that a city must be free to be ideal. Paris was not ideal in 1793 or in 1940. No city is ideal where the citizens hide in corners, tremble before the fear of the anonymous denouncer, or look at each other in suspicion. All the other desirable qualities might reside in Buenos Aires, Madrid, Peking, Moscow or Prague. Yet suspicion residing there destroys the ideal. This also could happen in New York.

Appendix

First Bicentennial Conference

Columbia University in the City of New York

THE METROPOLIS IN MODERN LIFE

January 7–9, 1954

CHAIRMAN OF THE BICENTENNIAL ORGANIZATION COMMITTEE

Arthur Hays Sulzberger

DIRECTOR OF THE BICENTENNIAL

Richard R. B. Powell

Dwight Professor of Law

CHAIRMAN OF THE COMMITTEE ON CONFERENCES

Louis M. Hacker

Dean of the School of General Studies

CONFERENCE CHAIRMAN

Ernest M. Fisher

Professor of Urban Land Economics and Director, Institute for Urban Land Use and Housing Studies

CONFERENCE VICE CHAIRMAN

Leo Grebler

Professor of Urban Land Use and Housing Studies and Associate Director, Institute for Urban Land Use and Housing Studies

CONFERENCE SECRETARY

John M. Kernochan

Associate Professor of Law and Director, Legislative Drafting Research Fund

First Session

The Dynamic Role of the City in Social Development

CHAIRMAN: Kingsley Davis, *Professor of Sociology, Columbia University*

PRINCIPAL SPEAKERS

Stuart Piggott, *Professor of Archaeology, University of Edinburgh*

383

Louis Chevalier, *Professeur, Sciences Philosophiques et Sociologiques,*
   Collège de France, Paris
Albert J. Reiss, Jr., *Professor of Sociology and Anthropology,*
   Vanderbilt University

Second Session

The Impact of the Metropolis on the Spiritual Life of Man

CHAIRMAN: John M. Krumm, *Chaplain, Columbia University*

PRINCIPAL SPEAKERS

Joseph Folliet, *Professeur de Sociologie,*
   l'Institut Social des Facultés Catholiques de Lyon
J. V. Langmead Casserley, *Professor of Dogmatic Theology,*
   General Theological Seminary, New York

DISCUSSANTS

George N. Shuster, *President, Hunter College, New York*
Paul J. Tillich, *Graduate Professor of Philosophical Theology,*
   Union Theological Seminary, New York
Louis Finkelstein, *Chancellor, Jewish Theological Seminary, New York*
S. Muhammad Ikram, *Professor, School of International Affairs,*
   Columbia University
Swami Nikhilananda, *Ramakrishna-Vivekananda Center, New York*

Third Session

The Influence of the Metropolis on Concepts, Rules, and Institutions Relating to Property

CHAIRMAN: Howard R. Williams, *Professor of Law, Columbia University*

PRINCIPAL SPEAKERS

Harold L. Reeve, *Senior Vice President, Chicago Title and Trust Company,*
   Chicago
Myres S. McDougal, *Professor of Law, Yale University*

DISCUSSANTS

Russell D. Niles, *Dean, School of Law, New York University*
Charles M. Haar, *Assistant Professor of Law, Harvard Law School,*
   Harvard University

Fourth Session

Economic Advantages and Disadvantages of Metropolitan Concentration

CHAIRMAN: Leo Grebler, *Professor of Urban Land Use and Housing Studies,*
   and Associate Director, Institute for Urban Land Use and Housing
   Studies, Columbia University

PRINCIPAL SPEAKERS

P. Sargant Florence, *Dean, Faculty of Commerce and Social Science, University of Birmingham, England*

Richard U. Ratcliff, *Professor of Land Economics, University of Wisconsin*

DISCUSSANTS

Harold M. Mayer, *Professor of Geography, University of Chicago*

Larry Smith, *President, Larry Smith & Company, Real Estate Consultants, Seattle*

Fifth Session

The Influence of Science and Technology on the Metropolis

CHAIRMAN: Mario G. Salvadori, *Professor of Civil Engineering, Columbia University*

PRINCIPAL SPEAKERS

A. V. Hill, *Professor Emeritus of Biophysics, University College, London*

Richard J. Neutra, *Architect, Los Angeles*

DISCUSSANTS

Alan Gregg, M.D., *Vice President, Rockefeller Foundation, New York*

Harold M. Lewis, *Consulting Engineer and City Planner, New York*

Sixth Session

Contributions of the Metropolitan Community to the Political Institutions of a Free Society

CHAIRMAN: Schuyler C. Wallace, *Professor of Public Law and Government and Director, School of International Affairs, Columbia University*

PRINCIPAL SPEAKERS

William Anderson, *Professor of Political Science, University of Minnesota*

Luther H. Gulick, *President, Institute of Public Administration, New York*

Seventh Session

The Impact of the Metropolis on the Professions

CHAIRMAN: Robert K. Merton, *Professor of Sociology, Columbia University*

PRINCIPAL SPEAKERS

Sir Alexander Morris Carr-Saunders, *Director, London School of Economics and Political Science*

Donald Young, *General Director, Russell Sage Foundation, New York*

DISCUSSANTS

Thomas Parran, M.D., *Dean, Graduate School of Public Health, University of Pittsburgh*

Reginald Heber Smith, *Director, The Survey of the Legal Profession, Boston*
Dana W. Atchley, M.D., *Professor of Clinical Medicine,*
    Columbia-Presbyterian Medical Center, New York
Harry W. Jones, *Professor of Law, Columbia University*

Eighth Session

The Search for the Ideal City

CHAIRMAN: Lyman Bryson, *Professor of Education, Teachers College,*
    Columbia University

PRINCIPAL SPEAKER

Sir George Clark, *Provost, Oriel College, University of Oxford*

DISCUSSANTS

Catherine Bauer, *Lecturer, Department of City and Regional Planning,*
    University of California (Berkeley)
Steen Eiler Rasmussen, *Royal Academy of Fine Arts, Copenhagen*
John E. Burchard, *Dean of Humanities and Social Studies,*
    Massachusetts Institute of Technology
Charles Abrams, *Professor of Housing, New School for Social Research,*
    New York

Participants

CONRAD M. ARENSBERG, Professor of Anthropology, Columbia University

LEOPOLD ARNAUD, Dean, Faculty of Architecture, Columbia University

CHARLES S. ASCHER, Chairman, Department of Political Science, Brooklyn College, Brooklyn, N.Y.

TRACY B. AUGUR, Office of Defense Mobilization, Washington, D.C.

EDMUND N. BACON, Executive Director, City Planning Commission of Philadelphia, Philadelphia, Pa.

GEORGE W. BARCLAY, Assistant Professor of Sociology, Columbia University

JOSEPH W. BARKER, President, Research Corporation, New York City

SALO W. BARON, Professor of Jewish History, Columbia University

PIERRE BEDARD, President, Parsons School of Design, New York City

COL. JOHN J. BENNETT, Chairman, City Planning Commission, New York City

J. H. BEUSCHER, Professor of Law, University of Wisconsin, Madison, Wis.

GORDON W. BLACKWELL, Professor of Sociology, Director, Institute for Research in Social Science, University of North Carolina, Chapel Hill, N.C.

T. LEDYARD BLAKEMAN, Executive Director, Regional Planning Commission, Detroit, Mich.

WALTER H. BLUCHER, Executive Director, American Society of Planning Officials, Chicago, Ill.

DONALD J. BOGUE, Assistant Director, Scripps Foundation, Miami University, Oxford, Ohio

ERNEST J. BOHN, Chairman, Cleveland City Planning Commission, Cleveland, Ohio

GERALD W. BREESE, Director, Bureau of Urban Research, Associate Professor of Sociology & Economics, Princeton University, Princeton, N.J.

ESTHER LUCILE BROWN, Russell Sage Foundation, New York City

HENRY BRUÈRE, Former President, The Bowery Savings Bank, New York City

EDWIN S. BURDELL, President, Cooper Union, New York City

ARTHUR R. BURNS, Professor of Economics, Columbia University

EVELINE M. BURNS, Professor of Social Work, New York School of Social Work

R. M. BURNS, Bell Telephone Laboratories, Murray Hill, N.J.

HAROLD S. BUTTENHEIM, Editor, *The American City,* New York City

THEODORE CAPLOW, Professor of Sociology, University of Michigan, Ann Arbor, Mich.

THOMAS CARROLL, Director, Division of Economic Development & Administration, Ford Foundation, New York City

THE REVEREND DR. J. GORDON CHAMBERLIN, The Riverside Church, New York City

ELLIOTT E. CHEATHAM, Charles Evans Hughes Professor of Law, Columbia University

HENRY S. CHURCHILL, New York City

FREDERICK P. CLARK, Regional Plan Association, Inc., New York City

SHEPARD B. CLOUGH, Professor of History, Columbia University

HENRY S. COMMAGER, Professor of American History, Columbia University

CARLOS CONTRERAS, Mexico City, Mexico

LEONARD S. COTTRELL, JR., Russell Sage Foundation, New York City

THOMAS CREIGHTON, Editor, *Progressive Architecture,* New York City

HOWARD S. CULLMAN, New York City

LELAND C. DEVINNEY, Associate Director for Social Science, Rockefeller Foundation, New York City

PAUL B. DEWITT, Executive Secretary, Association of the Bar of the City of New York

ROBERT E. DICKINSON, Professor of Geography, Syracuse University, Syracuse, New York

JOHN DILLENBERGER, Professor of Religion, Columbia University

JOHN R. DUNNING, Dean, Faculty of Engineering, Columbia University

SHELDEN D. ELLIOTT, Professor of Law, New York University School of Law

ERNEST A. ENGLEBERT, Professor of Political Science, University of California, Los Angeles, Calif.

JOHN EVERETTS, JR., Philadelphia, Pa.

HENRY FAGIN, Planning Director, Regional Plan Association, Inc., New York City

MARTIN L. FAUST, Professor of Political Science, University of Missouri, Columbia, Mo.

CARL FEISS, Housing and Home Finance Agency, Washington, D.C.

JAMES FELT, President, James Felt & Company, New York City

HUGH FERRISS, President, N. Y. Chapter, American Institute of Architects, New York City

WALTER T. FISHER, Chicago, Ill.

THE VERY REVEREND GEORGES FLOROVSKY, St. Vladimir's Seminary, New York City

HORACE L. FRIESS, Professor of Philosophy, Columbia University

JEWELL M. GARRELTS, Professor of Engineering, Columbia University

ELI GINZBERG, Professor of Economics, Columbia University

CHARLES Y. GLOCK, Lecturer in Sociology, Columbia University

RABBI JUDAH GOLDIN, Jewish Theological Seminary, New York City

WILLIAM J. GOODE, Associate Professor of Sociology, Columbia University

CARTER GOODRICH, Professor of Economics, Columbia University

STIG G. V. GUSTAFSSON, The Stockholm School of Economics, Stockholm, Sweden

FREDERICK GUTHEIM, Washington, D.C.

WILBUR C. HALLENBECK, Professor of Education, Columbia University

TALBOT F. HAMLIN, Professor of Architecture, Columbia University

WALLACE K. HARRISON, Architect, New York City

DOUGLAS HASKELL, Editorial Chairman, Architectural Forum, New York City

GEORGE L. HASKINS, Professor of Law, University of Pennsylvania, Philadelphia, Pa.

WILL HERBERG, New York City

PENDLETON HERRING, Executive Director, Social Science Research Council, New York City

HILDA HERTZ, Bureau of Applied Social Research, Columbia University

BENJAMIN H. HIGGINS, Professor of Economics, McGill University, Montreal, Canada

HOMER L. HITT, Head, Department of Sociology, Louisiana State University, Baton Rouge, La.

ARTHUR C. HOLDEN, Holden, McLaughlin & Associates, New York City

EDGAR M. HOOVER, Washington, D.C.

REGINALD R. ISAACS, Norton Professor of Planning, Harvard University, Cambridge, Mass.

WALTER ISARD, Littauer Center, Harvard University, Cambridge, Mass.

ABRAM J. JAFFE, Lecturer in Sociology, Columbia University

HARLEAN JAMES, Executive Secretary, American Planning & Civic Association, Washington, D.C.

VICTOR JONES, Professor of Government, Wesleyan University, Middletown, Conn.

DUDLEY KIRK, Department of State, Washington, D.C.

CHARLES M. KNEIER, Professor of Political Science, University of Illinois, Urbana, Illinois

THE REVEREND JOHN LAFARGE, S.J., New York City

HAROLD D. LASSWELL, Professor of Law & Political Science, Yale University, New Haven, Conn.

JAMES T. LEE, President, Central Savings Bank, New York City

ALBERT LEPAWSKY, Professor of Political Science, University of California, Berkeley, California

FRANK LOPEZ, Senior Associate Editor, Architectural Record, New York City

STUART A. MACCORKLE, Professor of Government, University of Texas, Austin, Texas

ROBERT M. MACIVER, Lieber Professor Emeritus of Political Philosophy and Sociology, Columbia University

PEPPINO MANGRAVITE, Associate Professor of Painting, Columbia University

ALLEN MANVEL, Chief, Governments Division, Bureau of the Census, Washington, D.C.

THEODORE T. MCCROSKY, McHugh and McCrosky, New York City

R. LOUISE MCMANUS, Professor of Nursing Education, Columbia University

ARTHUR MCVOY, Director, Baltimore Department of Planning, Baltimore, Maryland

HOWARD K. MENHINICK, Regent's Professor of City Planning, Georgia Institute of Technology, Atlanta, Ga.

GLADYS MEYER, Assistant Professor of Sociology, Barnard College

HENRY J. MEYER, Professor of Sociology, New York University

J. MARSHALL MILLER, Associate Professor of Planning, Columbia University

JOHN D. MILLETT, President, Miami University, Oxford, Ohio

C. WRIGHT MILLS, Associate Professor of Sociology, Columbia University

ROBERT B. MITCHELL, Chairman, Department of Land and City Planning, University of Pennsylvania, Philadelphia, Pa.

WILBERT E. MOORE, Professor of Sociology, Princeton University, Princeton, N.J.

GEORGE P. MURDOCK, Professor of Anthropology, Yale University, New Haven, Connecticut

ROBERT J. MYERS, Chief Actuary, Social Security Administration, Department of Health, Education & Welfare, Washington, D.C.

C. McKIM NORTON, Vice President, Regional Plan Association, Inc., New York City

JOHN E. ORCHARD, Professor of Economic Geography, Columbia University

LAWRENCE M. ORTON, Commissioner, New York City Planning Commission, New York City

JOHN OSMAN, Fund for Adult Education, New York City

HERMAN F. OTTE, Professor of Economic Geography, Columbia University

JOHN A. PARKER, Chairman, Department of City & Regional Planning, University of North Carolina, Chapel Hill, N.C.

THE VERY REVEREND JAMES A. PIKE, Dean of the Cathedral of St. John the Divine, New York City

HUGH R. POMEROY, Director, Westchester County Department of Planning, White Plains, N.Y.

SHEPPARD T. POWELL, Baltimore, Md.

EDMUND A. PRENTIS, Chief Engineer, Spencer, White & Prentis, New York City

MALCOLM J. PROUDFOOT, Associate Professor of Geography, Northwestern University, Evanston, Ill.

THE REVEREND EDWIN R. QUAIN, S.J., Fordham University, New York City

IRA DE A. REID, Professor of Sociology, Haverford College, Haverford, Pa.

RUSSELL R. RENO, Professor of Law, University of Maryland Law School, Baltimore, Md.

LLOYD RODWIN, Associate Professor of Land Economics, Massachusetts Institute of Technology, Cambridge, Mass.

NATALIE ROGOFF, Bureau of Applied Social Research, Columbia University

WILLIAM J. RONAN, Dean, Graduate School of Training in Public and Social Administration, New York University

THE VERY REVEREND LAWRENCE ROSE, S.T.D., Dean, General Theological Seminary, New York City

MAURICE E. H. ROTIVAL, New York City

RAYMOND J. SAULNIER, Professor of Economics, Columbia University

LADISLAS SEGOE, Cincinnati, Ohio

CLARENCE SENIOR, Chief, Migration Division, Commonwealth of Puerto Rico, New York City

LOUIS SKIDMORE, New York City

T. LYNN SMITH, Professor of Sociology, University of Florida, Gainesville, Fla.

FOSTER D. SNELL, New York City

ANATOLE A. SOLOW, Chief, Division of Housing & Planning, Pan American Union, Washington, D.C.

CLARENCE S. STEIN, New York City

JOHN Q. STEWART, Associate Professor of Astronomical Physics, Princeton University, Princeton, N.J.

W. DUNCAN STRONG, Loubat Professor of American Archaeology, Columbia University

FRANK TANNENBAUM, Professor of Latin American History, Columbia University

HOWARD C. TAYLOR, M.D., Columbia-Presbyterian Medical Center, New York City

SHELDON TEFFT, Professor of Law, University of Chicago Law School, Chicago, Illinois

DOROTHY S. THOMAS, Professor of Sociology, University of Pennsylvania, Philadelphia, Pa.

THE REVEREND JOSEPH T. TINNELLY, C.M., Dean, School of Law, St. John's University, Brooklyn, N.Y.

DAVID B. TRUMAN, Professor of Government, Columbia University

RUPERT B. VANCE, Kenan Professor of Sociology, University of North Carolina, Chapel Hill, N.C.

THE REVEREND DR. HENRY P. VAN DUSEN, President, Union Theological Seminary, New York City

CHARLES WAGLEY, Professor of Anthropology, Columbia University

RALPH T. WALKER, New York City

DR. WARREN WEAVER, Director, Division of Natural Sciences, Rockefeller Foundation, New York City

MAX WEHRLY, Executive Director, Urban Land Institute, Washington, D.C.

EDWARD W. WEIDNER, Professor of Politics & Social Science, Michigan State College, East Lansing, Mich.

LOUIS B. WETMORE, Director, Center for Urban & Regional Studies, Massachusetts Institute of Technology, Cambridge, Mass.

EDWARD B. WILKINS, Professor of City & Regional Planning, Rutgers University, New Brunswick, N.J.

GORDON WILLEY, Bowditch Professor of Archaeology, Harvard University, Cambridge, Mass.

NORMAN WILLIAMS, JR., Department of City Planning, New York City

ROBIN M. WILLIAMS, Professor of So-ciology, Director, Cornell Social Science Research Center, Cornell University, Ithaca, N.Y.

JOSEPH H. WILLITS, Director for the Social Sciences, Rockefeller Foundation, New York City

HOWARD E. WILSON, Director, European Program, Carnegie Endowment for International Peace, New York City

ABEL WOLMAN, Professor of Sanitary Engineering, Johns Hopkins University, Baltimore, Md.

RICHARDSON WOOD, New York City

COLEMAN WOODBURY, South Kent, Conn.

HAROLD ZINK, Professor of Political Science, Ohio State University, Columbus, Ohio

Index